Macroeconomics and the Environment

ADVANCES IN ECOLOGICAL ECONOMICS

Series Editor: Jeroen C.J.M. van den Bergh, *ICREA Professor, Universitat Autònoma de Barcelona, Spain and Professor of Environmental and Resource Economics, Vrije Universiteit, Amsterdam, The Netherlands*

Founding Editor: Robert Costanza, *Gund Professor of Ecological Economics and Director, Gund Institute for Ecological Economics, University of Vermont, USA*

This important series makes a significant contribution to the development of the principles and practices of ecological economics, a field which has expanded dramatically in recent years. The series provides an invaluable forum for the publication of high quality work and shows how ecological economic analysis can make a contribution to understanding and resolving important problems.

The main emphasis of the series is on the development and application of new original ideas in ecological economics. International in its approach, it includes some of the best theoretical and empirical work in the field with contributions to fundamental principles, rigorous evaluations of existing concepts, historical surveys and future visions. It seeks to address some of the most important theoretical questions and gives policy solutions for the ecological problems confronting the global village as we move into the twenty-first century.

Titles in the series include:

Macroeconomics and the Environment

Essays on Green Accounting

Salah El Serafy

Formerly of the World Bank, USA

ADVANCES IN ECOLOGICAL ECONOMICS

Edward Elgar

Cheltenham, UK • Northampton, MA, USA

Published by
Edward Elgar Publishing Limited
The Lypiatts
15 Lansdown Road
Cheltenham
Glos GL50 2JA
UK

Edward Elgar Publishing, Inc.
William Pratt House
9 Dewey Court
Northampton
Massachusetts 01060
USA

A catalogue record for this book
is available from the British Library

Library of Congress Control Number: 2012946682

ISBN 978 1 78100 735 8

Typeset by Servis Filmsetting Ltd, Stockport, Cheshire
Printed and bound by MPG Books Group, UK

Contents

Figures and tables

FIGURES

TABLES

Preface

This book is about green accounting. Green accounting seeks to adjust the national income estimates to reflect ecological deterioration to the extent these accounts will allow. But it is also about macroeconomics since the national accounts and macroeconomics are intertwined. Hicks traces the birth of macroeconomics back to Cromwell's invasion of Ireland in the 1650s when William Petty, a precursor of national accounting, was tasked with making an estimate of the 'Irish estate' gained as a war booty. Not too long later, the classical economists from Adam Smith onwards, and perhaps taking their cue from the French school of the Physiocrats, approached the study of economics from the macroeconomic end, focusing on the national aggregate of the wealth (meaning income) which figured in the title of Adam Smith's book: *The Wealth of Nations*. But the focus of economics (or shall we say political economy) on macroeconomics was dilated in the course of the nineteenth century. The prevailing *laissez-faire* thinking and practices were not exactly conducive to counting national aggregates, and attention shifted for quite a while to analysis of individual commodity markets with a concentration on value theory which was conveniently analysed by the microeconomic apparatus of supply and demand. It was not until the beginning of the twentieth century, however, that we note stirrings back to the classical perspective. Sporadic estimates of national income began to be made in the United Kingdom with the availability of data including tax returns. But the real jump in the history of national accounting came with World War II in order to mobilize national resources for the war effort and allocate them to serve this vital purpose. In the United States the same drive came a little later, also associated with the war. The impetus to green the national accounts came later still and this is the main theme that will be investigated in detail in the following chapters.

In this book I challenge the veracity of the magnitudes produced by the national accounts, even those compiled after the major overhaul of the United Nations System that came out in 1993, to which I shall be referring as SNA93. The challenge will not affect all economies – not to the same degree anyway – but will relate especially to those poorer economies where primary production forms a significant portion of their industrial structure. Primary production comprises activities rooted in Nature and cover mining, agriculture, fishing, forestry and similar economic pursuits. The aggregate estimates produced in the national accounts provide the prime material the macroeconomists use for monitoring economic change, analysing its nature and causes, and for making economic policy prescriptions. These magnitudes include GDP and GNP, and their net parallels NDP and NNP, and also cover components within them such as consumption, saving and investment. A major claim I shall be pressing is that natural resources are part of a nation's economic capital, and their deterioration represents an economic loss that should be captured unambiguously in the national accounts to the extent the accounts would permit, and should thus be forced on the attention of economists. To view ecological or environmental deterioration as biological and physical losses – while certainly true – without appreciating the *economic* significance of that loss, is worse than a crime: it is a mistake![1] In what follows I shall be using 'ecology' and 'environment' interchangeably, stressing the fact that the environment is unquestionably part of a society's capital in the full sense of capital as used in economic analysis. Natural capital adds to the contribution other factors make to output and withdrawing it in whole or in part will lessen the product. One important aspect of this argument is that, similarly to other forms of capital, it should be maintained, and its maintenance must be seen as a prerequisite for the proper estimation of national income.

Whilst the ecological aspect of natural resource deterioration receives ample recognition from the environmentalists, it is their economic role that is curiously overlooked by the economists – or at least by a majority of them. And it is the attention of these I shall be trying to attract. When the System of National Accounts came up for a major update in 1993 the new version – SNA93 – treated the environment decidedly as non-economic, devoid of any economic quality or even relevance. To its authors the environment was merely an ecological entity meriting no place in the central 'economic' accounts. With the obvious economic relevance of natural resources, as will be elaborated throughout the next chapters, I shall be curious to find out by the end if readers will judge SNA93 justified in reserving the quality of 'economic' to the traditional estimates of GDP, while denying the same quality to ecological changes. Questioned also will be the place where these amendments to the accounts should be made: should they be in the 'mainframe' of the SNA, or banished out of sight into the newly created set of 'satellite accounts'?

Simultaneously with the release of SNA93, the United Nations Statistics Department issued a guide for the compilation of the Satellite Accounts. This guide came out as expected in the series of 'Studies in Method', bearing the title, *Integrated Environmental and Economic Accounting: An Operational Manual.* Significantly it was stamped by UNSD as 'An Interim Version' in recognition of the fact that controversy was still raging on account-adjustment methods, and in the expectation that a definitive version would later emerge. Subsequent updating of SNA93, and a number of attempts to firm up the Manual that would allegedly *integrate* (or re-integrate?) what is 'economic' with what is 'environmental' have failed. This has occurred despite heroic efforts led by UNSD and the consultants it recruited for the task. Two decades after initiating this Manual in 1993 it has not been finalized to everyone's satisfaction, and the Satellite Accounts still lack a standard format, and even their very purpose has not been clarified. Where they have actually been compiled, and many statistical offices throughout the world have striven to compile them, they seem to have emerged merely as a repository of relevant information, related in some fashion to the environment – doubtless potentially useful for research, but lacking a format conducive to the genuine integration intended. Importantly macroeconomic work continues to be based on the unadjusted accounts, which, for many developing countries dependent on primary production, do not accord with the reality of their situation.

I must stress that this book is in large part built upon a number of earlier essays dealing with environmental economics. These have now been updated, touched up, and complemented with other unpublished papers and with further thoughts relating to the interactions between the environment and macroeconomics. While the book naturally supports what has come to be known in some circles as the 'El Serafy Method', it takes up many other related topics while keeping as close as possible to current national income accounting practices. Significantly it very largely eschews an aspect of green accounting that has garnered amazing popularity in the ecological economics literature, namely the welfare implications of greening the accounts. Though certain aspects of welfare will receive critical coverage in this book it will not be pursued in any substance since I view welfare as irrelevant to the approach I am taking. National income is not meant to signify happiness – a view which the account estimators themselves have strongly emphasized. They stress that they are estimating output and its counterpart, income, and certainly not the state of mind that output may impart to the income recipients.

One cannot deny that associating output with welfare – an association that may be traced back at least to Pigou – has given rise to some impressive contributions recently made that have enlivened the discussion of greening the national accounts, and these will be touched upon later. What I shall be concerned particularly with is to rebut contributions coming interestingly from economic theorists who have rushed in to deploy heavy mathematical artillery to introduce what they believe as relevant inputs to national account reform. Most of these attempts it will be seen focus on 'welfare' which as I just said is a different topic. Welfare economics has of course been central to neoclassical economics for a whole century, and has gone through many phases of development as is well known. In one phase it dwelt in great length on cardinal and ordinal utility for welfare comparisons, and for interpreting the national dividend and its changes. In another phase it has led to the practical apparatus of cost–benefit analysis – a technique favored for project appraisal by many development agencies. My own position, I must declare at the outset, is that we may derive welfare from output to our hearts' content, provided that we get better readings of output first. Any derivation of welfare from output must wait until output has been properly estimated. And second, this should be done totally outside the SNA. The output estimates produced by the national accounts are clearly not sufficient to enable welfare judgments based on them. The estimates need to be supported by additional information that is not usually available to the national accountants, including the number of the income recipients, how income is distributed among them, their age and gender structures, and how they spread along the range of the income distribution. Armed with such information welfare questions may be pursued fruitfully but decidedly outside the SNA.

It will be seen that the method I am trying to propagate and which dominates what I am going to say in the following chapters began as a device I forged in the 1970s for estimating *income* out of the revenues obtained from the commercial exploitation of depletable natural resources, initially petroleum. I shall be showing that the user-cost method has since then proved to be quite versatile in that it has been successfully applied also to renewable resources when these are insufficiently replenished or not replenished at all. Successful applications of my method have been made for other minerals, forestry, soil, fisheries, and fossil water among other natural resources. Failure to renew renewable resources amounts in effect to 'mining' them so they become depletable. This method has had its supporters and detractors. The supporters, I like to think, have made the necessary effort to understand it properly, and the detractors in my view often failed to comprehend it or appreciate the assumptions upon which it is based. In my opinion opponents, often with good intentions, have played no small part in delaying a satisfactory greening of the national accounts along the lines I have been proposing. In this book I try to summarize their 'misunderstandings' in two chapters, citing instances of criticism I have come across, but clearly there are many more that I have not encountered. I am inclined to pose the question as to whether these detractors should not bear their share of responsibility for obstructing the progress of green accounting. But this is perhaps a question too early to pose at this stage, and should receive an answer by book end.

I now turn to the organization of the book in an attempt to show how I intend to proceed. I shall not elaborate here on the chapter contents, but sketch them only in outline. It is my intention to divide the presentation in six parts. Part I introduces the subject spread over three brief chapters. I begin by stressing the economic angle which defines my entire approach, followed by a brief historical account of how I got involved in green accounting in the first place, then I describe from my perspective how SNA93 came about, and end with a previously published essay on why the environment constitutes part of a nation's Capital. I had planned to include in this part my essay on 'the economic rationale for green accounting' (El Serafy 2006: Chapter 3 in Philip Lawn, ed., *Sustainable Development Indicators in Ecological Economics*, Edward Elgar, Cheltenham), which would give a bird's eye view of this book, but decided to exclude it to avoid repetition.

Part II consists of five chapters, the first of which examines the fundamental concepts of Income and Capital in relation to Nature's accounts, followed by two chapters, successively on Marshall's distinction between rent and royalty, then another on Hicksian income, concluding by an examination of the concept of income, properly defined, in application to mineral extraction. Part II finishes off with an example of a policy issue, namely adjusting investment downward, consequent upon greening the accounts.

Part III focuses on the user-cost approach to greening the accounts. It contains two chapters dealing with its rationale, and how to estimate it, examining the criticism levelled against it which I label 'Misunderstandings', and finally focus on one particular critic who had made a detailed study of my 'Contribution' to this issue.

Four chapters make up Part IV where I examine in detail certain methodological matters or rather 'instruments' associated with a user-cost approach, namely (1) treating declines of resource stocks in commercial exploitation as withdrawals from Nature's store and stressing the inappropriateness of likening these withdrawals to capital consumption; (2) outlining my views on Sustainability and the related topic of substitutability i.e. between natural and human-made inputs in production; and (3) that contrary to general perception, greening the accounts will not necessarily lead to a lower growth rate. Then I devote a short chapter to the demographic pressure on natural resources.

Part V gathers together important policy matters that need to be re-examined once the accounts have been greened. One chapter contains what in effect was a 'sermon' I addressed to fellow World Bank economists directing their attention to the natural resource foundations on which are based the macroeconomic estimates they use and mechanically project. The second chapter explores further green accounting and economic policy. A third chapter explodes the myth of the natural resource curse. A fourth brings in the case of Indonesia, which has been the field of a pioneering study on green accounting. And a fifth provides a short account of sovereign funds established in many cases to receive the proceeds of natural resource liquidation.

Finally Part VI, made up of a single chapter I call 'An afterword', tries to sum up the book's main messages.

NOTE

1. I am alluding here to the French adage that a mistake can be worse than a crime – a saying attributed to many people, but notably to Napoleon's Chief of Police, Joseph Fouché who apparently had said: *'C'est pire qu'un crime, c'est une faute!'*

Acknowledgements

Having outlined my plan of work it is now my pleasant duty to acknowledge the help and encouragement I received over the years from many individuals and institutions. It is not possible to list them all, and their help will be revealed by reference to private correspondence, memoranda and other citations to be found scattered throughout the book. But I would be remiss if I didn't mention in particular those who have been backing my views especially when I was trespassing for the first time on virgin territory trying to feel the ground. In the forefront of supporters I must mention Herman Daly and Robert Goodland, friends and former World Bank colleagues, on whom I tried earlier drafts, and who have been most obliging with valuable suggestions. I have not always heeded their advice so they cannot be blamed for the shortcomings that remain. From the beginning Herman signalled his endorsement in the book he authored with John Cobb (*For The Common Good*, 1989) where my method was described rather generously as 'elegant and parsimonious'. The latter adjective was meant to refer to the economy of data required for estimating my user cost. And Robert, among his many environmental accomplishments, was the one who had spotted my paper on 'Absorptive Capacity' (*Journal of Energy and Development*, 1981) where I had introduced my formula for estimating income from revenue realized in natural resource extraction, and persuaded me to join the then ongoing UNEP-World Bank International Workshops that led eventually to the development of green accounting.

As to helpful institutions I cannot over-praise the United Nations Environment Programme (UNEP), which sponsored the green accounting initiative from the beginning, and kept supporting it in a variety of ways over time. In this regard I must mention UNEP officials Mostafa Tolba, the late Yusuf Ahmad and also Hussein Abaza who merit special recognition. Hussein kept me involved in the difficult process of re-integrating the 'economic' and the 'environmental' for many years after I retired from the World Bank, treating me as if I were a UNEP insider. Besides UNEP, the World Bank must be credited with enormous support for the green accounts initiative, providing my time and covering international travel costs in addition to giving me the opportunity of exchanging views with gifted colleagues on its staff. Its contribution has also included making its premises available in Washington and Paris where crucial green accounting issues were debated. It was certainly my twenty-year spell at the Bank, working mostly as a macroeconomist and being involved in shaping 'country macroeconomic policies' that ignited my interest in having the SNA reformed. Natural resources, upon which the prosperity of many developing nations rest, had tended to be *terra incognita* to the Bank's economists, particularly those working on the macroeconomics of individual developing countries. Along with non-Bank economists many of them would perceive economic reality through the fogged-up lens of the inadequate national accounts available.

Among World Bank friends and colleagues with whom I discussed aspects of my work over the years, and who have been most sympathetic to my views, have been the late Michael Ward and also Ann Harrison, both national income specialists; Stanley Fischer, at one time World Bank Chief Economist; Vinod Dubey and the late Enzo Grilli. There were also many others whom I am not mentioning by name or who just slipped off my memory, but who would recognize their contribution in the following pages. But I must not forget the role played by the late Barber B. Conable, President of the World Bank 1986–91, who had a genuine interest in the environment. He enthusiastically added his name to that of Mostafa Tolba, then Executive Director of UNEP below the Foreword I had drafted for *Environmental Accounting for Sustainable Development*–A Joint UNEP-World Bank Symposium (World Bank, Washington DC, 1989). Outside the Bank although my method had many detractors it found strong support from various scholars throughout the world including Eric Neumayer, Jeroen van den Berg, Philip Lawn, and intermittently, though with occasional caveats, Jeffrey Vincent, Partha Dasgupta and also many others who took the trouble to apply the user-cost method in empirical studies. I must also add Neva Godwin's group at Tufts University, notably Jonathan Harris, who showed profound understanding of the user-cost method and helped to spread its message. It goes without saying that one of the greatest debts I must acknowledge is to the late Professor Sir John Hicks who had supervised my doctoral dissertation at Oxford in the 1950s with wisdom and encouragement, and who was to maintain interest in my career afterwards. Readers will not fail to notice that his name imbues practically all aspects of the current book. I am duty bound too to name the late Professor Zaki Hasan, Chartered Accountant and Dean of the Faculty of Commerce, Alexandria University, Egypt, where I took my first bachelor degree. It was he who kindled my interest in accountancy at an early age and had wished me to be an accountant.

But I must not conclude without mentioning the unfailing

encouragement and support given to me by my two sons, Joseph E. Serafy of the US National Oceanic and Atmospheric Administration (NOAA) and the University of Miami, and Sam Serafy of The Library of Congress, Washington DC particularly since the demise in 2008 of my wife of 50 years, Susan. She was always reluctant to be acknowledged in print, but occasionally I would slip in her name as 'Susan Hubert' without her knowledge. Her help with my previous publications has been profuse and profound, and to her memory this book is dedicated.

To the following publishers, the author and publisher are grateful for allowance to reprint earlier work by the author either as originally published or subsequently modified.

Columbia University Press for Chapter 3. 'The Environment as Capital', pp. 168–175, in Robert Costanza (ed.), (1991), *Ecological Economics – The Science and Management of Sustainability.*

Island Press, the World Bank and UNESCO for Chapter 8. 'Sustainability, Income Measurement, and Growth', pp. 63–79, in Robert Goodland, Herman E. Daly and Salah El Serafy (eds), (1992), *Population, Technology, and Lifestyle.*

The World Bank for Chapter 9. 'The Proper Calculation of Income from Depletable Natural Resources', pp. 10–18, in Yusuf J. Ahmad, Salah El Serafy and Ernst Lutz (eds), (1989), *Environmental Accounting for Sustainable Development* (A UNEP-World Bank Symposium).

The White Horse Press for Chapter 13. 'In Defence of Weak Sustainability', *Environmental Values*, 1996, Volume 5 number 1, pp. 75–82.

Elsevier Science B.V. for Chapter 15 'Pricing the Invaluable', *Ecological Economics*, 1998, Volume 25, number 1, pp. 25–27, and Chapter 17, 'Green Accounting and Economic Policy', *Ecological Economics*, 1997, Volume 21, pp. 217–228.

For

Susan Hubert

PART I

Introduction

1. Breaking the ground

I

THE ECONOMIC PERSPECTIVE

A chief purpose for this book is to argue the case for greening the conventional estimates of national income basing the argument on economic grounds. These estimates are not in a vacuum, but should make economic sense and serve economic purposes, while remaining faithful to the precautionary nature of accountancy. The approach I am espousing is not geared to serving the environment – not primarily anyway – but aims to help in obtaining more meaningful measurements for monitoring economic performance properly, improving economic analysis and guiding economic policy. In line with accounting ways, my goal is not for precise estimates, which the economists understandably seek, but for approximations for which the accountants strive, and which have become indispensable for macroeconomic understanding. In this respect, to borrow an expression of the late Professor Sir Dennis Robertson: 'It is better to be vaguely right than precisely wrong.'[1]

Inevitably this book endeavors to promote my favorite account-greening method, the user-cost method, which I have been advocating for decades and which is known to analysts and income estimators – albeit with an occasional misunderstanding and, more frequently, misapplication. Because the method is essentially simple, and is in harmony with common sense, it has gained certain popularity especially in graduate courses on environmental economics. In that milieu, it provides scope for critical assessment and for comparison with alternative greening methods, often built around arithmetical examples. A key characteristic of this approach – my approach – is that it avoids deriving the flow accounts from stock values. Important as this link is for theoretical analysis, it becomes a curse for accounting. In my method, stocks remain important, but are firmly placed in the background, to be reckoned in physical terms only. Comparing the physical stocks to physical extraction during an accounting period suggests the life expectancy of the resource from the perspective of the current account period. This life expectancy is obviously a fundamental indicator of resource 'sustainability'.

The overall objective, on which most accounting 'reformers' agree, is to reflect ecological losses in the national accounts to the extent the national accounts allow; but this objective has so far proved elusive owing to a seemingly unbridgeable gap that separates economics and ecology. On both sides of the divide there are impediments against convergence or even harmonization. But reconciliation of the two disciplines is not at all difficult considering the availability of the highly suitable medium of national accounts. Until fairly recently ecologists and economists conducted their own separate business without much exchange between the two, but things have changed. This is because over the past three decades a 'movement' has arisen for a new blend called environmental or ecological economics, and it is this movement that must be credited with giving vent to the 'green accounting' initiative.

Considering the deliberate separation between economics and ecology perpetrated by the System of National Accounts adopted in 1993 (SNA93), one is curious to know if its drafters were being mischievous or simply naïve in describing as *economic* the unadjusted, conventionally estimated, series of national income which overlooks the deterioration of the obviously *economic* natural resources, while labelling any attempted green accounts as *environmental* or in plain words as not economic? This wording may in effect work as a shield against integrating environmental deterioration in the accounts so that business would remain 'as usual' based on the unadjusted accounts.

'Green accounting' can, of course, just mean keeping track of the physical changes in natural resources using physical units, or more strictly physical units adjusted for quality differences. Such a course is a worthy endeavor that would help meet some fundamental 'sustainability' concerns, and in any case it amounts to an essential first step towards any monetary estimation. Although, for accounting purposes, the quantity of a resource stock varies, often with the state of technology, it may be taken as determinate from one account period to the next. If technological improvements raise stock size the accountants would just take this increase in their stride when it happens, treating it similarly to new discoveries. In this book 'green accounting' will mean integrating ecological changes valued in money into the System of National Accounts, and the path I'll be taking will unfold over the following chapters and will be seen as essentially taken from an economic standpoint.

I should add that failing to go forward with green-accounting reform will do damage to an initiative that began in hope and promised great potential. The drawbacks of refraining from taking effective action to safeguard natural resource sustainability have become too obvious and too important to neglect. Ecology is obviously not my specialty – a fact that will be only too noticeable in this book, but it does not need a specialist to observe that much uncharted terrain remains unexplored in ecology, and this will impair comprehensive coverage. However, taking in as much as possible will improve the estimation of the macroeconomic variables and will open up vast vistas for economic analysis, which are now hidden from view by faulty accounting.

Economically viewed – and a narrow view at that – it is not in fact the natural resources per se that need protection, but their services. In an effort to reduce the complexity of the issues involved and to form a bridge connecting the environment with economics, the work of the Dutch economist Roefie Hueting is remarkable. Imaginatively, he coined the concept of 'environmental functions' which are services provided by Nature and are being progressively stressed (Hueting, 1980). From my perspective, the cost of safeguarding, repairing and maintaining these environmental functions should be recognized explicitly in the national accounts simply by invoking the fundamental maxim of 'maintaining capital intact' (El Serafy, 1998). This issue was taken up in a brave attempt to attach a value to environmental functions worldwide, which is the subject of Chapter 15 entitled 'Pricing the Invaluable'. I pay a special tribute to Hueting in El Serafy 2001.

Regrettably, not many economists have familiarized themselves with national accounting and continue to use its numbers with unfounded confidence in their veracity and accuracy or near accuracy. When pressed, in my experience, they defend themselves by confessing no expertise in national accounts. And yet many analytical economic models have been constructed on rickety national income foundations, which can hardly support them, and indicate flawed or even harmful economic policies, which get applied with apparent innocence. At a minimum, faulty accounting that overlooks the deterioration of environmental capital overestimates income and results in exaggerated consumption, which erodes sustainability however defined.

Interest in macroeconomic issues, it may be recalled, reflects the aggregative approach that was given prominence in Adam Smith's *Wealth of Nations* (1776). Smith's emphasis on 'nations' in his analysis testifies to his concern of taking each nation one at a time: the same approach adopted later by the national accountants. In this regard, it is worth recalling that Smith's 'wealth' meant 'income' (Cannan, 1904; Kuznets, 1971; Hicks, 1975, among many others.) Adam Smith's approach was obviously a macroeconomic one. Though macroeconomics may be said to have begun earlier than microeconomics it seems to have had a fallow period lasting for several decades after John Stuart Mill (1773–1836). Its heyday was in the classical era of Smith, Ricardo, Malthus and Mill. What is especially interesting in our day is that the foundations of macroeconomics now get challenged afresh by contemporary writers who claim that it suffers from many weaknesses. They justifiably claim that macroeconomic theories now in use do not change in response to uncomfortably contradictory evidence, and that they continue to have a shaky relationship with empirical econometric work. Moreover, their policy applications, and particularly many forecasting forays, are said to leave much to be desired (see, for instance, Backhouse and Salanti, 2000). But these complaints get considerably enhanced when the *unadjusted* national income estimates are used routinely for macroeconomic analysis.

If for a moment national accounting were to be viewed merely as a tool somehow divorced from macroeconomics, it would be seen to be less problematic, though undoubtedly it would have its own difficulties as will be amply illustrated in due course. But perhaps it is not an exaggeration to state that without national accounting, however imperfect, modern macroeconomics could not have developed as fruitfully as it obviously has. The aggregative quantities of income, saving, consumption and investment, which are the staple magnitudes of macroeconomists, were certainly prominent in Keynes's path breaking book, *The General Theory of Employment, Interest and Money* (1936) and have dominated the writings of post-Keynesian economists since then. And these, it will be noted, are the very quantities that the national accountants have been striving to estimate for decades. Hicks (1990) goes so far as to credit the development of modern macroeconomics to the prior progress achieved by the national accountants, and in a subtle differentiation dismisses as alleged precursors of national accounting both Keynes's *General Theory* and earlier writings by Keynes himself (as well as by others) – a claim which has been put forth by some Keynesians. To Hicks, and specifically for Britain, the 'turning-point' in the development of macroeconomics was the booklet[2] published at the beginning of 1940 called *How to Pay for the War,* produced by Meade and Stone under Keynes's direction.[3]

THE GROWTH MANIA

Reference to a 'growth mania' will be repeated in the following chapters for it seems to have given economics, all economics, a bad name among environmentalists. Growth, bracketed with the environment, made an appearance at Stockholm in 1971 when Simon Kuznets received his Nobel Prize in Economic Science. He strongly denied the appropriateness of applying the term growth to describe economic expansion *that is not sustained*, interestingly citing the case of countries 'selling fortuitous gifts of nature to others' (Kuznets, 1971, p. 247). Kuznets was stressing the view that in order for economic expansion to qualify as 'growth' it must be 'sustained'. And yet macroeconomists, taking the national accounts at their face value, glibly label all economic expansion as 'growth', and applaud any increase in GDP, however shaky its foundations, as attesting to good economic policies. It is amazing how the mere expansion of economic activity irrespective of its origins, and disregarding its costs, is taken by economists as *the* badge of economic success.

The flourishing subdiscipline of macroeconomics over the past eight decades has in fact proved to be a mixed blessing for it gave birth to the emergence of a 'growth mania' that has dominated economic analysis and policy in recent times. There is much to be said for economic expansion if it could enhance the wellbeing of the income recipients. But at least the expansion observed must be genuine growth of *value added*, not based on natural capital disinvestment. Secondly, it should be growth whose costs, directly and indirectly, are taken into consideration. Put another way, in order for it to be genuine it must be within the capacity of our biosphere to provide the necessary inputs for it and absorb and assimilate the emissions unavoidably associated with a larger and larger scale of production and consumption. It is now clearly recognized by many economists, but sadly not by all, that the unfettered rise in economic activity, often hailed as unalloyed economic accomplishment, has been excessive and cannot be maintained. This excessive expansion has inflicted great harm on our ecology – harm which is often difficult, and in certain respects impossible, to reverse.

Behind economic growth and its negative effects has been the relentless increase in world population and the rising aspirations for a better life of billions of people in the poorer countries who understandably wish to elevate their consumption levels.[4] Recent economic expansion in countries such as China and India containing huge populations, though commendable in many ways, is ecologically alarming. Notwithstanding the fact that rates of population growth have tended downwards in recent decades, the population base remains sizeable enough to make annual population additions still substantial with a negative influence on income per head in many places. This is not forgetting the wasteful consumption of the rich in all nations, rich and poor, and at many levels of extravagance. Signs multiply continually including a seemingly insatiable demand for luxuries and a misguided enthusiasm for avoidable military adventures that are especially popular in places where the instruments of war are manufactured, and where they are viewed myopically as providing local employment and prosperity.

Many people tend to put their trust in technology imagining that its progress will lead the environment out of its predicament. But advances in technology, though considerable, have in some important respects failed us so far: they do not come on cue when needed or in the shape that would meet urgent requirements, and in application they are also frequently resisted. Population curtailment provides a good illustration. Many people had hoped that progress in birth control methods would curb excessive population growth. Yet it is often obstructed by religiously motivated aid donors, perhaps responding to their political constituencies, and frequently also by the would-be recipients themselves. Altogether technical progress has made little difference where it is most needed. Two centuries ago Thomas Malthus (1766–1834) had drawn attention to the imbalance then developing between the number of people and the means of nourishing them. If population growth is not rationally constrained, he opined, Nature will impose the balance harshly and painfully. For a while, and a long while at that, Malthus's views were disparaged as too pessimistic. Opportunities for food production appeared in the new territories of America and Oceania, but these seem to have gradually narrowed and the Malthusian 'pessimism' on a world scale has come back with force.

It must be admitted that reforming the national accounts cannot be expected to be a panacea for all our behavioral faults, but perhaps it can shed a better light on what is occurring on the ground at the nexus between ecological change and economic performance, and may in a small way induce the restraining of some of our excesses. Without proper accounting we imagine that we are consuming only what we produce when in fact we are frequently consuming our capital: natural as well as human-made – a sure recipe for worse things to come.

II

GENESIS OF THE USER-COST METHOD

The user-cost method will receive ample coverage in the course of the next chapters, but here a foretaste may be useful. As stated in the Preface, this book is built upon and around a number of papers, many of which have been published before, but now hopefully corrected, updated and integrated. Many of these papers had seen the light mostly as contributions to conferences and international meetings, invited by editors of journals or organizers of symposia to fit into a variety of initiatives in the field of environmental economics. They had been written mostly when my attention was focused on other macroeconomic work at the World Bank so in a sense they were ad hoc pieces, which I try now to mould into a coherent work with a concentrated purpose. They had appeared as journal articles or chapters in books, but a few are freshly composed. Some of the latter are based on exchanges over the years with colleagues working in the same field and have not been previously published. The overall output, spanning 30 years of involvement, may be said to have attracted attention from academic circles, research organizations, United Nations agencies, national income estimators and individual scholars. To repeat, the attention that my approach has attracted, though appreciable, has not always been uncritical.

It will be seen that opposition to my line of thinking has been voiced and maintained by certain official centers, notably the influential Bureau of Economic Analysis (BEA) of the United States Department of Commerce. BEA is the unit in the United States government that is responsible for national accounting. In my view the authors of SNA93 were so anxious to secure the adherence of the United States to a new *universal* SNA that they strove to accommodate the proclivities of BEA staff in matters pertaining to green accounting methods. I offer my purchase on this matter in Chapter 11 which I label 'Misunderstandings'. My interpretation of this matter will doubtless be challenged, but I put it forward at least as a plausible hypothesis.

Be that as it may, the interest in my user-cost method for re-estimating the macroeconomic numbers of the national accounts has been flatteringly worldwide: in developed as well as in developing countries. But support has been more evident in places such as the Netherlands, the United Kingdom and Australia than in developing countries with some significant exceptions. Researchers in South Africa, Brazil, Chile, Costa Rica, China and in many other places have made valuable contributions applying the user-cost method for recalculating their national accounts and comparing the results obtained using alternative approaches. At the official level, however, statistical offices in the less developed world have been hesitant to experiment with new methodological ways without the authority of the usual arbiters of national accounting procedures, traditionally located in the industrialized world. But many scholars in these countries have not been so constrained. Additionally a number of doctoral dissertations in several countries, rich and poor, have investigated my technique, applied it and compared its results with rival approaches. Not all these studies have been free from fault, but the collective judgment in my view has been favorable. Interestingly, one important group, the oil exporters, though aware of the user-cost method, practically from its inception, has mainly held back. While many researchers in the oil exporting countries have been intrigued by it and proceeded to test it against their data, their governments, by contrast, have shown disinclination to involve their statistical offices in such testing. Understandably, there has been a tendency on the part of many such countries to await the imprimatur of the United Nations, which had previously issued the SNAs. SNA93 did in fact offer the user-cost method as one possible way of greening the national accounts, but not quite with the enthusiasm I had expected.

More recently the UN and its specialized unit, the United Nations Statistics Department (UNSD), have had to collaborate over national accounting with other international institutions possessing more financial resources and housing greater specialized expertise. But the latter, including the European Community and the Organisation for Economic Co-operation and Development (OECD), have in my view tended to reflect the interests and power of the developed world. A major claim I shall be making repeatedly in the next chapters is that the concerns of the industrialized countries and of the less developed countries over greening the national accounts do not always coincide and in fact they may diverge in some important respects. This is particularly evident in regard to natural resources *as a source* of raw materials and energy, since these resources are far more important in the economic structure of the poorer nations than for the majority of the industrialized countries. On matters concerning pollution there should be little difference between the rich and poor countries' concerns. In my view, pollution does not need the SNA in the same way the deterioration of the natural sources of raw materials and energy does. Thus it is understandable that the industrialized countries on the whole are fairly content with their national accounts without much adjustment, comfortable with the minor modifications introduced by SNA93, which their own experts so obviously shepherded. In fact, the modifications introduced were largely prescribed (though with some notable reservations) by their nationals acting as *international* experts. These modifications fundamentally leave the gross product as traditionally reckoned, virtually unchanged, and confine any adjustments to the external set of 'Satellite Accounts' explicitly labelled 'environmental'. This was a premeditated strategy, which I have been slow to detect, but which now appears to me with clarity.

NOT A UNIVERSAL SYSTEM

It is important therefore to realize that if the SNA is to be taken as a universal system, especially with the United Nations prominently involved in the process, some special provisions should have been made specifically to accommodate the concerns of the primary producing economies that dominate the 'developing' world. Such special treatment would of course have been awkward to handle, hence what came out as SNA93, which, however, was inappropriately presented as a global blueprint. Sporadic participation of statisticians from developing countries at meetings on method, while giving the impression of a universal accord, does not in fact ensure a genuine consensus.

The user-cost method, it will be seen, is capable of providing a world approach with no exclusions or special qualifications needed. For the richer countries the adjustments it brings will tend to be slight in most cases, and could indeed be shunted for convenience into satellite accounts. But for many of the poorer countries the satellite accounts can hardly be sufficient. For countries where the needed adjustment to the conventional estimates is appreciable their traditional gross product estimates will continue to be economically worthless and misleading, and should not be left unadjusted under the false claim that the unadjusted numbers are economic not environmental. There is nothing *economically* valid about them where the economic assets of natural resources are eroding. The question here is not just a procedural one involving a choice between effecting the greening within the 'main frame' of the SNA or alternatively in subsidiary accounts. If the size of the needed adjustment itself is significant it should be shown clearly above board and not hidden in peripheral accounts, and the change should be highlighted as *economic* in substance and purpose. And even if the adjustment were to be made only at the stage of estimating the net product (as SNA93 and UNSD have been insisting) the alleged greening will be doubly misleading. The unadjusted gross estimates will be left flawed; and the re-estimated net product, based erroneously on strong sustainability, will be 'over-corrected', as this procedure wipes out from the adjusted net product all value added attributable specifically to the natural resource in question. In other words, both the gross product (that wrongly contains asset sale proceeds misidentified as value added) and the over-corrected net product will continue to be wrong.

III

SOME PRACTICAL PROBLEMS

It has been during the process of attempting to green the national accounts that many new issues have surfaced. And it is not by accident that my contributions to green accounting have often been set in *conceptual* terms because conceptual clarity helps to dispel irrelevancies, clarify arguments and sharpen debate. One major controversy that emerged was over whether account-reforming proposals based on the notion of optimality provide any practical help to the estimators. Another, already touched upon above, was taking the estimates of the national accounts as indicating welfare, perhaps under the impression that the account-greening initiative from the outset had been targeting happiness. Behind the last statement is the plausible assumption that a good environment, at least at the pollution end, makes people happier. Another very interesting development has been the arrival on the scene of analytical economists who rushed in to contribute to green accounting, but managed in the process to muddy the waters of debate. Their work has yielded a rich harvest of economic insights, but with hardly any guidance for improving the empirical estimates. Their output has kept referring to national accounting, but contributed relatively little by way of offering useful amendments to old concepts or guiding estimation methods. Despite their efforts and those of others the concepts of income and capital which are the mainstay of all accounting methods continue to be hazy in the perception of the estimators, and even the purpose of the national accounts, other than the wrongly emphasized welfare, has been questioned – a fact which has emerged with clarity during discussions over greening methods.

Against a background of methodological disputations, the economists and statisticians involved in natural resource accounting have struggled on, battling with apparently mundane, yet very important practical problems. The unadjusted accounts had habitually called for great efforts to string together often-fragmented data and weave them into some coherent fabric meant to spell out some macroeconomic estimates of which the estimators would be the first to admit their imperfection. Greening the accounts has obviously introduced more complications: What is to be changed, and how? And at which stage in the adjustment process should the change be made? What should be done when natural resource stocks are re-estimated? How do we value end-period natural stocks which are often many times annual extraction? Without being too sanguine, the user-cost method will give adequate answers to these questions. Fortunately the flows are economically much more important than the stocks, and estimating them in value terms is far easier than the estimation of stocks.

With the proliferation of diverse economist views, the estimators began to view familiar quantities such as income and capital, the costs of extraction, the nature of revenue, asset sales, new deposit discoveries and many others with a fresh look. Unless these 'concepts' are clear and given a determinate disposition, their treatment for national accounting, and especially for green accounting purposes, will vary and the accounts will not be standardized. In fact it is possible that the very existence of the extraneous apparatus of satellite accounting may be blamed. The satellite accounts have offered a soft option for 'reform', and unintentionally delayed the process of a rigorous standardization that would have taken the green initiative nearer to their hoped-for destination.

It is clear from the more recent theoretical contributions by analysts such as Mäler, Weitzman, Hartwick, and Asheim (see Hartwick, 1990; Mäler, 1991; Asheim, 1994; Weitzman, 2000) that theoretical reasoning and the practical estimation of the national product have remained quite far apart, often seemingly unrelated. Despite the fact that much of the recent theoretical work on the topic is enlightening, what I find missing is its failure to indicate the situations where theory may be applied if it is to be applied at all. In fact clever analyses, even ingenious ones, have been offered without their authors apparently contemplating their pragmatic application. The result is that the national accountants who are looking for analytical guidance from the economic theorists tend to find very little to guide their practical efforts. And no intermediary agents have emerged within or without the UN agencies, the multilateral development institutions, or for that matter in research establishments, to translate abstract analysis into practical procedures. This fault, if it may be called a fault, may be attributed to the theorists themselves who may not realize that their reference to national income is of little practical import. But such failure is at least paralleled by the practical estimators themselves misreading the proper setting or settings in which a theory is meant to be applicable. Not infrequently this gap between theory and practice has confused the green accounting efforts, leading to much waste of time and energy in argumentation over greening methods and also over interpreting the results of adjustment methods that should have sorted out the grain from the straw.

FOUR EXAMPLES OF INCONGRUITY

It is not difficult to find illustrations where national accountants, trying to pattern their measurements on theoretical models, have succumbed to theories that do not in fact apply. The record is not yet complete enough for me to offer a thorough examination of such errors, but I am anxious to draw attention to instances of incongruity between theory and practice at this early stage in the book. Additional instances of incongruities will be discussed in detail in appropriate chapters. Many have been committed by researchers in individual country studies, most clearly for African countries, financed in many cases by bilateral aid. The relevant studies frequently made comparisons between alternative greening methods – comparisons that have led to disparate results and dissimilar conclusions.

Examining some of their work, I came to realize that their authors did not always fully understand the methods they applied and what results they were comparing. A number of these studies, of course, were actually undertaken prior to SNA93, some with the specific purpose of assessing the merits and demerits of competing methods as an input for reforming the system. Examples included green accounting studies for Papua New Guinea and Mexico. But in practically all cases, I am bound to assert, the research was not done with the rigor that the task demanded, and with only partial understanding of the intricacies of the approaches being compared. I find this particularly clear in regard to the user-cost method as I explain in a later chapter. On the other hand, the literature does not lack examples of impressive work including that by Young and Serôa Da Motta (1995) on mineral extraction in Brazil; the study by Vincent and Hartwick (1997) on forestry for the FAO; or also for forestry by Renaldo Serôa Da Motta and Ferraz (2000). Lest it be said that I extol only work that supports my approach, I should add the FAO work on forestry was not uncritical of my method.

My first example of a gap between theorists and practitioners, which I am calling 'incongruity', is the accountants' reliance on Harold Hotelling's visionary model that upholds expectation of rising prices of a depleting natural resource. This mistaken belief in the applicability of the model to the accounts of individual nations has invaded some theoretical research and been incorporated in empirical investigations including the work of the US Bureau of Economic Analysis. It figures prominently in the volume labelled *Nature's Numbers* published in 1999 for the US Committee on National Statistics (Nordhaus and Kokkelenberg, 1999), which I discuss in Chapter 11 on 'Misunderstandings'. Apart from what is contained there by way of illustrative examples, I have seen no actual application of the Hotelling theory for empirically greening the accounts though I fear it has the potential of being so misapplied. Indirectly, however, the Hotelling model has inspired several studies to test its implications for a number of African countries, but these enquiries have on the whole been tangential to resource accounting (see Perrings and Vincent, 2003; Cynthia Lin and Wagner, 2007). I am not referring here merely to the simplifying assumptions of optimality, free markets and foreknowledge underlying the Hotelling model, which obviously do not materialize in reality, but I have in mind specifically the misconception of the actual situations where the Hotelling model would apply. My argument in this regard would proceed as follows. National accounting is accounting for an *individual* economy. Consider the case of a minor oil-extracting country whose stock of this natural resource is fast dwindling. Such a country cannot expect much comfort from the Hotelling model coming as a saviour with the promise of a future price escalation. Such escalation if it materialized would only occur after the resource had expired, and the higher prices would be irrelevant. While the resource lasts other suppliers of the same commodity may be able to feed the global market so that the international price may not rise at all. It is only if the world market were controlled by one owner that the Hotelling model would work faultlessly so that increased scarcity would translate into higher prices; or alternatively if the individual supply sources were separated by significant distances and prohibitive transport costs to bring about an independent market for each separate locality. But these limitations of the model do not often present themselves in real life, and are seldom appreciated by the practitioners.

A second example that separates theory from practice is the controversy in the green accounting literature over whether marginal or average costs should be used for estimating the surplus that is commonly, but I believe inaccurately, known as 'resource rent'. This has emerged as a bone of contention among some analysts and will receive further attention later. It is advanced as a criticism of some adjustment methods that affect the estimation of 'resource rent'. Assessing resource rent is of vital importance since it directly influences the contribution of extraction that appears in the national income – not that measurements of marginal costs have actually been successfully made, but the criticism is advanced as a theoretical stick with which to beat empirical estimators, including the World Resources Institute. Determining marginal costs in extractive activities is well nigh impossible owing to discontinuities, joint products, contractual restraints on flexibility of action, and many other reasons. Adjustments based on average costs, which are the costs available to the accountant at period end – and may simply be obtained by dividing total costs by the volume of output extracted – have been condemned as overestimating the surplus. This argument is not only pedantic but, as I show when discussing sustainability in Chapter 13, is misguided. For one thing, average costs may in fact be falling instead of rising, in which case average costs will be higher than marginal costs. This will occur in situations where the prospective richness of a mine had been optimistically overestimated beforehand so that excessive investment was sunk in to create capacity that in retrospect could not be fully used up. Furthermore, in natural resource extraction a cost margin can rarely be identified in practice – a fact that renders the concept of marginal costs, though analytically promising, pragmatically irrelevant. Whether marginal or average costs ought to be used for estimating the surplus realized in natural resource exploitation is thus often pointless where costs in practically every case are discontinuous, the capital equipment used lumpy and indivisible, and the concept of the margin is simply a chimera. Furthermore, political situations surrounding resource-extraction activities are often obscure, and often unpredictable, and the contracts under which the work is carried out constrain the flexibility of operators who are typically expatriate corporations. Thus the assumption of a suppliers' output proceeding along smooth cost curves, though theoretically appealing, becomes not just incongruent, but divorced from reality. It is understandable that the mathematically inclined analysts should have a strong preference for continuous functions that would describe costs as totals, averages or at the margin, but the accountants dealing with the same subject matter have to make do with data that are incomplete and discontinuous, and occur not in continuous time but in the accountants' discrete periods. To the accountants, costs appear usually in *totals* on the basis of which averages may be calculated, and the concept of the margin would be alien to the nature of the available information. Averages tend also to be reached through shortcuts and across data gaps and approximations, and are available only after the accounting period has closed. Thus the criticism that has been heaped on some pragmatic estimators who had used average rather than marginal costs for greening the national accounts appears to me unwarranted and superfluous. The French engineer/economist Gabriel Dessus (1949 [1951]), analysing the structure of costs in the related field of power production, denounced the economists' obsession with continuous cost curves, citing several practical difficulties against their occurrence, including the existence of multiple products with joint costs; the instability of the cost functions themselves; discontinuities in production; and other considerations that are paralleled even to a greater degree in extractive operations. But even in a remote and unrelated field, the field of retail trading, continuous cost functions have been found to be impossible to materialize in reality (see Dean, 1942). In all this we should remember that the strictures over marginal and average costs for greening the accounts were not theoretical qualms, but specifically geared to actual estimates in concrete situations.

A third example of incongruity between theory and practice is the attempt to derive income estimates from stock changes in an ambitious attempt to link accounting flows tightly with stocks. Stocks do indeed change in volume as well as in value, and volume changes have many complex origins including reserve re-assessments, fresh discoveries, improvements in technology, and obviously the result of actual extraction. Such a watertight accounting procedure linking flows with stocks may make sense for abstract economic analysis, but creates insurmountable accounting difficulties. The national accountant's primary task is to estimate the flow of income and its cohorts, valuing them in the tradition of national accounting at market prices; and it is the flows, not the stocks, that for them are of primary importance. For accounting purposes the stocks serve only as a background datum, and their valuation is subject to accounting 'golden rules' designed primarily to keep capital intact for guiding income estimation. To the accountant, opening stocks are the same as the closing stocks of the previous period, and closing stocks for the current period should be valued at their cost of acquisition or market prices at the time, whichever value is less. When applied to the practical estimation of national income the prices favored by economists for valuing stocks are current prices throughout, and this procedure requires endless efforts of 'reconciliation' to bring about an unnecessary stock-flow value integration.

A final example, which I have already touched upon, is the mathematical arguments geared to 'refined' *welfare* estimates to be derived from the available GDP data. Deriving welfare from output is a worthy endeavor, no doubt, but it is an elaborate and complex task that requires a great deal of additional information not always available to the national accountants, and obviously missing in the national accounts themselves. Reading joy or happiness from national income must wait until *output* had been sorted out correctly. Many of the attempts so far made to translate output estimates into welfare estimates have tended to address the two tasks simultaneously. The proper sequence is first to adjust output, and then try to derive welfare from the result which will always remain debatable. The two undertakings, estimating output and estimating welfare, can more fruitfully be pursued separately, with the adjustment of output decidedly taking precedence over welfare which is obviously outside the SNA framework.

There are many similar instances of incongruity, that will receive attention in the course of this book, where theory, clever as it may be, has failed to guide practical estimation simply on account of the analysts' failure to understand the crudeness of the national account estimation process, the crudeness and incompleteness of the information usually available to the national accountants, and also the theorists' own refraining from clarifying the context where theory should apply. No less to blame is the estimators' inability to recognize the concrete settings that would accommodate the often-brilliant economic theories they would wish to have employed.

PRESENTING THEORETICAL WORK

It may be worthwhile to elaborate the last mentioned argument further. Quite frequently theorists highlight 'national income' or the 'national accounts' in the coverage of otherwise valuable theoretical contributions. In this regard I need only cite the names of Weitzman, Hartwick, Asheim and Mäler as examples of a multitude of distinguished authors anxious to join the green accounting debate. For some of them national accounting has represented only a fraction of their published work, and it may be unfair to select them for criticism here. In their work they rely on theoretical assumptions such as perfect foresight and an optimum trajectory of resource exploitation, however the optimum is defined, which are among the problems theory presents to the practitioners of the 'art' of computing the national accounts, and subsequently their greened accounts.

Whether the objective is estimating welfare, or simply reckoning output, is another area where the income estimators are often at a loss, baffled perhaps by the ingenuity behind the mathematical concepts on offer which are intended for *welfare* estimation and not for *output* estimation. A mathematical concept that provides a vivid example of abstraction is the 'Hamiltonian', which focuses on the estimation of the net rather than the gross product. As stated earlier those involved in the empirical estimation of the national accounts often misjudge the practical situation to which a theory may be applicable – in this case the welfare orientation of the Hamiltonian, which obviously has no place here (see for example Weitzman (2000)). And the theorists, seemingly carried away by the ingenuity of their models, often disdain to guide the estimators to where their theories may be relevant in practice. This issue may be compared to medical practice where a diagnosis made by a clinical practitioner would largely depend on the correct reading of actual symptoms in a concrete situation, whilst therapeutic theories abound in textbooks. Which theory to pull out involves primarily a diagnostic skill which depends on observation, experience and common sense – all needed to identify a concrete situation. A similar flair, I believe, is required for greening the national accounts convincingly, sorting out what is relevant for application out of the cornucopia of theories available and which is continually being augmented by clever theories.

IV

PLANNING THE BOOK

Lastly, a word should be added regarding the contents of this book over and above the structure given in the Preface. I reiterate that the original papers that now make up the bulk of the text had been scattered in one form or another in many publications, and some had not been published before. Attempting to bring them together in one place should make them accessible to researchers in the field of environmental economics. In the process I have managed to clear up some ambiguities and address misapprehensions of my approach, which have gained confirmation with repetition. To decide on the format of this book I had to choose between two options. One was republishing the previously published pieces in their original form in a collection of essays, and this was certainly tempting since it involved a minimum of effort. However, the original essays had often attempted to introduce more or less similar material to an unfamiliar audience, and thus in many respects overlapped with one another. Whether or not I have succeeded in pruning them sufficiently to eliminate duplication is debatable. On the other hand there is perhaps no real harm in some replication remaining, especially if it comes from different directions and if it succeeds in clarifying and reinforcing the thrust of my arguments.

Another good reason warranting the presentation now selected for these pages is that the subject of green accounting which is a common denominator in many of the papers contained in this book was at the beginning unfamiliar to the varied audiences I was addressing. At the time national income adjustment methods, which would alter estimates of fundamental macroeconomic quantities, were diverse and controversial so that when initially presented my approach frequently needed to be argued from first principles. With the passage of time, however, many scholars got a better grip on the subject and simultaneously my focus shifted to elucidating the basic reasoning underlying my method and to discussing the merits and demerits of alternative green accounting methods. Gradually, I also came to realize that an unfortunate chasm had developed within the national accounting reforming camp – a chasm that later widened and became a wide gulf that obstructed progress. This was between a few, including me, who sought green accounting for *economic* purpose on one side, and on the other perhaps a plurality of would-be reformers whose overriding interest was not economic but *environmental*. Attempting to articulate this divide in the following chapters will hopefully assist in guiding selection of a proper approach from among alternative methodological options, and perhaps also help to bring harmony between the two divisions of reformers who should be working in tandem instead of opposition. From my standpoint, I see the divide originating from the distinction between weak and strong sustainability – a theme that will be elaborated again and again in the following chapters.

NOTES

1. I remember hearing Robertson utter this aphorism in a talk he gave at the London School of Economics in the early 1950s. Others have credited it to Keynes without exegesis, but it is the kind of saying that was in the air at Cambridge, England, when Robertson and Keynes were contemporaries.

2. Richard Stone in the Foreword of 'Meade and Stone', 1948, cited below says that an earlier edition was published in 1944 by the Oxford University Press and refers to yet earlier official precursors along the same lines beginning in 1940.
3. Hicks's 'The unification of macro-economics' was a posthumously published article where Hicks asserts that it was the availability of data rather than the development of aggregative analysis (which could indeed be found in earlier writers) that began modern macroeconomics. Here also, Hicks stresses the influence of the 'socialization' brought about by the war effort, and the availability of income tax data that made the estimation possible.
4. See Paul Ehrlich, *The Population Bomb*, written more than four decades ago, which remains as relevant today, if not more so, since world population has soared from 3 billion in 1960 to 7 billion in 2011 and the incidence of famine has increased and deprivation has markedly worsened.

REFERENCES

Asheim, Geir B. (1994),'Net national product as an indicator of sustainability', *Scandinavian Journal of Economics*, **96**, 257–265.

Backhouse, Roger E. and Andrea Salanti, (eds) (2000), *Macroeconomics and the Real World, Volume 1: Econometric Techniques and Macroeconomics, and Volume 2: Keynesian Economics, Unemployment, and Policy*. Oxford: Oxford University Press.

Cannan, Edwin (1904), 'Introduction' in A. Smith (1776), *An Inquiry into the Nature and Causes of the Wealth of Nations*, Modern Library Edition (1937). New York: Random House, pp. xxiii-lvi,

Costanza, Robert et al. (1997), *Nature*, **387**, May 15, 253–60.

Cynthia Lin, C.-Y. and Gernot Wagner (2007), 'Steady state growth in a Hotelling model of resource extraction', *Journal of Environmental Economics and Management*, **54** (1), 68–83.

Dasgupta, Partha (2008), 'The welfare economic theory of green national accounts', *Environmental and Resource Economics*, **42**(1), 3–38.

Dean, Joel (1942), 'Department-store cost functions', in Oscar Lange, Francis McIntyre and Theodore O. Yntema (eds), *Studies in Mathematical Economics and Econometrics*. Chicago, IL: University of Chicago Press, pp. 222–254.

Dessus, Gabriel (1949), 'The general principles of rate-fixing in public utilities', International Economic Association, *International Papers No.* 1 (1951). London and New York: Macmillan and Co., pp. 5–22.

Ehrlich, Paul R. (1968), *The Population Bomb*. New York: Ballantine Books.

El Serafy, Salah (1998), 'Pricing the invaluable', *Ecological Economics*, **25** (1), 25–27.

El Serafy, Salah (2001), Chapter 8, pp. 189–210 in Ekko C. van Ierland, Jan van der Straaten and Herman Vollebergh, eds, *Economic Growth and Valuation of the Environment – a Debate*, Edward Elgar, Cheltenham UK and Northampton, MA, USA.

Hartwick, John M. (1990), 'Natural resources, national accounting and economic depreciation', *Journal of Public Economics*, **43** (3), 291–304.

Hicks, John Richard (1975), 'The scope and status of welfare economics', *Oxford Economic Papers*, **27** (3), 307–326.

Hicks, John Richard (1990), 'The unification of macro-economics', *The Economic Journal*, **100** (401), 528–538.

Hotelling. Harold (1931), 'The economics of exhaustible resources', *Journal of Political Economy*, **39** (2), 137–175.

Hueting, Roefie (1980), *New Scarcity and Economic Growth*. Amsterdam, New York and Oxford: North-Holland Publishing Company.

Keynes, John Maynard (1936), *The General Theory of Employment, Interest and Money*. London: Macmillan.

Kuznets, Simon (1971), 'Modern economic growth: findings and reflections', Nobel Lecture, *American Economic Review*, **63** (3), 247–258.

Lin, C.-Y.C. and Wagner, G. (2007), 'Steady-state growth in a Hotelling model of resource extraction, *Journal of Environmental Economics and Management*, 54 (1), 68-83.

Mäler, Karl-Göran (1991), 'National accounts and environmental resources', *Environmental and Resource Economics*, 1(1), 1–15.

Meade, James E. and Richard Stone (1948), *Income and Expenditure*. Cambridge: Bowes and Bowes.

Nordhaus, William D. and Edward Charles Kokkelenberg (1999), *Nature's Numbers: Expanding the National Economic Accounts to Include the Environment*. Washington DC: National Academy Press.

Perrings, Charles and Jeffery R. Vincent (2003), *Natural Resource Accounting and Economic Development*, Cheltenham, U.K. and Northampton, MA: Edward Elgar.

Serôa Da Motta, Ronaldo, and Claudio Ferraz do Amaral (2000), 'Estimating timber depreciation in the Brazilian Amazon', *Environment and Development Economics*, **5** (1), 129–142.

Smith, A. (1776 [1937]), *An Inquiry into the Nature and Causes of the Wealth of Nations*, Modern Library Edition. New York: Random House.

Vincent, Jeffrey and John Hartwick (1997), 'Forest resources and the national income accounts: concepts and experiences', Report to the FAO Forestry Department, Rome.

Weitzman, Martin (2000), 'The linearised Hamiltonian as comprehensive net domestic product', *Environmental and Development Economics*, **5** (1), 55–68.

Young, Carlos Eduardo Frickmann and Ronaldo Serôa Da Motta, (1995), *Resources Policy*, **21**(2), 113–125.

2. Green accounting: history and prospects

PRELUDE

This chapter covers some of the ground of Chapter 1 but from a different angle. In part it is a piece of personal history regarding my getting involved in green accounting. It also tries to assess the current status of green accounting and speculates on its likely future course. The personal history part will understandably differ from other people's recollections, but this should be expected. A rival method to the user cost, the 'net price method', has triumphed, having been backed in influential circles. Without a determined effort to extricate green accounting from its present stagnation, it will almost certainly not survive as a convincing tool for achieving what green accounting was meant for. Despite all, there continues to be considerable interest in green accounting worldwide. The assessment of empirical results and even the purpose of greening the accounts remain blurred. Importantly, the impact of national accounting reform on macroeconomic policies does not seem to have attracted much interest. This raises the question as to the very purpose of greening the accounts. As I see it, a web of confusion and unhelpful contributions has shrouded this once promising tool, and this short chapter aims to trace its chequered course from its inception. It will briefly identify what I consider to be confusion and negative contributions advanced for and around it. With some overlap with the previous chapter, this chapter will speculate about future prospects of green accounting, while sketching an approach that might revive it and restore its past momentum. A *sine qua non* for such restoration would be a forceful and disinterested sponsorship by a leading institution with adequate resources and sustained determination. But until this occurs, the best that I can offer is to try to take stock of its current status and chart a tentative way ahead.

FROM PHYSICAL TO MONEY ACCOUNTING

Before its association with economics, green accounting began sensibly enough in physical terms using physical units appropriate to each natural resource. Indicators were sought for CO_2 emissions; loss of forest cover; erosion of soil; pollutants in air and water, etc., employing appropriate *numéraires* such as tonnage, acreage, cubic feet, and a variety of metrics of concentration and erosion. Such indicators were often converted into ratios, time rates of change, indices and occasionally into years of projected life expectancy of a natural resource. During the past quarter century, however, green accounting has become more ambitious, moving from the physical to the monetary, and the phrase is now generally identified with expressing the physical changes in value terms and aiming to embody them in the framework of the national accounts. Even the environmentally driven current activities for the satellite accounts are being pursued within the orbit of the SNA – a quintessentially *economic* system. Like all accounting, and particularly in the case of national accounting, green accounting does not claim comprehensive coverage and large tracts of the environment will always be left outside the accountant's perspective, whether estimated in physical or value terms. The economists concerned for the environment had looked at the SNA as a possible venue for reform. Insufficient attention, it seemed, was being given to environmental deterioration, noted only piecemeal by ecologists and expressed in a variety of separate physical indicators. Reform-minded environmental economists wished to see environmental losses grouped together, added up in some form and inserted, if possible, into the powerful medium of the SNA.

From the perspective of the macroeconomists, the traditional national accounts were producing aggregate estimates, which, while on the whole useful, imparted false messages about the economic prosperity of many countries. Among the latter, some of the poorest countries were affected. These have tended to be disadvantaged and 'under-developed' nations, which rely significantly on primary production. Where the sources that fed these primary activities were undergoing significant decline, the accounts would perversely show misleading indications of macroeconomic progress. In some cases these indications were not just misleading, but also harmful. Better accounts were needed to monitor progress and inform macroeconomic management.

Whether the search for better accounts was motivated by ecological apprehensions, or by concern for more meaningful macroeconomic measurements, the well-tested and highly valued system of national accounts was beckoning as a promising medium for the purpose. If handled appropriately the system could convey aggregate estimates of changes occurring in the environment expressed periodically in value terms. Government, citizens, business interests and other users of the adjusted estimates, it was thought, would then appreciate the enormity of the environmental damage and be motivated to do something about it. Yet identifying and calibrating environmental losses and bestowing values on them were not expected to be easy. The task, however, appeared interesting and challenging. With better information and improved methods, the goal did not seem untenable.

Many economists were aware of the fundamental dependence of economic activities, all activities in fact, on natural resource availability, and of the negative impact that pollution inflicts economically on people's life longevity and morbidity, and on the quality of health, and hence economic productivity. Yet on the whole, greening the national accounts had not been thought of previously as a possible tool for reform. In this respect, reform meant that the level and year to year variations in economic activity – interpreting the rises indiscriminately as desirable 'growth' – would have to be re-estimated to identify the hidden costs underlying the observable growth. In other words, environmental deterioration needed to be acknowledged explicitly and 'internalized' in the economic calculus. Thus the notion of green accounting, valued in money, was born.[1]

LACUNAE IN ECONOMIC ACCOUNTING

Without invoking any environmental argument, it did not make much *economic* sense to treat as value added the entire revenue raised by selling natural assets (such as fish, forestry products or petroleum) and include them in GDP simultaneously as the remaining stocks of these resources were known to be declining. And they were declining in the most obvious way, by the very act of extraction. Additionally, there were those resources that deteriorated collaterally, as it were, while supporting regular activities in agriculture, manufacturing, transportation and consumption. Examples include declining water tables, thinning soil cover, rising land salinity, silted waterways, additionally polluted by run-offs of toxic pesticides and chemical fertilizers; not to forget noise, congestion and urban wastes, as well as many others. All this deterioration had tended to be left out of economic reckoning.

It was a sad commentary on economic measurement in an age that boasted mathematical refinements and wide strides in the application of statistical methods to economic analysis that the decay of such important economic assets was overlooked when it should have commanded intense attention. As to natural resource dependent economies – many of them countries struggling to come out of poverty and backwardness – since the proceeds of their asset sales were regularly conflated with income, they were falsely portrayed as enjoying exaggerated domestic and national products. By indicating exaggerated levels of income, the national accountants were inadvertently giving license to excessive consumption which had frequently to come out of capital – a sure recipe for worse things to come.[2] Economists who set themselves up as specialists in 'Development Economics' were especially at a disadvantage, continually having to use inadequate national accounts to gauge macroeconomic change, assess the results of their recommended policies and reformulate their advice in light of what the national accounts told them of what was happening on the ground. Little wonder that the record of economic and social development, particularly in sub-Saharan Africa, has been disappointing. Had the economists access to better macroeconomic numbers their reading of change would have improved, and the effect of the prescribed policies more realistically evaluated. But, of course, faulty accounting cannot be singled out for blame for obstructing progress. And yet I find it amazing that the near-universal SNA, as sponsored by the UN, had remained for decades oblivious to the special position of the majority of the natural-resource-dependent developing countries whose macroeconomic variables were being estimated by a flawed system.[3] Even more amazing is the post-SNA93 insistence that nothing was wrong with the historical accounts: they were 'economic' despite the obvious impact of environmental deterioration on economic performance.

In view of the fact that the product of many countries was being portrayed inadequately in the national accounts, it is surprising that many analysts seem to focus on a welfare interpretation of the greened accounts, but there was also no scarcity of reformers who wanted to amend the SNA on grounds other than environmental. Defects were found in the leaving out of non-marketed transactions; virtually overlooking subsistence production; excluding unpaid domestic and voluntary work; and failing to count leisure in output. These gaps, or perceived gaps, if bridged, will not make an appreciable difference, and must be judged in the present context to be of secondary importance. Adjustment for environmental change if done properly will turn out to be substantial and thus economically far more important.

A QUESTION OF ATTITUDE

Even more important than the size of the required adjustment is the attitude of economists towards the methods of national accounting. Economists on the whole do not think much of the historical prices that the accountants must use in their profession. These are the actual prices at which the assets in the books had been acquired and at which transactions have been made during an account period that has just closed. By the nature of their work, the accountants come in after period-end to estimate the period's income or profit. To economists 'bygones are bygones', preferring current and projected future prices instead. On the whole, they are also happier with sorting out problems within idealized models constructed behind simplifying assumptions. This method has unquestionably yielded numerous economic insights and has helped to create what makes up much of economic theory today, yet it is at odds with accounting methods. Furthermore, economists tend to be uncomfortable with the accountants' reliance on 'impure' or – in their view – 'distorted' market prices for valuing the various components that make up the national dividend. These prices are held to be impure on account of their being 'contaminated' with taxes and subsidies, produced under imperfectly competitive markets (monopoly, oligopoly, bilateral monopoly and so forth), among many other reasons.[4] The economists' preference would be for optimum or 'Pareto-efficient' prices which the accountants have no way of ascertaining, nor indeed any wish to employ if they knew them. Accountants do not deal with ideal magnitudes or setups, but with actual situations, and their efforts are essentially historical and not analytical. In the writings of many mathematically minded economists, the ideal is set up as a standard and contrasted with the practical, and the practical is often found wanting.[5] However, notwithstanding their unhappiness with the 'distorted' numbers of the national accounts, economists on the whole have not been averse to setting great store by them. They take them at their face value and try to squeeze all kinds of inferences from them. They feed them nonchalantly into sophisticated models arriving at dubious outcomes that inevitably reflect the quality of the inputs. Few leading economists are actually known to have criticized the quality of the national accounts they use. Even when they venture into subjects directly related to the environment such as the alleged 'Resource Curse' (see Chapter 18 in Part V) they use the flawed national income estimates glibly as evidence, trusting the estimates produced by the accounting system.

All told, it is tempting here to conclude that with or without its flaws the system of national accounting has been found by a majority of economists to be serviceable, meeting most economic needs, and thus deserves highly to be kept alive. Gross domestic product (GDP) is much too valuable to be discarded as some recent iconoclasts have been urging. However, it should not be left unadjusted without some drastic environmental corrections.[6]

UNEP AND THE WORLD BANK: A STORY OF INSTITUTIONAL COOPERATION

During the 1980s debates continued in earnest among interested parties to have the system of national accounts adjusted to show environmental deterioration, and this led to suggestions of some fundamental modifications to the system. But a guiding institutional hand for this important task was missing. The grand age of Hicks, Kuznets, Meade and Stone had gone, and the task had fallen to a new breed of specialists in national income *procedures* who, on the whole, turned out to be too conservative to entertain radical changes. Hope, however, had earlier emerged when the United Nations Environment Programme (UNEP) came into being in 1972 with strong representation on its board of developing countries, many of which were sensible to the decline of their ecological wealth. In the early 1980s UNEP formally invited the World Bank to collaborate over a task related to natural resources, which was not precisely defined, and the World Bank responded positively. In the framework of this collaboration a series of international workshops was organized, and after two initial meetings led to the idea of exploring the possibility of amending the SNA so that it could meet the growing environmental concerns.[7] To begin with, the search aimed at finding some 'metric' to show the predicament of the environment – a predicament which was felt by many, but not sufficiently appreciated by governments, business communities or the citizens at large. It was not, however, until the third workshop Paris meeting in 1986 that the SNA was identified as an ideal medium for that purpose.[8]

Between 1984 and 1988, six international workshops and expert meetings were held, which brought together environmentalists, national income statisticians and economists, many of whom submitted papers and held discussions in an effort to sift through options and explore reform possibilities.[9] A landmark along the way that eventually led to SNA93 was the publication of the UNEP–World Bank Symposium, *Environmental Accounting for Sustainable Development* (Ahmad et al., 1989), which printed a selection of papers presented at these gatherings. This was later followed by a decisive step taken by the Austrian Statistical Society, which in cooperation with the Austrian Central Statistical Office, organized a special conference on environmental accounting in May 1991. The conference was shaped by the International Association for Research in Income and Wealth (IARIW) and led to the publication in 1993 of *Approaches to Environmental Accounting* (Franz and Stahmer, 1993) containing an anthology of papers presented at that meeting. The initiative had by then matured, passed the stage of conceptual debate, and entered the practical world of statistical estimation. It was at that meeting that I represented my paper on inventories (El Serafy, 1993). The basic arguments I presented at that conference are summarized in Chapter 12.

THE NEW SNA AND THE SATELLITE ACCOUNTS

Meanwhile an Inter-Secretariat Working Group on national accounts took shape, consisting of representatives of relevant institutions among which the United Nations Statistics Department played an important role. For its work, substantial inputs were provided by EUROSTAT and OECD, and experts largely recruited from European and American institutions.[10] This group worked on revising the structure of the system, and addressed several weaknesses that had been indicated over the years. It was this group that really authored the new SNA which was issued in December 1993 to supplant the UN's 1968 System. This time, however, the system's sponsorship had widened to comprise five leading institutions (see Commission of the European Communities et al.,1993).[11] In respect of natural resources, it initiated the sub-system of satellite accounts as described in Chapter XXI of SNA93 and retold in Chapter 1 above. Also as previously stated, this sub-system was elaborated for the environment in a companion publication by the UNSD. It was the intention that, besides the environment, satellite accounts would also be compiled for 'health' and 'education'. But these were strange bedfellows to be lumped with the environment. It was not clear what accountants were expected to do with them, and obviously they had no constituency comparable to UNEP and the 'environmental movement' to support them. It seems, however, that they offered scope for broadening the concept of investment to cover investment in 'human capital' (see Jorgenson, 2010). To guide the development of the environmental satellite accounts UNSD composed the 'manual' or 'guide book' on how to compile these accounts as related in the previous chapter.

The justification for relegating the adjustment to satellite accounts, it was claimed, was to avoid burdening the main frame of the system.[12] At the time it was not clear, however, whether shunting the adjustment to satellite accounts would be the end of the road for greening the accounts or whether it was a temporary step until the sharp disputes over appro-priate adjustment methods had subsided and consensus prevailed. If this was to happen and consensus prevailed, it was hinted that the adjust-ments would then be incorporated in the 'main frame'. I for one, as I said before, was under the impression that this was only a temporary step, especially since the UNSD 1993 manual was described as an 'Interim

Version'. But I certainly failed to notice a signal that should have been obvious. It was a signal that was explicit in the very title of the handbook: *Integrated Environmental and Economic Accounting*, which declared that the environment was not economic. And the use of the word 'integration' cynically kept environmental accounting at arms' length, away from the core accounts. As it happened, this manual or *Blue Book* was found to be too elaborate to be employed by statistical offices worldwide and had to be simplified and made more 'user friendly'. But the very purpose of the satellite accounts continued to be blurred and this has retarded the efforts to prescribe for them any definite format. In practice, when compiled they seem to have become a depository of relevant information, closely or remotely relevant information, that one day may become of use. Some of the information is expressed in money values and some in physical units, but deliberately they do not figure at the SNA core.

FRESH ROUNDS OF GUIDELINES

To my knowledge few attempts were made to implement the 1993 Guidelines for the 'Integrated Environmental and Economic Accounting' (or IEEA as it is sometimes referred to) even in developing countries where outside 'technical assistance' has been made available to national statistical offices mostly through bilateral aid. The lack of a standard format, or even a model list of what should be contained in them, must have been a handicap. But it is also their purpose which has remained unclear from the beginning: unless, of course, their creation was deliberate as a diversion to deflect attention away from making changes in the core accounts.

With the slow progress being made, UNEP decided to prod the guidelines out of their slumber, aiming for a clarification of their role and the production of a simple manual that would induce implementation. It was natural that it should turn to the UNSD, which had issued the original version and also provides regular links with national statistical offices throughout the world. But as the account-greening field did not cease to be controversial, and as SNA93 had restrained flexibility of action, further refining of the guidelines proved difficult. Two subsequent versions of the guidelines were issued. The first, prompted by UNEP, came out in 2000 under the same title, *Integrated Environmental and Economic Accounting: An Operational Manual.* This was followed three years later by another version, *Integrated Environmental and Economic Accounting 2003* which seems to have advanced no further than 'a final draft before printing'.[13] Significantly, this latest version (UNSD 2003, p. 415) states that the 'whole of this handbook is likely to be subject to significant revision in the short to medium terms . . .'.[14] The hesitation over, and the constant revisions of, the guidelines, which are meant to clarify ambiguities and accelerate implementation, reflect a lack of clear purpose for greening the accounts. They also reveal basic contradictions in the whole approach of satellite accounting. Further work along the lines already established in my view is unlikely to lead to more workable guidelines.

DIFFERENCES IN OUTLOOK

During the 1980s the participants at the UNEP–World Bank workshops were probably under the illusion that they all had the same objective in mind, but there were two camps with two separate motives: one environmental and the other economic. It is now obvious that the environmental group had won. Greening the accounts has now meant 'no change' in estimating the gross output, and adjusting for the environment has become a side environmental issue. I may have been unconsciously aware of this latent fault line, but thought that getting agreement on changing the SNA might succeed in hitting two birds with one stone, so to speak. I thought that pursuing the environmental objective did not necessarily preclude achieving the economic one also. But in reality the economic emphasis has been downplayed in the process and the environmental one uplifted. Ultimately the split became unmistakable as disputes raged over such issues as 'sustainability': whether it should be weak (economic) or strong (environmental), and which greening method had implicitly assumed that natural capital and produced capital were substitutes or complements. The user-cost method has been wrongly criticized as based on infinite substitutability between natural resources and human-made capital.

To explain this dichotomy differently: the environmentalists were looking for indicators of natural resource deterioration, whereas the economists, though their intentions were not yet formulated, were targeting the macroeconomic estimates. What weakened the 'economist camp' further was its split over whether the economic purpose of greening the accounts was to gauge *welfare* changes, or less ambitiously, to get a firmer grip on output and the other macroeconomic magnitudes associated with it. Welfare is the joy or satisfaction associated with acquiring or consuming output. It is a state of mind that cannot be directly measured or even observed. Much more than aggregate output has to be known before any welfare inferences can be made from it, including the size of the population and income distribution. Besides, some drastic assumptions have to be made regarding the comparability of individual satisfactions. Such factors are normally absent from the macroeconomic aggregates of the national accounts. Users of the accounts may indeed try to distill from output levels and output changes presumed changes in welfare if they like, but it is a mistake to think that output and welfare are synonymous.

This last point is rather important since in the name of reforming the national accounts several economists have targeted welfare as the quantity that should be 'sustained' over time and further identified this quantity with net, as distinct from gross, output. Occasionally welfare would be conflated with consumption, excluding investment from output. All such speculations are not without interest, but their relevance is doubtful to greening the accounts. Worse, they divert attention away from addressing the practical problems of adjusting the macroeconomic estimates, and fog the vision of the income estimators who try to keep up with what the economists are saying. And then there is the issue of greening the accounts for environmental purpose. National accounting in any case is a poor instrument for achieving environmental sustainability however defined. And accounting, to stress this point once more, is a historical, not a forward-looking process. To estimate a year's income, the accountant has to wait until the year has closed. Its connection with the future is limited and is made through a narrow gate allowing consideration of keeping capital intact. For keeping capital intact, now widened to include environmental capital, 'depreciation' is estimated and deducted from gross income. The estimate of 'depreciation' of course varies according to whether strong or weak sustainability is targeted. But whichever level of sustainability is invoked this process of keeping capital intact has to be seen as pertaining to a short span of time. It is done from one account period to the next, and is meant only for ensuring the continuity in operation of the entity for which the accounts are being drawn. There is no reason, however, why analysts should refrain from extrapolating the national accounts of any country into the future for longer periods – even for a distant future – but such extrapolation has nothing to do with accounting, and alternative assumptions may be made regarding future technology, input substitutions, the composition of demand for ultimate goods among others. While such assumptions have everything to do with sustainability, they are irrelevant to greening the national accounts, which merely *describe* what actually happened in a period that has already closed. All that the SNA can offer in this respect are estimates of income based on what has been called 'weak sustainability': a degree of sustainability based on maintaining capital so that income will not be diminished.

To recapitulate, supporters of strong sustainability focus on natural resource stocks and would charge any decline in them against gross income to arrive at a greened net income. The sustainability they seek is geared to the environment and not to the economy. Their outlook may further be characterized as not only stock-focused, but also long term with different assumptions regarding the future. Applying a strong sustainability approach to the national accounting, always recommended by its advocates to adjust the net (and not the gross) magnitude will wipe from net income all value added by the resource itself, while leaving the gross income uncorrected. As a result neither the gross nor the net product will be properly estimated. The superiority of weak sustainability in this regard is clear. The gross product will be adjusted downwards, and the net product will need no further correction. The oft-repeated charge that weak sustainability urges the destruction of natural capital is baseless. Methods using weak sustainability, such as the user cost, do not recommend future action. The future is not addressed at all save through the narrow chink of maintaining capital intact, and this only from one account period to the next. Though called weak, there is nothing feeble about it as an instrument for greening the accounts. Remember also that it is not the business of accountants to recommend future investment, either in the aggregate or for specific activities – nor for that matter its spread over future time.

THE HEAVY HAND OF MATHEMATICS

This section is important, not just for national accounting, but also for economic scholarship generally which to a growing number of economists has become too mathematical for a discipline that is essentially a social subject.[15] One of Hicks's penetrating comments on the misuse of mathematics in economics is to be found in his review of Carl Menger's *Principles of Economics* when that book appeared in English in 1951 (Hicks, 1951 [1983], p. 334). He praises Menger highly saying that his lack of mathematics actually benefited his analysis:

> the absence of mathematical simplification gives him a beautifully direct approach to some problems which are again in our day being forced upon the attention of economists – problems which do not go into mathematics easily, so that we are tempted to deal with them by the use of higher and higher mathematics!

In a similar vein, the late Chicago Professor Milton Friedman thought that mathematics in economics 'is often used to impress than to inform' (Friedman, 1991). I have a feeling many contemporary economists will see the validity of this argument. Interpreting national income, the *social* product, in mathematical terms as some version of the Hamiltonian, and an indicator of welfare has not just diverted attention away from the central purpose of greening the accounts – which is essentially to get the right estimate of output while taking note of environmental deterioration – but in some small way it diverted the green initiative in the direction of the 'cloud-capped castles of the mathematicians'.[16] The pragmatic pursuit of greening the accounts got thus side-tracked by influential economists who raised interesting, but hardly relevant, welfare issues. The new contributions, by stressing 'national income' in their headings, have not helped the national income statisticians who try to heed what the economists are saying and seek to adjust their estimation methods accordingly. In fact it is only through welfare analysis that the concept of the 'Hamiltonian' trespassed on the discussion of national income. With its versatility in the dynamic analysis of optimization problems it was brought into green accounting incongruently to further refinements of measurements which cannot be attained in pragmatic work, besides the focus on welfare which the national accountants do not pursue. The constraining assumptions behind the Hamiltonian's usefulness in the present context – particularly assumptions of perfect foresight – limit its applicability or even relevance. In economics it was probably introduced by Samuelson and Solow (1956), but for national accounting it was later articulated by Weitzman who gave it an unmistakable 'welfarist' flavor. (Weitzman, 1976; see also Asheim, 1994, 2000).[17]

To me it is highly significant that Weitzman, despite his focus on welfare and his concern for refined measurements, was co-opted as a member of the Nordhaus Panel that produced *Nature's Numbers* in 1999, which was subtitled *Expanding the National Economic Accounts to Include the Environment* (Nordhaus and Kokkelenberg, editors). Membership of this panel included theoretical economists who had little familiarity with practical accounting methods, and a sample of income estimators who favored 'strong sustainability' – the same strong sustainability that, in my view, had previously wrecked the United States' initial efforts to green the American accounts (Survey of Current Business, 1994; see El Serafy, 1997). The association of welfare-oriented theoretical economists with this report, though they had much of value to say, and despite the fact that the panel came out in support of the resumption of green accounting, inevitably led the report along a strong sustainability path focused on ecological change with scant attention to macroeconomic needs. To repeat, pursuit of strong sustainability ends in wiping out from a greened net product any contribution made by 'mining'– a result that was later judged inappropriate even by the chairman of this panel.[18]

V

WEALTH VERSUS INCOME

It seems almost self-evident that the 'wealth' of an individual or a group has more bearing on welfare than income, which may fluctuate from year to year. In lean years a person of wealth can draw on that stock to sustain annual wellbeing. Whether this obvious fact needed mathematical proof is questionable. Yet wealth became the focus of a line of thinking that has been another diversion of attention away from the flow accounts, and reinforced the mistaken strong sustainability approach rooted unavoidably in the attempted valuation of wealth. An important supporter of the wealth approach has been Dasgupta who could find no better way of estimating the 'wealth' of a number of countries than multiplying the available income estimates – though considered 'inadequate' for the purpose – by a factor of four (Dasgupta, 2001, p. C11). To emphasize his preference of wealth over income, Dasgupta appealed to Adam Smith, mistakenly asserting that Adam Smith's *Wealth of Nations* was about the stocks of wealth not the flows of income.[19] A strong argument against reliance on wealth is that hardly any country has successfully estimated its wealth – not even that portion of its wealth that is made up of 'produced assets' which include the public assets of ports, roads, dams, bridges and other structures. The book-value of some of these may be available, but economists, and hence the national accountants, are justifiably reluctant to set much store by such a value. It may be safely asserted that a comprehensive measure of wealth has not been made for any country, however 'advanced', and in my view that is not a great loss for economics. As to ecological wealth, which even Dasgupta would count in the national wealth, it comes in a vast variety of genres and shapes, extending from a share in the earth's protective ozone layer to the almost infinite variety of biodiversity: from fish in streams, lakes and adjacent oceans, to forests of many types; from natural springs to rainfall, to subsoil aquifers; and to complex ecological systems that are not easy even physically to delineate. How can we be expected to be able to count the fish, quantify forestry stock, or get a handle on biodiversity in physical terms – let alone attach economic values to them to arrive at a country's stock of wealth? And yet, the guidelines for compiling the satellite accounts (United Nations, 2003) in Chapter 7 and again in Chapter 10, cheerfully gloss over these obvious difficulties and reiterate the following theoretical approach in relation to natural assets, put forward as if it were a practical method for assessing wealth. Projections are to be made of the future products of this wealth, year by year, with annual prices predicted for valuation before discounting this hypothetical stream of conjectures to arrive at a current value of society's natural wealth. Obviously overlooked here is the fact that that wealth is not needed for the estimation of the flow accounts, and changes in wealth, even if they could be reliably estimated, should not be mixed with the vastly more important annual product. What is obviously more relevant is the *change* in the physical stock, not the stock itself; and the value of the change, not the value of the stock. The physical changes in market-transacted stocks due to economic activity are valued in the normal way at current market prices. The total value of the stocks will always be debatable, and in fact it is of little use to economists, and can be totally ignored. In sum, wealth understandably would interest its owners, individual or corporate, the authorities assessing inheritance tax, and lending institutions when assessing loan collaterals, but is hardly indispensable for economic analysis. If the economists need to estimate wealth they can do this by speculating outside national accounting. The imaginative view, originally proposed by Irving Fisher, that national income is in fact the interest society earns annually on its wealth, which seems to have been freshly discovered and rediscovered by contemporary economists, is undoubtedly true, but it is of little operational significance.[20] It is also historically true that William Petty (1623–87), a pioneer of social accounting (and from whose work macroeconomics is said to have descended), tried to assess wealth, but that was only for a limited purpose. He had gone to Ireland with Cromwell's army in the 1650s and was asked to estimate the prize of the conquest: the wealth of Ireland (see Hicks, 1990).

AN ASIDE ON POLLUTION

Pollution appears to be a major environmental concern for the richer economies, more so than source resources like petroleum or forests – at least for those countries without significant stocks of the latter sort to worry about. Reducing pollution in practice does not require much assistance from national accounting. Over the longer term moderating the rate of expansion of economic activity will certainly help, especially if coupled with encouragement of technological changes that will lessen demand for natural inputs and reduce emissions associated with production, transport and consumption. Initiatives for raising awareness, identifying polluters and encouraging less wasteful consumption habits, including curtailing armed conflicts, will all be helpful. So will arresting population growth, which in many parts of the world has been sapping the forces of economic and social development. For the shorter and medium terms, pollution

problems can still be addressed by regulation, policing, taxation, inducement and penalties.

Where pollution matters have been covered, or attempted to be covered,
as corrections to national income, the size of the adjustment has been
found to be relatively limited and the impact on actual behavior even
less impressive. Pollution of course is not a negligible matter, and its
damage, if properly assessed – counting secondary and tertiary rounds of
impacts – will be seen to be enormous. For it can undermine biological
life-support systems and the very lives these systems sustain. However, it
still makes some sense to try and use the agency of national accounting for
the purpose. An imaginative practical suggestion has been made by Roefie
Hueting to associate pollution with GDP. This begins by setting standards
of 'tolerable' pollution, assessing the cost of reaching them, and charging
this cost against GDP.[21]

VI

A CONCLUSION

This chapter overlaps in many ways with the previous one though it comes
with a different slant. It describes the dilemma of green accounting at
present and the different directions in which it is being pulled by diligent
economists of varied interests. It does contain a bit of history relating to
my association with the green accounting effort. This is obviously a blink-
ered history and a subjective one, but we are informed by the historians
themselves that subjectivity and limitedness of perspective are inherent
in all histories.[22] If my story is challenged I shall not change it except on
factual grounds. My narrative has not been confined to the past as I have
been going back and forth to discuss various aspects of green accounting,
which I thought were relevant to this history. More substantively I hope
the important message has come through in this chapter that I have viewed
green accounting all along as an economic initiative, conducted through
the economic medium of the national accounts, with outcomes expected
to affect the estimation of the macroeconomic variables produced by the
accounts. This economic outlook is one that is very largely missing in the
literature, and I plan to maintain it throughout this book. It will be seen
that the *purpose* of greening the accounts will come up again and again,
and unless clarity is gained by all who are engaged in the green accounting
process nothing much of value will be achieved. The concepts of 'wealth'
and more relevantly 'capital', though difficult to estimate empirically, still
remain crucial for economic analysis. These again will come up repeatedly

in the following chapters. To reinforce the economic thrust of this chapter my next task will try to articulate the argument that the environment does indeed qualify as an important part of a nation's capital.

NOTES

1. The thought of using the SNA for greening the national accounts must have occurred to others besides myself, but its adoption by the Workshops was due I believe to my involvement. There was certainly a strand within the joint UNEP–World Bank Workshops held in the 1980s who had much less interest in economics and were wary of valuing environmental losses in monetary terms. Members of this group favored the collection and analysis of physical data instead. The Fifth Workshop meeting held in Paris, 20–21 November 1986, represented that variation (see Ahmad et al., 1989, p. 95). Participants in that Workshop attached a low priority to using the medium of SNA on the grounds that it offered little by way of 'practical resource management needs in developing countries' (cf. Garnåsjordet, 1986).
2. At the micro level extractive projects were similarly assessed for prospective investment by the same flawed methods, viewing their estimated future benefits as unfettered gain without allowing for the stock declines brought about by extraction. The overestimation of investment returns in these activities hastened the depletion of the natural resources involved, and misdirected scarce investment funds away from other lines that might have accelerated development.
3. Prior to SNA93 most countries with some notable exceptions (e.g. the United States and USSR) were following the UN's SNA, which had had remained virtually unchanged since 1968.
4. There is a variant of national income that estimates it at 'factor cost' avoiding valuation by market prices so that taxes, subsidies and the like are excluded. These are viewed as 'transfer payments' from some income recipients to other income recipients. Using market prices for valuation in national accounting is now predominant.
5. Prominent examples are Weitzman (1976) and Hartwick (1994).
6. On 7 December 1999 the Department of Commerce of the United States Government (the parent of the Bureau of Economic Analysis which produces the national accounts) formally designated the national income and expenditure accounts as its 'achievement of the century', noting their contribution to winning World War II and helping the American economy 'along a path of prosperity and stability' (Daley et al., 2000).
7. This unusual institutional collaboration perhaps needs some explanation. As already said, it was UNEP that took the initiative of inviting the World Bank's collaboration at a time when the World Bank had only a fledgling Environmental Unit with little operational experience or policy clout within the Bank. The ecologist Robert Goodland, a member of that Unit, breathed life in the collaborative project. With Yusuf Ahmad from UNEP they co-chaired the first international gathering that heralded a number of subsequent meetings, which eventually became an established series. What is interesting, and perhaps unrepeatable, was the readiness of the Bank to commit resources including personnel time, travel expenses and conference venues in Washington and Paris for the exploration of this novel territory. Behind the scenes was perhaps the pressure from environmental non-governmental organizations (NGOs) on the United States Treasury, which played a constructive role. The Bank was in fact being urged to become more environmentally minded. Personally, I had no connection with the Bank's environmental work at that time, but my interest in the environment's impact on macroeconomic policy was known to many Bank colleagues. And the Bank was obviously eager to participate in this effort to help improve its economic and social development image. Later compartmentalization of the Bank that brought about, inter

     alia, the establishment of a Vice Presidency for Sustainable Development, which hosted the 'Environment Department', seemed paradoxically to dampen this earlier innovative and investigative spirit.

8. This was the first Workshop I attended and I believe it was I who directed the initiative towards using the SNA as a vehicle.

9. For details of attendance and topics discussed at these gatherings see Ahmad et al. (1989, pp. 93–95).

10. From personal correspondence, I understand that EUROSTAT (of the Commission of the European Communities) and OECD were vying for dominance, and the former prevailed.

11. Commission of the European Communities; International Monetary Fund (IMF); OECD; UN; and the World Bank.

12. Contrary to the intentions of SNA93, there has been no follow-up on devising satellite accounts for health or education either in 'Studies in Method' or elsewhere. Some national accountants were viewing expenditure on health and education as investment in 'human capital', but there were no constituencies to push for health or education coverage in the national accounts and no research done on them similar to the environmental issue. Grouping them with the environment as suitable candidates for satellite accounting is revealing in that all three subjects were not being considered as central issues to affect the core estimates, though they were areas of 'curiosity' to be covered if possible with supplementary information.

13. See Alfieri and Olsen who in a 2007 paper still referred to this 'final draft before printing'. Alfieri should know the status of this publication as she was writing as the chief of the Environmental Economic Section of UNSD.

14. One revealing feature of the difficulties encountered is that successive handbooks gained steadily in length as they lost in clarity. The initial 1993 guidelines (the 'interim version') had come out in 182 pages; the 2000 version (UN, 2000) in 235 pages; and the latest, the 2003 update (final draft before printing) has no less than 572 pages – more than triple the first version. It is noteworthy that this final version, while intended for the familiar series of UNSD's 'Blue Book' series, appears to carry the 'authority' of all five institutions in whose name the original SNA93 was issued.

15. See 'Economic education after the crisis', pp. 14–16 in the Royal Economic Society newsletter (2012) describing an initiative sponsored by the Government Economic Service and the Bank of England to explore economics teaching at UK universities. Lack of history, institutions and economic doctrines in curricula were identified as weaknesses.

16. This memorable phrase was 'coined' in a different context by Hicks (1966, p. 21). I believe it refers to the impermanence of much unnecessary mathematical work which Hicks considered as a 'baseless fabric' similar to the 'Cloud-capp'd towers, the gorgeous palaces, the solemn temples' which all 'shall dissolve' as Prospero says in Shakespeare's Tempest, Act IV.

17. The Hamiltonian, which began to appear in the literature on green accounting with some frequency, has been described as equal to a level of 'stationary utility' obtained by discounting future utilities, using discount rates as weights (see Heal and Kriström, 2001 [2005]). A number of mathematically argued papers began to appear with some regularity referring to national income following Weitzman (1976), including Hartwick (1994) and Asheim (1994).

18. An e-mail from Professor Nordhaus to the author, dated 19 December 2002, contained the statement: 'It is going too far to argue that there is zero value added in the extractive sector.' Needless to say that this 'outlandish argument' was the very one favored by the Nordhaus Panel. Reference should also be made to a different, yet comparable, work by Heal and Kriström (2001), which interestingly combines admirable theoretical analysis with a less satisfactory handling of practical approaches to greening the accounts. Here again 'strong sustainability' is implicitly accepted as the guiding principle for adjusting the accounts. In both these works the user-cost method makes an appearance, but is not actively advocated.

19. On p. C4 Dasgupta writes, 'The moral is this: whether we are valuing or evaluating, the object of study should be wealth. Viewed in terms of this finding, it should not surprise that Adam Smith inquired into the wealth of nations, not the gross or net national product of nations, nor the Human Development Index of Nations.' Contrast this with Hicks's statement, reinforcing other authorities on Smith: 'We are nowadays so accustomed to thinking of wealth as capital wealth that it may not be easy to realize that in Smith wealth is normally taken in a 'flow' sense (Hicks, 1975, p. 224n). Interestingly when Dasgupta made this false interpretation of the *Wealth of Nations* at a World Bank seminar prior to publication I corrected him publicly.

20. Dasgupta (2001), instead of multiplying national income by a factor of four to arrive at wealth, could have divided income by a hypothetical interest rate, but of course the choice of a meaningful interest rate would be awkward. The factor-of-four assumption implies an interest rate of 25 per cent if human and ecological capital are excluded, but it is not clear how the exclusion of ecological capital can be justified when the subject is natural resources as assets.

21. Under the method proposed by Hueting (see Tinbergen and Hueting, 1992) standards are to be set for acceptable levels of pollution. The cost of meeting these standards may be theoretically estimated and imputed as a charge against the unadjusted GDP. Controversy, however, gets in when defining such standards, and further in respect of the technology to be applied for attaining them and, of course, technology does not stand still. If such standards are met autonomously by the polluters themselves, or forced upon them by legislation, no correction of GDP for pollution would be needed. See also El Serafy (2001).

22. I recall an early project of United Nations Educational, Scientific and Cultural Organization (UNESCO) for the production of an objective world history by a committee of eminent experts selected for the task. The process began with one distinguished historian writing a piece of text and allowing other distinguished historians to record their qualifications or dissent in footnotes. The footnotes kept expanding until they swamped the text, and the project had to be abandoned.

REFERENCES

Ahmad, Y. J, S. El Serafy and E. Lutz (eds.) (1989), 'Environmental accounting for sustainable development. A World Bank UNEP Symposium', Washington DC: The World Bank.

Alfieri, Alessandra and Thomas Olsen (2007), 'Integrated environmental and economic accounting', paper prepared for the second meeting of the Oslo group on Energy Statistics, Delhi, 5–7 February, available at http://milleniumindicators.un.org/unsd/env/accounting.

Asheim, Geir B. (1994), 'Net National Product as an Indicator of Sustainability', *Scandinavian Journal of Economics*, volume 96, number 2, pp. 257–265.

Asheim, Geir B. (2000), 'Green National Accounting: Why and How?', *Environment and Development Economics*, volume 5, pp. 25–48.

Commission of the European Communities (EUROSTAT), International Monetary Fund, Organisation for Economic Co-operation and Development, United Nations; and World Bank (1993), *System of National Accounts 1993*. Brussels, Luxembourg, New York, Paris, Washington DC: EUROSTAT.

Daley, W.M., A. Greenspan, M.N. Bailey and R.J. Shapiro (2000), Press conference announcing the commerce department's 'achievement of the century', *Survey of Current Business*, **80** (1), 10–14.

Dasgupta, Partha (2001), 'Valuing objects and evaluating policies in imperfect economies', *The Economic Journal*, **111** (471), C1–C29.

El Serafy, Salah (1993), 'Natural resources: fixed capital or inventories?' in A. Franz and C. Stahmer (eds), *Approaches to Environmental Accounting*. Heidelberg: Physica Verlag, pp. 245–258.

El Serafy, Salah (1997), 'Green accounting and economic policy', *Ecological Economics*, **21** (3), 217–229.

El Serafy, Salah (2001), 'Steering by the right compass: the quest for a better assessment of the national product', in Ekko C. van Ierland, Jan van der Straaten and Herman Vollebergh (eds), *Economic Growth and Valuation of the Environment: A Debate*. Edward Elgar: Cheltenham, UK and Northampton, MA, USA, Chapter 8, pp. 189–210.

Franz, A. and C. Stahmer (eds) (1993), *Approaches to Environmental Accounting*. Heidelberg: Physica Verlag.

Friedman, Milton (1991), 'Old wine in new bottles', *The Economic Journal*, **101**(404) 33–40.

Garnåsjordet, Per Arild (1986), Rapporteur's Memorandum dated 5 December on the Fifth Workshop held in Nairobi, Kenya, 20–21 November, mimeo.

Hartwick, John M. (1994), 'National wealth and net national product', *Scandinavian Journal of Economics*, **96**(2), 253–256.

Heal, Geoffrey and Bengt Kriström (2001), 'National income and the environment', Columbia Graduate School of Business, No 98.01.

Hicks, John Richard (1951), 'Review of Carl Menger, principles of economics', *Economic Journal*, December, 852–853.

Hicks, John Richard, (1966), 'A memoir: Dennis Holme Robertson 1890–1963', reprinted from the *Proceedings of the British Academy: Sir Dennis Holmes Robertson, Essays in Monetary Theory*. Manchester, UK: Collins Fontana Library.

Hicks, John Richard (1975), 'The scope and status of welfare economics', *Oxford Economic Papers*, **27** (3), 307–326.

Hicks, John Richard (1990), 'The unification of macro-economics', *Economic Journal*, **100** (401), 528–538.

Jorgenson, Dale W. (2010), 'A new architecture for the US national accounts', Harvard University, Department of Economics, September, available at http://post.economics.harvard.edu/faculty/jorgenson.

Nordhaus, William D. and Edward Charles Kokkelenberg, (eds) (1999), *Nature's Numbers: Expanding the National Economic Accounts to Include the Environment*. Washington DC: National Academy Press.

Royal Economic Society (2012), 'Economic education after the crisis', *Newsletter*, **157**, April 2012, 14–16.

Samuelson, Paul A. and Robert M. Solow (1956), 'A complete model involving heterogeneous capital goods', *Quarterly Journal of Economics*, **70** (4), 537–562.

Survey of Current Business (1994), 'Accounting for mineral resources: issues and BEA's initial estimates', US Department of Commerce, Washington DC.

Tinbergen, Jan and Roefie Hueting (1992), 'GNP and market prices: wrong signals for sustainable economic success that mask environmental destruction', in Robert Goodland, Herman Daly and Salah El Serafy (eds), *Population, Technology and Lifestyle*. Washington DC and Covelo, CA: Island Press, Chapter 4, pp. 52–62.

United Nations Statistics Division, Department for Economic and Social

Information and Policy Analysis (UNSD) (1993), *Integrated Environmental and Economic Accounting (Interim Version), Studies in Methods*, Handbook of National Accounting, Series F, No. 61. New York: United Nations.

United Nations (2000), *Handbook on National Accounting, Integrated Environmental and Economic Accounting: An Operational Manual. Studies in Methods*, Handbook of National Accounting, Series F, No. 78. New York: United Nations.

United Nations, Integrated Environmental and Economic Accounting (2003), *Handbook on National Accounting, Integrated Environmental and Economic Accounting: An Operational Manual. Studies in Methods*, 'Final draft' circulated for information prior to official printing, to be issued in the series Studies in Methods, Series F, No. 61, Rev.1.

Weitzman, Martin L. (1976), 'On the welfare significance of national product in a dynamic economy', *Quarterly Journal of Economics*, **90**, 156–162.

3. The environment as capital

PROLOGUE

This chapter reproduces an invited paper read in Washington DC to the first meeting of the newly formed International Society for Ecological Economics held at the World Bank in May 1990. I had no formal connection at the time to the Bank's Environment Department although I had kept a close watch on ecological deterioration while helping to shape the Bank's development strategies for individual borrower countries. Projections of future exports, an important element in country policy formulation and for assessing borrower creditworthiness for Bank lending had to be made. In many cases future exports were assumed to grow simply by projecting older numbers regardless of ecological feasibility or even world market opportunities. Other duties at the Bank unfortunately limited my participation in the conference and hence any contribution I might have made to the follow-up discussion. Some environmentalists with disdain for economics have resented the appellation of 'capital', wary of economists trespassing on their turf. But I wished to establish the fact that taking note of ecological deterioration should be a primary concern for macroeconomic analysis and projections, and that a ready vehicle was available in the national accounting system. This chapter is included here with minor changes from Chapter 12, 'The environment as capital', in Robert Costanza (ed.), (1991), *Ecological Economics: The Science and Management of Sustainability*, Columbia University Press, New York, pp. 168–193. It proposes a gradual national accounting reform, which, however, was not adopted in the 1993 SNA. Of note is my endorsement of the then unborn 'Environmental Satellite Accounts'.

INTRODUCTION

Inasmuch as the environment contributes to the productive process, even when it is not appropriable, it should be considered as a factor of production. This chapter will consider the contribution the environment makes to production, and examine the substitutability between environmental elements and the conventional factors of production, notably capital. The chapter emphasizes the necessity of keeping environmental capital intact for proper national income measurement while distinguishing between renewable and nonrenewable natural resources. To keep renewable environmental capital intact, provision has to be made for its 'depreciation'. Depreciation along established accounting lines for fixed capital however is inappropriate for depletable resources, and this chapter will explain why. The chapter will end with a recommended approach for integrating capital conservation concerns in national accounting. The recommendations stress that we should proceed without delay to incorporate ascertainable environmental degradation into the national accounts, however imprecisely estimated, fully realizing that such an approach will remain partial, but is bound to be expanded gradually as our knowledge of the facts improves, and as we bring more environmental concerns 'into relation with the measuring rod of money.'

The capital of an economy is its stock of real goods, with power of producing further goods (or utilities) in the future. Such a definition of capital will probably be acceptable to most economists (Hicks, 1974). Viewed as such, capital would comprise land, considered in classical economic thinking as a separate factor of production. Land would qualify as part of the stock of real goods that is capable of producing further goods. And it is only a short step to extend such a definition to Nature in general, both as a source of raw materials and as a receptor of wastes generated in the course of economic activity. Alfred Marshall viewed the distinction between land and capital in their capacity as factors of production as rather artificial, just as he viewed the distinction between rent and profits.[1]

Marshall, who is generally regarded as the father of Neoclassical Economics, was so conscious of the contribution of Nature to production that he inscribed the adage *Natura non facit saltum* (which may be translated as 'Nature does not make a leap', or that it only proceeds slowly) on the frontispiece of his magnum opus, *Principles of Economics*, of which the 8th edition was published in 1920. Although he subscribed to the Ricardian theory of rent, which ascribes rent to the 'inherent' and 'indestructible' properties of the soil, and accepted the distinction between these original properties of land and the 'artificial properties which it owes to human action', he expressed his reservations thus: 'provided we remember that the first [i.e. land's inherent properties] include the space-relations of the plot in question, and the annuity that nature has given it of sunlight and air and rain; and that in many cases these are the chief of the inherent properties of the soil.' (Marshall, 1920, p. 147).

Stressing the capital quality of land, Marshall had on the same page written:

all that lies just below the surface has in it a large element of capital, the produce of man's past labor. Those free gifts of nature, which Ricardo classed as the 'inherent' and 'indestructible' properties of the soil, have been largely modified; partly impoverished and partly enriched by the work of many generations of men.

We have only to think of the 'impoverishment' of land in the passage just cited, as disinvestment, and of land as a proxy for Nature to conclude that the father of neoclassical economics himself was not unmindful of the contribution of Nature to the production of goods and services and would not be averse to the notion that the degradation of the environment should be charged against production as capital depreciation. It is not therefore in any sense revolutionary to think of Nature as a factor of production. The acid test of what makes a factor of production:

> is that it should make a contribution to production, in the sense that if it were removed, production (or output) would be diminished. Or more usefully, if a part of it were to be removed production would be diminished. Which comes to the same thing as saying that the factor must have a marginal product. (Hicks, 1983, p. 122)

That Nature has a marginal product is not difficult to demonstrate and therefore can be acceptable in the neoclassical economic framework as a factor of production. Even when Nature is held in common, such as international waters, the ozone layer or the air we breathe, it can still be viewed as a factor of production: even if it is not tradable and does not carry a market price. In the words of Hicks (*loc. cit.*), 'In order that a thing should have a price, it must be appropriable, but it is not necessary that a thing should be appropriable for it to be a factor of production.'

Which factor of production should Nature come under in order for it to be included in the economic calculus? The answer is that, for *theoretical* reasons, it does not matter. We may recall that Marshall applied the concept of rent to machines, inventing the category of 'quasi-rent' to denote income derived from capital that is in short supply in the near term. Also, Hicks questioned the traditional demarcation of factors: 'The factors of production are Land, Labor and Capital; or just Labor and Land; or just Labor and Capital; or just Labor' (Hicks 1983, p. 121) and queried their supposed independence of each other. For practical reasons, however, there are compelling reasons why Nature should be treated as capital. That it contributes to economic activity is beyond dispute. To subsume it under land, might trivialize its contribution, recalling Herman Daly's strictures against economics having reduced land's contribution to production to rent, and rent to a surplus that is excluded from the determination of prices (Daly and Cobb, 1989). After all, the most fecund form of the production function is provided by the Cobb–Douglas model which most commonly reduces the factors of production to only two: capital and labor. Under capital, one could bring in all kinds of things, including land and technology.

THE POWER OF TECHNOLOGY

In the debates between the environmentalists and traditional economists, a great deal has been made of the notion as to whether capital and natural resources are substitutes or complements. This issue appears important not just theoretically, but empirically also, as the environmentalists who are viewed often as doomsayers – very much as Thomas Robert Malthus has been viewed on population – insist that our planet's capacity to absorb our wastes and to provide raw materials and energy is limited, and that this limitedness cannot be assumed away in the belief that advances in technology are bound to ease out the constraints. Technology has been remarkably successful in that it substituted synthetic rubber for natural rubber, plastics for copper, and may well replace non-renewable fossil fuels with renewable energy. It has recycled some of our wastes and will probably recycle others. The electronic revolution is allowing much work to be carried out at home rather than on business premises, and is thus bound to reduce road congestion and cut down on transport.

In all this, technology seems to have consistently economized on material inputs as well as labor. And yet, overoptimistic views about the power of technology have failed us over the population problem worldwide – a major source of environmental stress – and are bound, if they continue to prevail, to fail us yet again in regard to the environment. Enough has been said in the first part of this chapter to show that theoretically all factors are substitutable for each other at least in some degree, but it is empirical substitution that is in question here, as reflected in, say, the elasticity of substitution between energy and capital in production processes. It would be foolhardy to argue that such elasticity is zero, even for the shortest of all runs. That it is bound to rise with time, in common with all elasticity relationships, is undeniable but trite, but this is not here the issue.

The issue, in my judgment, is whether in practical terms technology is developing rapidly enough to solve our environmental problems and the answer is clearly no. And it is the duty of the economist to play the role of the pessimist. If things are left to go the way they are going, repairing the damage would be far more costly than attempting to avert it before it has occurred. As all can see, too much damage has taken place already for complacency to continue to prevail.

NATIONAL ACCOUNTING FOR NATURE

The foregoing suffices to show that there is much in modern economics that is in harmony with ecological thinking. This, as I have shown, is particularly evident in the writings of John Hicks, a Nobel Laureate in economics who has had a profound influence on the profession. Not only has he supplied an excellent definition of sustainability by defining income, but he has also striven to give economic meaning to business practices, including accounting.[2] Besides, his copious work on capital theory contains fertile notions about the role of time in production from which environmental economics will eventually benefit. For me, it was his reflections on income from wasting assets in his magnum opus *Value and Capital* (1946) that led me to develop a model for calculating income from depletable natural resources (El Serafy, 1981). It is not, however, the contribution to production of natural resources that I wish to address here, but simply how to reflect, in national accounting measurements, the changes in the stock of available natural resources brought about by economic activity.

Quite clearly, if what is conventionally measured as income ignores the deterioration of the environment, either as a source of materials or as a sink into which we pour emissions which result in environmental degradation, then such an income is overstated. It is now pretty well established that national accounting should reflect such environmental deterioration, but there are still a number of controversies on how to make the required adjustments. Before addressing these controversies, however, it is necessary to point out that accounting has, on the whole, a limited function; it merely assesses the implications of past behavior for estimating profits or income, thus providing a measurement of performance, and therefore indicating 'net worth' since the accountants usually also produce balance sheets of assets and liabilities for the entity concerned, whether an individual, a corporation and sometimes bravely for a nation.[3] On the basis of the accounts, entrepreneurs can make decisions about the future, relying also on many other factors, including their expectations. Where the accounts are wrong, in the sense that the accountant's income contains elements of capital (representing the running down of natural resource stocks, or polluted air or water), such an 'income' exaggerates true income, and if consumed, could lead to inevitable ruin. In other words, accounting would be encouraging behavior that cannot be sustained. Meanwhile, since macroeconomic policy makes use of national income as a 'touchstone' against which various economic aggregates are tested (money supply, savings and investment, fiscal and current account deficits, etc.), false income measurements lead to faulty economic policies, besides failing to gauge true economic performance. Thus a country may be presumed to be achieving a high economic growth rate on the strength of the account-ant's flawed measurements, whereas in reality its true growth would be slower, nonexistent, or even negative than if the accounts were properly to reflect the diminution of the natural resource stocks and the deterioration and degradation of the environment. See, however, Chapter 13 below for caveats relating to this statement.

PARTIAL ADJUSTMENTS TO NATIONAL ACCOUNTS

I find it interesting that most people who see the necessity of adjusting standard national income calculations to reflect environmental concerns would wish to do so subject to two constraints. First, they wish to have a totally integrated system starting with a complete inventory of environ-mental assets, and setting money values on these assets which appear in the debit side of a balance sheet, whether these assets are natural – or human-made. Changes in such a balance sheet from year to year, as a result of degradation, renovation, locating new deposits, as well as economic exploitation, would be reflected in the end-period balance sheet. The impact on the flow of income would simply be derived from the change in wealth from one balance sheet to the next. The second constraint I see, which again seems to be quite popular, is the view that the GDP as con-ventionally calculated needs no adjustment at all. All that is needed is to reflect environmental degradation only in net income, by deducting from the gross values calculated, a magnitude for 'depreciation'. This course would leave the GDP (gross domestic product) and GNP (gross national product) series, as previously calculated, without alteration, and adjust only NDP (net domestic product) and NNP (net national product).

The first constraint is self-imposed and unnecessary; it is also so con-strictive that it is likely to impede progress on the adjustment of the national accounts. It should be obvious that no balance sheet can be con-structed which would not only cover the totality of natural assets in quan-tity and quality, but also put a money value on all these assets. Moreover, to attempt to reflect the year-to-year changes in the value of environmen-tal assets in the flow accounts would introduce large adjustments, which can dwarf the annual economic activities that should be the legitimate basis for income calculation. Re-estimation of mineral deposits, either as a result of new discoveries or a reassessment of reserves (remembering also that reserves are often orders of magnitude greater than annual extraction), can thus play havoc with the more solidly based income calculations without, in my view, being at all essential.

I have made two suggestions in this regard (El Serafy, 1991). First this 'holistic approach' should not be attempted at all, not even as an eventual goal, because it is impossible to attain and attempting its adoption is bound to impede progress on adjusting the national income estimates. All that is required is to take advantage of the satellite accounts, which have now been agreed to be developed under the forthcoming United Nations System of National Accounts, so that partial adjustments to income can be made there. On this, I have taken my cue from Pigou who, in *The Economics of Welfare* (1924, pp. 10–11), was facing a similar problem. Pigou perceived that economic welfare was only part of human welfare, but saw that human welfare was such a vast and complex subject – just, I would say, like the environment – that it could not be profitably studied by economists. Choosing a partial approach, he proposed that economists should focus on those aspects of human welfare that can be 'brought into relation with the measuring rod of money'.

I see the road clearly ahead: we must not be too ambitious at this stage aiming for a comprehensiveness that will forever remain elusive. Let us adjust national income gradually for depletion and degradation of petroleum, forestry and fisheries, fresh water availability, soil erosion, taking one step at a time until our methodologies firm up and the physical basis of our calculations improves, leaving economic valuation of thorny areas such as biodiversity to the last. We must also bear in mind the fact that accounting has a limited function, in that it should be complemented by sound environmental policies including proper incentives for conservation, disincentives against pollution and eventually regulation, if neither a carrot nor a stick is effective.

Apart from the holistic approach, the other major concern I want to stress is 'depreciation'. I find no fault in applying the accounting convention of depreciation of assets that wear out in the process of production to natural resources that can be repaired, renovated or replaced. In respect of resources such as forests and fish, sustainable yields can be estimated, and exploitation over and above such yields may be considered as comparable to depreciation. 'Positive depreciation' may be possible if replanting or restocking exceeds exploitation, but this should more appropriately be treated as capital formation. Where I think depreciation is not applicable is in the case of nonrenewable natural resources such as fossil fuels that cannot be recycled or reused once they have been combusted. I have argued elsewhere (El Serafy, 1989) that in their case we need to adjust gross income itself and not just net income. It is wrong to reckon receipts from the sale of such nonrenewable assets as value added, to be included in GDP. And deducting from it the whole part, representing asset diminution, would wipe out from net income the entire value added (due to the natural resource) by extractive activities. Sustainability, which is the hallmark of income, compels us to adjust GDP itself along the lines I am proposing.[4]

FUNDISTS VERSUS MATERIALISTS

The controversy on this issue, if I may call it thus, recalls two different views of capital, which have been lucidly demarcated by Hicks (1974). He distinguished between two schools of thought, the 'fundists' and the 'materialists'. The former view capital as a fund, a sum of money that can be embodied in physical goods, which is revolved over time in the process of production, whereas the latter, the materialists, think of capital in physical terms as machinery and equipment, goods in progress, and stocks of raw materials and finished products. Among the fundists, Hicks listed Adam Smith, Marx, Jevons, as well as the *accountants* who, up to the present, regard capital as a sum of values that may be embodied in physical goods in different ways. Hicks believed that fundist thinking had emerged from the pattern of economic activities (largely mercantile) that preceded the Industrial Revolution. Among the materialists, he classed later influential members of the profession: Cannan, Marshall, Pigou and J.B. Clark. Keynes, he thought, was brought up as a materialist, materialism being a post-industrial school of thought to which practically all neoclassical economists belonged, but his writings led to a revival of fundism. According to Hicks (*loc. cit.*): 'if the Production Function is a hallmark of materialism, the capital-output ratio is the hallmark of modern Fundism'.

As accountants have remained fundists, they naturally have had difficulty dealing with material capital, such as machines, which do not circulate like traded stocks and often last considerably longer than one accounting period. The imputation for depreciation of machinery and equipment is done on simple assumptions with which the economist feels uncomfortable. This probably explains, at least in part, why economists prefer to use GNP rather than NNP for macroeconomic analysis. The accountant, anxious to keep capital intact, uses rules of thumb, approximations and, above all, the assumption that technology remains constant over the life of the asset being depreciated. He or she resorts to approximation and shortcuts, because his or her primary concern is to indicate a level of income that can be safely consumed, leaning always to the side of caution: underestimating income if in doubt, in order to protect the intactness of capital. The accountant's income is primarily a level that indicates prudent and sustainable behavior though it often lacks the precision the economist is usually seeking.

When it comes to the treatment of exhaustible resources in the national accounts I find myself using the fundist approach to capital. The method I devised which converts receipts from mineral exploitation into a permanent stream representing true income, I did almost unconsciously, using the methods of the accountant. Petroleum reserves are part of a stock. They can be sold *in toto* or in part, and the proceeds can be sunk in other assets. I asked the accountant's question: what proportion of the total stock does the annual sale represent? In the light of the answer, and with the aid of a discount rate, I could convert the proceeds into a permanent income stream.[5] That Keynes (1936 [1949]), according to Hicks, became a fundist is clearly evident from his treatment of the user cost in *The General Theory of Employment, Interest and Money* (Appendix to Chapter 6). Very clearly, I treated sales of exhaustible natural assets as sales out of stock, not as production that creates value added which they are not. It was later that I called the capital element I calculated a 'user cost' to correspond to Keynes's approach which, interestingly (as he says) he brought over from the world of using up 'copper stocks', intending to apply the user-cost concept to the wear and tear of machinery.

CONCLUSIONS

Finally, I want to end on a practical note. Accounting has never found a totally satisfactory way of treating capital consumption for the purposes of net income estimation. Problems of inflation and changed technology have remained difficult to handle. To the economist, who is by nature forward looking, the value of capital lies in its ability to generate future production, and this may have little relation to the historic cost of making the capital in question. This latter cost is recorded in the books at inception, and is the stock-in-trade of the accountant. The accountant, also by nature, is backward looking, and it is wrong, as frequently happens, for people to confuse his/her functions with those of the economist. But the accountant performs a most useful task, and the accounting results are at once approximate and cautious. If we follow this reckoning, we strive to keep capital intact so that we can make use of it to give us a 'sustainable' income in the future. All we need to do now is to try to apply accounting to environmental capital, without waiting, focusing on income flows and leaving aside the valuation of the total stock of environment. Our approach should be gradual, attempting to bring measurable elements into the process as our knowledge improves. But to wait until everything falls properly into place will mean that we shall have to wait forever.

NOTES

1. Marshall (1920), see in particular p. 432 where he draws attention to the views in this regard of Nassau Senior and John Stuart Mill.
2. Hicks was the product of the English Neoclassical School of Economics, and was also greatly influenced by Pareto and more profoundly by the Austrians. His great interest in accounting is reflected in many contributions including *The Social Framework: An Introduction to Economics,* (Oxford: Clarendon Press, 1942; 2nd edition, 1952). An article about him published by Arjo Klamer (1989) after his death was titled, 'An accountant among economists: conversations with Sir John R. Hicks'.
3. The net worth of a nation's wealth, however, is likely to remain elusive to estimate for some considerable time to come.
4. As stated elsewhere all the sustainability accounting is capable of offering is a year-to-year sustainability (if the accounting period is a year); but if this process continues year after year a longer perspective of sustainability may be attained.
5. The discount rate has also relevance to the *ex ante* optimization of extraction, for it should guide the owner of a resource as to whether he should leave his resource in the ground to appreciate per Hotelling or extract it and reinvest the proceeds in alternative assets. See El Serafy (1989) and Hotelling (1931).

REFERENCES

Costanza, Robert (ed.), (1991), *Ecological Economics: The Science and Management of Sustainability.* New York: Columbia University Press, pp. 168–193.

Daly, Herman E. and John B. Cobb Jr. (1989), *For the Common Good.* Boston, MA: Beacon Press.

El Serafy, Salah (1981), 'Absorptive capacity, the demand for revenue, and the supply of petroleum', *The Journal of Energy and Development,* **VII** (1), 73–88.

El Serafy, Salah (1989), 'The proper calculation of income from depletable natural resources', in Y.J. Ahmad, S. El Serafy and E. Lutz (eds), *Environmental Accounting for Sustainable Development: a UNDP–World Bank Symposium.* Washington DC: The World Bank.

El Serafy. Salah (1991), 'Natural resource accounting: an overview', in James T. Winpenny (ed.), *Development Research: The Environmental Challenge.* London: ODI, Chapter 21, pp. 205–220.

Hicks, John Richard (1942), *The Social Framework: An Introduction to Economics,* (2nd edition 1952). Oxford: Oxford University Press.

Hicks, John Richard (1946), *Value and Capital: An Inquiry into Some Fundamental Principles of Economic Theory*, 2nd edition. Oxford: Oxford University Press.

Hicks, John Richard (1974), 'Capital controversies: ancient and modern', *American Economic Review*, **64**, 301–316.

Hicks, John Richard (1983), 'Is interest the price of a factor of production?', in *Classics and Moderns: Collected Essays on Economic Theory*. Cambridge, MA: Harvard University Press, Chapter 9, pp. 113–128.

Hotelling. Harold (1931), 'The economics of exhaustible resources', *Journal of Political Economy*, **39** (2), 137–175.

Keynes, John Maynard (1936 [1949]), *The General Theory of Employment, Interest and Money.* London: MacMillan.

Klamer, Arjo (1989), 'An accountant among economists: conversations with Sir John R. Hicks', *The Journal of Economic Perspectives*, **3** (4), 167–180.

Marshall, Alfred (1920 [1947]), *Principles of Economics*, 8th edition. London: Macmillan.

Pigou, A. C. (1924), *The Economics of Welfare*, 2nd edition, London: MacMillan.

PART II

Concepts of income and capital

4. Income, capital and wealth

I CONTROVERSIES

MEASURING INCOME

Income is a difficult quantity to define and problematic to measure. Capital is even worse; and yet both are important concepts with which economists and accountants have to struggle. Their relevance to national accounting is obvious for they directly impinge on the estimations of the macroeconomic values that are read from national income. Controversy surrounds discussion of both quantities, and yet, the meaning of both concepts has been fairly clear for some considerable time. This is not to say that either of them, especially capital, is yet free from debate.[1] Disputes have also surrounded a capital-related quantity, 'wealth', which has received much attention in environmental economic discussions of late. A source of some confusion is that wealth in classical economics often meant a flow of income. The recent popularity of the stock of wealth derives from the claim that it is superior to income as an indicator of welfare – a claim that can hardly be disputed. But welfare is not the primary reason, or even the reason, why national income is estimated.

Wealth and capital though closely related are sometimes differentiated, and the very meaning of 'wealth' has itself undergone change. In line with common usage in the time of Adam Smith (*The Wealth of Nations*, 1776) wealth denoted *income* as a flow. In current usage, however, it is a stock. As to capital, there has been a tendency, not always sustained, to regard it as a part of the stock of wealth: that part which combines with land and labor to produce income. On this view the rest of wealth over and above 'capital' comprises such things as works of art, musical instruments and similar possessions which, though yielding utilities to their owners, are not employed in production and thus do not create money income. Such a demarcation between wealth and capital, it is worth mentioning, was not favored by Fisher (1906). All told there is no dispute now over the fact that both wealth and capital are stocks while income is a flow. In some theoretical interpretations income is a kind of interest or dividend that society periodically earns from its stock of capital or wealth. This view, while analytically illuminating, is scarcely operational, defying empirical estimation.

MEASURING CAPITAL

The value of capital has sometimes been inferred from income estimates which are more readily available. Multiplying income by an arbitrary number assumed to indicate some capital–income ratio yields an estimate of capital. In the accounting books capital, as perceived by the economists, appears as assets, valued usually at historical costs and periodically adjusted upward by additional investments and downward by estimated depreciation.[2] How do national capital and income relate quantitatively to each other? Keynes in the 1930s would challenge his students to put a value on Britain's capital in comparison with its national income, and would provide his answer that two or three years of national output would make up the entire national capital (see also Chapter 16 on 'Sundry observations on the nature of capital' in Keynes's *General Theory*). It is interesting that some 70 years later Dasgupta, who prefers wealth over income as an indicator of welfare, had no precise answer to this Keynesian pedagogical quiz, and just employed a multiplication factor of four to conjecture capital (or wealth) from output estimates. He applied the same multiplicand – a factor of four – to a group of economies he called 'imperfect', varying from China to Bangladesh and from India to 'Sub-Saharan Africa' (see Dasgupta, 2001, Table 1).

There is also a tendency for economists to argue that a present value of the elusive quantity of capital may be inferred from capital's future contribution to production as if that can be ascertained. But this contribution not only has to be guessed at, but must also be discounted by some arbitrary interest rate. Yet the future will always be murky so that the robustness of such a valuation will ever be questioned. There are too many imponderables involved, including: (1) Will a good or service, foreseen as the product of a specific piece of capital equipment, continue to be in demand? (2) At what price will that product be sold and bought? and (3) Will the technology associated with that piece of machinery remain safe from being supplanted by newer processes that make the equipment redundant? These uncertainties caused Hicks once to doubt the appropriateness of such a speculative approach and made him argue that the book-keeping value of a piece of machinery as set at its historical cost might after all possess a validity that surpasses the conjectures of the economists. Despite the obvious shortcomings of these historical values, 'they may not be all that inferior to values obtained by sheer guesswork'.[3]

In national accounting income is not an ambiguous quantity since it is taken by convention as synonymous with output or product. From one angle it is seen as the sum total of consumption and investment; from another angle it is the aggregate of consumption and saving. But this makes no difference since saving and investment in a closed economy are always equal *ex post*, which in effect is the accountant's perspective. From another angle, national income is simply the sum total of incomes received by all members of society – a thought that can be traced back to the French late-eighteenth century Physiocrats. An important point always to keep in mind is that national income has to be made up entirely of *value added* – that is added by the services of land, labor and capital – the very factors employed in productive activities. The providers of these services, the owners of the factors of production, share the product among themselves, which they receive as their respective incomes: rent, wages, interest and profits.

The uncertainty inherent in capital valuation is of crucial importance for green accounting since it undermines a popular method that tries to infer income from capital stock changes. This is an approach favored by those who seek to link income and capital through what they perceive as 'capital theory'. While there is little harm to attempt this link theoretically, it is the wrong method empirically. The attempt to do just that by many economists writing on green accounting, including Hartwick and Vincent, and also those national accountants who try to keep up with the wisdom of the economists, undermines income estimation in practice. Controversial stock estimates are obviously poor foundations on which to base the far more important income estimates. For long the accountants had separated stocks from flows, and have devised strict rules for the valuation of stocks. To them opening stocks are the same as end-period stocks of the preceding period, and end-period stocks of the current period are to be valued at the lesser of two quantities: cost of acquisition or current market prices. This precautionary accounting rule aims at avoiding the possibility of overestimating income, which would induce excessive consumption and thus threaten the 'sustainability' of the entity for which the accounts are being drawn. And this is a rule that should be observed in *national* accounting also.

The convention has been established to confine the national output (GDP and GNP) very largely to *transacted* activities, using market prices for valuation. True, some controversy emerges now and then as to whether output should be valued by utility (demand) or by cost (supply) – each of these views having validity depending on purpose. My understanding is that, since the enunciation of 'Marshall's Scissors', market prices are essentially the product of demand and supply: like a pair of scissors cutting a sheet of paper, where it is useless to know which of the two blades actually does the cutting.[4] In practice, valuation of output in the national accounts has for long been based on a combination of cost and utility. The consumption part is valued in the manner of Marshall by both cost and utility as reflected in market prices, whereas investment and government services are valued differently since these are not traded in the market. In their case they are valued by cost.

II   CAN CONSUMPTION DEFINE INCOME?

CONSUMPTION AS INCOME

Readers familiar with the literature will observe that the substance of what I am going to say in this chapter goes over much of the same territory explored by Irving Fisher in his book, *The Nature of Capital and Income* published as early as 1906. The meticulousness of Fisher's scholarship, the originality of his analysis and the breadth of his sources combine to make this work of lasting importance in the present context. It is not surprising therefore that some ecological economists have tried to find in Fisher a pretext for attacking GDP as a useful macroeconomic instrument, questioning the basic convention of viewing income, or product, as the sum of consumption and investment.[5] Investment, on that view, should be excluded from income which should be synonymous with consumption. It may be useful here to mention that Fisher's work was, according to Schumpeter (1954), a first step toward coordinating the economist's and the accountant's work.[6]

Fisher undoubtedly had a welfare conception of income in mind, which he saw as a magnitude that denotes 'desirability'. Fisher distinguished between 'desirability' of acquiring an object at a point of time, and the pleasure *later* enjoyed from having acquired it – a pleasure which he conflated with 'utility' (Fisher, 1906, p. 43). In this vein he argued for the exclusion of current investment from income, thus in effect identifying consumption as income. For him, while investment indicated an act of acquisition, the returns to be enjoyed from it would only come later. This splitting of hairs was obviously not followed in modern national accounting, now with the emphasis placed on assessing output rather than welfare.[7] Output, or GDP, became the accepted quantity in mainstream economics, made up of consumption plus investment, and regarded as the fundamental magnitude that economic statisticians were to estimate. More recently, the Fisherian line of thinking was resurrected, and unsuccessful attempts have surfaced to make consumption the very objective of economic endeavor, and thus the quantity that should be identified with income and used in the national accounts to target 'sustainability'. This implied the claim that 'Hicksian income' (see below) should be discarded in favor of a Fisherian income that would exclude investment. But these attempts have not succeeded and are unlikely to succeed, particularly for national accounting and for the macroeconomic magnitudes that have become the standard means of economic analysis and policy. Nevertheless it cannot be denied that consumption may justifiably be considered as the ultimate goal of economic activity. Aside from national accounting, there is no harm in accepting the view that investment may be construed, in the language of Fisher, as a 'desired' means for attaining some future consumption.[8]

It may be useful here to add that Fisher, who was doubtless influenced by Jevons,[9] considered income as a subjective or a 'psychic' utility yielded by goods and services *when consumed* and thus he could conflate income with consumption.[10] He had in mind, he said, a body of healthy consumers who could enjoy this psychic quality to its fullest; that is why he paid considerable attention to 'human capital'. Fisher argued that investment was not part of current income since it did not yield immediate utility. It represents an intermediary step leading to later consumption, which only then will become part of income. The implicit reference to welfare is clear since income is seen by him as a conduit to satisfaction. As stated earlier, Fisher's view of treatment of income as identical with consumption was not readily accepted, and has not stood the test of time. Even Fisher himself is said later to have repudiated that view: see the references to Tobin below.

III   IS WEALTH SUPERIOR TO INCOME?

The superiority of wealth over income can only be claimed if the objective is the estimation of welfare, but it certainly has no superiority for the assessment of output. That wealth is often more important than income, when welfare is considered, is obvious. A rich family in possession of a stock of wealth of some size can in hard times sustain its consumption (*alias* welfare if we wish) by drawing on its wealth. But is such replenished consumption equivalent to a higher *income* in the fallow periods concerned? Suppose alternatively that the same family chooses to live frugally and not draw on its wealth: does this mean its income automatically becomes lower? Fisher's unconvincing approach to this issue lost much ground to the so-called 'Haig–Marshall' concept of income which includes investment and which has become the standard adopted for national income estimation. Those who still hanker after Fisher's early definition of *actual* consumption as synonymous with income have probably failed to realize that Fisher himself, in a 1946 memoir, repudiated his earlier definition. According to Tobin (1991, 2005a), Fisher:

> confesses some regret that he lost some acceptance of his idea by insisting too strongly on identifying income with actual consumption. At that time, he agreed that actual consumption plus capital accumulation, positive or negative, was a useful definition.

MAINTAINING CAPITAL INTACT

There is hardly any disagreement now over the notion that the central purpose of national accounting is the estimation of income, and the latter depends fundamentally on 'maintaining capital intact'. Income and capital are entwined in any discussion or estimation of income. Thus we find Alfred Marshall asserting (1920, p. 78) the existence of a 'correlation of income and capital', and drawing attention to the fact that 'Adam Smith said that a person's capital is that part of his stock from which he expects to derive an income', adding:

> And almost every use of the term capital, which is known to history, has corresponded more or less closely to a parallel use of the term income: in almost every use, capital has been *that part of a man's stock from which he expects to derive an income.* (Marshall, 1920; italics in the original)[11]

To summarize: despite some confusion found in recent writings many things have been clear regarding income and capital for a long time. Income is a flow and capital is a stock; capital is part of wealth: that part which is employed along labor and land to produce output; wealth includes items that may not be employed for generating money income, but nevertheless yield utilities to the wealth owners: examples are works of art and musical instruments; the value of capital or wealth is much more difficult to estimate than income; and finally though the stock of wealth may be more important for *welfare* purposes than the changeable flows of income, it is much less important for gauging output. Some of these points are taken up in the following pages.

IV   INCOME FROM CAPITAL

More than a century ago both Alfred Marshall in Cambridge, England, and Irving Fisher in Yale, United States, viewed income as a stream of 'dividends' periodically yielded to society by its stock of wealth of all kinds.[12] Both knew and appreciated each other's work and their fundamental views on income were close. It is not difficult to discern that both held that the stream of income could be reckoned per unit of time such as a year, a month or a week, or even at a point of time to be read from the first derivative of a continuous flow over time. Neither would dispute the fact that capital as a stock may be reckoned at any point of time: in business accounting commonly on 31 December of each year, though it may also be counted quarterly or at shorter intervals. To present-day economists and accountants, capital is a collection of goods, rights and claims on outsiders that may be seen on the 'asset' side of a balance sheet that would list buildings, machinery, inventories, bank accounts as well as debts due for collection. These assets are matched in the balance sheet by counter-claims known as liabilities. The difference between assets and liabilities can be used to estimate the net worth of the enterprise concerned. However, some writers on national accounting, who should know better, would sloppily refer to a list of assets as a balance sheet.

Wealth and income are clearly understood today by most people as respectively stocks and flows although Adam Smith's *Wealth of Nations* managed to confuse some present day economists who mistook Smith's famous work as referring to stocks of wealth, not to flows of income. One notable example of this confusion is provided by Partha Dasgupta, a prolific writer on ecological economics (see Dasgupta, 2001). The gravity of his mistake, in my view, cannot be over-emphasized since it was made in his Presidential Address to the Royal Economic Society while trying to advance the argument that *for welfare assessment*, asset stocks are superior to income flows. He rather too strongly asserted:

> it should not surprise that Adam Smith inquired into the Wealth of Nations, not the gross or net national product of nations, nor the human development index of nations. (Dasgupta, *op. cit.*, p. C4)

For the record, there is no dispute at all among economists that Adam Smith's 'wealth of nations' was meant as the 'income' of nations.[13] Dasgupta's preference for wealth over income for the specific purpose of evaluating welfare is perfectly plausible except that, as already stated, national income estimates are not meant to indicate welfare – not directly anyway – but only to denote the product. Because of the importance of the distinction between income and wealth in the present context a brief note on the topic is appended to this chapter.

V   INCOME AND SUSTAINABILITY

It is worth remembering that economists came to the definition and estimation of income much later than the accountants. The issue of income estimation confronted the accountants in the late Middle Ages, roughly around the 1500s, well before the advent of the Industrial Revolution. That was a time when commercial capital was made up largely of inventories of trading wares, and the often ocean-faring craft that conveyed them between countries and continents. In the mercantile ports of the Mediterranean, both north and south, the maritime traders sought the advice of their bookkeepers to indicate for them the amount out of their financial receipts that could safely be spent on family consumption. Thus the concept of income as a quantity available for consumption was born. The accountants had initiated the method of double-entry bookkeeping, which viewed every transaction simultaneously as a debit from one angle and a credit from another. To answer the question about income estimation the accountants came up with the concept of 'keeping capital intact'. Out of the complexity of the trading financial flows a surplus could be identified which constituted income. This could safely be withdrawn for consumption without endangering the *sustainability* of the business by eating into its capital.

The intactness of capital in that context was not 'normative' in the sense that it was not advice to the owners to refrain from eroding their capital though it could certainly imply that sense also. It was merely a device for estimating *ex post* income, and was intended to be free from any recommendation regarding sensible behavior, which, needless to say, is not usually the function of accountants. Additionally, it was clearly understood that any such definition of income was only approximate. In his famous discussion of income Hicks (1946, chapter XIV, p. 171) was careful to stress, as will be detailed in a later chapter, that concepts such as income and its related cohorts of saving, depreciation and investment have 'far too much equivocation in their meaning, equivocation which cannot be removed by the most painstaking effort'. Hicks went further to elaborate that these were not 'logical categories' at all, but 'rough approximations, used by the business man to steer himself through the bewildering changes of situation which confront him'. The early accountants had clearly perceived this fact, and had proposed a golden rule: when in doubt income should be *under*estimated rather than *over*estimated since the durability of the business was at stake and hinged on safeguarding its capital against decline. For this purpose the accountants have also been paying special attention to the valuation of end-period stocks and have devised a strict rule. If end-period stocks were overvalued 'income' would be exaggerated, and over-consumption would undermine the intactness of capital. To repeat, the relevant accountancy rule is that end-period stocks are to be valued at current prices (that is prices prevailing at December 31 of the year concerned) or the opening period prices (12 months previously at January 1st) *whichever are less*. By contrast, economists have tended to be unhappy with this method of stock valuation, preferring current prices throughout – a stance that has crept into national accounting, threatening the fundamental objective of 'keeping capital intact' — besides setting off accounting difficulties that require reconciling variations in stock values with income estimates. It is perhaps worth repeating that income accounting and its 'device' of 'keeping capital intact' aim to ensure a limited sustainability from one account period to the next. But if observed, period after period, the span of sustainability can be lengthened.

VI   MEASURING CAPITAL

> The measurement of Capital is one of the nastiest jobs that economists have
> set to statisticians.
> (Hicks, 1969, p. 204)[14]

As previously stated, capital, sometimes used synonymously with wealth, is a stock that usually comes about through accumulation. Saving out of current income adds to the stock of wealth via investment. An individual saves by refraining from consumption so that consumption plus saving will add up to income. But capital assets can also be transferred from one individual to another by trade, gift or inheritance. In almost every case wealth can be traced to an act of original saving. But it is also possible, as sometimes happens, that one's wealth increases (or decreases) fortuitously through windfalls, accidents, disasters or war. But for a new owner, in order to be able to purchase an already existing asset, some savings, or an exchange of assets, have to be involved. Obviously wealth may also be acquired by force through aggression, exploitation, confiscation, games of chance or even theft. But again the origins of wealth are traceable in most cases to someone's original savings.

It is needless to add that capital assets come in many forms: bank accounts, financial claims on others, land, buildings, metals, machinery, tools or inventories of raw materials, work in progress and finished goods. To this, for national accounting purposes, must be added the public networks of roads, railways, bridges and other infrastructures that make up national property. In practice, putting a meaningful value on national wealth has been virtually impossible; hence the attempts at deriving it in approximate terms from national income. With natural resources in mind as part of the national wealth it is worth mentioning that Marshall was always eager to point out that under 'land' – for him a principal category of capital – should be reckoned its natural endowment of place, topography, rain, sunshine, rivers and lakes, soil and subsoil deposits. Fisher, Marshall, Pigou and others were in agreement that income is theoretically the dividend owners obtain from their capital – a dividend identified by Marshall as a 'usance'. Turned around, the flow of 'usance' may be capitalized into wealth, and Fisher had the intellectual audacity to turn the services of labor, namely wages, into 'human capital' by capitalization. To Fisher wealth bears income, and income consists simply of the services of wealth (p. 58 in his chapter on Capital).[15] Fisher had a clear vision that flows should be separated from stocks, upbraiding economists, not excluding John Stuart Mill, for confusing stocks and flows in considering wages and 'wage funds' (*loc. cit.*), adding that '[a] little attention to business bookkeeping would save economists from such errors' (p. 59).

PUTTING A MONEY VALUE ON CAPITAL

One difficulty in valuing capital, which Fisher considers under the rubric 'wealth', is that capital assets do not always exchange hands, or not very frequently, so their market price may not be easily ascertainable from transactions. This makes guessing at prices very difficult. 'In fact some people make a living by simply appraising wealth on which, for one purpose or another, a price of some sort must be set' (Fisher, *op. cit.*, p.12). The purpose of valuation, he emphasizes, 'makes a great difference' to the appraised value. He counts various ways in which purpose affects values: there is a value assessed by government for taxation; another value set by insurance companies for compensation for loss; there is the price expected at a forced sale; and the price to be obtained by a patient owner willing to wait. Fisher mentions the stark case of a family ancestor's portrait whose owner would appraise it for insurance purposes at a high price, whereas it would fetch next to nothing if he were to offer it as collateral to obtain a loan. To Fisher therefore the value of capital is not always determinate, and would vary quite widely for different purposes. Hicks (1961, p. 19) confirms this view stating that while the valuation of 'income goods' is characteristically a market valuation, the valuation of goods that enter into the capital stock are characteristically imputed values.

Fisher, along with Marshall, knew very well that the rate of interest acts as a link between income and capital, asserting that capitalizing income is a simple matter obtainable by a 'straightforward process'. But to do this,

Fisher cautioned, the rate of interest should be foreknown *and constant* during the successive years. Yet Fisher later qualified this view in his Appendix to Chapter XIII by producing a formula to average out fluctuations in the anticipated interest. Using capital and wealth synonymously he again asserted that wealth is nothing other that the present worth of future income, and that this is true whether income accrues continuously or discontinuously in spurts; whether it was uniform over time or oscillating; or finally whether the income instalments were few or infinite in number (p. 202). Hicks certainly went forward with this Fisherian approach, developing it in useful directions in *Value and Capital*. For me, Fisher's contention is particularly important, namely that irrespective of the constancy or variability of future income streams the discounted outcome remains the same. This refutes some spurious criticisms of the user-cost formula I proposed for estimating income from natural resource extraction as I argue in Chapter 10 below.

In the light of the foregoing one may raise the following questions: Should national statistical offices expend time and resources to put a value on natural resources? Is it not sufficient just to survey the available resources in physical terms and ascertain how their stocks are changing? And do we really gain much by putting a value on this stock? The arduous experience of the Australian Bureau of Statistics in this regard should serve as a warning to others.[16]

VII   A DIGRESSION ON HUMAN CAPITAL

I have not shown much enthusiasm in my work for what has been labelled 'human capital' — much less for so-called 'social capital'. I have viewed the latter as a network of institutions and connections that, valuable as they may be, fall without the domain of economics (see Chapter 18 on the 'resource curse' which is frequently blamed on inadequate institutions). As to 'human capital' I have always had the view that that kind of 'capital' does not present a critical problem that needs attention in the framework of national accounting. It does not seem to be threatened by deterioration similarly to the way ecological capital is deteriorating. Human health, surely a component of such capital, has generally been improving over time with signs of longer life spans. More relevantly, perhaps, the store of knowledge available to humankind, instead of eroding, seems to be growing all the time. The stock of information, experience, scientific knowledge and technology that would make up such capital is effortlessly bequeathed undiminished by every generation to subsequent generations without raising worries about its 'sustainability'. This transfer across generations is being eased with the help of education and research, and increasingly with rapidly advancing means of archiving and communications. But we should not totally ignore Irving Fisher's view on this topic for he did set much store on 'human capital'. This defined for him the very capacity available to humans for *enjoying consumption*, which, as mentioned earlier, he regarded as the target of all economic activity. Fisher considered the possibility of capitalizing wages into a stock similar to other categories of capital that should be kept intact through expenditure on health and education. Here he raised the issue as to whether a premium should not be deducted from wages and invested in a sinking fund 'sufficient to provide for the continuance of this income after the destruction by death of the laborer' (*op. cit.*, p. 111). On this point Fisher sums up as follows:

> If the annuitant or laborer should *actually* set aside such an annual sum as to maintain the capital value of his property unimpaired, we should be quite justified in considering the net sum, and not the gross sum, as income.

But mention of Fisher's pertinent thoughts on this topic will not be complete without mentioning his view regarding the effort exerted to produce income. This is a point stressed by Pigou too and generalized later by ecology-conscious writers addressing welfare issues who drew attention to the damaging aspects of economic activity generally, and to economic growth in particular. Fisher recognized the disservices behind the creation of income and the adverse psychic sensations associated with effort, which he argued must be set against income. Humorously, James Tobin (2005b) remarks that Fisher actually enjoyed his own work and derived much satisfaction from it. Enjoying work is quite a common phenomenon often experienced by professionals. [17]

TOBIN'S CRITICISM OF FISHER

Fisher's erstwhile definition of income as consumption was criticized by Tobin on the following grounds:

> The implication that a wealthy household or society has a low 'income' in periods when it chooses to live frugally and accumulate capital, and a high 'income' in periods when it is depleting its capital is difficult to swallow. Some concept of sustainable consumption seems preferable. That is why what came to be known as the Haig–Marshall concept of income, namely that the rate of consumption consistent with maintaining capital intact, gained wider acceptance than Fisher's proposed definition.

Stressing Fisher's later change of mind, Tobin then adds:

> Fisher was well aware of the problem, and in *The Nature* he called the hypotheti-
> cal intact-capital rate of consumption 'standard income' (1906, p. 110). In his
> 1946 memoir, he confesses some regret that he lost some acceptance of his idea
> by insisting too strongly on identifying income with actual consumption. At that
> time, he agreed that actual consumption plus capital accumulation, positive or
> negative, was a useful definition (see Barber, 1997, Appendix to Volume 2).

VIII   ECONOMISTS AND ACCOUNTANTS: DIFFERENT PERSPECTIVES

National accountants try to harmonize their methods with what the economists are saying. But there is a fundamental difference between what economists and what accountants regard as income and this difference has adversely affected green accounting. It brought much confusion to SNA93 and subsequently to the guidelines for compiling the satellite accounts for the environment. Many of the inconsistencies in these documents will be elaborated later, but here it suffices to point out a set of fundamental conflicts. From the accountant's point of view, the main product of the national accounts is income, not wealth or capital, and this is to be estimated for a period that has already closed. By convention, no ideal, optimum or 'shadow' prices are relevant. The accountants take market prices at their face value. Further, for estimating GDP or GNP no attempt is made within national accounting to assess the wellbeing or welfare of the income recipients. No precision is sought in or claimed for the income estimates the accountants produce. The accountant follows precautionary methods for the estimation of income so that it must not be overestimated. In general there is an accountant tendency where in doubt to underestimate income rather than overestimate it. The purpose is to check overconsumption so that capital erosion is avoided. The accountant's focus, it should be emphasized, is on the *flow of income* while stocks of capital are only used as stepping-stones along the road leading to the estimation of income. Capital stocks do appear at the beginning and end of the accounting period, however, and are important for income estimation. At January 1st of the accounting year they are the same as at 31 December of the preceding year. Valuing stocks at the current year-end is of crucial importance as it affects the estimation of income. *Ceteris paribus* end-period stocks are to be valued at current market prices or at the opening stock prices, whichever are less. A last point to emphasize is that the accountant's income is historical and descriptive, and is in no sense to be taken as 'normative' or 'prescriptive'.

The economists on the other hand tend to have a different outlook on income. Above all they seem to seek precision in estimation, not being content with the precautionary approximations of the accountants. Their analysis often illuminates concepts, but quite often defies empirical estimation. They are happier with *current* price valuation throughout. For them *income* is a dynamic concept closely related to *wealth* and whose value may be inferred by discounting prospective consumption which the stock of wealth is expected to create. And income is the 'interest' (or dividend) society earns annually from that stock so that the valuation of income and of wealth is interdependent. It is also undeniable that there is now a tendency for (many) economists to give national income a normative interpretation identifying income with wellbeing. This trait of thinking has led inevitably to placing more significance on the estimation of net income in preference to gross income. Unwittingly, this has caused gross income to be virtually neglected for proper 'greening'. And it is gross income that is commonly reckoned and ubiquitously used for economic analysis in preference to net income, which has become the favorite of mathematicians for indicating welfare.

IX   THE END OF GDP?

On 7 December 1999, the Department of Commerce of the United States Government designated the development of the national income and product accounts as its 'achievement of the century', noting its contribution to winning World War II, and helping the American economy along a path of prosperity and stability (Daley, 2000).

With such a certificate of merit, it is unlikely that GDP will be terminated; neither, for that matter, the whole apparatus of national accounting. GDP is the undisputed star in the national accounting firmament and it is most unlikely that it will meet its demise any time soon. But there is no denying that there has been a rising tide of hostility against GDP coming to a great extent from exasperated ecological and environmental economists. Presumably despairing of having a reformed GDP that would faithfully reflect ecological deterioration, they seem to abandon hope of reforming it, and see no better alternative than dumping it altogether. Aside from its ecological faults and obvious lacunae, the failings of GDP as it stands unadjusted are legion, and little has been achieved so far by way of adjusting it to the satisfaction of its ecological critics. In particular, the 'popular' wish for growth with GDP expanding year after year contradicts the ecological stress witnessed everywhere. Critics see GDP being used by economists (or most economists anyway) who take it for granted that the rate of GDP growth indicates economic progress. To those who have argued for the abolition of GDP the 'growth mania' that pervades macroeconomic thinking has been particularly irritating, and terminating GDP would pull the rug from under their feet. There is no dearth of argument leveled by contemporary ecological economists against the impossibility of economic expansion given the finiteness of the biosphere that contains the whole economy. A devastating criticism on grounds other than ecological had been offered by Hicks who has written extensively on economic growth:

> Why should we be interested in economic growth – an increase in the social product, however measured? It is clearly not always 'good' in an ethical sense – not only because greater production may be accompanied by worse distribution, but for many other reasons. A richer society may be a more stupid society, or a more discontented society – one does not have to go far to find examples (Hicks, 1975, p. 318).

While we are still on the topic of GDP abolition, it should be made clear that the fault here does not lie with GDP itself but with some of its users. The dissatisfaction of the GDP abolitionists is based chiefly on its ostensible failure to account for the adverse impact of its expansion on wellbeing. And yet, even as it stands with all its blemishes, including its incomplete coverage and its imparting misleading economic messages for natural-resource-based economies, GDP still performs certain functions quite usefully. For countries where natural resources do not figure as contributing *significantly* to the economy, GDP is very useful, particularly for short-to-medium term macroeconomic monitoring, analysis and management. GDP has certainly been found helpful, if not actually indispensible, for devising monetary and fiscal policy in particular. In general, and for many countries, it at least indicates whether an economy is expanding or shrinking. But as stressed in many parts of this book it fails that function spectacularly when the liquidation of ecological capital is read as economic growth.

It is probably worth repeating that spurious criticisms of GDP have come persistently from those who wrongly conflate GDP with welfare. Bluntly speaking, if critics wish to read an increase in GDP as signifying greater happiness and a decrease as reflecting misery, they lack understanding that GDP is a metric of *output*, not of happiness. This wrong conflation of output with welfare though apparently popular does not become the professionals. There is undoubtedly some association between output and happiness, but much more information is needed to enable the interpretation of GDP changes as welfare changes. Clearly a rising social dividend or output will not necessarily signify 'economic success' or greater happiness if the numbers of income recipients have risen to depress income per head; or if income distribution has 'worsened' in the interval; or if the cost of growth is overlooked by neglecting the effort exerted in making a larger GDP or more relevantly here if the expanded GDP has added to stress on the physical environment – stress that is not counted. Some of these shortcomings may be bridged in a reformed GDP, but many of them will defy coverage and these will tend to fall outside the accounting system altogether. However, these could be handled for economic purpose without difficulty by knowledgeable analysts in complementary studies outside the SNA.

It is worth adding here that a mistake is sometimes made when specified sectors within GDP, such as agriculture, are identified as standing for the ecology or the environment in GDP estimates so that if agriculture were to vanish, as it were, the loss to the economy would be limited to its share in GDP. This is because the contribution of natural resources to GDP far exceeds the share of the agricultural sector (about 3 per cent for the United States). This ignores the fact that natural resources in one form or another provide the basis on which value is added in practically all sectors of an economy – an argument that has repeatedly been advanced by Herman Daly.

To recapitulate: the thought of doing away with GDP must be seen as well meaning but utopian. For GDP has become part of our contemporary culture, and is extensively used by citizens, government and business alike, and its estimates prior to publication are eagerly awaited equally by workers and employers, by entrepreneurs and stock market dealers, by bankers and by public officials, who all try to adjust their economic behavior and forward plans in light of the new numbers. Rather than seeking to abolish it, which seems to be 'overkill', GDP should be recognized as imperfect, but also amenable to reform, specifically to address its identified faults. Once identified (as this book attempts to do) these faults may be dealt with piecemeal and seriatim. For ecological purposes, *greening* the national accounts seems more feasible, and potentially more useful, than shutting one's eyes to the importance of GDP as a central macroeconomic magnitude. Abolishing GDP, as van den Bergh appears to be saying, though put forward with subtlety and careful caveats, might in his view be easier than 'greening' it; but I happen to think otherwise for, if abolished, there would be nothing left to 'green'. See van den Bergh (2007, 2009).

NOTES

1. In more recent times theoretical debates have intensified over capital when in the 1960s Massachusetts Institute of Technology (MIT) economists, notably Samuelson and Solow, were disagreeing with English Cambridge economists, especially Joan Robinson, who were using arguments derived from Ricardo and Piero Sraffa over capital productivity and its effect on distribution. The Robinson–Sraffa school denied the measurability of capital altogether. For them the fact that new capital often comes mixed with new technology makes capital impossible to measure. Hence they argued for separating the contribution to economic growth of capital from that of technology. On this see for example Maddison (1987). It is worth mentioning that Christopher Bliss (1975) then at Cambridge, England, once remarked that 'when economists reach agreement on the theory of capital they will shortly reach agreement on everything'. Hicks, of course, while recognizing the great difficulties standing in the way of estimating the stock of capital, distinguishes between a backward look (the historical, national accounting, valuation) and a forward looking valuation which is based on conjecture.
2. Those familiar with accountancy know that 'capital' appears in a balance sheet of a concern as a liability that is owed by the business to its founders. In economics, capital, as used here, is not a liability and comprises cash and bank accounts, buildings, machinery, debts to be collected and inventories that the accountant shows on the asset side of a balance sheet.
3. Hicks (1948) reviewing F. Sewell Bray's *Precision and Design in Accountancy*.
4. The classics valued national wealth (i.e. income) by cost or labor inputs, but Jevons in the late-nineteenth century, and thence Pigou in much of his writings, preferred valuation by 'utility'. See Hicks (1975, p. 312).
5. Or consumption plus saving. Saving and investment are of course equal *ex post*, which accounting usually is. This conception of income, which has become standard in national accounting, is sometimes referred to in the literature as the Haig–Marshall definition.
6. Schumpeter (1954, p. 872) states that Fisher took a first step toward coordinating the economist's and the accountant's work. Schumpeter adds that *The Nature of Capital and Income* was much admired by Pareto, besides presenting 'the first economic theory of accounting', suggesting that it 'is (or should be) the basis of modern income analysis'. Schumpeter was aware that Fisher's cotemporaries underestimated his contributions, doubtless reinforced by Fisher's own reluctance to assert his originality. In a backhanded way, p. 873, Schumpeter describes Fisher as 'a reformer of the highest and the purest type', but whose achievement did not make for quick success, adding with regret that the 'contents of *Capital and Income* were considered by most people as elaborate trivialities'.
7. Without going further back there is to be found in Britain an earlier stream of work preceding Keynes which includes estimates by Arthur Bowley (especially Bowley and Stamp), Pigou, and Colin Clark in the earlier decades of the twentieth century. Worthy of special citation are the following works: Bowley and Stamp (1927) and Clark (1932, 1937). See Hicks (1990, p. 537) and Stone (1984).
8. By his own admission, Fisher's conception of income as confined to consumption seems to follow an earlier progenitor cited as Henry Rogers Seager in his *Introduction to Economics* (1904); on this see Fisher (1906, p. 349).
9. William Stanley Jevons (1835–82) the author, among other works, of *The Coal Question* (1865) is often credited with ushering in the 'marginalist revolution' with emphasis on valuation of goods by utility (strictly his 'value in exchange' or 'catalactic value' as Hicks came later to name it). But Hicks rejects the 'marginalist' quality of this 'Revolution' insisting that the margin had always existed in economics as it is no more than an expression of the mathematical rule for a maximum or a minimum. More significantly the 'Revolution' Jevons claimed was about shifting valuation away from cost (Hicks, 1975, p. 322).

10. The word 'psychic' seems to have been current in economics at the time and was famously used by Francis Ysidro Edgeworth (1845–1926) in his book *Mathematical Psychics*, 1881. This polymath (classicist, philosopher, ethicist, mathematician, lawyer, economist and statistician) held the University of Oxford's Drummond Professorship of Political Economy (later assumed by Hicks) and the editorship of the *Economic Journal.*
11. As will be explained later 'capital' on this view is that part of wealth that may be employed to create income. Wealth, a wider concept, may include the possession of a piano or a painting which, though giving useful service, is not strictly speaking part of 'capital' that may be so employed in productive processes.
12. Marshall (1898, p. 56) and Fisher (1906). See also Marshall (1920, Book II, Chapter I, pp. 49–53) where he considers various categories of wealth.
13. See Edwin Cannan's introduction to Smith's *The Wealth of Nations* (1776 [1937], pp. lvii–lix). In his first footnote (p. lvii), Cannan draws attention to Smith's description of 'wealth' not as a stock but as an *annual* quantity following the usage of the Physiocrats. See also Hicks (1975) where he states (footnote to p. 312): 'We are nowadays so accustomed to thinking of wealth as capital wealth that it may not be easy to realize that in Smith wealth is normally taken in a flow sense.'
14. Hicks (1969) was addressing the International Statistical Institute of London, raising a number of questions the statisticians may legitimately put to the economists, perhaps the most pertinent of which is: 'Do we really need a measure of capital?' Hicks was laying emphasis on the importance of 'income', rather than 'capital', from the angle of the practical need of 'guiding the business man through the bewildering changes in circumstances' (Hicks, 1946, p. 171) and raising doubt regarding the practical usefulness of facing the daunting task of measuring capital. In this Hicks was obviously treading in the footsteps of Marshall (1920, p. 80) who had stated that 'The money income, or inflow, of wealth gives a measure of a nation's prosperity, which, untrustworthy as it is, is yet in some respects better than that afforded by the money value of its stock of wealth.'
15. Fisher (1906, p. 58) disagreed with the view propagated by Adam Smith and others that capital is that part of wealth that is productive, calling this demarcation 'futile'. On the previous page he quotes Marshall approvingly who had some doubts about this separation between productive and unproductive wealth. For Fisher, all utilities signified income whether expressed in money or not.
16. In 1995 the Australian Bureau of Statistics (ABS) published in its Australian *Economic Indicators* 1 August issue, an article entitled, 'Valuing Australia's natural resources: Part 1', the first of two articles reporting on the ABS's work on the valuation of natural resources. This was said to be based on an earlier effort: 'Occasional paper: national balance sheets for Australia, issues and experimental estimates 1989 to 1992'. Natural resources there covered land, forests and subsoil deposits. It contains the statement, 'The value of natural resources has not previously been included in the Australian national accounts, and these experimental estimates represent the first attempt by the ABS to value consistently a diverse range of Australia's assets.'
17. Cited in Eisner (1989).
18. See also the iconoclastic paper of Eisner (1989).
19. After all it was Pigou who had persuaded Hicks to leave the London School of Economics for Cambridge in 1935. Samuelson (1950) also attests to Pigou's greatness.

REFERENCES

Barber, William J. (1997), *The Works of Irving Fisher*. London: Pickering Master Series, Pickering and Chatto, Ltd.

Bliss, Christopher (1975), *Capital Theory and the Distribution of Income*. Amsterdam: North Holland, p. vii.

Bowley, Arthur L. and Josiah Stamp (1927), *The National Income 1924*. Oxford: Clarendon Press.

Clark, Colin (1932), *National Income 1924-31*. London: Macmillan.

Clark, Colin (1937), *National Income and Outlay*. London: Macmillan.

Daley, William (2000), United States Secretary of Commerce, Press Conference on December 7, 1999 announcing the achievement of the Bureau of Economic Analysis, *Survey of Current Business*, January.

Dasgupta, Partha (2001), 'Valuing objects and evaluating policies in imperfect economies', *The Economic Journal*, **111** (471), C1–C29.

Edgeworth, Francis Ysidro (1881), *Mathematical Psychics: An Essay on the Application of Mathematics to the Moral Sciences*. London: C.K. Paul.

Eisner, Robert (1989), 'Divergences of measurement and theory and some implications for economic policy', *American Economic Review*, **79**, 1–13.

Fisher, Irving (1906), *The Nature of Capital and Income*. London and New York: The Macmillan Company.

Haig, Robert M. (1921), 'The concept of income: economic and legal aspects' cited by Richard A. Musgrave and Carl S. Shoup, (eds) (1959) *Readings in the Economy of Taxation*, Homewood, IL: Irwin, pp. 54–76.

Hicks, John Richard (1942a), 'Maintaining capital intact: a further suggestion', *Economica,* May, 174–179.

Hicks, John Richard (1942b), *The Social Framework: An Introduction to Economics*, 1st edition. Oxford: Clarendon Press.

Hicks, John Richard (1946), *Value and Capital*, 2nd edition, Oxford: Clarendon Press.

Hicks, John Richard (1948), 'Review of F. Sewell Bray, *Precision and Design in Accountancy*', *Economic Journal*, **58** (232), 562–564.

Hicks, John Richard (1961), 'The measurement of capital in relation to the measurement of other economic aggregates', in F.A. Lutz and D.C. Hague (eds), *The Theory of Capital* (Proceedings of a Conference held by the International Economic Association). London: Macmillan & Co. Ltd, Chapter 2, pp. 18–31.

Hicks, John Richard (1969), 'The measurement of capital: in practice', *Bulletin of the International Statistical Institute*, **43**, reproduced in *Wealth and Welfare, Collected Essays on Economic Theory*, Vol. I. Cambridge, MA: Harvard University Press, Chapter 9, pp. 204–217.

Hicks, John Richard (1975), 'The scope and status of welfare economics', *Oxford Economic Papers*, **27** (3), 307–326.

Hicks, John Richard (1990), 'The unification of macro-economics', *Economic Journal*, **100**, 528–538.

Jevons, William Stanley (1865), *The Coal Question*. London: Macmillan and Co.

Keynes, John Maynard (1936), *The General Theory of Employment, Interest and Money*. London: Macmillan.

Maddison, Angus (1987), 'Growth and slowdown in advanced capitalist economies: techniques of quantitative assessment', *Journal of Economic Literature*, **XXV** (2), 649–698.

Marshall, Alfred (1898), 'Distribution and exchange', *Economic Journal*, **viii** (March), 37–59.

Marshall, Alfred (1920), *Principles of Economics*, 8th edition. London: Macmillan and Co.

Pigou, Alfred C. (1932), *The Economics of Welfare,* 4th edition. London: Macmillan and Co.

Samuelson, Paul A. (1950), 'The evaluation of "social income": capital forma-tion and wealth', *Oxford Economic Papers* (New Series), pp. 1–29. Reprinted in Joseph E. Stiglitz (ed.) (1966), *The Collected Scientific Papers of Paul A. Samuelson*, Vol. 1. Cambridge, MA, and London: MIT Press, pp. 299–324.

Schumpeter, Joseph (1954), *History of Economic Analysis.* New York: Oxford University Press, p. 872.

Simons, Henry (1938), *Personal Income Taxation*, Chicago, IL: University of Chicago Press.

Smith, Adam (1776 [1937]), *An Inquiry into the Nature and Causes of the Wealth of Nations*, Modern Library Edition. New York: Random House.

Stone, Richard (1984), 'The accounts in society', Nobel Memorial Lecture, 8 December, Section 2 Precursors.

Tobin, James (1991), 'Irving Fisher, 1867–1974', in Steven N. Durlauf and Lawrence E. Blume (eds), *The New Palgrave: A Dictionary of Economics*, Vol. 2. London: Palgrave Macmillan, pp. 369–376.

Tobin, James (2005a), 'Irving Fisher, 1867–1947', *American Journal of Economics and Sociology*, **64** (1), 1–20.

Tobin, James (2005b), 'Fisher's the nature of capital and income', *The American Journal of Economics and Sociology*, **64** (1), 19–42.

Van den Bergh, Jeroen C.J.M. (2007), 'Abolishing GDP', Tinbergen Institute Discussion Paper Number 07-019/3, University of Amsterdam.

Van den Bergh, Jeroen C.J.M. (2009), 'The GDP paradox', *Journal of Economic Psychology,* **30**, 117–135.

APPENDIX

WEALTH AND WELFARE

Misreading Adam Smith's Wealth

Professor Dasgupta misreading Adam Smith's 'wealth' as a stock, and not as it should properly be read, as a 'flow', may not be an isolated case. In this he may get some solace from Samuelson who nevertheless was well aware that wealth in *The Wealth of Nations* meant income. In a light-hearted mood he chose to emphasize that those who misread Smith's wealth as a stock might be 'on to something'. He went as far as saying that 'Adam Smith is often these days criticized for writing about the *wealth* of nations and not about their incomes. But the present discussion [Samuelson's] reveals that he was (inadvertently?) right' (Samuelson, 1950 [1966], pp. 320–321. Page references are from the 1966 reprint). Samuelson's use of the word 'inadvertently' suggests that Smith could have been thinking of wealth as a stock, but one may surmise that Samuelson's quizzical '?' is almost 'tongue-in-cheek'. More seriously the stock of wealth for Samuelson performs a future *welfare* function for its owners. But for wealth to fulfill that function a great deal depends on future periods' unpredictable use of the inherited stock, and also on the then prevailing complex conditions that would enable the wealth owners to make use of it. Invoking the authority of Pigou from whose book (*The Economics of Welfare,* 4th edition, 1932) Samuelson repeatedly quotes, he concludes that 'Careful reading of Professor Pigou's argument suggests to me that it does establish the following point [sic]. (i) Current consumption does *not* fully reflect the welfare effects of policies now being initiated. (ii) It is necessary, even though difficult, to consider effects on future consumption (suitably discounted?); i.e. welfare changes are to be measured by wealth changes' (Samuelson, 1966, p. 322). Samuelson goes on to dispute, albeit rather hesitantly, Pigou's extra point (iii), namely that 'adding the rate of net capital formation to the rate of consumption does adequately measure the sought-after wealth'. Here Samuelson seems to spot a minor contradiction. Pigou was extolling the value of wealth stocks for welfare assessment, but in this last quoted statement Pigou would only make sense if wealth were to be taken as a flow.

In the same essay Samuelson (pp. 323–324) has much to say on the definition of income proposed by Hicks as the 'level of consumption flow permanently attainable', and also by Hicks's predecessors: Marshall, Fisher, Haig (1921 [1959]) and Simons (Henry Simons 1938).[18] In a footnote (pp. 321–322) Samuelson draws attention to Pigou's approval of

Fisher's notion that income defined as current consumption gives a 'better objective index of correlation with economic welfare which a community obtains from its wealth over a long series of years'. Especially to be noted here is the fact that Samuelson never advocates any valuation of *total* wealth, but only *changes* in wealth. Current attempts to put values on the stock of wealth of nations are, in my view, as pointless as they are misguided, and they only muddy the waters for estimating income. They also can be misleading to the proper estimation of income.

A refreshing view of Pigou in this respect is offered by Hicks (1975, p. 312) where he states that despite its title, Pigou's book was not at all about welfare: it was the classical theory of production and distribution which Pigou was taking over and turning into the *Economics of Welfare*. This was *The Wealth of Nations* in a new guise. Hicks continues:

> For remember the exact title of Adam Smith's Book – An Inquiry into the Nature and Causes of the Wealth of Nations. If we take that title, not as a mere label in the modern manner, but as a description which means what it says, it corresponds to what we have found in Pigou. Wealth is production; the Wealth of a Nation is what we now call the National Product. Adam Smith is to tell us what the Social Product of a Nation is; what is meant by its being large or small; what is meant by its growing. That is 'nature' (Pigou Part I). Then he is to tell us why the Social Product is large or small, and why it grows. That is 'causes' (Pigou Part II). There is a close correspondence.

Hicks's Conversion Away from Welfare

It is possible to discern from one or two of Hicks's earlier pieces that he was initially hoping that national income, when estimated, could be made to perform a double role: indicating output as well as welfare. Pigou obviously associated the national dividend with welfare. Hicks's closeness to Pigou's thinking is attested by several references he made to the 'greatness' of Pigou as an economist.[19] In his 1975 *Oxford Economic Papers* (p. 318), Hicks confesses a change of position, renouncing the welfare connection altogether, saying:

> We are perhaps a little further forward than Pigou appears to be, in view of our decision to treat the Social Product as primary, and to banish 'economic welfare'. For there is no doubt that the Social Product, the measurable Social Product, is a magnitude in which people *are* interested. There are legions of statisticians measuring it.

A few pages later Hicks affirms his conversion, remarking (p. 324) that: 'We have indexes of production; we do not have – it is clear we cannot have – an Index of Welfare'. Hicks's renunciation of the welfare function of the national product seems to have come as early as 1942 when he was writing *The Social Framework* (Hicks, 1942b) but he dropped welfare with obvious regret. Hicks (1942a, p. 179) wrote: 'But comparing economic welfare is not the only purpose (nowadays, alas! it is not even the main purpose) of measuring the National Income'. Recent writers who insist on reading national income estimates as welfare indicators should perhaps make some serious acquaintance with the rich literature available on national income and its evolution in economic thinking.

The elaboration of the concepts of income and capital in this chapter leads us to explore the difference between rent (income) and royalty (capital) in the composition of revenue obtained from the exploitation of natural resources, and to this we must now turn.

5.   Rent and royalty

THE ISSUE OF RENT

In the literature on environmental economics there is a prevailing tendency to refer to surpluses realized in natural resource extraction as 'rent', sometimes specified as 'resource rent'. In Solow's (1974) seminal article on 'The economics of resources or the resources of economics' he used the more precise expression 'scarcity rent' to denote what I interpret as my user cost. But rent seems to be a common appellation used in the literature without reflection. There is nothing fundamental against such a language if taken as a broad-brush expression, but for economic analysis, and specifically for national accounting, it has spelled confusion. For economists 'rent' connotes income or value added and thus warrants being included in GDP. Chiefly since Ricardo, rent is taken as a surplus accruing to the owners of land employed as a factor of production and does not constitute a cost of the produce that the land yields. It can be determined only *ex post* after the value of the product had been set by the market, and it is the latter value that determines rent not *vice versa*. Marshall (1920), of course, extended the concept of rent and introduced the notion of 'quasi rent' applicable principally, but not exclusively, to machinery that becomes temporarily in short supply – an appellation later adopted by Keynes in his *General Theory*.[1] When it comes to natural resources, however, whether renewable or depletable, the picture gets a little complicated. This is discernible from debates over what determines the supply price of a mining product, the decomposition of the surplus into capital disinvestment and income, and how this relates to the life expectancy of the resource.

MARSHALL'S ANALYSIS

The analysis here should start with Marshall. Addressing the economics of mining, Marshall tells us that there was a conflicting view between Adam Smith and Ricardo (Marshall, 1920, p. 439n). Smith apparently held that the long-term supply price of the produce is determined (at least on occasion) by the most fertile mine, whilst Ricardo insisted that it is the least fertile mine that sets the price. Marshall tried to adjudicate between the two, siding mainly with Ricardo. But with astute judgment Marshall also ushered in the concept of 'royalty' as playing a decisive role in the determination of prices. His royalty, of course, corresponds to what I have called a user cost and to what Solow (see below) has termed 'scarcity rent'. Marshall perceived correctly that the surplus realized in natural resource exploitation is made up of true income and a royalty, and the share of royalty in the mine's produce expands as the mine approaches exhaustion. In other words income falls as a proportion of the surplus while royalty increases. Comparing Adam Smith with Ricardo, Marshall (*loc. cit.*) refines his judgment as follows:

> But in fact when the charge for the use of a mine is mainly in the form of a royalty, neither proposition seems to be applicable. Ricardo was technically right (or at all events not definitely wrong) when he said that rent does not enter into the marginal cost of production of mineral produce. But he ought to have added that if a mine is not practically inexhaustible, the income derived from it is partly rent and partly royalty; and that though the rent does not, the minimum royalty does enter directly into the expenses incurred on behalf of every part of the produce, whether marginal or not.

This statement does not need clarification save to state that both Smith and Ricardo appear to have ignored the exhaustibility of the mine, whereas Marshall was acutely conscious of it and introduced the concept of royalty as an analytical tool to decompose the surplus into income (rent proper) and capital disinvestment (royalty). Needless to add that Marshall's vision of this fits neatly in my formula for user-cost estimation.

THE CONTRIBUTION OF HAROLD HOTELLING[2]

About a generation after Marshall came Hotelling. For me, Hotelling's work shows two outstanding features. (1) He laid the foundations for a mathematical argument for conservation, and (2) he favored monopoly over competition as serving the 'public good'. Hotelling's paper, 'The economics of exhaustible resources' (1931) has been recognized, albeit after considerable delay, as path-breaking by many economists, and described by Kenneth Arrow as providing the base on which all subsequent papers on the growing sense of natural resource scarcity were built (Arrow, 1991). Hotelling insisted that natural resources are *assets* that should be managed on the same principles as other assets are managed. He applied the calculus of variations to the problem of allocating a fixed stock of a natural resource through time under simplifying assumptions.[3] Hotelling's aim was to arrive at some optimal level of periodic extraction that will not compromise future availability. His simplifying assumptions were elaborated adroitly by Robert Solow (1974) 40 years later, who took up and adumbrated many interesting points earlier raised by Hotelling and thus resurrected interest in a paper that had remained neglected for a long time.

Hotelling recognized the inadequacy of a free market to regulate resource management through time. He pointed out a divergence between private and social benefits with emphasis on the effect of market structure (i.e. monopoly, duopoly, competition, etc.) on the pace of resource exploitation. In this respect, Hotelling favored monopoly, stating that a monopolist may produce high prices, which the consumer resents in the short run, but these would restrain extraction, which is socially beneficial. He regarded restraining extraction as always working for the public good. He lamented the disappearing supplies of minerals and of forests, and expressed the 'feeling' that these products were now too cheap for the good of future consumers. He supported the prohibition of extraction at certain localities and at certain times such as the imposition of fishing seasons. He is on record as stating that the exploitation of an exhaustible natural resource 'can never be too slow for the public good' (Hotelling, 1931, p. 138). Whereas consumers may prefer a lower price, the restraints a monopoly imposes may in fact be preferable. Open to compromise, Hotelling outlines a practical middle channel between high and low current prices as 'really aimed at two distinct evils, a Scylla and Charybdis between which public policy must be steered'.

On the method of analysis, Hotelling recognized that 'the economics of exhaustible assets presents a whole forest of intriguing problems'. He emphasized that the static equilibrium which was popular at the time in economic theory was 'plainly inadequate' since it was physically impossible to maintain a steady rate of production. He recalled the fundamental question that Marshall had previously raised: 'How much of the proceeds of a mine should be reckoned as income, and how much as a return to capital?' (p. 139). He went on raising questions that needed answers, such as:

1. What is the value of a mine when its contents are supposedly fully known and what is the effect of uncertainty on the estimate?
2. From a mine owner's perspective what is the golden mean between too rapid extraction that would depress prices now and too slow extraction that, while raising prices and short-term profits, may be postponed farther into the future than the rate of interest warrants?
3. How can the State force the mine owner by taxation and regulation to adopt a schedule of extraction more in harmony with the public good?

4. What of the plight of laborers and subsidiary industries when a mine is exhausted?

Hotelling's attention to this line of query, his stated approval of the conservation movement and his apparent pessimism about the future of natural resources – all undermined a general acceptance of his views, particularly by those who adulated free market forces, believing that these forces were capable of addressing the problems he flagged. That's why the importance placed particularly by Solow on Hotelling's contribution, though coming rather late in the day for Hotelling, was particularly valuable in 1974 when confusion was rife over higher petroleum prices and the financial surpluses they produced for the exporting countries.

KRISTRÖM ON DEPRECIATION

Perhaps as a footnote to Hotelling (1931) it would be useful to cite Bengt Kriström (2002) who drew attention to a 1925 Hotelling paper on depreciation which defines capital erosion as the decrease in the discounted value of its future returns. This view, attributed now to Hotelling though it obviously descended from Irving Fisher's analysis, is seen by Arrow as original and defining 'a turning point both in capital theory and in the reorientation of accounting towards a more economically meaningful magnitude' (Arrow, 1991, pp. 670–671). Arrow hailed Hotelling's definition of the value of an asset, such as a machine, as its annual rental value plus a scrap value, and its depreciation as the decrease in value over time where a machine's worth is defined as the present value of the discounted stream of annual rental values over an infinite horizon. For a further discussion of this issue see the following section on 'Arrow'.

In the same paper, Kriström has a section on 'El Serafy's approach to depreciation'. This is worth citing because it conceives accurately what my user cost is about and in effect defends it against recurrent charges that it assumes a constant rate of future extraction. There Kriström ends up with the judgment that 'El Serafy's approach is equivalent to the more general Hotelling result, but because X, the stream of income $(x_0, x_1, x_2 \ldots x_n)$ is a constant, while annual revenue $(R_0, R_1, R_2 \ldots R_n)$ is not, this equivalence holds only at time t $(t_0, t_1, t_2 \ldots t_n)$. The stream of 't' is the sequence of periods underlying the calculation of the user cost, and here Kriström realizes correctly that my method is an *ad hoc* method to be applied afresh every year when new parameters, including the new size of the reserves and the rate of extraction, have become known. In Chapter 10 below it will be seen that this point of view escapes many critics who fancy that the estimation of the user cost relies on the assumption of a constant level of 'R's, year after year, thus making nonsense of the whole approach. Any constancy has been assumed only within the formula to simplify calculation, and does not apply to actual extraction.

ARROW'S CULPABILITY?

As an aside to this digression, Arrow's endorsement of Hotelling's view that asset values should reflect the discounted future flows from their services (1991) may in effect have deluded many national income accountants. There is obviously nothing wrong with Arrow's view on a theoretical level, but Arrow may have gone too far in claiming that Hotelling managed to reorient accounting towards 'more economically meaningful magnitudes'. No such reorientation was either needed or proposed. That claim may be meaningful to economists, but has been misleading for national accountants who are anxious to pattern their estimation methods on what economic theorists say. Arrow's hidden hand may therefore be identified behind the faulty approach that is evident in the work of the US Bureau of Economic Analysis and others who try to discover asset values by projecting arbitrary and time-bound future flows of capital services and discounting them to get a present value of the assets concerned. And, as mentioned before, additionally compounding this error by deriving the economically more important income flows from changes in such precarious conjectures of stock values. Having said this I realize that Arrow may not be singled out for blame as the notion to which he subscribed had been in the air for a long time, though his assertion of a reorientation of *accounting* towards more economically meaningful magnitudes was obviously overstated.

SOLOW'S INSIGHT

In his 1974 paper entitled, 'The economics of resources or the resources of economics' Solow revived the work of Hotelling referred to above, lavishing high praise on his 'Economics of exhaustible resources'. Solow's was an important address to fellow economists reminding them of Hotelling's path-breaking contribution made four decades previously, but which had remained largely overlooked. As already stated, Hotelling viewed natural resources as assets that should be 'managed' by their owners in the same way as all other assets should be managed. In his presentation Solow reiterated Hotelling's views and summarized them as follows:

1. Mines are assets.
2. For a resource to be left unmined it must compensate its owner by appreciating in value.
3. Equilibrium in the asset market is achieved only when all assets 'in a given risk class' earn the same return.
4. This return is partly a current dividend and partly a capital gain.
5. Net price (i.e. market price minus marginal extraction cost if competition prevails) should increase exponentially over time at the rate of interest.
6. In non-competitive situations net price is the difference between marginal revenue and marginal cost, this difference being the marginal profit which is the quantity that has to grow exponentially.

Solow claims that Hotelling's model focused on equilibrium in the flow of asset services (i.e. extraction) whilst Solow broadened the analysis to seek an equilibrium both in the flow and stock markets. In this respect, Solow may be said to take Hotelling a step forward, and appears to have mastered the arguments of both Marshall and Hotelling, reformulating them with simplicity and clarity. Solow's presentation may also be interpreted as baring the roots of the user-cost method with amazing lucidity.

To complete his analysis Solow brought in the demand curve for the mine's ore. Prices rise over time due essentially to the rise of 'scarcity rent' (or, if we like, the user cost) as extraction moves in steps from the lowest cost mine towards the highest. In a stylized gradated approach, in the beginning the lowest cost operator captures the whole market until 'his' cost is high enough to bring onto the market the next lowest cost operator. This process continues, ushering in successively higher and higher cost operators selling their ore in smaller quantities at rising prices that gradually reduce demand and eventually chokes it off completely. In effect the operators climb up the negatively sloping market demand curve step by step as demand shrinks in response to higher prices until the price is high enough to reduce the quantity demanded to nothing. At that point the supply dries up as the ore is totally exhausted.

In his analysis Solow introduces a refinement that has since been elaborated by Nordhaus (1973), which would curtail the price rise before the vanishing point is reached. That is when the price had risen sufficiently to bring in supply elastic substitutes, designated as a 'back-stop' technology. This will stop the rise of prices and stabilizes it at the level of a flat cost along an infinitely elastic supply curve emanating from the new technology. Solow adds several refinements and provisos to this illustration, but the above is sufficient to outline some main features of exhaustible resource economics.

This simple and elegant model while convincing on a broad front is too stylized to provide an explanation of reality. Marshall, in particular, always strove to temper abstract economic reasoning by bringing it down to face real situations. It is not clear if Solow was contemplating an isolated country with different mines – a country that is situated far away from other sources of the same ore. Or alternatively was looking at the world as a whole without sufficiently considering quality differences and variations in transport costs between source locations and demand destinations. But these may be viewed as mere details in a useful overall model. Yet there are also other problems. Mining operators working in different parts of the world tend to be large foreign corporations acting under constraining contracts frequently against uncertain local conditions. They are quite often ignorant of the dimensions of their own deposits, let alone the deposits of their rivals. Their operating equipment and other necessary facilities are lumpy and take a long time to lay down, and they are often difficult to adjust in reaction to change. Working under concessions they tend to be in a hurry to hasten extraction in the face of political uncertainty, paying little regard to optimizing their operations as the economic theorists envisage. Besides they are generally ignorant of their rivals' plans, their rivals' costs or their rivals' contractual obligations with any certainty. So the gradual transition from lower cost extraction to higher cost may not in practice take place smoothly as assumed, and the concept of marginal cost in this context becomes incongruous if not altogether pretentious. Solow's model may also be said to be essentially a static construction with a given demand curve, and with supply functions that behave effortlessly according to what is expected of them. A cursory glance at the real market reveals simultaneous supplies coming on stream at any point in time from sources that vary greatly in extraction costs and in reserves life expectancy that would influence the size of 'scarcity rent'. The arrival of a backstop technology to curtail rising prices is presented by Solow with scholarly hesitance, but as he himself recognizes, it is bound up with unknowns and uncertainties. However, his approach is enlightening and reinforces the earlier work of Marshall and Hotelling.

It may be thought that the strictures I bring forth to the stylized model of Solow also detract from the very analysis I have proposed for estimating the user cost. But evidently my approach does not require marginal costs or marginal revenues; nor does it envisage any process of sequential exploitation from low cost to higher cost operators. It does not in fact analyse theoretical behavior but only describes what has already taken place for one country in a given span of time. Its requirements are only two numbers: the size of reserves, however approximate, and the number of years remaining based on current extraction. No optimization is premised, and the method simply reads past behavior and tries to give it an accounting interpretation. These values (size of remaining reserves and volume of extraction) usually vary in practice from one account period to the next in light of new information. In helping to refine a workable approximation of income the accountant's golden rule in this regard is to avoid the consumption of capital – an avoidance that would seek *income* sustainability but only a short period sustainability between two successive account periods.

USER COST AND DEPRECIATING MACHINERY

In the interval between Hotelling and Solow attention to user cost by interested economists focused not on exhaustible resources but on the depreciation of fixed capital. Attention was given to the estimation of depreciation in the context of national income estimation. Depreciation of fixed capital obviously related to 'maintaining capital intact' for the assessment of income. A wide range of views emerged in a controversy that brought in Pigou (1941), Hayek (1935, 1941), Hicks (1942, 1948) and Kuznets (see Hicks, 1948). The question of obsolescence loomed large in the discussions as machines that had not fully deteriorated physically were becoming otiose due to the introduction of new technology. A related question that was echoed by Keynes (1936) was the effect of intensity of use on the wear-and-tear of machinery. The basic idea behind that line of thinking was that if a piece of equipment is driven hard to meet a short term surge in demand its depreciation will accelerate. Keynes actually introduced the phrase 'user cost' in Chapter 3, entitled 'The principle of effective demand' in a rather convoluted fashion, promising clarification later. He takes up this issue in Chapter 6 on 'The definition of income saving and investment', and devotes nearly five pages to the subject in an 'Appendix on user cost' (pp. 66–73) without delivering his previously promised clarity. It is significant that Keynes does not use his user cost in any meaningful way in the *General Theory* but his treatment seems relevant to the discussion undertaken here. There is little doubt in my mind that Keynes was then mindful of the later discussions over 'keeping capital intact' although he kept away from the battlefield.

Keynes identifies the user cost as 'simply the equivalent of the current disinvestment involved in using the equipment' (p. 67). Proceeding along a Marshallian path he adds 'For the short period supply price is the sum of the marginal factor cost and the marginal user cost.' He further avers that the user cost constitutes one of the links between the present and the future, suggesting (p. 70n) that 'To-day's user cost is equal to the maximum of the discounted values of the potential expected yields of all to-morrows.' In this he recognizes correctly that the user cost is fundamentally a temporal opportunity cost. A fair comment to make here is that Keynes's attempted clarification fails to edify. His language is convoluted, and his analytical purpose obscure. He brings in Marshall again and again and uses Marshallian terminology, referring to Marshall's 6th edition of *The Principles* where 'a part of user cost is included in prime cost under the heading of extra wear-and-tear of plant'. He disapprovingly quotes Pigou who was saying that the difference in wear-and-tear between using the equipment and not using it is negligible in practice – a valid point of view that seems to me incontrovertible. So Keynes (p. 73) hurriedly leaves machinery and turns to the user cost of raw materials:

> In the case of raw materials the necessity of allowing for user cost is obvious; if a ton of copper is used up to-day it cannot be used to-morrow, and the value which the copper would have for the purposes of to-morrow must clearly be reckoned as a part of the marginal cost . . . The essential difference between raw materials and fixed capital lies . . . in the fact that the return to liquid capital consists of a single term [the interest rate]; whereas in the case of fixed capital, which is durable and used up gradually, the return consists of a series of user costs and profits earned in successive periods.

It is remarkable how Keynes's inadequate attempt at 'clarification' of the user cost contrasts with Marshall's lucidity on this matter (see note 1), and which was available to Keynes when he addressed the topic in *The General Theory*.

SAMUELSON AND ACCOUNTING

The gulf separating accountants and economists does not seem to have been dug in one direction and the economists themselves may be faulted on this score. In an article published in 1950 in *Oxford Economic Papers* (republished in Stiglitz, 1966) Samuelson, with an explicit emphasis on welfare, explores theoretical problems raised for national income estimation by issues relating to investment, technological change and windfalls. Elements of his argument that are relevant to the discussion here are that wealth as a stock is more meaningful for welfare comparisons and welfare policies than current income. This is a theme, as stated earlier, which has re-emerged in subsequent work by others decades later, and is certainly valid theoretically but impossible to pin down in practice since wealth however defined eludes objective measurement. Samuelson curiously challenges the accountant's division of time into discrete portions, which he claims to have resulted in 'an arbitrary change in the level of GNP' (p. 301n). This 'unreasonableness' on the part of the accountants leads him to assert an obvious non sequitur: 'this is one of the most important arguments for NNP, the net magnitude remains invariant under changes in accounting conventions'. How NNP, which is a derivative of GNP and unquestionably relates to a discrete time span, can withstand Samuelson's 'challenge' while GNP cannot is not clear. The use of discrete time is not a matter of choice. It is dictated by business (and national) accounting modes, and intimately relates to fiscal time divisions and other public conventions and interests. How the use of discrete time periods can lead to arbitrary estimates of the gross product is not at all clear and must be taken as unconvincing. Even a great economist of Samuelson's caliber gets into trouble when addressing accounting matters.

Samuelson's argument seems further to relate to the role of inventory changes, which he believes wrongly are dealt with in accounting at the level of the *net* product estimation. Contrary to his view, the accountants consider changes in inventories when ascertaining *gross* income while fixed capital depreciation is not addressed until *net* income is being estimated. And it is obvious that dividing time in discrete portions should have no effect on reckoning either the gross or the net magnitude. Furthermore, Samuelson seems to be carried away in his criticism of Irving Fisher when he attacks Fisher's contention that the national dividend is the interest society earns from its capital. According to Samuelson, to impute all production to capital alone constitutes a 'theory of value' that is a non-labor, non-land theory 'of little relevance'. Here Samuelson ignores the fact that in Fisher's conception all factors of production, even labor, have to be capitalized in the stock of wealth to make sense of Fisher's insight. To Fisher, society's capital does indeed include land and capitalized labor (alias 'human capital'), in addition to machinery and other assets.

Remembering that Samuelson's discussion of these matters centers on welfare and not output it is understandable that he thought that a better indicator of a welfare change is to be found close to what is called 'wealth'. By wealth he meant not the present discounted future earnings (à la Haig–Marshall as he puts it), but 'the present discounted value of all future consumption' (p. 318) – in which case Fisher's broad view could not be faulted. Samuelson then concludes rather triumphantly, but wrongly, that '[o]ur rigorous search for a meaningful welfare concepts has led to a rejection of all current income concepts and has ended up with something close to wealth'. Interestingly, he adds a comment on Adam Smith's *Wealth of Nations*, which either reveals his unfamiliarity with Smith or alternatively was put forward with 'tongue-in-cheek': 'Adam Smith is often these days criticized for writing about the wealth of nations and not about their incomes. But the present discussion reveals that he was (inadvertently?) right' (pp. 320–321).

The question mark in this quotation is Samuelson's and this curious view is one adopted later by Dasgupta (2001), but it is at odds as explained before with scholars who had read and understood their *Wealth of Nations* including Cannan, Hicks and Kuznets, for whom *The Wealth of Nations* very clearly meant the 'income of nations'.

Finally, having in this chapter explored the evolution of Marshall's royalty into user cost, and having considered a collection of economists' views on accounting in general and national income accounting in particular, I turn now to the complement of the user cost, genuine income, which is the other portion of revenue associated with natural resource exploitation. In the next chapter I discuss the estimation of this genuine income, often dubbed 'Hicksian Income' in the ecological economic literature.

NOTES

1. Marshall (1920, p. 427n) writes, 'That part of the income which is required to cover wear-and-tear bears some resemblance to royalty, which does no more than cover the injury done to a mine by taking ore out of it.'
2. Hotelling (1895–1973) apparently published 87 papers of which only six were devoted to economics, all becoming 'landmarks which continue to this day to lead to further developments'. (See entry by Kenneth Arrow in the *New Palgrave Dictionary of Economics* (1991).
3. Interestingly Arrow (1991) mentions that the *Economic Journal* turned down Hotelling's paper because it was 'too mathematical'. Heightened interest is invoked by the fact that Keynes (who had graduated in mathematics) was then the editor of the *Economic Journal* with an occasional stand-in by the mathematician Edgeworth.

REFERENCES

Arrow, Kenneth (1991), *The New Palgrave Dictionary of Economics*, Vol. 2, entry on 'Hotelling'. London: Macmillan. pp. 670–671.

Dasgupta, Partha (2001), 'Valuing objects and evaluating policies in imperfect economies', *The Economic Journal*, 111 (471), C1–C29.

Hayek, Friedrich A. (1935), 'The maintenance of capital', *Economica*, **II**, 241–276.

Hayek, Friedrich A. (1941), 'Maintaining capital intact: a reply', *Economica*, **VIII** (31), 276–280.

Hicks, John Richard (1942), 'Maintaining capital intact: a further suggestion', *Economica* (New Series), 9 (34), 174–179.

Hicks, John Richard (1948), 'The valuation of the social income: a comment on Professor Kuznets' Reflections', *Economica* (New Series), **15** (59), 163–172.

Hotelling, Harold (1925), 'A general mathematical theory of depreciation', *Journal of the American Statistical Association*, **XX**, 340–353.

Hotelling, Harold (1931), 'The economics of exhaustible resources', *Journal of Political Economy*, **39** (2), 137–175.

Keynes, John Maynard (1936), *The General Theory of Employment, Interest and Money*. London: Macmillan.

Kriström, Bengt (2002), 'Harold Hotelling (1925) on depreciation', in Bengt Kriström, P. Dasgupta and K.-G. Löfgren (eds), *Economic Theory for the Environment: Essays in Honour of Karl-Göran Mäler*. Cheltenham, UK and Northampton, MA, USA: Edward Elgar, 195–204.

Marshall, Alfred (1920), *Principles of Economics*, 8th edition, London: Macmillan.

Nordhaus, William (1973), 'The allocation of energy reserves', *Brookings Papers on Economic Activity*, **3**, Washington DC: The Brookings Institute.

Pigou, Arthur Cecil (1941), 'Maintaining capital intact', *Economica*, **VIII** (31), 271–275.

Samuelson, Paul A. (1966), 'The 'evaluation of the "social income": capital formation and wealth' in Joseph E. Stiglitz (ed.), *The Collected Scientific Papers of Paul A. Samuelson*, Vol. I. Cambridge, MA: MIT Press, Chapter 27, pp. 299–324.

Solow, Robert (1974),'The economics of resources or the resources of economics', The Richard T. Ely Lecture, *The American Economic Review, Papers and Proceedings*, **LXIV** (2), pp. 1–14.

6. Hicks's income and Hicksian income

I TERMINOLOGY

It should be clear from the discussion in the previous two chapters that maintaining capital intact is a necessary requirement for estimating income. If capital, whether produced or natural, is deteriorating, then what passes as income in the national accounts will be overestimated. National accounting conventions had restricted the maintenance of capital to produced assets, but the new ecological economics movement has sought to extend the concept of capital to embrace natural resources. However, this has encountered some resistance from 'purist' environmentalists who expected no good to come from any association with economists, and resisted using concepts such as capital for ecological matters. And yet, once the economic avenue of national accounting has been taken, the economic link strongly asserts itself since the apparatus of national accounting, as said before, is inescapably economic. Before I go any further, the distinction needs to be made between what I intend to say in this chapter distinguishing what I have called 'Hicks's income' from 'Hicksian income' which has become familiar to environmental economists. The former is what can be culled from Hicks's writings on the concept and estimation of income and the latter is the view that proper estimation of income should include keeping 'environmental capital' intact – *pace* the dissention of some environmentalists.

My own work on the user-cost method – work that was begun in the late 1970s – explicitly treated natural resources as capital that needed to be maintained undiminished for the purpose of estimating income (see El Serafy, 1979, 1981). Initially my focus was on petroleum, but I later developed the same argument on a wider front to cover natural resources in general. This widening of coverage occurred during my association with the UNEP–World Bank workshops as previously told, culminating in El Serafy (1989): 'The proper calculation of income from depletable natural resources'. Similar reasoning was put forward in Herman Daly's chapter 'Toward a measure of sustainable social net national product' in the same publication (1989, Chapter 2). In May 1990 I read my essay on 'The environment as capital' (Chapter 3, this book) to the first international conference of the newly founded International Society for Ecological Economics, which was held at the World Bank, Washington DC (see El Serafy, 1991).

During the UNEP–World Bank collaborative workshops in the 1980s much discussion centered on the correct estimation of income so that keeping the natural resource 'capital' intact became a key issue that naturally brought up Hicks's analysis of income. It is to be noted in passing that Daly, who may be credited with popularizing 'Hicksian income' among environmentalists, had not mentioned it until he wrote his book with John Cobb, *For the Common Good*, published in 1989. For my part, I do not use the expression 'Hicksian income' which is what I thought of all along to be 'income', and I never qualify income by the adjective 'sustainable' since income by definition has to be sustainable to merit being called income. Working on natural resources, I had seen clearly that it was wrong to reckon receipts obtained from their commercial exploitation as income without recognizing that their stocks diminish as they are extracted. I proposed the user-cost method, which dominates the current book, for the estimation of income from depletable natural resources, and by extension also from renewable resources when these are being 'mined', i.e. when they are not being sufficiently renewed.

Hicks had given a lot of thought to the concept of income and its estimation in several of his earlier publications, but his chapter on 'Income' in *Value and Capital* (1946, second edition) contains his most detailed thoughts on the subject.[1] There he also discusses income from 'wasting assets' which is another name for natural resources being depleted. Hicks would not leave his discussion of income alone, but would come back to it again and again, always finding something fresh to add or qualify.[2] This was most significantly done in the course of his seminal paper, 'The scope and status of welfare economics' (Hicks, 1975). Reference to welfare is germane here since much is made of welfare in the green accounting literature.

Aside from *Value and Capital* (first published in 1939), Hicks's attention to income found systematic treatment in his book, *The Social Framework: An Introduction to Economics* (first published in 1942). This book was totally devoted to national income in theory and practice. He intended the *Social Framework* to be an introductory textbook to the study of economics starting from the macroeconomic end. He thought this was a better end to start from, supplanting the standard microeconomic approach that begins with 'supply and demand'. In the *Social Framework* Hicks elaborated the relevant concepts and examined their interconnections, covering consumption, investment, factors of production, population, the national product and foreign transactions. He also confronted the formidable task of tabulating, practically for the first time, the social accounts of the United Kingdom for the years 1938 and 1949 (the latter year not appearing until the 1952 second edition). All along he explained related quantities and definitions in simple terms as might be expected in an elementary textbook.[3] In that work he went back and forth in time to offer useful comparisons, pointing out practical estimation difficulties, and explaining how he dealt with them. This was often a difficult terrain to be covered, and the obstacles he had to surmount should reveal to the uninitiated economist how hard it is to come up with acceptable estimates of national income. What a far cry this is from the mathematicians who have been trying to pin down income with razor-edge precision. The same difficulties in practical estimation are familiar to national income estimators every day.[4] It will be seen that both as a concept and as a magnitude to be empirically estimated income always eludes precision.

II   THE INCOME OF *VALUE AND CAPITAL*

Because of the importance of Hicksian income for environmental economics it may be useful to consider its place in Hicks's broad analysis. His consideration of 'income' in *Value and Capital* was essentially conceptual, and intended to apply alike to the income of individuals, corporations and nations. The income chapter in that book consists of two parts: the main discourse (pp. 170–181), and 'Notes to Chapter XIV' (pp. 181–188) – the latter analysing income in conjunction with saving and investment, together with a discussion of the interest rates to be used for capitalizing future income streams. In the wider scheme of *Value and Capital* the income chapter came at the conclusion of Parts I–III, devoted to 'static' analysis, with the author intending the income discussion as a springboard to the dynamic analysis of the later parts. This separation of statics from dynamics, it will be seen, sheds light on his income definitions. In statics, Hicks asserted, 'the difficulty about income does not arise: a person's income can be taken without qualification as equal to his receipts' (p. 172). Interestingly, he saw here a similarity between statics and the 'stationary state' of the classical economists. For Hicks, a stationary state meant an economy progressing at a constant rate of expansion, not a state of zero growth, which is currently favored by some environmental economists. He viewed a 'stationary state' as a branch of dynamic economics where everything had come to rest. The same income chapter contained a consideration of the income-related concepts of 'saving, depreciation and investment', which Hicks insisted were 'not logical categories at all', but merely approximations needed to indicate 'prudent behaviour' by the income recipients. After considering income from various angles, he thought it pointless to seek any *precise* definition of it since that 'would put upon it a weight of refinement it cannot bear' (p. 171). Something rougher, he maintained, was 'actually better'.

Hicks's analysis of income proceeded in steps, first offering a general definition he judged as 'basic' or 'central', namely 'the maximum value which "he" [the income recipient] can consume during a week and still expects to be as well off at the end of the week as he was at the beginning' (p. 172). The use of the week was a Hicksian simplification so that nothing much could be expected to change during this short duration. Worthy of notice is the loose wording such as 'maximum *value*',[5] 'still expect', 'as well off' – all rather vague expressions though consistent with the roughness he attached to income estimation. Hicks then went on to discuss *variations* around this basic concept, which he named 'Income Number 1'. For him these variations were 'approximations' regularly made by 'business men and economists alike'. Thus his 'Income Number 2' emerged, derived from the capitalized money value of an individual's prospective receipts. Noting its flexibility, however, since expectations of interest rates would vary, he concluded that the second definition was more appropriate to income from property than to income from wages. At this juncture he went back to elaborate 'Income Number 1', basing it explicitly on the maintenance of capital. 'Income No. 1 is the maximum amount which can be spent during a period if there is to be an expectation of maintaining intact the capital value of prospective receipts (in money terms)' (p. 173), adding that Income Number 2 was theoretically 'a closer approximation to the central concept than Income No. 1.' But he went on further to consider 'Income No. 3' which depends explicitly on price expectations. If prices are expected to rise, the income recipient must expect to be less well off at the end of the week and consequently 'his' current income would be lower. That is because income is the maximum that a recipient can spend and still expect to be able to spend the same amount *in real terms* in subsequent periods. Therefore Income Number 3, he judged, is subject to 'indeterminateness' (p. 175). Hicks's 'Income Number 4' then enters the discussion with the introduction of 'durable consumption goods'. Here Hicks emphasized the distinction that should be made between 'spending' and 'consuming'. Income is the maximum amount that can be *consumed*, not just spent, while keeping capital intact. If part of the expenditure goes for acquiring durable consumer goods then expenditure will in this case exceed consumption. Only if the fresh acquisition of durable consumption goods matches the use (or consumption) of 'durables' acquired in the past will consumption and spending coincide. But if the old stock is being used up and there are no new acquisitions the income recipient must be worse off.

After all this probing it may be fair to conclude that Hicks's approximations around the central concept of income yielded little extra illumination, and we are therefore forced back onto the central definition (p. 172) that 'a man's income [is] the maximum value which he can consume during a week, and still expect to be as well off at the end of the week as he was at the beginning'. This is the definition that many environmental economists have embraced, and have named 'Hicksian income'.

It is interesting that the valuation of stocks (or accumulations) held by the income recipient receives no mention in Hicks's income chapter, but since his income period was very short he could overlook changes in the unit value of stocks held at the beginning and end of the week. But with a longer period, that problem could not be ignored. He was of the opinion, however, that the stocks – both at the period's beginning and the period's end – should be valued at *current* prices.[6] His view, as stated in Hicks (1976, p. 284), that the valuation of opening stocks 'depends in part' upon the expected end-period value seems mistaken and at odds with his general position (see below). Stock valuation at current prices is the view generally favored by economists, and this view has been followed by the national income statisticians who have sometimes to go through tortuous exercises of 'reconciliation' to accommodate changes in stock values to make sense of the income estimates. In accounting the value of beginning-period stocks is unambiguously the same as that of the previous period-end, and the stocks held at the end of the current period, according to a long-standing accounting rule, are to be valued at purchase prices (here including the period-beginning valuation) or current market prices *whichever value is less*. Refraining from overvaluing end-period stocks is a precautionary measure that may sometimes underestimate the estimated income, but the accountants see no harm in such underestimation as it will check undue consumption, safeguard capital and ensure sustainability from one account period to the next. Natural resources were not specifically covered in *Value and Capital*, except obliquely under the subtopic of 'wasting assets', but they figured two decades later in Hicks (1983a) when he addressed the work of John Stuart Mill (see later in this chapter). For national accounting purposes it is not too radical to propose that natural resources – sources as well as sinks – should be viewed as part of society's capital that needs to be kept intact for the estimation of income.

III   INCOME FROM WASTING ASSETS

Embedded in Hicks's income chapter in *Value and Capital* (1946) is the important notion that whichever of the 'approximations' to the concept of income we choose to use, the calculation of income consists in finding some sort of *standard stream* of values whose present capitalized value equals the discounted value of the stream of receipts which is actually in prospect. To Hicks the current receipts from a *wasting asset* should not be viewed as income that the income recipient would be receiving if he were getting a standard stream of the same present value as his expected receipts. Hicks further explained that any stream of values has a capitalized value, which is a function of the rate of interest. In this respect he put forward the important thought to be found on p. 187 of *Value and Capital*:

> If a person's receipts are derived from the exploitation of a wasting asset, liable to give out at some future date, we should say that his receipts are in excess of his income, the difference between them being reckoned as an allowance for depreciation. In this case, if he is to consume no more than his income, he must re-lend some part of his receipts; and the lower the rate of interest is, the greater the sum he will have to re-lend in order for the interest on it to make up for the expected failure of receipts from his wasting asset in the future.[7]

It is remarkable that this insightful notion of income from wasting natural resources – a notion put forward more than seven decades ago and which has inspired the user-cost method – has yet to find adequate expression in the official estimates of national income.

IV   HICKSIAN DOUBTS AND REVISIONS

As previously mentioned Hicks's view of income did not rest with *Value and Capital*. On at least two later occasions he came back to explain or slightly modify what he had meant to say before. This related in particular to what he termed the place of *income in time*, and the place of *income in growth theory*. In some sense he was only tinkering at the borders with what he had said about income in *Value and Capital*, and in another sense he wanted to justify what he thought were shortcomings of that earlier exposition.

Hicks expressed these doubts in the *Festschrift* for Nicholas Georgescu-Roegen – a name well known to environmental economists interested in entropy. There, Hicks contributed a chapter on 'Some questions of time in economics' (Hicks, 1976). This was almost a review of all his own past work on income, including his major achievements, but with emphasis now on weaknesses therein which he could discern. However, for the purpose of defining and estimating income what he had previously said remained virtually intact. This 'revanchist' piece, however, contains gems of wisdom about economics being a humanist discipline not a scientific one; about statics and dynamics; 'equilibrists' and others; and much more. But specifically on income, where he failed to string his 'weeks' into a longer sequence, he is most critical. Most pertinent is the issue he raises anew on the irreversibility of time as it relates to the valuation of stocks in social accounting. This is odd for he asserts, wrongly as I claim, that the value of the opening stocks reflects in part the value to be expected for the closing stock (p. 136).[8] Along the way he spreads his iconoclasm broadly to other areas of his influential work, repudiating the whole apparatus of indifference maps which he had helped to propagate in the early 1930s, denying that all options open to a consumer could form a stable scale of preferences to be hierarchically ordered and mapped by indifference curves. For consumer behavior, he sided with Marshall against the more elaborate conjectures of Samuelson and others. He also denounced his famous references to 'in time' and 'out of time', meaning, respectively, a difference between a dynamic movement and a static snapshot of a stationary state (p. 139). His view of a stationary state as mentioned earlier meant an economy expanding at a constant rate of growth. He accused both himself and Keynes of 'muddling' in that they mixed statics and dynamics, specifically where Keynes considered liquidity as a stationary state phenomenon, but this is altogether a different story.

Significantly Hicks looked back on his 'Income' chapter in *Value and Capital*, identifying what he thought were weaknesses common to him and Keynes (specifically Keynes's income in *The General Theory*) who, Hicks asserted, was merely expounding Marshall's short period analysis: 'The Keynes theory and *Value and Capital* theory were weak in corresponding ways. They both lacked, at one end, a satisfactory theory of *markets*; and at the other end, they lacked a satisfactory theory of *growth*.' These may be valid qualms, but hardly affects his careful treatment of income in *Value and Capital*. Several pages later he explained that his (Hicks's) 'steady state' was a 'growth equilibrium model' where the balance of macroeconomic variables, technology and investment (both autonomous and induced – see Hicks (1950)) – was made to produce a constant rate of economic expansion. This he judged in retrospect to have been a futile exercise though it produced many lessons. His alleged failure to develop a theory of markets in *Value and Capital* is not convincing: he simply assumed (he says) that prices were determined by demand and supply. In both these cases of self-criticism a fair critic would conclude that Hicks was exaggerating his own shortcomings, or may simply have been attempting to widen the analytical context while sketching future paths for others to further the study of income.[9]

V   THE PRIMACY OF OUTPUT OVER WELFARE

There is yet another aspect of Hicksian income which relates to welfare that needs discussion. 'Welfare' has received a lot of attention in the green accounting literature as much work has been done to read happiness from the national product. Hicks found fault in Pigou's insistence that the national dividend should be taken as identical with national welfare. But what is 'welfare'? Hicks asked. For Hicks 'welfare' is a technical term of economics which is to be as far as possible dissociated from its meaning in ordinary speech (Hicks, 1975, p. 310). But Pigou had strongly asserted that it was the substance of 'economic science' no less – an assertion Hicks could not abide. If this were only a matter of words, he says, the problem could easily be dismissed. But digging deep, Hicks came to the surprising conclusion that Pigou's welfare economics had little to do with welfare as commonly understood. Pigou was merely taking over the Classic Theory of production and distribution and turning it into the Economics of Welfare. To Hicks '*The Economics of Welfare* is *The Wealth of Nations* in a new guise' (p. 312) as I have already mentioned in the Appendix to Chapter 4 on 'Income, Capital and Wealth'.

The story of Hicks's income would not be complete without mentioning that he once entertained the thought that the social dividend, or the national income, could indicate both output (the product) and the joy or utility ('welfare') derived from it. In the same year he published the first edition of his *Social Framework* he wrote in the *Economic Journal* (Hicks, 1942b, p. 179): 'But comparing economic welfare is not the only purpose (nowadays, alas! it is not even the main purpose) of measuring the National Income.' Three and a half decades later in *Oxford Economic Papers*, Hicks (1975, p. 324) comes down clearly on the side of national income as an index of output, discarding any association between it and welfare, viewing output estimation as 'objective' and welfare as 'subjective':

> Partly as a result of the Keynesian revolution, but more (perhaps) because of statistical labours that were initially quite independent of it, the Social Product has now come right back into its old place. Modern economics – especially modern applied economics – is centered upon the Social Product, the Wealth of Nations, as it was in the days of Smith and Ricardo, but as it was not in the time that came between. So if modern theory is to be effective, if it is to deal with

questions that we in our time want to have answered, the size and growth of the Social Product are among the chief things with which it must concern itself. It is of course the objective Social Product on which attention must be fixed. We have indexes of production; we do not have – it is clear we cannot have – an Index of Welfare.

Justifying this position Hicks (p. 318) stated that we were 'perhaps a little further forward than Pigou' in view of 'our decision to treat the Social Product as primary, and to banish 'economic welfare'.

VI   STEADY AND STATIONARY STATE ECONOMICS

The 'steady state' and the 'stationary state' have crept into the above discussion without adequate clarification. Herman Daly's (1991) steady state (which has many admirers who wish to protect the environment by arresting economic expansion) is obviously different from that of Hicks who described it in no uncertain terms: 'I shall not say much about Steady State economics; for in spite of all that it has meant for the economics of the fifties and sixties, it is my own opinion that it has been rather a curse' (Hicks, 1976, p. 142).

But to Hicks, as already mentioned, the *steady* state meant expansion at a *constant* growth rate. And his opinion of the '*stationary* state' of the Classics was even worse: it was moribund with no growth at all. Unlike the static stationary state, Hicks's steady state was a dynamic process of a 'regularly progressive economy', and the assumption of a *constant* rate of growth was a challenge for him to discover the factors that would produce such a 'steady' rate. He was following on from the dynamic growth models of 'Harrod and Domar (or perhaps . . . von Neumann)'. How such steady growth might be achieved had also been Hicks's quarry in his book on *The Trade Cycle* (1950).

Looking further back it is interesting to see how earlier economists treated their *stationary* state. Adam Smith had described the stationary state as a 'final' economic state in which a country 'had acquired that full complement of riches which the nature of its soil and climate, and its situation with respect to other countries, allowed it to acquire; which could, therefore advance no further' (Smith, 1776 [1937], p. 94).[10] Marshall later picked up the theme (1920) where he called the stationary state 'a famous fiction').[11] To Marshall it was a monotonous state where all was predictable (p. 810) with population stationary, the average age constant, and the character of man himself was a constant quantity (pp. 367–368). Marshall contrasted the progressive reality of economic activities around him with the stationary state world where 'every plain and single doctrine as to the relations between cost of production, demand and value is necessarily false: and the greater the appearance of lucidity which is given to it by skilful exposition, the more mischievous it is' (p. 368).

Marshall wanted a state that would illuminate economic scholarship, believing that a stationary state was analytically barren. But he also briefly attempted a relaxation of some of its rigid assumptions, mainly in respect of a steady population and a constant stock of capital, with a view to bringing it closer to reality and therefore rendering it more useful for economic analysis.

Between Smith and Marshall had, of course, notably come John Stuart Mill (see below). It was Mill who had extolled the virtues of the stationary state (1848, Book iv, Chapter vi) looking forward to a future where the progress of society would relax before the utmost physical limit had been reached. He pleaded for the enjoyment of solitude, the beauties of nature, and the pursuit of moral and social progress instead of material expansion. Later echoes of the same sentiment are to be found in Keynes (1930) as he also looked forward to a future when the economic problem had been largely solved, and humanity settled down to the pursuit of the higher ends of leisure and enjoyment, and economics had become a humble vocation like dentistry.

After adopting Hicks's definition of *ex post* income Daly moved forward to confront the future of income change. Impelled by the dangers he foresaw in the continual expansion of economic activity as advocated by most economists he used his powers of persuasion in support of 'steady state economics' as an alternative to 'growth economics'. Daly's steady state emphatically means no growth at all. More strongly than Hicks (but see below), Daly dismissed future economic expansion as untenable, whether at a constant or a variable pace, focusing on the incompatibility between exponential economic growth and the finite biosphere that contains all economic activity, following along the path that Donella H. Meadows *et al.* (1972) had blazed earlier. He argued convincingly that the scale of world production and consumption had reached or exceeded limits that the earth can ill afford. In this he touched a sensitive nerve among economists who not only idolize growth but have made it the principal – sometimes the sole – criterion for judging economic success. Daly, however, made one subsidiary concession: on the way to arresting growth, it is only the 'throughput' of material and energy that needs to be constrained not the final product. Daly's steady state is, however, a little vague on population. The classics had followed a Malthusian vision that expected population to be controlled by wages falling below subsistence. Daly's (1974) paper, admittedly put forward tentatively, talked of imposing 'population quotas' to restrain population increases, an idea Daly presumably took from Boulding (Daly, 1974, p. 19; see also Daly, 1996, *passim*.) A clearer exposition of the population issue is to be found in Daly (1991, p. 17) where he advocates a stationary population requiring births to offset the inevitable deaths at low, rather than high levels, allowing for increased life spans. This is of course an altogether sensitive subject to many, and if I am not mistaken it has been left out of Daly's later writings. Steady state economics as stressed in Daly's work is covered in greater detail in other chapters of the present book and, of course, is to be found in Daly's own book, *Steady State Economics* (1991; see also Daly, 2008).[12]

VII HICKS ON J. S. MILL, POPULATION AND THE ENVIRONMENT

Hicks's brief comments on the environment may be found in an essay on John Stuart Mill principally aimed at restoring Mill's place in the triumvirate of classical economists beside Smith and Ricardo from which he had been expelled (Hicks, 1983b). After parading various contributions by Mill, which anticipated aspects of the modern theory of international trade and some of the work of Marshall and Keynes, Hicks focuses on Mill's attitude to growth. Mill, according to Hicks, disagreed with the 'optimism' of both Smith and Ricardo who believed in a 'progressive, growing, economy, in which capital and population are increasing more or less in step.' Like Malthus before him – Hicks observes – Mill believed that it was the 'increase in population that was the Devil' which could be exorcised by birth control. While Ricardo foresaw a situation where land was the fixed factor and the product of society went progressively to the land owners, Mill, according to Hicks, believed that with a fixed population there was no need for the economy to go on expanding. To Mill a stationary state with zero growth was no longer a horror. On the contrary, it was a desirable objective to be happily anticipated. (Hicks, 1983b, p. 68). Hicks concludes this essay on Mill with 'a message to present-day environmentalists, who have risen up in opposition to the new growth economics, just as he did to the old'. From Mill's *Principles of Political Economy* (1848), Hicks (1983b, chapter 5, p. 70) picks up a long passage containing the following:

> (There is not) much satisfaction in contemplating the world with nothing left to the spontaneous activity of nature; with every rood of land brought under cultivation, which is capable of growing food for human beings; every flowery

waste or natural pasture ploughed up, all quadrupeds or birds which are not domesticated for man's use exterminated ... If the earth must lose that great portion of its pleasantness which it owes to things that the unlimited increase of capital and population would extirpate from it, for the mere purpose of enabling it to support a larger, but not a better or happier population, I sincerely hope, for the sake of posterity, that they will be content to be stationary, long before necessity compels them to it.

Hicks, who had written so much on growth theory, perhaps unexpectedly, wished to stress the *ecological* harm of unfettered economic expansion. He had previously warned against the mindless pursuit of growth ('a richer society may be a stupider society' he once wrote) but now he championed the cause of the environment and aptly quoted John Stuart Mill. Although this piece on Mill appeared in his *Collected Essays* of previously published contributions, this particular contribution was composed afresh.

Before I go forward let me backtrack a little by tracing my own steps towards Green Accounting, which I do in the next chapter, which for me began with the petroleum crises of the 1970s.

NOTES

1. The first edition of *Value and Capital* came out in 1939.
2. As Frank Hahn (1990) observed, this was a recurrent trait in Hicks's work: 'He returned to the same problems over and over again over many years because he brooded on them and became dissatisfied with his earlier answers.'
3. There were of course 'mighty' predecessors of whom he mentions Adam Smith himself. It is interesting that in this regard Hicks conflates the development of macroeconomics with the development of national income estimation. The latter he traces back to a 1940 booklet by Keynes, *How to Pay for the War*, produced under Keynes's supervision, which led to the first official estimates of the British National Income and Expenditure issued in the same year by Meade and Stone. Lack of even rudimentary data had stymied the first attempt by Bowley and Stamp to estimate Britain's national income for 1911 and 1924, and handicapped the pioneering work of Colin Clark. On this see Hicks (1940, 1990).
4. See also Meade and Stone (1949).
5. Emphasis added.
6. Though his view – as stated in Hicks (1976, p. 136) – that the valuation of opening stocks 'depends in part' upon the expected end-period value seems in my view to be wrong and at odds with his general position; but see note 8.
7. It was this thought that guided me to formulate what became known as the 'El Serafy method'.
8. From a less critical angle, it is possible to read Hicks as having meant by 'value', not money value, but 'usefulness' so that holding a stock at the beginning of the year would be an indication that such a holding is foreseen as being useful later in the year.
9. Hicks's self-criticism in this regard is akin to his partial repudiation of his famous Investment–Saving/Liquidity preference–Money supply (IS-LM) apparatus which he had put forward in 1937 to explain Keynes's *General Theory*.

10. Adam Smith, *Wealth of Nations*, Book I, Chapter IX entitled, 'Of the profits of stock'. Smith envisaged that in a stationary state profits would drop and wages decline sufficiently to quell population growth.
11. Schumpeter in his *History of Economic Analysis* (1954, p. 966) comments sarcastically that though it was a fiction yet 'as a methodological fiction the stationary state was not at all "famous" in 1890'. Schumpeter in fact traces the stationary state back to Plato. (pp. 55–56.)
12. Hicks, strictly speaking, was not a neoclassical economist but the eclectic product of different schools associated with the names of Pareto, Walras, Menger, Böhm-Bawerk and the Swedes, with a fundamental grounding in the English tradition of Marshall and Pigou. In a sense he was also a Keynesian as he had similar views to what came out as *The General Theory* of Keynes in 1936. In a word, his school was 'Economics'. See Hicks's autobiographical essay, 'The formation of an economist' (1983, Chapter 31, pp. 355–364).

REFERENCES

Daly, Herman E. (1974), The economics of the steady states', *American Economic Review, Papers and Proceedings*, **LXIV** (2), 15–21.

Daly, Herman E. (1989), 'Toward a measure of sustainable net national product', in Yusuf J. Ahmad, Salah El Serafy and Ernst Lutz (eds), *Environmental Accounting for Sustainable Development, A UNEP-World Bank Symposium*. Washington DC: The World Bank, Chapter 3.

Daly, Herman E. (1991), *Steady State Economics*, 2nd edition. Washington DC: Island Press.

Daly, Herman E. (1996), *Beyond Growth, The Economics of Sustainable Development*. Boston, MA: Beacon Press.

Daly, Herman E. (2008), 'Growth and development: critique of a credo', *Population and Development Review*, **34** (3), 511–518.

Daly, Herman E. and John B. Cobb (1989), *For the Common Good: Redirecting the Economy toward Community, the Environment and a Sustainable Future*. Boston, MA: Beacon Press.

El Serafy, Salah (1979), 'The oil price revolution of 1973–74', *Journal of Energy and Development*, **IV** (2), 273–290.

El Serafy, Salah (1981), 'Absorptive capacity, the demand for revenue and the supply of petroleum', *Journal of Energy and Development*, **7** (1), 73–88.

El Serafy, Salah (1989), 'The proper calculation of income from depletable natural resources', in Yusuf J. Ahmad, Salah El Serafy and Ernst Lutz (eds), *Environmental Accounting for Sustainable Development, A UNEP-World Bank Symposium*. Washington DC: The World Bank, Chapter 3, pp. 10–18.

El Serafy, Salah (1991), 'The environment as capital', in Robert Costanza (ed.), *Ecological Economics: The Science and Management of Sustainability*. New York: Columbia University Press, Chapter 12, pp. 168–175.

Hahn, Frank (1990), 'John Hicks the theorist', *The Economic Journal*, **100** (401), 539–549.

Hicks, John Richard (1940), 'Valuation of the social income', *Economica*, **VII** (New Series), No. 26.

Hicks, John Richard (1942a), *The Social Framework: A Introduction to Economics*. Oxford, UK: Oxford University Press at the Clarendon Press.

Hicks, John Richard (1942b), 'Maintaining capital intact: a further suggestion', *Economica*, **IX** (New Series) (34), 174–179.

Hicks, John Richard (1946), *Value and Capital*, 2nd edition. Oxford, UK: Oxford University at the Clarendon Press (2nd edition 1950).

Hicks, John Richard (1950), A *Contribution to the Theory of the Trade Cycle*. Oxford, UK: Oxford University at the Clarendon Press.

Hicks, John Richard (1975), 'The scope and status of welfare economics', *Oxford Economic Papers*, **27** (3), 307–326. Reprinted in John Richard Hicks (1981), *Wealth and Welfare, Collected Essays on Economic Theory*, Vol. 1. Cambridge, MA: Harvard University Press, Chapter 10, pp. 218–239.

Hicks, John Richard (1976), 'Some questions of time in economics', in Anthony M. Tang, Fred W. Westfield and James S. Worley (eds), *Evolution, Welfare and Time in Economics (Essays in Honor of Nicholas Georgescu-Roegen)*, Lexington, MA: Lexington Books, Heath and Company, Chapter 6, pp. 135–152.

Hicks, John Richard (1983a), 'The formation of an economist' in *Classics and Moderns, Collected Essays on Economic Theory*, Vol. III. Cambridge, MA: Harvard University Press, Chapter 31, pp. 355–364.

Hicks, John Richard (1983b), 'From Classical to Post-classical: the work of J.S. Mill', in *Classics and Moderns, Collected Essays on Economic Theory*, Vol. III. Cambridge, MA: Harvard University Press, Chapter 5, pp. 60–70.

Hicks, John Richard (1990), 'The unification of macroeconomics', *Economic Journal*, 100, No. 401, pp. 528–538.

Keynes, John Maynard (1930), 'Economic possibilities for our grandchildren', in *Essays in Persuasion* (1963). New York: W.W. Norton & Co., pp. 358–373.

Marshall, Alfred (1920), *Principles of Economics*, 8th edition, London: Macmillan.

Meade, James. E. and Stone, Richard, (1949), *National Income and Expenditure*, 2nd edition. Cambridge: Bowes and Bowes.

Meadows, Donella H., Dennis L. Meadows, Jørgen Randers and William W. Behrens (1972), *Limits to Growth, A Report for the Club of Rome*. New York: Potomac Associates.

Mill, John Stuart (1848), *Principles of Political Economy*. London: Longmans, Green and Co., Book iv, Ch. vi.

Schumpeter, Joseph E. (1954), *History of Economic Analysis*. New York: Oxford University Press.

Smith, A. (1776 [1937]), *An Inquiry into the Nature and Causes of the Wealth of Nations*, Modern Library Edition. New York: Random House.

7. Income from extracting petroleum and controversies over keeping capital intact

A HISTORICAL PERSPECTIVE

There is nothing 'green' about petroleum but it was one of two things that triggered my interest in having the system of national accounts reformed, and both occurred during the 1970s. One was my becoming acutely aware from my work on macroeconomics at the World Bank that the deterioration of the natural resource base which sustains many economies, rich or poor, but primarily the latter, was being overlooked by the macroeconomists. The other, the focus of this chapter, was the upheavals that rocked the international petroleum market. Many must have forgotten – if they had been of age then – the emotional reactions, even within academic circles, to the rises in petroleum prices during that decade. The petroleum price rises of the 1970s appear now to have been quite moderate if compared to the now prevailing prices and their projected future trajectory. It will be recalled that the petroleum market upheavals of half a century ago were set off by two events: a Middle East war of 1973–74 and the Iranian revolution of 1978. But it was largely the first event's impact that got me started on the road of reforming the national accounts. True there was a short-lived embargo in the air, but this had nothing to do with the Organization of the Petroleum Exporting Countries (OPEC; see below). To me, confusion was rife as the oil revenues were conflated with oil incomes, together with an exaggerated role of OPEC as a monopolist. OPEC comprised a group of oil exporters that had emerged a decade earlier and had no experience in controlling supplies. Apart from its alleged market power, which I discuss later, I was anxious to extricate the proper income of its members from the revenues they were collecting.[1]

Against a strong tide of contrary opinion, I took particular exception to the use of 'rent' to characterize the financial surpluses the oil exporters were gathering from the commercial extraction of their natural resource. Practically always these revenues were misnamed 'resource rents'. To me, 'rent' since Ricardo has been associated with the surplus produced by land due, in his familiar phrase, to the 'original and indestructible powers of the soil'. The rent of land is genuine income that is seen as perpetual or nearly perpetual, whereas the surpluses obtained from natural resource extraction are in most cases transitory, liable to give out when the resource has expired. In that early paper (El Serafy, 1981) I sketched my method, and put forward an algebraic formula to extricate true income from revenue, and this formula has stayed unchanged. What remained after deducting income from revenue I later named a user cost.

The 1981 paper had appeared a few years prior to my involvement with the quest for reforming the United Nations System of National Accounts (SNA). This quest had developed – as stated earlier – from UNEP's search for some unitary indicator of ecological deterioration that would attract attention, and this search unexpectedly spurred the cooperation of the World Bank, thanks to the efforts of Robert Goodland, the Bank's principal environmentalist at the time. As already mentioned, a series of international workshops under the joint aegis of UNEP and the World Bank began searching for an effective way to arouse public awareness of the environment's predicament. The search was still alive when for the first time I participated in the third workshop meeting held in Paris in September–October 1985. That meeting took place two years after this initiative had started, and I was voted as rapporteur for that meeting. I was at the time not involved in any environmental work whatever, but was immersed in macroeconomic analysis and policy efforts through which I had become acutely aware of the inadequacy of the traditional GDP estimates for many developing countries. I believe my participation at that Paris meeting helped to sway the workshops in the direction of using the SNA as a useful vehicle for the sought-after purpose.[2]

Note that in the present context I use GDP as a proxy for national income. Strictly speaking national income is the NNP, which equals the GNP adjusted downward for 'capital' depreciation. In turn the GNP adjusts GDP for factor service payments and receipts across national boundaries. Such transboundary transactions, as is well known, include interest on foreign debt and workers' remittances, both positive and negative. But all these estimates must begin with GDP, which is the basic quantity in national income estimation, and in most cases GDP does not deviate appreciably from GNP.

As stated earlier, my method also sprang from my own reaction to the frenzied analysis of the upheavals that beset the international petroleum market during the 1970s. I was particularly concerned to point out that the oil exporting nations, members of OPEC, which was then a fledgling institution with little coherence and less experience, was trying to improve the terms of trade for their principal product. The members of OPEC – which was popularly, but inaccurately, referred to as a cartel – were mostly poor and less developed countries whose aggregate market share as suppliers in the international oil market, though considerable, did not amount to a monopoly which technically the epithet of a cartel conveys. In the world context OPEC countries commanded only about half of all oil extraction in 1974, and this is the relevant proportion that is significant for judging market power. Oil was, and is still, extracted and consumed in numerous countries, so that domestic supply and consumption provide room for flexibility of the quantities traded by non-OPEC members on the international market.[3]

The influence of OPEC over the volume of petroleum extracted worldwide, and hence its impact on the price fetched on the international market, were evidently limited though not negligible. For a long time previously powerful international petroleum corporations (known in the international oil market as 'The Seven Sisters') had the upper hand in these matters, and often formed a coalition to bargain with individual suppliers. But the 'post-colonial' era had begun to dawn in the 1960s though the powers of the newly independent nations were later countered by powerful opposite forces. The notion of a cartel was belied also by the fact that the individual economic interests of OPEC's member countries were in many cases contradictory or at the very least not identical.[4] Countries with modest reserves had a near horizon and favored smaller volumes of extraction and higher prices, whereas others with more abundant supplies had a longer view, preferring greater extraction volumes now and lower prices. Even later, when OPEC for a short while decreed supply restrictions with quotas allocated for individual member exports, 'cheating' was rife, and the OPEC limitations were in practice ineffective – a familiar pattern of behavior well known to cartel analysts.

REVENUE MINUS INCOME EQUALS USER COST

From the perceptive of a macroeconomic analyst it was of great importance to appreciate the reality that incomes derived from the exploitation of 'wasting assets' were overestimated in the national accounts (El Serafy, 1979, 1981). Emphasizing the fact that petroleum was not being 'produced' as it was (and still is) commonly being described, but only 'extracted', I argued that the revenues of the petroleum exporting countries were an admixture of income and capital disinvestment – more or less echoing Alfred Marshall (see the next section). The revenues, wrongly conflated with income, both in the public perception as well as in many 'learned' economic tracts, in fact consisted partly, and in certain cases principally, of the proceeds of asset sales. By the very nature of the act of extraction the assets being exploited get diminished, and *ceteris paribus*, the time will inescapably come when these assets will exist no more. The question of the 'unsustainability' of commercially exploited natural resources was evidently inherent in my argument, but tended to be absent from much of the macroeconomic analysis that appeared in the literature. Resource exploitation meant disinvestment, which in the national accounts had been, and continues to be, perversely portrayed as value added and counted in income. Conventional national income estimates appeared in many cases to say that the faster the rate of extraction the rapider the growth of the economy concerned – an error that spectacularly conveys the wrong economic message.

My own argument (El Serafy, 1979), to put it mildly, failed to gain immediate acceptance,[5] but it gradually gathered momentum, especially when a few years later I dressed it up in an ecological garb and applied it to depletable natural resources in general. Getting away from the emotionally charged petroleum market was a great help, and whatever popularity it gained afterwards must be credited to the 'environmental movement'. I had not given it a name previously, but now began to call it a 'user-cost' method, having in mind that in its essentials user cost and true income add up to revenue. In my new exposition a fresh emphasis developed: in prior publications my concern had been to show that *income* was lower than *revenue*, but later I began to emphasize the natural resource *loss* involved in extractive activities. This was a slight change in emphasis, but in both cases I was intuitively following Hicks, searching like him for a way to reckon 'true' income out of what in *Value and Capital* he labeled 'wasting assets'.

'RESOURCE RENT' AS VIEWED BY MARSHALL[6]

Many environmental economists are aware of Hicks's work on income, but are understandably less familiar with the writing on the same topic of Alfred Marshall the acknowledged father of 'neoclassical economics' – a discipline that incidentally has been maligned by non-economist environmentalists. And for the national accountants the user cost incurred in mining natural resources has for long escaped their attention and this was naturally carried over to most users of the macroeconomic magnitudes produced. Marshall had clearly perceived this 'cost' as a disinvestment, and called it a 'royalty', which he thought should be included in the price of the mined ore. Marshall had a profound understanding of the distinction between rent (income), and royalty (disinvestment) (see Marshall,

1920, in particular Book v, x, 6, page 438). We should bear in mind the fact
that Marshall had been writing prior to the emergence of modern national
accounting, and in his argument about royalty he was focusing on the
economics of mining from a microeconomic perspective. In his words:

> A royalty is *not* a rent, though often so called. For, except when mines, quar-
> ries, etc., are practically inexhaustible, the excess of their income over their
> direct outgoings has to be regarded, in part at least, as the price got by the sale
> of stored-up goods – stored up by nature indeed, but now treated as private
> property; and therefore the marginal supply price of minerals includes a royalty
> in addition to the marginal expenses of working the mine. [Emphasis is in the
> original.]

On the following page Marshall calls attention to the capital nature of the
opportunity cost implicit in extraction:

> the royalty . . . on a ton of coal, when accurately adjusted, represents that dimi-
> nution in the value of the mine, regarded as a source of wealth in the future,
> which is caused by taking the ton out of nature's storehouse.

It is remarkable that these two citations from Marshall, written several
decades before I came to address the issue, perceptively capture the essence
of my user-cost method. Marshall, however, held back from proposing a
formula for estimating what he termed 'royalty' (my user cost). However,
it was with the help of my understanding of Hicks's *Value and Capital* that
I was able to devise my formula.[7] Marshall's reference to the case where
stocks are (practically) inexhaustible – leading to equality between income
and revenue, or in other words to a zero user cost – is a result obtainable
by my formula (see Chapter 9 below on the 'Proper calculation of income
from depletable natural resources'). This, taken together with Marshall's
hint of a temporal opportunity cost implicit in mineral extraction, puts in
a nutshell the basic analytical rationale behind my user-cost approach. It
is truly interesting that Marshall, assuming the role of a micro-economist,
wanted the user cost (his royalty) to be included in the price of the mined
product – a precursor perhaps of OPEC's quest for higher prices? From
my own angle, however, I wanted to promote a correct macroeconomic
estimation of income.

Keynes, Marshall's pupil, added an Appendix on user cost to the
chapter on income (Chapter 6 in his *The General Theory of Employment,
Interest and Money*, 1936) though he could find no practical use for it
elsewhere in the book. Keynes was looking at the user cost from a very
narrow perspective, simply as 'depreciation' of a piece of machinery. To
him it is the cost in wear-and-tear of using a machine rather than not using

it. In this he was taking his cue, as he says himself, unconvincingly from Marshall's royalty. For this he sought to emphasize two points: first, that an estimate of this user cost was not determinate, but 'debatable', which in his view would undermine any precision that could be attached to net income if estimated. So he expressed preference for the unambiguousness of gross income over net income as a serviceable macroeconomic variable. The second point Keynes raised in this context was in the Appendix to Chapter 6. There he traced Marshall's footsteps (notably Marshall, 1920, p. 427) describing the user cost as 'That part of the income which is required to cover wear-and-tear' and, as just mentioned, he suggested its resemblance to Marshall's royalty 'which does no more than cover the injury done to a mine by taking ore out of it.'[8] In *The General Theory* Keynes interestingly compared the user cost specifically to the using-up of copper (see Keynes, 1936, page 55n in Appendix on user cost, pp. 66–73). However, by limiting the user cost to machinery depreciation Keynes in effect diminished its importance, and Pigou quite rightly thought that such an adjustment could be neglected (see the next chapter).

To repeat, income, properly reckoned, and Marshall's royalty (the user cost) are in fact complements that add up to the totality of the net revenue realized in extraction. If one is known, so is the other, once revenue has been ascertained. It should be emphasized once more that when *renewable* natural resources (such as fish or forests) are exploited in a manner that does not ensure their renewal, then they are in effect being 'mined'. This will require that a user cost be estimated along similar lines, and deducted from the revenue which appears wrongly as income in the national accounts.

PETROLEUM AS A WASTING ASSET

Petroleum is only one example, though an obvious one, of a 'wasting asset' that fails to be accounted for properly in national income estimates. It belongs to a category of natural resources that includes other minerals, and extends to so-called renewable resources such as fish and forests when these are not being renewed. To the extent they appear in the national accounts these are resources that are commercially exploited and their output is transacted in the marketplace without due attention given to changes in their stocks. The actual stocks need not be known with any precision, but the stock changes, when they are transacted, are *flows* that are conventionally recorded in the national accounts. The concept of wasting assets is a more general one which may easily be extended to cover soil, water, the quality of the atmosphere, and even the ozone layer, which cannot be neatly fitted in a *national* context. Many of these assets qualify as 'wasting assets' when their quantity or quality deteriorates and are ripe candidates to be brought eventually into the SNA orbit. But it was the petroleum problems of the 1970s that gave birth to my method, which could be applied generally to all the above-mentioned resources for purposes relating to sustainability, even if they are not transacted, have no market price, and therefore have failed to be covered in the national accounts. For monitoring sustainability, therefore, we need not remain constrained by the limitations of the conventional national accounts.

ABSORPTIVE CAPACITY

Tracing back its history, the 'El Serafy method' – as it later came to be known – made its first appearance in an article perhaps oddly titled, 'Absorptive capacity, the demand for revenue and the supply of petroleum' (El Serafy, 1981). This originated as an invited paper to a conference on 'Absorptive Capacity' organized in October 1980 by the University of Colorado at Boulder. The argument was then being made that the oil exporters were accumulating balance of payments surpluses, which were upsetting the 'world financial system'. Such balances, so the reasoning went, could be reduced or eliminated if they were sunk into domestic investments. These investments would then activate imports, reduce the balance of payments surpluses and thus contribute to the restoration of 'balance' to international payments. However, since the capacity of the relevant countries to 'absorb' such new investments was obviously limited (and thus if the new investments were vetted with a cost–benefit method as they should) low or negative rates of return would discourage undertaking them. So it made sense to seek ways to enlarge the domestic absorptive capacity of the oil exporters so that domestic investments would become economically justifiable. This assumption of a strategy of rational scrutiny of domestic investments was in fact rather academic, considering the vast waste that characterized much of these countries' economic behavior. However, it provided a good context to examine theoretically some important economic issues. A counter argument I advanced during the conference against focusing on absorptive capacity was that these financial surpluses could be lowered or even eliminated at the source by the reduction of oil extraction – an option that was obviously viewed as inimical to the interests of the petroleum importers. And it was even harder to gain acceptance of the notion that the national accounts of the oil exporters, as those of other natural resource-extracting countries, which were similarly liquidating their natural assets through commercial operations, exaggerated their true income by misleadingly including the net proceeds gained from natural asset sales in GDP. Furthermore, I was anxious to point out that the environmentalists' popular view of excluding from NDP, when reckoned, the entirety of asset declines was wrong and tantamount to 'overkill'.

NAÏVE TRUST IN GDP ESTIMATES?

It is amazing how many clever economists put so much trust in the national income estimates. To me, the then-current UN SNA, as well as comparable national accounting systems, were defective in the treatment of income from wasting assets. Truly remarkable was the blind trust that macroeconomists had in the accuracy or near-accuracy of the national accounts which for one thing wrongly presented disinvestment (associated with the exploitation of both renewable and depletable resources) perversely as income. This blind trust became abundantly clear when the problem of higher petroleum prices emerged in the 1970s. Many economists indulged in dubious comments, overlooking the peculiar problems of the petroleum exporters *qua* developing countries, focusing concern almost exclusively on the hardships inflicted on the generally richer importing nations. True there was insecurity of supply and apprehension over more price hikes in future engendered by a short-lived embargo;[9] and true, hardships were indeed inflicted on the poorer importers of petroleum whose difficulties were compounded by higher prices of food and manufactured goods imports on top of weaker prices they were obtaining for their own primary product exports. I argued in El Serafy (1979) that the hardship caused by the latter imports were greater than that of the higher petroleum prices, and to alleviate part of the suffering incurred by the poorer importers the oil exporters gave generous development assistance as attested by successive reports of the Development Assistance Committee of the OECD.[10]

For OPEC members the option of regulating the oil supplies to mop up excessive revenues was of course constrained by contractual obligations towards the operating companies. These contracts seldom allowed flexibility, and even on the assumption of technical feasibility, abating extraction was likely to raise prices and these would counterbalance the effect of reduced extraction. In other words, higher prices would defeat volume reduction and revenue would not be reduced. There was also the possibility that the more industrialized oil importers might allow the inflow into their economies of the oil revenues in support of their own domestic investments. This latter route, however, was generally disparaged by both sides. The oil importers were wary of creating future economic claims on their domestic economies, and the oil exporters were themselves fearful of future expropriation of their investments by the host countries – a possibility that did not lack precedents.

In the politically charged atmosphere of the 1970s the fundamental notion was seldom contemplated that petroleum is a fossil fuel that took geological time for it to form, and that the great bulk of its deposits had in all probability been already located. Few appreciable discoveries were being made or expected – a thought that began to sink in only gradually in later years. This, despite a memorable contribution by Robert Solow of MIT in 1974 in an essay entitled, 'The economics of resources or the resources of economics' which reminded fellow economists of the depletability of petroleum. Solow recalled the almost neglected work of Harold Hotelling (1931), which had been rather discounted partly on the false charge that it was too pessimistic. Hotelling had applied the calculus of variations to the optimal allocation through time of a fixed stock of a natural resource while simultaneously treating the natural resource as an asset to be managed in the same way as other forms of assets are to be managed. Hotelling's work, though analytically ground breaking and closely related to income estimation, was seen wrongly as having no bearing on national accounting since it was constrained by assumptions of optimality and foreknowledge – assumptions not normally associated with accounting.

Besides Solow (1974, see also Solow, 1992), the contribution of John Hartwick was greatly significant. Not long after Solow (1974) he published two articles urging the investment of 'resource rents', by which he meant the net financial gains realized in the extraction of depletable resources, in new income-yielding ventures for the benefit of 'future generations' (Hartwick, 1977, 1978). Hartwick's estimated 'resource rents' had thus to be adjusted downward for individual resource owners though not explicitly for incorporation in a national accounting framework. A weakness of Hartwick's position in my view was his inclination to adjust resource revenues downwards by the full decline in stock values (not just by my user-cost equivalent). For me, this stamps him as an advocate of 'strong sustainability' – a concept I have expounded elsewhere in this book. Curiously, however, he is regarded as a proponent of 'weak sustainability' under the mistaken impression that, like myself, we support, or at least tolerate, the liquidation of natural capital to be replaced by other forms of capital. Be that as it may, it is obvious that Hartwick's purpose here was 'normative', or policy-oriented, whereas the accounting approach I have taken is *ex post*, descriptive and 'positive', and does not urge or prescribe any policy. An obvious distinction between our two positions is that he would deny the resource owners any consumption out of their current resource revenues, expecting them to wait until the recommended new investments had matured and begun to yield income. This is why I believe Beckerman considers Hartwick's stance as 'immoral'. I address this feature and other aspects of Hartwick's work in more detail in Chapter 11.

Another interesting issue is the (normative) recommendation by some ecologists that resource revenues, gained say from petroleum exploitation, be reinvested in ventures to generate *petroleum* substitutes. While sensible at its face value, such a proposal is marred by the fact that many natural resources, particularly petroleum, are not single-purpose products. Oil, for instance, performs many functions. While in many circles petroleum is viewed narrowly as a fuel, in reality it serves several purposes including the making of plastics, lubricants, paints, textiles and other products. As a fossil deposit, it is being depleted in our own fraction of time at an alarming rate, encouraged no doubt by its relatively low prices which have lured us to establish a way of life built around the combustion engine and the convenient transport it has provided. Apart from the general problem of facing its exhaustion before substitutes have been found to replace it in adequate quantities and at acceptable costs, there is of course the specific problem of its being an economic asset located in a few 'fortunate' countries'.[11] For many of these countries it has raised interesting economic issues that needed to be considered analytically quite apart from the general problem of whether or not the resource is being depleted unwisely on a world scale. As previously mentioned its extraction is being mislabeled 'production', and the cost of extraction has been regularly misnamed a cost of production. Debate would occasionally address whether there was enough petroleum in the world to satisfy the avid appetite for it that is inherent in the prevailing lifestyle of industrial economies and which are being emulated by the rich in developing countries. A great dependence on power, generated to an appreciable extent by cheap petroleum, is all-apparent; so is the addiction to the automobile as a predominant means of conveyance. Even the recent automotive vehicles, described as 'hybrid', rely on electric power that requires inputs of fossil fuels including coal, though increasingly the cleaner input of natural gas whose transportation via long pipelines is far from being free from hazards. When all this is added to a seemingly relentless global population growth, and expectations of higher and higher standards of individual consumption everywhere, it is easy to understand the ecologists' alarm about the future of Planet Earth, which is already greatly stressed, though denied by skeptics.

Despite growing concern, much false optimism has also been abroad emanating, among others, from those economists who seem to have unquestioned faith in the power of the market to lead to satisfactory outcomes. Technology, it was thought, would help to reduce fuel requirements, facilitate future oil discoveries and squeeze more oil from already declining deposits and from deposits yet to be discovered. This optimism rides in tandem with an indiscriminate belief in the ability of the market to limit and rationalize demand among the most urgent uses, and encourage supply from alternative sources. In the interim, however, false optimism manages to discourage the development of substitutes in the expectation that the dwindling supplies of fossil fuels would raise their prices and activate equilibrating reactions. Even some petroleum economists, who should be aware of the impending scarcities, have been known to side with the optimists, claiming that petroleum deposits in the earth's crust are practically limitless (cf. Adelman, 1990; Adelman et al., 1990.) The obvious flaw in that view, which is strictly speaking correct, is the fact that it is contradicted by the reality of extraction operations. Scattered deposits in small quantities may forever remain unexploited since commercial exploitation will likely require investment in physical amenities, including transportation facilities, pipelines, ports, storage structures and others which involve capital outlays that would render small-scale exploitation uneconomic and therefore for practical purposes non-existent. Until very recently, the opposing powers of the anti-environment sentiment, rooted frequently in the corporate and individual pursuit of short-term gains, have frustrated the formation of meaningful national energy policies, even in countries, such as the United States, where dependence on outside sources is great and openly resented, and where many citizens have become aware of the seriousness of the problem.

Over the last four decades or so awareness of the growing scarcity of petroleum has fluctuated with gyrations of its prices, especially with increasing recognition of the deleterious impact on climate change of fossil fuel combustion and its carbon dioxide releases. Much interest was generated in the 1970s when two upheavals occurred in the crude petroleum market, the first in 1973–74 in association with yet another Middle East war that triggered the denial of some Arab oil exports to certain importers, and the other in 1977–78 when the Iranian Revolution dethroned the Shah and ushered in an Islamic regime. It is significant that both upheavals had political origins, although the economic lessons derived from the later disruption were better understood and more clearly analysed. Looking back, the price rises of the 1970s appear fairly modest in real terms, and have been followed intermittently by later declines. As stated earlier much misreading of the earlier 1970s' events gave rise to alleged cartel power residing in OPEC and exercised through supply manipulation – possibly as an emotional reflex to the demise of the importers' monopsonist cartel that, in my view, had kept oil prices too low. There was also the importers' resentment of the rise of a group of developing-country exporters, which appeared to be bent on acquiring control over their own natural wealth in a largely post-colonial era. From the start, OPEC threatened the hegemony of the more powerful cartel of the international oil corporations (mainly American, British and Dutch) which were popularly known as the 'Seven Sisters' (see Sampson, 1975).[12]

ON OPEC AS A CARTEL

Lost in much of the analysis was the internal inconsistency of OPEC's members' interests, as stated above, which impeded its actions as a monopolist (see Razavi, 1984.) Countries within OPEC, sitting on large oil reserves, were more interested in the long run, and anxious to keep prices fairly low to ensure the continuation of demand. Other members of the group, those possessing small reserves and therefore with a shorter temporal horizon, were more eager to obtain higher prices in the short run – the only run obviously available to them. When in the early 1980s OPEC declared supply limitations in the form of export quotas, these were frequently flouted in practice by 'cheating' in various ways, including using arcane barter agreements – a weakness that is common to such supply coalitions. The persistent epithet of a 'cartel' attached to OPEC seems to mirror the displaced power of the 'Seven Sisters' that had dominated the industry for decades. That power was eroded by the entry into the market of a number of 'minor' rivals who secured concessions by offering better terms to the crude petroleum owners. The emergence of OPEC in 1960 had been prompted by the machinations of the Cartel of the Majors, cutting the oil prices they offered twice (in 1959 and 1960) without host country consultation. There may have been good reasons for these cuts but the emergence of OPEC naturally caused alarm in the oil importing countries, which in some cases viewed it as a threat to their 'national security'. Previously, the group of American, British and Dutch companies led by the United States had met regularly to plan common strategies vis-à-vis the oil countries. In America they managed to obtain special waivers from successive US administrations allowing such collusion which is said to have legally violated existing antitrust regulations (Sampson, 1975; Rubino, 2008, p. 235. See also Sampson, 1982, especially Chapter 7 on the impact of all this on international financial flows).

HICKS AND PIGOU ON NET INCOME

To round off this chapter, the contribution of Hicks to income estimation in the context of ecological economics needs some explaining. Hicks published his economic path-breaking work, *Value and Capital*, (subtitled 'An inquiry into some fundamental principles of economic theory') in 1939, with a second edition seven years later (Hicks, 1946). His famous chapter on 'Income' (Chapter 14 in Part III of the book) has since been widely quoted in the rising discipline of ecological economics, with the expression 'Hicksian income' cited with approval by environmentalists. Between the first and second editions of *Value and Capital*, Hicks produced *The Social Framework* (1942; of which a second edition came out in 1952). This was a work entirely devoted to national accounting, which he believed would make an excellent introduction to the study of economics beginning from the macroeconomic end. This was meant to complement if not to supplant the traditional microeconomic approach based on supply and demand of individual commodities. In fact Hicks subtitled this work 'An introduction to economics'.

Hicks was deeply interested in accounting methods, and it may be stated confidently that in his income chapter of *Value and Capital* he was simply articulating in economic language what the accountants had been saying about the determination of income for centuries. Thus writing about income, I have always been reluctant to use the expression 'Hicksian income' or 'sustainable income' being aware of the fact that the estimation of income had been pioneered by the accountants using pragmatic methods that aimed at 'sustainability'. The sustainability involved was not the sustainability advocated by ecological economists, but that of the individual entities for which the accountants were drawing the accounts. It was a sustainability geared to the survival of the entity from one accounting period to the next. For this purpose the accountants had devised a benchmark standard, which the economists happened to stumble upon much later, namely the concept of 'keeping capital intact'. Striving to estimate income from mercantile revenues in the late Middle Ages, the accountants based their income estimation on this concept – a concept that was to attract the analysis of major economists including Pigou, Hayek, Hicks and Kuznets in the 1930s.

In his income analysis Hicks pays high tribute to Pigou for his efforts to elucidate the concept of 'net income'. To Pigou net income is lower than gross income by an allowance for capital 'depletion' (his term). There is much in Pigou's (1932) *Economics of Welfare* that is germane to the topic, but perhaps the most pertinent piece of his work appeared in a later article entitled, 'Net income and capital depletion' (Pigou, 1935).[13] By depletion,

Pigou meant all forms of deterioration or depreciation, not just the decline in the capital stock of non-renewable natural resources as the expression is used in the ecological economic literature of today. In line with the conventional practice of the accountants, the concept of 'keeping capital intact' appeared to Pigou as necessary, though not without a major caveat. He correctly distanced himself from maintaining the *value* of capital, as later writers would assert, offering a general definition (*op. cit.*, p. 235): 'Net income consists of the whole of annual output minus what is needed to maintain the stock of capital intact; and this stock is kept intact provided that its physical state is held constant.'

An important prerequisite of this definition – a prerequisite that should ward off facile criticism – is that it applies only to a 'stationary state' where for him the future is simply a repetition of the past. However, in a more realistic setting where the future is not known, the physical capital to be kept intact becomes, in Pigou's view, an uncertain quantity, and net income loses its precision as a result. Pigou identified two barriers against objective assessments in this respect: (1) defining the precise point in time at which capital should be held intact, and (2) the time preference dimension (the discount rate) needed for discounting future quantities. In this regard he considered a very wide range of possibilities within which capital consumption would lie: wear-and-tear of machinery on the one hand, and total destruction by an event such as enemy action or an earthquake on the other, where the damage could actually exceed the total value of the asset. Significantly he contemplated also a variety of perspectives including a large change in people's rate of discount of future satisfactions leading to a corresponding change in the value of the existing capital stock in terms of current production while the physical stock of capital still remained unchanged. Summing up, Pigou stated (*op. cit.*, p. 240):

> there is plainly no definition to which we are ineluctably compelled. In the last resort we shall be forced to rely on a more or less arbitrary fiat. Net income is not a precise entity given in nature. It is a portion of gross output selected and marked off from the rest by a boundary line, which our own choice, not objective fact, imposes.

Fundamental probing of the concept of 'keeping capital intact' for the purpose of estimating income is seen to have been extensive and shows how elusive it is in both theory and practice. This corroborates Hicks's emphasis on the unavoidably rough nature of income estimates, whether in gross or net terms. The search for precise measurement importantly flies in the face of recent attempts by mathematically inclined economists to set a precisely defined 'net income' concept, wishing to place it at the heart of welfare 'sustainability'. Two examples of this are papers by Asheim (1997) and Weitzman (2000): as if welfare itself, which is a 'state of mind' unlike output, which is concrete, could be measured without much equivocation. In this respect we should recall also Hicks's comments on Pigou's introductory chapter on 'maintaining capital intact' in the third edition of *Economics of Welfare* (Hicks, 1974). On a practical level, obsession with precision also exposes the naïveté of some analysts who tabulate the industrial structure of GDP and NDP and their rates of growth using percentages with obsessional eagerness to show such measurements, not just in round numbers as they should, but with the addition of one or even two decimal points.

It is now high time to embark on the analysis of the user cost, and describe what has been said about it by way of criticism and try to rebut opponents' arguments where I feel they have been misguided. Before that however, I address in the next chapter, in general terms, the impact of greening the accounts on the estimates of the macroeconomic variables.

NOTES

1. Note how I avoid calling the extraction of such a resource 'production' which is a common appellation even among environmentalists.
2. It is remarkable how the World Bank at the time was so supportive of this initiative that it provided my time and incurred the cost of my participation at a time when I had no official connection with environmental work.
3. I can claim to speak with some authority on this matter since my Oxford doctoral dissertation, written under the supervision of Professor Hicks, had the subtitle: 'A study in the regulation of supply'.
4. See Razavi (1984).
5. El Serafy (1979); but it was its sequel, El Serafy (1981), that met with hostility when I read it in draft to a conference at the University of Colorado, Boulder, in 1980.
6. When I began my serious economic training in the 1950s in London, a recurrent phrase used by my teachers was 'It's all in Marshall' – a phrase which understandably lost its validity gradually, though precious gems are still to be found in Marshall (1920) ready to be mined by attentive researchers.
7. I should perhaps mention that I had a thorough grounding in accountancy as part of my first degree in business at Alexandria University, Egypt, in the 1940s.
8. This citation comes from Marshall (1920), Chapter X on 'Marginal costs in relation to agricultural values', which is in his Book V, entitled *General Relations of Demand, Supply, and Value*. In that chapter we find Marshall's differentiation between rent, quasi-rent, and royalty (the latter being my user cost).
9. There were in fact two oil embargos, both short lived and ineffective. They were wrongly blamed on OPEC (and sometimes the Organization of Arab Petroleum Exporting Countries (OAPEC) which never had any role in deciding extraction or export). Both were Arab (not OPEC) embargos and were associated with two Middle East wars in 1967 and again in 1973–74. Neither garnered unanimity and were short lived and applied only against perceived war adversaries. The first lasted from June to August 1967 and the latter from October 1973 to March 1974. During the last one, OPEC exports in fact increased as some Arab countries actually expanded their exports in disregard of the embargo.

10. In the period 1973–77 total official aid flows from OPEC member countries, on the basis of net disbursements, aggregated US$31.5 billion and amounted to over 3 per cent of their combined (and overestimated) GDP (OECD, 1978). Obviously, this aid would have amounted to considerably more than 3 per cent of GDP if income had been more accurately estimated.
11. A whole literature has arisen claiming that a country endowed with subsoil wealth is in fact 'cursed' – a quaint claim that ignores the possibility that with appropriate policies the endowment could be made advantageous to the country concerned. In Chapter 18 I try to refute the existence of this alleged curse.
12. Adelman (1990) has expressed the contrary opinion that these oil corporations which made up the 'Seven Sisters', far from seeking low prices, had every reason to gain from higher prices, but this point of view has found few supporters.
13. See also Keynes (1936, pp. 59–60), who confirms Pigou's judgment on the subjectivity of net income.

REFERENCES

Asheim, Geir B. (1997), 'Adjusting green NNP to measure sustainability', *Scandinavian Journal of Economics*, **99** (3), 355–370.

Adelman, M.A. (1990), 'Mineral depletion with special reference to petroleum', *Review of Economics and Statistics*, **72** (1), 1–10.

Adelman, M.A., Harindar De Silva and Michael F. Koehn (1990), *User Cost in Oil Production*. Cambridge MA: MIT Center for Energy Policy Research.

El Serafy, Salah (1979), 'The oil price revolution of 1973–74', *Journal of Energy and Development*, **IV** (2), 273–290.

El Serafy, Salah (1981), 'Absorptive capacity, the demand for revenue and the supply of petroleum', *Journal of Energy and Development*, **7** (1), 73–88.

Hartwick, John M. (1977), 'Intergenerational equity and the investing of rents from exhaustible resources', *American Economic Review*, **67** (5), 972–974.

Hartwick, John M. (1978), 'Investing returns from depleting renewable resource stocks and intergenerational equity', *Economics Letters*, **1**, 85–88.

Hicks, John R. (1942), *The Social Framework: An Introduction to Economics*. Oxford: First Editions, Clarendon Press.

Hicks, John R. (1946), *Value and Capital, An Inquiry into Some Fundamental Principles of Economic Theory*, 2nd edition, Oxford: Clarendon Press.

Hicks, John R. (1974), 'Capital controversies: ancient and modern', *American Economic Review*, **64** (2), 307–316.

Hotelling, Harold (1931), 'The economics of exhaustible resources', *Journal of Political Economy*, **39** (2), 137–175.

Keynes, John Maynard (1936), *The General Theory of Employment, Interest and Money*. London: Macmillan.

Marshall, Alfred (1920), *Principles of Economics*, 8th edition. London: Macmillan.

OECD (1978) 'Review, Report by the Chairman of the Development Assistance Committee, Paris', November, p. 160.

Pigou, Arthur C. (1932), The *Economics of Welfare*, 4th edition. London: Macmillan.

Pigou, Arthur C. (1935), 'Net income and capital depletion', *Economic Journal*, **XLV** (178), 235–241.

Razavi, Hossein (1984), 'An economic model of OPEC coalition', *Southern Economic Journal*, **51** (2), 419–428.

Rubino, Anna (2008), *Queen of the Oil Club: The Intrepid Wanda Jablonski and the Power of Information*. Boston, MA: Beacon Press.

Sampson, Anthony (1975), *The Seven Sisters*. New York: Viking.

Sampson, Anthony (1982), *The Money Lenders*, Coronet edition. London: Hodder and Stoughton.

Solow, Robert M. (1974), 'The economics of resources or the resources of economics. Richard T. Ely Lecture', *American Economic Review, Papers and Proceedings*, May, 1–26.

Solow, Robert M. (1992), *An Almost Practical Step Toward Sustainability*. Washington DC: Resources for the Future.

Weitzman, Martin (2000), 'The linearized Hamiltonian as comprehensive NDP', *Environmental and Development Economics*, **5** (1), 55–68.

8. Adjusting for disinvestment: in the wake of Brundtland

PROLOGUE

This chapter originates in a paper that appeared in 1992 under the heading: 'Sustainability, income measurement and growth' in a book published by Island Press and edited by Goodland, Daly and El Serafy. The book was titled, *Population, Technology and Lifestyle*, and sub-titled *The Transition to Sustainability*. As our introduction to that book explained we used the Brundtland Report as a springboard for further explorations of the concept and estimation of 'sustainable development'. For the present chapter the original text had to be trimmed, though its main argument is retained. My purpose was to show that investment, which is seen by most economists as a main instrument for future output, should be scaled down in the national accounts to reflect natural resource deterioration. Such a correction will not be exhaustive since a great deal of natural resource losses occurs outside the market place and escapes national accounting altogether. Nevertheless the argument is important, not only to take care of the activities that are already entered inadequately in GDP, but also others that are candidates for future inclusion. The activities affected would include commercial fishing, mining and logging. It should be noted that the original paper had been published before SNA93 came out and contains prior expectations of the SNA that have not all materialized.

SUSTAINABILITY

Sustainability is a concept that has gained much popularity in environmental economics. It is a concept that figured prominently in the World Commission on Environment and Development, *Our Common Future* (1987) known informally as the Brundtland Report. Within the Brundtland Report itself we find more than one definition of sustainability, but the definition that has since been most quoted is one that combines 'sustainability' with 'development': 'Sustainable development is development that meets the needs of the present without compromising the ability of future generations to meet their own needs'.

'Need' is not exactly a word used in economic analysis. Economists tend instead to use 'preferences' which could be taken as an approximation. The more recent work on 'poverty', however, is replete with references to 'basic needs' exemplified by food and shelter.

The Report goes on to clarify 'sustainable development' as containing within it two key concepts (World Commission on Environment and Development, 1987, page 43):

- the concept of 'needs', in particular the essential needs of the world's poor, to which overriding priority should be given; and
- the idea of limitations imposed by the state of technology and social organization on the environment's ability to meet present and future needs.

The reference to limitations of technology and social organization, and to meeting 'essential needs of the world's poor' in the above quotation, and also a later statement that 'concern for social equity between generations . . . must logically be extended to equity within each generation,' are appealing to many people. But these statements reveal the complexity of Brundtland sustainability, both as a concept and as a pragmatic guide to policy action. As will presently be discussed, the vagueness of definition of Brundtland sustainability should not detract from its commendable concern for addressing distributional issues, which are viewed rightly as an integral part of sustainable development. Such definitional ambiguity is by no means confined to the Brundtland Report. A subsequent attempt to clarify what sustainability meant to different authors yielded a wide array of definitions.[1]

A precise definition of sustainability has remained elusive, with a growing awareness that for practical purposes sustainability should be perceived in approximate terms only.[2] It is certainly evident that the use of the expression 'sustainable growth' has become more frequent in recent development literature, replacing the older unqualified 'growth' as a policy objective. Such a use often reflects an attempt to impart the notion that growth should be kept within environmental limits. The Brundtland Report represents one of the early attempts at this usage. It is true, however, that the environmental limits implicit in such 'sustainable growth' remain undefined in a manner conducive to practicable policy guidelines, but I return to this point later.

In retrospect it seems that while the Brundtland Report made a great impact on world leaders and environmentalists alike, its impact on economists has been rather modest. This is not to deny some indirect influence it has had on economic policy through the political forces it motivated.[3] The attention that has been given to global environmental issues since the publication of *Our Common Future* may therefore be a product of its political, not economic, impact.[4] There is also the growing reference to environmental issues in economic development work practically everywhere, which may be traced back, at least in part, to the Brundtland publication.

ENVIRONMENTAL ACCOUNTING FOR SUSTAINABLE DEVELOPMENT

While the Brundtland Report was being written an initiative was developing, spurred by the United Nations Environment Programme (UNEP) in association with the World Bank, to revise national income estimates in order to draw attention to environmental concerns. The coincidence in timing is remarkable between the World Commission on Environment and Development, which began its work in December 1983 and reached conclusion in mid-1987, and the UNEP–World Bank Workshops, which sought improved national income measurements. This parallel effort also began in 1983, reached a crucial stage in 1988, and led to proposed changes in national accounting in a number of directions.[5]

During the two and half decades prior to 1993 most countries had been estimating their national income according to guidelines issued in 1968 by the United Nations and known as the SNA. These guidelines paid practically no attention to the fact that, in order to reckon income properly, the estimates should account for natural resource erosion and environmental degradation. The old system treated much of the anti-pollution expenditures as final expenditures that would raise income estimates, instead of regarding them as necessary intermediate costs that should be charged against the final product. It also failed to take account of environmental disasters when they occurred. It treated natural resources, particularly those exploited in the public sector, as a free gift from nature, reflecting in the accounts mainly the activities relating to development and extraction costs. No value was attached to the extracted product itself. The entire surplus realized in extractive activities over and above extraction cost had been treated as 'rent' and therefore part of GDP.[6]

More fundamentally the 1968 SNA had failed to distinguish between value added by factors of production, and proceeds of natural assets sales such as forestry products and petroleum. Through income measurements patterned on the SNA, many natural-resource-based developing countries were made out to have higher income than they actually had and to be growing at rates that reflected resource exploitation but obscured their true economic performance. Besides, the accounts failed to reflect the fact that the current levels of prosperity these countries were said to be enjoying could not last since the basis for such prosperity was progressively being eroded. False accounting has resulted from mixing in the flow accounts elements of natural capital that should have been kept separate and excluded from current income estimates. Such flawed income estimates, where they occurred, covered up economic weaknesses that needed attention, thus misdirecting economic policy. Countries where natural resources contributed significantly to fiscal and external balances failed to make essential economic adjustments which better economic accounting would have indicated. They ended up allocating to consumption too much of the receipts they obtained from selling their natural assets. Besides, many of them assumed excessive external debt the servicing of which was to become an intolerable burden later. Domestically, relative prices moved against tradable goods, leading to a lamentable shrinkage of domestic productive activities apart from those based on the extraction of natural resources, which offered few work opportunities. Little wonder that so many resource-rich developing countries that should have benefited materially from the exceptional improvement of their terms of trade during the 1970s found themselves in the 1980s hardly better off than they had been previously.[7]

At the UNEP–World Bank Workshop held in Paris in November 1988,[8] experts from various national statistical offices met with economists and others who had been investigating the topic of environmental national accounting, and for the first time a consensus was reached that natural resources and the environment were indeed important and likely to become more so in the future; that natural accounts should reflect the stress on the environment that had become increasingly evident; and that a set of environmental satellite accounts would need to be compiled and attached to the core accounts in the new SNA with the view of reflecting environmental considerations. That 1988 meeting was a watershed from which significant developments were to flow. Further work was subsequently conducted in cooperation with the United Nations Statistics Office, and this led to the acceptance of the notion that when the revised SNA (expected in 1993) came out, it would recommend compiling a set of satellite environmental accounts showing to the extent possible the changes that occur from year to year in the state of the environment and (presumably) attempting a recalculation of national income to reflect such changes. This national accounting adjustment initiative, which still continues, provides a bridge between some of the objectives of the environmentalists and the work of the economists.

SUSTAINABILITY AND INCOME

If properly measured, income is sustainable by definition. From an environmental angle, errors in measuring income can be viewed as coming largely from wrongly mixing in income certain elements of natural capital and when greening the accounts from conflating natural asset liquidation with depreciation of fixed assets.[9] A person or a nation cannot continue to live at the same material level if present enjoyment is obtained at the cost of capital disinvestment. As capital erodes, the ability to maintain the same level of consumption into the future is undermined. That is why, from its inception, the accounting profession has insisted that for profit and loss calculations, whether for individuals or corporations, capital must be 'kept intact'. To the accountant, keeping capital intact never meant that capital should be preserved in its original state (the preservationist argument), but only that allowance be made out of current revenues, sufficient to restore capital to the extent that it has eroded during the account period. Unless capital is 'maintained', future income would inevitably decline. By extension the same argument applies to *national* accounting. Keeping capital, including environmental capital, intact for accounting purposes requires adjusting any magnitude pretending to be income to make it reflect capital deterioration. Again, this does not mean that the accountant is advocating that capital should be kept undisturbed, or in the language of some environmentalists, that it should be 'conserved' in its existing state, since the very essence of sustaining economic activity relies on utilizing capital for the generation of future profits or income. There is little disagreement now on extending the same principles that apply to human made capital to environmental capital save on the application of those principles to the special case of depletable resources which cannot be renewed or recycled, but whose stock (*ceteris paribus*) steadily dwindles as it is used up in the productive process. By a further extension the same argument applies to 'renewable' resources that are being mined in the sense that their erosion exceeds renewal either by Nature or by a combination of Nature and human efforts.

That the environment can be viewed as natural capital is easy to perceive, both as a sink for wastes and a source of materials and energy (see El Serafy, 1991). Wastes have been dumped in rivers and seas, buried on land, and dispersed in the atmosphere in the belief that such natural receptors had an unlimited capacity to deal with them. As production and consumption have grown, this capacity has clearly been seen to be limited and has also become limiting. There is thus a growing acceptance of the notion that the polluting activities should bear the full costs to society of their pollution. If standards are set for acceptable levels of pollution, the cost of achieving such standards, even if not actually incurred, may be used as a measure of environmental deterioration due to pollution and be charged against income as depreciation.

As a source of materials, the environment should also be brought into income calculation. A distinction is clearly needed between resources that can be regenerated and others that cannot. Nature, and society in cooperation with nature, can amend, restore or regenerate fish stocks, forests, soils and the like. Where such regeneration falls short of theoretical or practical rates that would maintain such capital intact (that is, restoring to its original level at the beginning of each accounting period), shortfalls should be deducted, as depreciation, from gross income calculations. Some problems of valuation would present themselves, but the guiding principle throughout should be pragmatism and approximation, since precise measurement is still, and likely to remain, a difficult goal to attain. In respect of renewable resources, such as fish, ecologists likewise should attempt measurements of 'sustainable yields' in the same spirit of providing pragmatic and prudential estimates instead of letting their quest for precision become an obstacle that would delay application and render their measurements irrelevant for environmental policy.

As to depletable minerals such as fossil fuels, which cannot meaningfully be restored once they are used, applying the same approach of depreciation in parallel with renewable resources would be inappropriate. Other things being equal, such resources represent (roughly) known wealth that can be liquidated over a *variable* time span depending on their owners' needs, their expectations of future prices, and the state of the market as well as practical constraints such as contractual obligations towards foreign or domestic operators. Whereas productive capacity, such as machinery, depreciates in the books according to rough accounting norms, existing inventories of subsoil deposits do not depreciate, but are used up or liquidated, and it would be wrong conceptually to treat the proceeds from selling inventories, which are assets as income, even as gross income. And it is equally wrong to believe that, in order to correct for their inclusion in gross income, all that is needed is to deduct the decline of the stock from the wrongly calculated gross income to arrive at a presumably correct estimate of net income. If such an approach is adopted, neither the gross nor the net income will be correctly measured. The gross will be inflated by asset sales that do not represent value added, and the net will be underestimated since the whole contribution of the extracting activity to income is removed as capital consumption or depreciation. If, on top of such erroneous accounting we add windfalls from upward re-estimation of reserves, and deduct from income the downward adjustments of these reserves, we arrive at very dubious and gyrating estimates of income that are as meaningless as they are useless for economic analysis, either for gauging economic performance or for guiding economic policy. A depletable resource's contribution to income requires special handling.

ACCOUNTING FOR DEPLETABLE RESOURCES

In as much as the reserves of depletable resources can be ascertained, they should be treated as inventories, not as fixed capital. Inventories can be drawn down to exhaustion if that is perceived by their owners to be economically desirable. The proceeds from their exploitation in any one accounting period should, as a first step, be viewed as proceeds from asset sales, not as value added. This may be illustrated with a simple example. If the owners draw down all their known reserves in one year because they believe this to be their best action, it would obviously be wrong to include all such proceeds in their gross income for that year, and to deduct the diminution of the asset, equivalent to the same amount that had been included in gross income, so that net income from this activity is shown as zero. Now that the owners have substituted for the subsoil asset, say a bank account, true income would be the interest that can be earned on that new account. Alternatively, the owners may sink the proceeds from selling the mineral assets in new material investments, returns from which would represent true income. In this way capital liquidation would be kept, as it should, outside the *flow* accounts.

Following a proposition which the late Professor Sir John Hicks put forward more than seven decades ago (Hicks, 1946, p. 187), it was possible for me to calculate that part of the proceeds from a 'wasting asset' that must be reinvested in alternative assets so that the yields obtained from such reinvestments could compensate for the decline in receipts from the wasting asset. Using a discount rate and the amount extracted from the reserves in any one year relative to total reserves, I was able to indicate the proportion of the proceeds that can be reckoned as *true* income, the remainder – a kind of a Keynesian user cost – having to be set aside and reinvested to produce a stream of constant future income. The user-cost part is a capital element that should be expunged from the GDP and gross income, and therefore would automatically disappear from the net domestic product or net income either. If fresh deposits were to be located, these would affect the flow accounts only indirectly through the change of the reserves-to-extraction ratio in the formula I proposed. The augmented stock will provide a longer lifetime of the asset so that the income part rises and the user-cost part falls.[10]

This proposal, which is slowly gaining ground among economists, is still by no means generally accepted, either by them or by the national income statisticians.[11] Many of the latter, even if convinced, would still prefer to preserve the old-time series of erroneously calculated GDP along conventional lines on the argument that all that is required is to deduct natural resource 'depreciation' (equivalent to the entire diminution of the stock) from the gross product to show a more sustainable net product that could amount to nil as shown by the simple example offered above. The conceptual confusion implied by such procedures has already been mentioned. If one must persist with this confusion for the sake of preserving the old time series, the user cost, as explained above, would be the appropriate estimate of 'depreciation' for the estimation of the net product.

THE LIMITED FUNCTION OF ACCOUNTING

Accounting, by its nature, has a limited function. It is essentially a backward-looking activity that attempts to sort out from the behavior of economic units during a past period those elements from which a numerical history may be compiled. This usually takes the form of a snapshot at a point in time (a balance sheet of assets and liabilities) and a flow during a certain period (most commonly a year). The latter will show the net results of the economic activity concerned: profits and loss for an individual or a corporation, and value added or GDP for a nation. Economists have often misunderstood the function of the accountant, and his or her concern (perhaps even obsession) with keeping capital intact, often challenging the accountant's precise meaning of 'keeping capital intact', and the accuracy of the accountant's measurements since any concept of capital maintenance inevitably conjures up issues of its future productivity. The Hicksian definition of income itself, whose author insisted that it was merely a rough guide for prudent behavior, has itself been wrongly criticized owing to critics' concern with precision and the economists' forward orientation against the accountants' historical function. Hicks's income has been said to be incapable of being 'directly measured' and even that it is 'not suited to an accounting of what happened in the past' either (Bradford, 1990). Whereas Hicks stressed the accountants' quest for approximately defining a level of *income* that can be devoted to consumption with concern for a sustainability built around reusing capital in the future, other economists have tended to hanker after a precise level of sustainability that the Hicksian approach, with its emphasis on *future* income sustainability, obviously cannot meet, partly because the future will always remain unknown.

  Economists and accountants have different but perfectly reconcilable objectives. In their measurements the accountants seek approximations, assume constant technology from year to year, and posit that the future will be a continuation of the past. In practice, technology does change, and the future is a little different from the past. But this does not matter much since the accountants' perspective is seldom more than one year, and every new year brings with it new facts and some fresh technology that the accountants have to, and certainly do, take in their stride.

BUSINESSES AND GOVERNMENTS

The approach I have proposed for estimating income from depletable natural resources, which relies on setting aside part of the proceeds from the sale of natural capital to be sunk in alternative investments so that they may yield a constant stream of future income, begs the question as to what kind of alternative investments are to be sought, and whether for the sake of sustainability such investments will always be available. Here we leave the *ex post* world of the accountant and enter the realm of *ex ante* analysis.

Prudent individual owners of depletable resources, even without help from economists or national income specialists, often see to it that part of their receipts, whether in the form of depletable allowances or set-asides, are reinvested so that the owners can continue in business or as the phrase goes take care of 'future generations'. Whether or not their new investments should be in the same line of business they are already in, or diverted toward other lines, will depend on many factors. If the price of the natural resource they own is rising in reflection of its growing scarcity, this indicates an opportunity for investing in activities to produce substitutes for the same product. So if such a course is economically feasible, the owners may well continue in the same line of business. But frequently the market would fail to reflect the resource's growing scarcity, and the price would fail to rise. Besides, technologies for producing substitutes may not be available, and if available may not be economic at the prevailing set of prices. Thus we often observe a tendency for diversification away from single-product business on the part of large corporations that exploit natural resources.

Some environmentalists would prefer that the user cost entailed in the exploitation of a depletable natural asset be invested in a 'twin' project that would supply a renewable substitute for the same resource that is being depleted.[12] But in light of the considerations just mentioned, such 'twinning' or 'pairing' may not be attractive to private owners. On the other hand, there is nothing against society as a whole indicating its desire to raise the overall level of saving and investment so that these become consistent with the objective of maintaining future income and additionally subsidize pioneering and experimental ventures in search of renewable sources to replace the declining ones. This can be achieved by insisting, via appropriate monetary and fiscal policies, that the user cost of depletable resource exploitation should be re-invested. The extra investments could be guided to socially desirable ventures, such as natural resource maintenance and restoration, through a carefully designed system of taxation and subsidization.[13]

USER COST AND INCOME IDENTITIES

Consider what happens to the usual identity that says that income, Y, is the sum total of consumption, C, and investment, I. Denoting user cost by the letter U, we can write:

$$Y = C + I \qquad (3.1)$$

Adjusting for user cost, income in Equation (3.1) falls and becomes:

$$Y - U = (C - U) + I \qquad (3.2)$$

But if the user cost is devoted to fresh investments income rises back and we get:

$$Y = (C - U) + (I + U) \qquad (3.3)$$

Equation (3.3) is identical to Equation (3.1) except that the user cost is now taken (as it should) out of consumption, which now becomes lower and added to investment, which becomes higher.

Equation (3.2), however, depicts the correct level of income if the user cost is not reinvested. But if C is unchanged, then the true level of investment that has been attained is only $I - U$ since U represents a disinvestment. In this latter case we have:

$$Y - U = C + (I - U) \qquad (3.4)$$

Equation (3.4) thus indicates that as traditionally estimated both current income and estimated investment are higher than they genuinely are, and that the excess of consumption has taken place at the expense of true Investment which the equation shows to be lower than had previously been assumed.

POLICY AND THE PROBLEM OF SCALE

While the approach of sinking part of the proceeds into new investments seems perfectly valid for individuals, businesses, and even small countries, which also have the option of acquiring foreign investments if profitable domestic opportunities are not available, is it workable if it is done on a large scale so that significant portions of global natural capital might be liquidated to be substituted for by human-made capital?

Once the problem is posed in this way, the realization of the objective of creating a permanent income stream from wasting assets becomes questionable. Individuals, corporations and even nations can run out of a natural resource – even if their livelihoods depend materially on it – in the knowledge that future income may be maintained through carefully selected new investments at home or abroad. When considering better accounting for depletable resources, my focus was on the *income* of their owners. It did not matter what form the new investments might take provided they guaranteed for the owners a steady stream of future income. The form of the new investments would be guided by the opportunities the market offers. And if the market indicates that the new investments should be in the same line of business, so be it. It was Daly and Cobb (1989) who suggested that the new investments should aim at creating substitutes for the very natural resource being depleted. This seems to be a sensible proposition that might satisfy some ecologists, except that the recommended line of business may not be all that clear. Crude oil, for instance, when refined is used for fuel, making lubricants, paints, textiles, plastics and other products. Out of these, which usage should the new investments aim to replace?

Furthermore, if the problem is considered not just as one of better accounting for the resource owners, but as a forward guide to economic policy on a global scale, we have to face the issues raised by Brundtland and the various constraints and propositions we find there for future environmental directions. We also encounter the problems of scale and of ultimate substitutability between natural resources and human made capital to which ecologists have been drawing our attention. If we perceive the problem of stressed natural resources globally, then it is clearly necessary to replace, for example, dwindling natural energy sources, not just with other sources of *income,* but with other sources of *energy* that are renewable, and the issue of 'twinning' natural sources with artificial ones becomes relevant. If the market fails to signal rising energy prices to justify investing in renewable energy sources, then society may wish to give the market a helping hand through appropriate policies. Again, viewed globally, society should have a broad interest in the creation and application of new technologies that would substitute renewable sources for diminishing nonrenewable ones.

But what should be done about the search for a balance between the state of the environment and global economic activity? World economic 'organization' has been functioning on the basis of economic agents seeking perpetual economic growth, a pursuit that has traditionally been seen not only as desirable for raising material welfare all around, but also as essential for energizing the development of the less developed countries and thus assisting in the alleviation of world poverty. If technology could be organized so that it gave us substitutes for natural resources through the instrument of human-made capital formation, we would be able to continue 'business as usual', hoping that the market would reflect scarcities into higher prices and thus induce and guide the process of substitution. This certainly appears to be one of Brundtland's fundamental assumptions. However, we have reached a stage where the state of the environment has become so stressed, and technology and social organization have clearly lagged, at least so far, that some drastic alternative solution deserves to be explored. Brundtland offered one solution, which leans toward maintaining the current emphasis on growth while using the fruits of growth to lessen the material 'throughput' of materials and energy that enters economic activity. This would go some way towards protecting the environment, and also towards redistributing income, both intranationally and also internationally from the richer to the poorer nations, with the objective of alleviating poverty. I join with the other contributors to the volume *Population, Technology and Lifestyle* (1992) in contending that this strategy is questionable: partly because much of the damage to the environment caused by indiscriminate growth is irreversible; partly because the process of substitution of human made capital for natural resources is slow and erratic; and also in view of the enormous increase projected for global economic activity as compared with the advanced state of environmental stress already reached. And this is not to overlook the consequences of the steadily increasing world population. If we are serious about saving our planet, we must seek a steady state for the economies of the rich thus providing room for the poor to grow and develop so that poverty may be eradicated and income disparity, which is the source of so much environmental damage, is reduced. Meanwhile technology development and dissemination should be accelerated and population growth urgently constrained by appropriate policies.

If the Brundtland path is rejected as impractical, can the proposal to arrest growth in much of the world economy be viewed as anything short of utopian? It is difficult specifically to perceive the sociology and political economy of maintaining a steady level of income, taken here as per head of population, in the richer countries. These countries rely primarily on free market forces to guide the mobilization and allocation of economic resources. For them the essential profit motive is geared unavoidably to business expansion in search of economic opportunity. The impact of the richer countries' economic expansion on developing countries has also often been seen as benign, but this is only valid in an 'empty world' context of nonbinding environmental constraints. In fact it can be observed that every time growth slows down in the richer economies the poorer countries appear to suffer from lower exports, adverse terms of trade, and depressed incomes. And yet it cannot be denied that the richer countries use the bulk of the world resources to support a minority of world population. If the rich are to grow richer merely to provide markets for the poor, not only are there more economical ways to achieve the same objective, but maintaining such a course would accelerate international income inequality. Clearly something drastic has to take place in social and industrial organization and in the modalities of international relations if a steady state of economic activity, involving a constant level of throughput, is to prevail in the developed world. Drafting a blueprint for this vision of the future is therefore needed. Its economic content will have to address the problem of obtaining growth and/or development in the poorer countries simultaneously as the economies of the richer countries are kept on an even keel. In addition, the richer countries would be asked to transfer to the less developed nations the economic means necessary to redress the negative effect of the richer countries' arrested growth and to alleviate poverty. Furthermore, it is necessary to plan for the kind of economic policy that would have to apply in the richer countries to produce the target of a steady state: as some activities will have to expand, others must contract. What criteria would be used to modulate aggregate activity in a free market economy that also has to be managed in pursuit of many other policy objectives? The issues this scenario raises will have to be faced by the advocates of such a strategy. The Brundtland Report avoided all these complex issues and opted instead for a non-revolutionary, rather optimistic, but seemingly untenable course.

CONCLUSION

Finally, a word about the importance of proper income accounting, since it is income measurements that will indicate what kind of growth or expansion of economic activity is being experienced and projected. Today's income changes, which probably lie behind Brundtland projections of growth, relate to the gross domestic product (GDP) as conventionally estimated and as valued at factor cost or market prices.[14] But if we shift the focus from the gross product to an environmentally more sustainable *net* product (from which the user cost of depletable resources has been eliminated), put a value on natural disasters and deduct this from income, and develop the habit of valuing activities at their full environmental cost when prices reflect true scarcities, we are bound to get a very different reading of income and its growth. In which case it might well turn out that the five-to-ten-times expansion in economic activity, as envisaged by the Brundtland Report, will have to be less. A hint of this is to be found in the contribution by Tinbergen and Hueting in the volume edited by Goodland, Daly and El Serafy (1992) Chapter 4, but clearly much work is needed to clarify this issue.

POSTSCRIPT

In the context of the general tenor of the book where this chapter was first published, I viewed sustainability from an economic angle, and a narrow economic angle at that, being discussed only from the perspective of national accounting. When attention began to be given to sustainability in affluent societies – ecological sustainability apart – there was concern that the current level of prosperity and the happiness derived directly from a clean environment might not be available for subsequent generations. It made sense to aim for 'sustaining' the current living standards enjoyed by contemporaries so that our descendants would not be worse off. For the poorer countries, however, sustainability of their current standards of living does not make sense especially at the lower end of the per capita income scale. Would they wish to perpetuate their current deprivation? Of course they would not want to fall downward further, and sustainability for them would be better than a downward slide towards greater misery. Here the distribution issue emphasized by the Brundtland Report becomes crucial especially as many of the poorer economies had a modicum of traditional pragmatic resource sustainability (e.g. in farming or fishing). These efforts were often upset by 'development programs' under the guise of 'structural adjustment' that urged dismantling autarkical production patterns and reorienting their economies towards commercial crops for the external market. The failures of many such programs to enhance development raise the issue of 'justice' against 'charity' for correcting some of the previous 'advice' offered by the development experts.

ACKNOWLEDGEMENT

This chapter is adapted from 'Sustainability, income measurement and growth' in *Population, Technology and Lifestyle*, edited by Robert Goodland, Herman E. Daly and Salah El Serafy. Copyright © 1992 The International Bank for Reconstruction and Development and UNESCO. Reproduced by permission of Island Press, Washington DC.

NOTES

1. Differing definitions of sustainability are surveyed by Pezzey (1989).
2. As the reader will note presently the search for a precise meaning of 'sustainability' is akin to the vain quest for defining 'income' in exact terms. No unanimity is possible, since both concepts depend among many things upon one's vision of the future. For practical purposes, however, and as a guide for prudent behavior, we must be content with some useful degree of approximation.
3. Whether it was due to the Brundtland Report itself, or the political forces that have been gathering momentum independently in various parts of the richer nations, it is remarkable how the impact of the Green Movement as reflected in the declarations of recent economic summits of the Group of Seven (G-7) leading industrial nations, and through the latter's influence has given vent to a number of environmental initiatives. The July 1989 Economic Declaration of the G-7 Economic Summit (section 37) contained the statements: 'In order to achieve sustainable development, we shall ensure the compatibility of economic growth and development with the protection of the environment' and 'We encourage the World Bank and regional development banks to integrate environmental considerations into their activities.'
4. The July 1990 Economic Declaration of the G-7 Economic Summit referred to global environmental stress (ozone depletion, climate change, marine pollution, and loss of biological diversity) and stated that 'one of our most important responsibilities is to pass on to future generations an environment whose health, beauty and economic potential are not threatened.'
5. It is interesting that in their initial stages the UNEP–World Bank workshops were seeking to establish national physical indicators of environmental stress, and hoping to combine these eventually into one national index that would reflect the state of the environment, but participants very quickly realized that a system of 'weighting' (or valuation) was necessary to produce such a single index. This moved the concern of the workshops quite early on in the direction of reforming national income measurement. cf. El Serafy (1986).
6. The 1993 SNA has not much changed this approach banishing any adjustment to satellite accounts and to the net product when estimated.
7. cf. Alan Gelb and Associates (1988).
8. I was the chairman of that 1988 meeting held at the World Bank offices in Paris.
9. I am abstracting here from a number of activities that have traditionally been excluded from national income reckoning, such as household services by family members. That the environment can be viewed as capital, contributing to the productive process is a notion that is entirely in harmony with neoclassical economic thinking. See Salah El Serafy, 'The Environment as Capital,' *Ecological Economics: The Science and Management of Sustainability*, R. Costanza, ed. (New York: Columbia University Press, 1991).
10. Hicks's all too brief coverage of this topic in *Value and Capital* (1946) shows that he regarded such a user cost as an allowance for 'depreciation'. In a personal

communication in 1987, however, he indicated approval of my line of thinking and that I had 'made good use of the income chapter in *Value and Capital*.'

11. A qualified acceptance of this approach may be found in Adelman et al. (1990). This work uses the calculations of El Serafy to adjust national income for a number of countries in support of arguments made in their text, but states that 'El Serafy . . . err[s] in supposing that production can proceed at a constant rate, then abruptly cease. The decline rate stands at the center of every reservoir engineering calculation. Moreover the rate of extraction is limited by sharply rising marginal costs . . . However, this correction would not basically change the problem.' It should be mentioned, however, that (1) I did not propose that extraction would remain constant and then abruptly cease, and (?) Adelman belongs to the camp that sees no scarcity developing in the supply of minerals, which he views correctly as inventories, but believes that 'only a fraction of the minerals in the earth's crust, or in any given field, will ever be used' (*op. cit.*, p. 1). The approach I have been advocating is one that relies on a standard accounting rule of thumb that is carried out every year with fresh parameters including actual extraction in the year that is already past and does not assume any future profile of extraction. Extraction is treated as drawing down inventories out of a remaining stock in an attempt to approximate reality. I stated in my 1981 *Journal of Energy and Development* article that factors such as the ones mentioned by Adelman et al. could be accommodated under the approach I proposed. The so-called reservoir-engineering rule of always keeping a constant ratio between reserves and extraction is of dubious authenticity, besides not being essential for the calculations in any case. See El Serafy (1981).

12. Ecologists tend to define substitutes more narrowly than economists, who appear to favor a broad definition that allows freedom to the market to define what a substitute is. David Pearce, Anil Markandya, and Edward Barbier, in their *Blueprint for a Green Economy* (1989) advocated 'pairing' or 'twinning' but within a program of many projects rather than for each product at a time.

13. A vision of a possible course is offered in Daly and Cobb (1989). However, many aspects of such a course need to be more carefully examined as the authors actually urge.

14. The convention of valuing GDP at factor costs, and not at market prices derives from the notion that taxes and subsidies represent deviations from 'genuine' values produced by the market that should provide weights for the various activities that make up the domestic product. But if a new set of environmentally inspired taxes and subsidies is viewed as necessary to correct the market's failure to put proper values on the services of natural resources, then we should regard the new, environmentally adjusted 'market prices' as better weights than factor costs for the purpose of estimating income in the present context.

REFERENCES

Adelman, M.A., Harindar De Silva and Michael F. Koehn (1990), *User Cost in Oil Production*. Cambridge, MA: MIT Center for Energy Policy Research.

Bradford, David F. (1990), 'Comment on Scott and Eisner', *Journal of Economic Literature*, **28**, 1183–1186.

Daly, Herman E. and John B. Cobb (1989), *For the Common Good*. Boston, MA: Beacon Press.

El Serafy, Salah (1981), 'Absorptive capacity, the demand for revenue and the supply of petroleum,' *Journal of Energy and Development*, **7** (Autumn 1981), 73–88.

El Serafy, Salah (1986), 'Rapporteur's report of the September–October, 1985 Paris Meeting', Washington DC: The World Bank, mimeographed.

El Serafy, Salah (1991), 'The environment as capital,' in Robert Costanza (ed.), *Ecological Economics: The Science and Management of Sustainability.* New York: Columbia University Press.

El Serafy, Salah (1992), 'Sustainability, income measurement and growth', in Robert Goodland, Herman E. Daly and Salah El Serafy (eds), *Population, Technology and Lifestyle, The Transition to Sustainability.* Washington DC and Covelo, CA: Island Press.

Gelb, Alan and Associates (1988), *Oil Windfalls: Blessing* or *Curse?* World Bank Research Publication. Oxford: Oxford University Press.

Goodland, Robert, Herman E. Daly and Salah El Serafy (1992), *Population, Technology and Lifestyle*, Washington DC and Covelo, CA: Island Press.

Hicks, John Richard (1946), *Value and Capital*, 2nd edition. Oxford: Clarendon Press.

Pearce, David, Anil Markandya, and Edward Barbier (1989), *Blueprint for a Green Economy*. London: Earthscan Publications.

Pezzey, J. (1989), 'Economic analysis of sustainable growth and sustainable development', World Bank Environment Department Working Paper 15, Washington DC, Appendix 1.

World Commission on Environment and Development (1987), *Our Common Future* (The Brundtland Report). Oxford: Oxford University Press.

PART III

The user cost and its detractors

9. Proper calculation of income from depletable natural resources

PROLOGUE

With minor alterations this chapter reproduces a paper that has been the most cited of my work (El Serafy, 1989). Its genesis goes back to the 1970s when I tried to point out that most of the oil exporters were poor developing countries, and their putative incomes, reckoned along traditional SNA lines, were exaggerated, and should not be confused with their revenue. This I had outlined in an essay on 'The oil price revolution of 1973–1974' (El Serafy, 1979) and developed in a subsequent paper titled 'Absorptive capacity, the demand for revenue and the supply of petroleum' (El Serafy, 1981). The last mentioned paper contained an appendix showing my formula for estimating 'true income' out of petroleum revenues – the same formula I later reproduced in El Serafy (1989) for estimating the user cost. 'True income' and 'user cost' are complements that add up to revenue. It was not until November 1986 at the fourth UNEP–World Bank international workshop, which I happened to chair, that I presented a draft of the paper that now makes up the present chapter. I had widened my coverage to address natural resources in general, not just petroleum, and asserted that the same approach was applicable also to renewable resources when these were being 'mined'. Mine had been a lonely voice earlier on, and in fact, when I first presented my paper on 'Absorptive capacity'[1] at the University of Colorado, Boulder, in 1980, Professor Penrose of London University, who was chairing the session, denounced my presentation as 'economic nonsense'. By the time I read a similar paper in London ten years later (El Serafy, 1991), she had changed her mind and was indeed fulsome with praise. It is important to bear in mind that this paper was written five years prior to SNA93, which, as I show in various places in this book, did not usher much change.

I

PRELIMINARY

Recognition seems to be growing that income is not being accurately estimated for economies based on natural resources. Some would even say
that for these economies national accounting methods produce misleading
estimates. They turn out measurements that neither faithfully describe
economic performance *ex post*, nor can they be employed usefully as a
basis for forward economic policy proposals. For such economies, current
accounting practices exaggerate income, encourage unsustainable levels
of consumption, and obscure the necessity to implement greatly needed
economic policy adjustments.[2] The problem is relevant to practically all
countries where nonrenewable natural resources are being exploited and
where *renewable* resources are being run down without being restored.
But it is most acute where such resources loom large in an economy, and
exploitation is carried out in the public sector, either directly or through
foreign intermediaries. In the more industrialized countries extraction
typically occurs in the private sector, and tax allowances for depletion,
where they exist, tend to correct the calculation of the 'value added'
believed to be generated by such activities. Such correction, of course, is
effected as 'depreciation' carried out in the national accounts at the level
of estimating the net product, reducing the gross product by an element
to cover depletion. This correction is frequently inexact, but it is a step in
the right direction. And the process is helped by the fact that when properties containing marketable natural resources, such as subsoil deposits,
exchange hands, their market value tends to reflect their natural-resource
content. By contrast, no such correction is made in most of the developing
countries whose economies depend in greater degrees on the exploitation
of natural resources such as mineral extraction or the commercial logging
of forests to make timber and paper. This problem, therefore, is one of
paramount importance for the developing world.

The practice in these countries has followed the United Nations SNA,
which treats revenue derived from the sale of natural resources as income,
or 'rent' that is available for consumption. When the revenue accrues to
the public sector, it is often used to finance expenditure just like revenue
from any current source such as the proceeds from income taxes. Given
their typically short perspective, the politicians in charge of these economies often do not want to be told that the revenue derived from liquidating
their country's natural assets is neither recurrent nor sustainable. Many a
developing country witnesses its leadership being praised by international
institutions for illusory rapid economic growth, apparently high rates of

saving and investment, and deceptively stable or near-stable price levels – all brought about through imports that are sustained only by unrepeatable exports. Such apparent prosperity is bought at the cost of asset erosion – a sure recipe for future economic decline. Thus natural resources are used up and exported to prop up a truly unbalanced, but seemingly comfortable, external balance. An overvalued exchange rate inevitably develops, and relative prices at home get upset as a 'Dutch disease' syndrome sets in, whereby the prices of non-tradable goods and services rise in relation to the products of tradable activities.[3] Consequently, the economy's capacity is reduced to produce and export the products of non-natural-resource-based activities that could provide badly needed employment and a sustainable level of income. Any comparative advantage the country may already have gets sacrificed during a period of ephemeral affluence, peppered up with illusory growth. This is particularly true where the total exhaustion of the resource is imminent. Needless to say, the citizens of these countries find it only too easy to adjust to a higher level of consumption, which, however, cannot be maintained.

When the bonanza ends and the natural resource is exhausted, or almost exhausted, standards of living have to fall, and intolerable pressures develop on the external balance. Quite often the country additionally finds itself saddled with excessive external debt, which it had contracted in the deceptively prosperous years when it had overestimated its capacity to borrow, and its creditors had mistakenly assumed that the prosperity would continue. The government then finds itself in a difficult situation in which there are no margins left to provide a cushion for urgently needed policy adjustments that should have been initiated years before. The halcyon period of plenty will have come to an end, and all the putative economizing that had been done during those years is seen in retrospect to have been false and futile. Defective accounting had led economic behavior and policy analysis astray.

The fundamental principle that is flouted by applying conventional national income accounting to depleting resources is the separation that must be maintained between income and capital. This principle tells us that if you liquidate your assets and use the proceeds for consumption, you are living beyond your means, and in doing so you are undermining your ability to create future income. The accounting profession was born in the late Middle Ages in the city states of the Mediterranean basin largely to separate from the proceeds accruing to the maritime merchants that part which they could use to finance their families' expenditure needs. Those merchants had to guard against consuming their capital, the source of their continued wellbeing. From its infancy the accounting profession has specifically addressed this task. In present-day language the accountants had been asked to define sustainable levels of *consumption*, and they could do so by attempting to *keep capital intact*.

The same principle was taken up by Adam Smith (1776 [1937]), who saw capital as a means 'to increase the productive powers of labor', and as an asset whose maintenance was imperative since it 'is always repaid with great profit, and increases the annual produce by a much greater value than that of the support which such improvements require.' Bearing in mind that 'wealth' to Adam Smith meant a flow of income, he says in *The Wealth of Nations* (1776 [1937], p. 271):

> The gross revenue of all the inhabitants of a great country, comprehends the whole annual produce of their land and labor; the neat revenue, what remains free to them after deducting the expense of maintaining; first, their fixed; and, second, their circulating capital; or what, without encroaching upon their capital, they can place in their stock reserved for immediate consumption, or spend upon their subsistence, conveniences, and amusements. Their real wealth too is in proportion, not to their gross, but to their neat revenue.

The SNA, in failing to distinguish between unsustainable receipts derived from the sale of natural assets, and sustainable income produced by the original factors of production, disregards the fundamental concept of 'neat revenue', which should guide consumption and the assessment of the 'wealth' of the revenue recipients.

The distinction between capital and income has remained crucial throughout the development of economics. In the present day Hicks paraphrased this principle into a definition of income as that amount which a person can consume during a given period and still be as well off at the end of the period as at the beginning.[4] More specifically, we are told in no uncertain terms that: 'if a person's receipts are derived from the exploitation of a wasting asset, liable to give out at a future date, we shall say that his receipts are in excess of his income' (Hicks, 1946, p. 187).

The natural resources being exploited are indeed 'wasting assets'. If they are nonrenewable (for example, most minerals) or if they are renewable (for example, forests or fisheries or agricultural soil), but are not actually being renewed through careful restoration, they are also wasting assets. This means that receipts from their exploitation will give out in the future, and the revenue they generate is greater than income associated with them. Ignoring this elementary fact makes a mockery of what has been passing as economic analysis and policy prescription for economies based on natural resources and for which no effort has been made to compensate for draining their national wealth. Maintaining capital intact is not a marginal issue. It is central to economic behavior and analysis, and it is a poor economist indeed who is unable to tell the difference between capital and income.

II

CONCEPTUAL BACKGROUND

The confusion of capital with income, which unfortunately derives support from the SNA, has been the standard approach to national income estimation, and this confusion has become untenable. This chapter offers a way to estimate the true income content of the proceeds obtained from the sale of depleting resources and it is this magnitude that should appear in GDP. The treatment of income from renewable resources such as forests, which have to be maintained through replanting, or fisheries, which have to be restocked, is more straightforward. Where such replanting or restocking is effected at technologically acceptable rates that would keep capital intact, the cost of this maintenance could be charged against the gross returns from the natural resource to obtain the accurate value added generated; and this comes close to the way capital consumption is treated in the national accounts. Soil erosion also belongs to the same category of a natural resource the depletion of which can be offset by restoration, and the cost of restoration should be charged against the gross product of the soil in order to obtain a true estimate of the product.

But quite often, particularly in poorer countries, the resource is not restored to the status quo ante. As a result, the 'value added' that appears to be generated contains capital elements that should be removed. In this case those who estimate national income should impute a capital consumption estimate, based on technically acceptable criteria, to be charged against current receipts, to obtain the true *gross* income from these activities. For soil erosion, some estimate may be necessary of the declining power of the soil to produce, and this can be based, for example, on declining land yields over time. However, it is conceivable that yields may not fall until rock bottom has been approached, and vigilance would be needed to estimate the depth of the productive soil remaining. This chapter, however, addresses only the problem of estimating income generated from depletable, nonrenewable, resources.[5]

My thinking on this topic began to be shaped by a sense of discomfort over what I thought to be an inappropriate use of economic concepts when the pricing of petroleum began to attract the attention of macroeconomists in the early 1970s. To my mind the oil market had long been an oligopolistic market, dominated by powerful multinational conglomerates. Economic analysts, even if they had correctly read the petroleum market structure as an oligopoly, contributed little to understanding how prices were determined in that sort of market, beyond the traditional models of oligopoly theory, which concentrated on how equilibrium was reached rather than on the level of prices produced by it.[6] Later, when oligopsony in the petroleum market gave way to an alleged monopoly instituted by the OPEC the price increases were too facilely attributed to the powers of this exporters' 'cartel'.

It was curious that many analysts overestimated the degree of competition prevailing in that market before 1973 and underestimated it afterwards, choosing to emphasize OPEC's monopoly power. It was even more curious that many analysts in the 1970s appeared to think that if free competition were 'again' to prevail competitive equilibrium would indicate a price nearer the marginal cost of *extraction*, which was, and is still often referred to as *production*; and that it was only because of the alleged cartelization of supply that the price was able to rise well above that cost.[7]

This construction was later challenged by those who were aware that the price of a seemingly irreplaceable natural resource, such as petroleum, should perhaps contain a user cost or a capital element representing the erosion of the resource. Even under free competition, the marginal cost of extraction could not possibly indicate an equilibrium price level, since the cost of extraction is tantamount to the cost of asset liquidation and cannot determine the value of the very asset being sold. Hotelling had to be resurrected and used with great dexterity by an important economist like Robert Solow for a more convincing explanation of petroleum price increases before the economic profession could be persuaded.[8] But it has not been completely persuaded, and doubters still abound.

Parallel to the microeconomic confusion about the pricing of natural resources, other inaccuracies have also been perpetrated and have distorted thinking about macroeconomics in countries where the exploitation of depletable natural resources is significant. If the marginal cost of extraction was the only cost, then any surplus accruing to the sellers was pure rent and represented value added to be included in the GDP. This certainly is implied by the accounting practices currently being used under the SNA. Based on these practices, the expansion of economic activity as a consequence of accelerating the liquidation of subsoil assets is applauded as good economic performance and is confused with the growth that comes from labor, capital formation, technological progress, and efficient organization. The revenue accruing to countries that deplete their natural resources in this way is reflected in increased saving rates and investment coefficients and in improved parameters such as incremental capital-output ratios (ICORS), which shed deceptively favorable light on the economic performance of such economies. Policy advice based on these calculations becomes dulled at best and downright wrong at worst.

The concept of rent in this situation is profoundly misused and frequently misapplied. In the perception of the classical economists the rent that qualifies as value added is derived from the indestructible powers of nature.[9] Such revenue is clearly sustainable where the powers of nature to reproduce it are not impaired and it can therefore legitimately be counted as income. The surplus, net of extraction costs, emanating from liquidating natural resources, however, has little kinship with either rent or quasi-rent as defined by Marshall (1920).

There seems to be no alternative to bringing the capital nature of such exploitation into the open and integrating this notion in all economic thinking and measurements, not just to gauge welfare adequately, but to monitor economic performance and rescue economic analysis from folly. Even non-economists have on occasion rightly perceived that mineral extraction revenues are not wholly income. A small and underdeveloped country such as Libya could thus legislate as early as 1963 (when it first began to extract petroleum in commercial quantities) that at least 70 per cent of petroleum proceeds must be allocated to development. The perception was strong in that very poor country at the time that this unique wealth truly belonged to 'future generations' and should not be squandered on consumption as would be implied by treating the proceeds of oil sales as current income. To recall Hicks's standard definition, current income is that part of receipts which, if devoted to consumption, would leave the earner no worse off at the end of the accounting period than at its beginning.

III

WEAKNESS OF THE DEPRECIATION APPROACH

I use the expression, 'depreciation approach', to refer to a method of adjusting the national accounts by treating the depletion of a natural resource similarly to the depreciation of fixed assets. This would leave the gross product unadjusted and deduct from it an estimate for wear-and-tear to arrive at an estimate of the net product. Like other economists of the same bent, I thought first of using 'capital consumption' or 'depreciation' to adjust income from depletable mineral resources. As the resource is depleted by the quantity of extraction during the year, the amount of depletion, valued at current prices, may be deducted from the gross proceeds, just as, for example, the depreciation of capital equipment used in manufacturing is subtracted from the gross value added by manufacturing activities. The mineral extraction earnings can still be reckoned in GDP, provided that the value of the depletion is deducted from it for calculating net income. The problem of the exact valuation of capital consumption in this case appears to be of secondary importance. Much more important is to try to make some adjustment. Various methods are already used to treat inventories and other capital assets used up in the process of production. Shortcuts, approximations and arbitrary estimation are used throughout national income calculations, and no special harm, I thought, could come from adding the depreciation of natural resources to the list.

On reflection, however, I moved away from this approach, both for practical as well as conceptual considerations. First, the conceptual: it is wrong to describe as current production that which is not current production. GDP is an important measurement and is much more in use than NDP. Even if NDP and its national parallel NNP are correctly measured, the whole apparatus of GDP with its sectoral structure, input–output connections, and changes over time would remain incorrectly calculated if revenues from depletable resources were to continue being counted as value added in GDP.

It is not by chance that the gross product, rather than the net product, is the preferred quantity for macroeconomic analysis. And it is often used as a denominator for crucial macroeconomic ratios, with the nominator being money supply, exports, imports, external debt, debt service, savings, capital formation and so forth. As Hicks has suggested, the concept of net income is usually eschewed because it is always arbitrary. It relies on estimates of depreciation and inventory use that are a mixed bag of historical costs and estimation based on accounting conventions, tax laws and allowances, insurance company practices, as well as subjective valuation by economic agents who do the reckoning and who have a variety of expectations about the future (Hicks, 1969; see also Keynes, 1936).[10] From my perspective, if an income correction is to be made, it should apply to the gross product itself, and it is not enough to effect the adjustment at the net product level.

Another reason why I discarded the depreciation approach for rectifying income accounting for depletable resource activities is the fact that countries with marketable natural resources are evidently better off than those without such resources, and they can enjoy a higher and sustainable standard of living than the latter by virtue of their resource endowment. Such an advantage should be reflected in calculating the income of both groups. If we deduct from the gross receipts from mineral sales in any one year an amount equal to the depletion along the lines described above, the value of net income from this activity becomes zero. Where a country derives 100 per cent of its receipts from, say, petroleum extraction – an extreme case of a Saudi Arabia – the depreciation approach (ignoring the multiplier effect of ancillary activities related to extraction as well as the contribution of other sectors to value added) would give us a GDP of 100 and an NDP of zero – a measurement that is not particularly edifying.

Under this approach the gross product would not incur any adjustment and the net product would be eliminated altogether. Such a measurement of net income would belie the observable fact that having subsoil mineral deposits to exploit gives their possessors an income edge over those who do not have that advantage. An added reason why the depreciation approach will not do is that accountants have standard depreciation profiles for buildings, machinery, etc. roughly based on their assumed life expectancy. Depleting natural resources does not follow any asset lifetime pattern, and could vary from 0 to 100 per cent. See Chapter 12 on 'Depletable resource: fixed capital or inventories?'

IV

CONVERSION TO A PERMANENT INCOME STREAM

Mineral deposits and other comparable marketable natural resources are assets. Selling assets does not create value added and the revenue obtained from the sale should not be included, unadjusted, in GDP. The sale, however, does generate liquid funds, which can be put to alternative uses. A country may choose to spend the proceeds (net of extraction costs) on consumption or investment or any combination of the two. But this is neither here nor there. From an accounting point of view, however, an income content of the net receipts can be estimated. This income content should be part of GDP since it represents value added. The argument for this approach proceeds as follows.[11]

If an owner of a wasting asset is to consume no more than 'his' income, he or she must re-lend some part of the receipts so that the interest on it will make up for the eventual failure of receipts from the wasting asset in the future. This proposition, which can be found in Hicks (1946, Chapter 14), suggested to me the need to convert the mineral asset concerned into a perpetual income stream. The finite series of earnings from the sale of the resource, say a ten-year series of annual extractions leading to the extinction of the resource, has to be converted to an infinite series of true income, such that the capitalized values of the two series are equal. From the annual receipts from sales, an income portion that can be spent on consumption should be identified. The remainder, a capital element, should be set aside year after year and invested to create a perpetual stream of income that would provide the same level of true income, both during the life of the resource as well as after the resource has been exhausted. The two constituent portions of current receipts need to be defined: the income portion and the capital portion. Under certain assumptions, which are neither too restricting nor too unrealistic, the ratio of true income to total receipts is:

$$X/R = 1 - \frac{1}{(1 + r)^{n+1}}$$

$$(9.1)$$

where X is true income, R the total receipts (net of extraction cost), r the rate of discount, and n the number of periods during which the resource is to be liquidated. $R - X$ would be the user cost, or depletion factor, that should be set aside as a capital investment and totally excluded from GDP. On the expenditure side, this depletion factor would represent a disinvestment that should be set against capital formation in new assets, so that total expenditure would still be equal to the true income. If all of the receipts were devoted to consumption and if new capital formation fell short of the depletion factor, the accounts should show a negative value for capital formation, thus reflecting the disinvestment that had occurred during the accounting period.

The ratio X/R depends only on two values: the reserves-to-extraction ratio, that is, the life expectancy of the resource measured in years (as viewed from the current period's perspective) and the discount rate. A country that liquidates its mineral reserves over 50 years needs to set aside for reinvestment a smaller portion of its receipts than another country that liquidates its reserves more rapidly, say over 20 years, and thus it can count a larger portion of its receipts as income. Similarly, if the receipts set aside can be invested at a high interest rate, say 10 per cent, a higher portion would be reckoned to income than if the interest used was 5 per cent. According to this formula, with a discount rate of 5 per cent, a country that liquidates its natural resource over ten years can consider as income only 42 per cent of its annual receipts, while another with a 50-year horizon can reckon as much as 92 per cent of its annual receipts to current income. At a 10 per cent discount rate the former's current income would be 65 per cent of the receipts and the latter's 99 per cent, which would require almost no correction to GDP estimates as currently made. See Figures 9.1 and 9.2 and Tables 9.1 and 9.2.

Figure 9.1 shows the ratio X/R (the portion of total receipts that is true income) as a function of the life expectancy of the resource, N, measured in years, at ten alternative discount rates, decreasing from 10 to 1 per cent. The same relation is given numerically in Tables 9.1 and 9.2. Table 9.1 shows the income content of mineral sales at eleven alternative discount rates from 0 to 10, for resource life expectancies of 1 to 200 years. This is shown as percentage shares of the receipts that are currently being treated under the SNA as if they were wholly income. Table 9.2 is the complement

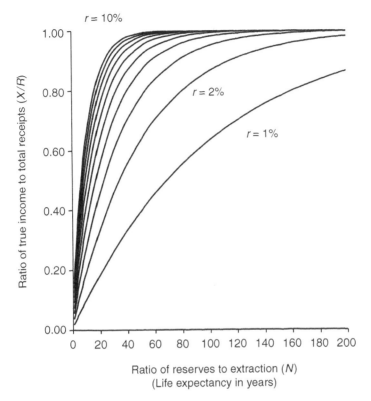

Figure 9.1   Ratio of income to total receipts at various discount rates and life expectancies

of Table 9.1 and presents the user-cost content of the annual sales, expressed also as a percentage of total receipts, for the same discount rates and life expectancies. This percentage represents the capital element that, I believe, should be excluded from GDP as a depletion factor.

The calculations show that the present practice of counting mineral sales proceeds as current income implies that the fraction

$$\frac{1}{(1 + r)^{n+1}} \tag{9.2}$$

equals zero in my formula. For only then would $X/R = 1$ and revenue becomes identical with income. This would be obtained, irrespective of the discount rate, by having $n = \infty$; or alternatively, where n is finite by having a very high value of the discount rate so that r tends to infinity. Such a

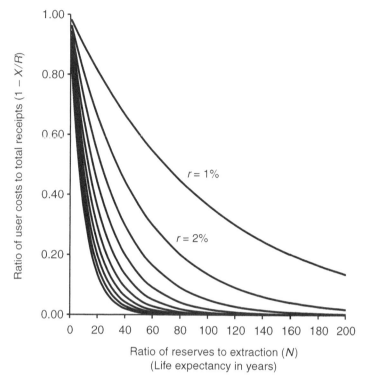

Figure 9.2   Ratio of user cost to total receipts at various discount rates and life expectancies

high rate of discount implies a very strong time preference of the resource owners and is tantamount to setting a very low value on the utility of the resource to future generations. Current practices for calculating GDP according to the injunctions of the SNA are thus seen to be built on one of two untenable premises or a combination of both: (1) that the natural resource being liquidated would last forever, and (2) that the interests of future generations do not matter.

V

CLARIFICATION OF THE USER-COST APPROACH

In defense of this approach, the following points should be emphasized.
   A discount rate must be chosen. This choice has to be arbitrary, but

Table 9.1 Income content of mineral sales *(X/R)*, life expectancy *(N)* at various discount rates *(per cent)*

N	Discount rate *(r)*										
	0.00	0.01	0.02	0.03	0.04	0.05	0.06	0.07	0.08	0.09	0.10
1	0	2	4	6	8	9	11	13	14	16	17
2	0	3	6	8	11	14	16	18	21	23	25
3	0	4	8	11	15	18	21	24	26	29	32
4	0	5	9	14	18	22	25	29	32	35	38
5	0	6	11	16	21	25	30	33	37	40	44
6	0	7	13	19	24	29	33	38	42	45	49
7	0	8	15	21	27	32	37	42	46	50	53
8	0	9	16	23	30	36	41	46	50	54	58
9	0	9	18	26	32	39	44	49	54	58	61
10	0	10	20	28	35	42	47	52	57	61	65
15	0	15	27	38	47	54	61	66	71	75	78
20	0	19	34	46	56	64	71	76	80	84	86
25	0	23	40	54	64	72	78	83	86	89	92
30	0	27	46	60	70	78	84	88	91	93	95
35	0	30	51	65	76	83	88	91	94	96	97
40	0	33	56	70	80	86	91	94	96	97	98
50	0	40	64	78	86	92	95	97	98	99	99
60	0	46	70	84	91	95	97	98	99	99	100
80	0	55	80	91	96	98	99	100	100	100	100
100	0	63	86	95	98	99	100	100	100	100	100
120	0	70	91	97	99	100	100	100	100	100	100
140	0	75	94	98	100	100	100	100	100	100	100
160	0	80	96	99	100	100	100	100	100	100	100
180	0	83	97	100	100	100	100	100	100	100	100
200	0	86	98	100	100	100	100	100	100	100	100

Note: Figures are rounded to the nearest digit.

the arbitrariness of the discount rate is not in principle any different from the arbitrary estimation methods used extensively under the SNA. A rate of 3-4 per cent may be chosen as approximating a precautionary yield to be expected from the new investments.[12] This could be changed periodically, say every five years or so, guided by changes in the market rates.

Under the proposed formula, the setting-aside of part of the proceeds for reinvestment is only a metaphor. It is merely a theoretical step needed for the estimation of current income. The owners may dispose of their

Table 9.2   *Capital content (user cost) of mineral sales (1 – X/R), life expectancy (N) at various discount rates (per cent)*

N	Discount rate (r)										
	0.00	0.01	0.02	0.03	0.04	0.05	0.06	0.07	0.08	0.09	0.10
1	100	98	96	94	92	91	89	87	86	84	83
2	100	97	94	92	89	86	84	82	79	77	75
3	100	96	92	89	85	82	79	76	74	71	68
4	100	95	91	86	82	78	75	71	68	65	62
5	100	94	89	84	79	75	70	67	63	60	56
6	100	93	87	81	76	71	67	62	58	55	51
7	100	92	85	79	73	68	63	58	54	50	47
8	100	91	84	77	70	64	59	54	50	46	42
9	100	91	82	74	68	61	56	51	46	42	39
10	100	90	80	72	65	58	53	48	43	39	35
15	100	85	73	62	53	46	39	34	29	25	22
20	100	81	66	54	44	36	29	24	20	16	14
25	100	77	60	46	36	28	22	17	14	11	8
30	100	73	54	40	30	22	16	12	9	7	5
35	100	70	49	35	24	17	12	9	6	4	3
40	100	67	44	30	20	14	9	6	4	3	2
50	100	60	36	22	14	8	5	3	2	1	1
60	100	54	30	16	9	5	3	2	1	1	0
80	100	45	20	9	4	2	1	0	0	0	0
100	100	37	14	5	2	1	0	0	0	0	0
120	100	30	9	3	1	0	0	0	0	0	0
140	100	25	6	2	0	0	0	0	0	0	0
160	100	20	4	1	0	0	0	0	0	0	0
180	100	17	3	0	0	0	0	0	0	0	0
200	100	14	2	0	0	0	0	0	0	0	0

Note: Figures are rounded to the nearest digit.

receipts any way they choose. But they should be made aware of the fact that their true income is only a fraction of their total receipts. Proper accounting should clearly convey this fundamental message.

- Equally metaphorical is the process of calculating the yields from investing the set-aside part of the proceeds at the arbitrarily chosen interest rate. As stated previously, the rate should approximate an available market parameter that would indicate yield on the new investments and simultaneously guide decisions about extraction. Thus the owner may decide to delay extraction if for instance the market interest rate available for financial investment appears lower than the rate at which the resource would appreciate if left in the ground. But the owner need not in practice sink his/her funds in physical or financial assets at that interest rate. However, the owner would be wise to seek such a rate as a minimum yield on the new investments. The so-called Hotelling rule states that if a depletable natural resource is left alone, it will appreciate at the market discount rate because of its growing scarcity.

- Likewise, the future extraction schedule, assumed to be at a constant rate over some time horizon, is also a paradigm, and is used only for devising the formula. The owner has a given resource. He or she may extract it over two years or 20. Every period the owner may decide to alter the extraction plans, depending on current prices and the expectations thereof by increasing or decreasing the annual extraction rate. The owner is at liberty to do so. All the formula needs is the ratio between the total reserves and the amount extracted in the current period, both denominated in physical units. Suppose an owner, who had been planning to liquidate the available reserves over a ten-year period, decides now to accelerate extraction because of an expected decline in future prices (reckoning that, since his/her market share is small, this may be done with impunity, that is, without depressing prices) and now decides on a five-year horizon instead. All that is necessary is to use the new ratio of reserves-to-extraction, and this can be decided, period-by-period, and changed every year if need be.
- The same applies to the discovery of new deposits or a downward adjustment in reserves – usually a tough nut to crack. The new discovery does not have to be counted as income as some have suggested. All that is necessary, if this approach is followed, is to alter the reserves-to-extraction ratio (N) in the calculations, that is, if it is decided to keep the extraction schedule unchanged. In this case, the discovery will reflect itself in higher income than before, as shown by moving from left to right on the x-axis in Figure 9.1. However, the owner may very well keep the reserves-to-extraction ratio unchanged by raising annual extraction when he or she realizes that the reserves are larger than had been thought. This will also translate into a higher income.
- It is not at all necessary to estimate the absolute value of the physical reserves, or to resort to what is known as 'wealth accounting.' Neither is it necessary to predict future prices. The owner of the resource does all the predictions necessary, and these are reflected in annual extraction, which the accountant has to relate to the size

of the total reserves in order to estimate income. By implication (if a value is set on the stocks which my method eschews) the unit value of the total resource will be the same as the current price. Such valuation, appearing in both the numerator and denominator of the formula given earlier, cancels out, and what remains is the ratio between two physical quantities: the size of the reserves and the annual extraction, that is, the number of years remaining before the resource is totally exhausted. Speculation about the future course of prices, however, does in reality occur, and this, as mentioned above, affects the rate at which the resource is liquidated, but this is not the accountant's concern.

- The problems of the terms of trade or of changed technology that might lead to drastic changes in the size and valuation of the resource are not addressed here. Such changes have to be acknowledged by the income accountants when they occur. The focus of this approach is on the volume of extraction in the accounting period as it relates to the total volume of the reserves. In the manner of national accounting, the market valuation of the product is taken as given and is used merely to weight the volume in order to assess the activity's contribution to GDP.

- This proposed method could be applied immediately to mineral deposits that are more or less ascertainable, such as petroleum, for which the industry estimates proven reserves and publishes these estimates regularly. But even for petroleum, and certainly for metals, owners tend to mine richer and more accessible deposits first and this means that later extractions involve progressively higher extraction costs. Rising extraction costs can undermine the sustainability of the activity as much as its physical exhaustion. When market prices fall below extraction costs, many previous sellers, still sitting on large deposits, find profitable operation impossible. Estimation of the volume of reserves therefore should be adjusted downward by a factor that would reflect the rising future cost of extraction. Shortcuts for such adjustment need to be devised case by case.

- It is important to remember that the issue here is *national* income accounting. Even if the identified global reserves of a mineral get adjusted upward, the fact remains that the reserves of individual countries get inevitably depleted as they are exploited. National income accounting should reflect this individual national aspect of the activity.

VI

CONCLUSION

Although the user-cost approach appears radical in that it seeks to alter the estimation of GDP under the SNA for certain activities, it is economical and practicable. It is an effective way of impressing on natural resource owners, particularly developing countries that depend economically on the exploitation of their subsoil deposits and on 'mining' their renewable resources, the fact that their natural resources are being exhausted as they are exploited. The method proposed is in harmony with standard economic concepts. The national income accounting practices set out under the SNA distort these concepts when applied to depletable resources. They falsely call rent that which is not rent, and depict as value added that which is not value added. A second-best alternative, which I certainly do not favor, would be to use the depreciation approach of deducting a depletion factor from an exaggerated GDP to reach a corrected NDP. The user cost proposed in this chapter would be the correct estimate of such a depletion factor, not the 'full-value' decline in stocks, which, as argued above, would wipe out all the activity from the net product. However, we should remember that the net product is not always estimated, and the gross product is the magnitude commonly in use by economists: that is why correcting GDP and GNP seems to be the preferred course. It is not enough to record depletion in balance sheets or in reconciliation or satellite accounts. Additionally, the approach recommended here would make it unnecessary to show in such accounts the absolute value of total reserves – values that would be 'contingent' and as arbitrary as they would be unedifying. Its adoption would lead to the proper understanding and measurement of the special economic activity of natural resource extraction, and consequently to better economic policy analysis.

EPILOGUE

There was some vagueness in the exposition of this paper as originally published, and yet it served my intended purpose quite well. Lack of clarity in some places, however, neither invalidated the main argument nor blemished the validity of my formula. Nevertheless, the original paper did not just outline a method for reckoning income from mining a wasting asset, but also had to make the argument during a very turbulent time when the economics of monopoly and competition in the petroleum market was being invoked. By 1989, the same argument was presented by me as a contribution to ecological economics and thus became less objectionable. The original paper had contained remarks of a political nature, which now seem to be out of place. I have decided to leave them in, however, to recall the time (the 1970s) when this paper was conceived. Many economists, including late Harvard professor Hendrik Houthakker (1974), expected that oil prices would decline once the market had been given time to react to OPEC's supply manipulations. It was the depletability of the resource that was uppermost in my mind, well above the alleged monopoly power of OPEC. Had the original paper been written now I would have dropped all references to the political tensions prevailing in the 1970s and early 1980s, which had included threats of war made on behalf of some importers. Though I displayed a whole range of discount rates for estimating income and user cost, both graphically and in tabular form, my purpose was to show the sensitivity of the calculations to the discount rate and the sustainability span of the resource. An error I have now cleared up is the earlier reference to the 'social rate of time preference' to be used as a discounting parameter. This is much less relevant than the anticipated return on future investments, which is the appropriate magnitude to be used for discounting.

NOTES

1. At the time the financial surpluses amassed by some oil exporters were viewed as upsetting to the world payments system. The Colorado conference was mounted mainly to discuss the possibility of enlarging the absorptive capacities of the surplus economies by easing the path toward domestic investments that would mop up some of the surplus.
2. Note that this paper was delivered five years prior to SNA93.
3. The term 'Dutch disease' originated in the 1960s to refer to the adverse effects on Dutch manufacturing of natural gas discoveries. Generally speaking increased revenues from a natural resource encourages spending on non-traded goods and draws resources out of the traded, non-natural resource sectors, thus stifling diversification and retarding development. See, for example, Corden (1984).
4. See Hicks (1946, p. 172). See also Keynes (1936) Chapter 6 on 'The definition of the income, saving and investment' and that chapter's 'Appendix on user cost'. Note that Keynes's insistence that saving and investment were always equal – a claim that caused much controversy at the time – is consistent with an *ex post* view that now dominates national income accounting.
5. Luca Salvati and Margherita Carlucci (2010) of the University of Rome applied the user cost method to estimate the effect of land degradation in over 784 local districts covering the entire Italian territory, reaching the conclusion that land degradation in Italy amounted to 0.5 per cent of agriculture's gross product.
6. As Paul Samuelson once quipped, economists seem to be the opposite of Oscar Wilde's cynic: they know the value of everything but the price of nothing.
7. OPEC admittedly met regularly to agree on the prices at which its members would sell oil. But such prices cleared the market without any quotas imposed to regulate supply. Not until 1982, however, did OPEC attempt to behave like a cartel with individual quotas indicated for its members, but like all cartels this attempt to maintain prices in a

declining market palpably failed. The interests of OPEC members often conflicted; see Razavi (1984).

8. See Solow, 1974 where he recalled Hotelling's path-breaking article, 'The Economics of Exhaustible Resources', *Journal of Political Economy*, Volume 39, Number 2, April 1931, pp. 137–175.

9. '[T]he original and indestructible powers of the soil' as formulated by Ricardo (1821, Chapter 2). Apparently Ricardo took this from Malthus: see Schumpeter (1954), and this is more clearly expressed in the entry on David Ricardo by De Vivo (1987) in *The New Palgrave, a Dictionary of Economics*.

10. Keynes in his *General Theory* (1936, p. 60), drew attention to the fact that net income is 'an equivocal criterion' which different authorities interpret differently and therefore is 'not perfectly clear-cut'.

11. I had been thinking along these lines for some time and first expressed my views on this topic in a paper delivered in March 1979 to the staff of OAPEC in Kuwait (later published as El Serafy, 1979). I elaborated these views and proposed my method for estimating income from depletable natural resources in a later paper on 'Absorptive capacity', presented in Colorado in 1980. The concern at the time was that the so-called 'capital surplus' economies which exported petroleum, had too low a domestic absorptive capacity. It was thought that if that could be expanded it would, through increased imports, restore equilibrium to the petroleum importers' balances of payments. I criticized this approach because it reflected the short-term interests of the petroleum consumers and not that of the owners of this scarce resource. See El Serafy (1981). An appendix to that paper entitled, 'How much of petroleum receipts can be reckoned to income?' contained the formula shown in the Appendix to the present chapter.

12. In the original paper I had suggested a 5 per cent interest rate, but I am leaning now towards a lower rate to minimize the risk of consuming capital. Others have picked the appropriate rate from the rate of growth of the domestic economy over some protracted period, but this sidesteps the possibility of investing abroad.

REFERENCES

Corden, W. M. (1984), 'Booming sector and Dutch disease economics: survey and consolidation', *Oxford Economic Papers*, **36**, 359–380.

De Vivo, G. (1987), *The New Palgrave, a Dictionary of Economics*, Vol. 4. London: Macmillan.

El Serafy, Salah (1979), 'The oil price revolution of 1973–74', *Journal of Energy and Development*, **IV** (2), 273–290.

El Serafy, Salah (1981), 'Absorptive capacity, the demand for revenue, and the supply of petroleum', *Journal of Energy and Development*, **VII** (1), 73–88.

El Serafy, Salah (1989), 'The proper calculation of income from depletable natural resources', in Yusuf J. Ahmad, Salah El Serafy and Ernst Lutz (eds), *Environmental Accounting for Sustainable Development*, A UNEP–World Bank Symposium. Washington DC: The World Bank, Chapter 3, pp. 10–18.

El Serafy, Salah (1991), 'Natural resource accounting: an overview', in James T. Winpenny (ed.), *Development Research: The Environmental Challenge*. London: Overseas Development Institute, Chapter 21, pp. 205–220.

Hicks, John Richard (1946), *Value and Capital*, 2nd edition. Oxford: Oxford University Press.

Hicks, John Richard (1969), 'Measurement of capital in practice', originally published in *The Bulletin* of the International Statistical Institute in London.

Reprinted in *Wealth and Welfare: Collected Essays on Economic Theory*, Vol. I, Cambridge, MA: Harvard University Press, Chapter 9, pp. 204–217.

Houthakker, Hendrik S. (1974), 'Policy issues in the international economy of the 1970s', *American Economic Review, Papers and Proceedings*, May, 140.

Keynes, John Maynard (1936), *The General Theory of Employment, Interest and Money*. London: Macmillan.

Marshall, Alfred (1920), *Principles of Economics*, 8th edition. London: Macmillan.

Razavi, Hossein (1984), 'An economic model of OPEC coalition', *Southern Economic Journal*, **51** (2), 419–428.

Ricardo, David (1821), *On the Principles of Political Economy and Taxation*, 3rd edition. London: John Murray.

Salvati, Luca and Margherita Carlucci (2010), 'Estimating land degradation risk for agriculture in Italy using an indirect approach', *Ecological Economics*, **69** (3), 511–518.

Schumpeter, Joseph A. (1954), *History of Economic Analysis*. New York: Oxford University Press.

Smith, A. (1776 [1937]), *An Inquiry into the Nature and Causes of the Wealth of Nations*, Modern Library Edition. New York: Random House.

Solow, Robert M. (1974), 'The economics of resources or the resources of economics', *American Economic Review, Papers and Proceedings*, **LXIV** (2), 1–14.

APPENDIX

Splitting Receipts into Income and Capital

In this chapter, receipts from the sales of a depletable natural resource are net of extraction costs. The extraction costs contain elements that do not directly generate value added, such as materials used up in the process of extraction, but would normally also contain payments for the services of factors of production such as labor which are included in GDP in the usual way.

A time series of expected net receipts R from the sale of a resource that, as a result of exploitation, will come to an end in a future year n contains a true income element X, where $X < R$, such that if $(R - X)$, the capital content, is invested year after year at interest rate r, the accumulated investment would continue to yield the same level of income X.

It is necessary to identify X/R, that is, the proportion of net receipts that can truly be called income, and its complement $1 - X/R$, the capital element, also as a proportion of net receipts. The capitalized value at interest rate r of the finite series of receipts R should equal the capitalized value at the same interest rate of the infinite series X. The capitalized value of the finite series R, accruing in equal amounts over a period of n years, would add up to:

$$\sum_{0}^{n} R^* = R \frac{\left[1 - \dfrac{1}{(1 + r)^{n+1}}\right]}{1 - \dfrac{1}{1 + r}}. \tag{9.3}$$

And the infinite series X would add up to:

$$\sum_{0}^{\infty} X^* = \frac{X}{1 - \dfrac{1}{1 + r}}. \tag{9.4}$$

Setting the two above equations equal and multiplying by the denominator in both quantities we get:

$$X = R \left[1 - \frac{1}{(1 + r)^{n+1}}\right]$$

$$X/R = 1 - \frac{1}{(1 + r)^{n+1}} \tag{9.5}$$

$$1 - X/R = \frac{1}{(1 + r)^{n+1}}.$$

In this formula it is assumed that the receipts R accrue at the beginning of each accounting period. If, alternatively, they accrue at the end, the fraction X/R becomes:

$$1 - 1/(1 + r)^n. \tag{9.6}$$

It is also assumed that the relative prices of the resource and the goods and services on which the stream of income will be spent do not change. If there is reason to believe, for instance, that such goods and services will appreciate over time relative to the resource output, the capital element to be set aside has to be larger (and the income content smaller) in order to make it possible to maintain a constant income stream in real terms. The converse is true if there is reason to believe that the resource product would appreciate relative to the goods and services that would make up future income. But these are refinements that could be incorporated in the method suggested and would not affect much the results obtained. The method proposed, with the implicit assumption of constant relative prices, seems adequate if the direction in which relative prices will change is uncertain.

10. Disagreements and misunderstandings

INTRODUCTION

This chapter continues the elucidation of the user-cost method for greening the national accounts, but approaches the topic from the standpoint of its critics. The chapter garners a number of disagreements and tries to address them. The instances cited I believe cover the whole range of adverse views. It will be seen that the claimed faults are in many respects repetitive and interdependent. Attempting to address them here should, however, throw greater light on the user-cost method and hopefully also confirm my belief that had this method been properly understood from the beginning progress towards a green accounting consensus might have developed faster. Again I am confining my coverage to monetary accounting, and overlooking physical accounting, which is obviously necessary in any case as a preliminary step. Physical accounting has been pursued with advantage in many situations and without much controversy. For presenting my arguments I have had two alternatives. One was a thematic approach, grouping censure by category of fault whether real or imagined. The other option was to identify critics, whether individuals or institutional, by name. I chose the latter, partly on grounds of convenience, but also to reveal some interesting interconnections between dissenters.

Some of the claimed shortcomings of the 'El Serafy method' may no doubt be attributed to ambiguities in my own exposition. Others may also be blamed on my reluctance to offer immediate rebuttals when errors of interpretation surfaced and came to my notice. I did, however, occasionally attempt to rebut perceived faults without taking special aim at individual detractors. But on the whole I tended to refrain from pointing out errors, imagining that misconceptions would be spotted by serious analysts and eventually cleared up. However, my passivity turned out in retrospect to have been misguided since errors, left uncorrected, created their own momentum. Fresh analysts would assume the validity of the critical views while occasionally adding their own dubious input. Subsequent researchers would quote earlier critics as well as each other in support of misconceptions that get perpetuated with repetition. In the process, false arguments that should have been stifled from the beginning lingered on, became entrenched, and gathered ungainly popularity by recurring endorsement. Although there were many positive views in favor, resistance to the user-cost method gradually hardened, especially among those national accountants who, for one reason or another, seemed committed to rival methods. To make matters worse some ardent environmentalists also joined the debate on the wrong side. They suspected 'weak' sustainability and preferred a stronger version. As I have argued previously the 'weak sustainability' associated with the user-cost method is the appropriate level of sustainability that is compatible with national accounting. But its avowed 'weakness' branded it in the eyes of some adversaries as inferior to an ostensibly stronger sustainability. Some environmentalists seem to like the 'over-correction' that 'strong sustainability' would bring to the accounts, imagining that it must be better for environmental awareness than an accounting approach that would produce less pronounced adjustments. Using strong sustainability for greening the national accounts would deduct the *entire* decline in natural resource stocks from the conventional estimates of the flow accounts (GDP, GNP and associated magnitudes). Moreover, such adjustments to the net product if made would be entombed in extraneous 'satellite' accounts. It is interesting to note that in the green accounting literature supporters of this over-correction include Hueting (1989), Repetto (1989), Victor et al. (1991) and Victor (1994). Even Hartwick (1990) seems to me to be a strong sustainability advocate though he is often classified as belonging to the weak variety camp. In the following chapter I shall explain my characterization of Hartwick's position in detail. Also among advocates of strong sustainability has been the World Bank (1997) with its estimates of 'genuine savings'. This led to the erroneous conclusion that a large number of developing economies were proceeding on an unsustainable path. Eric Neumayer took up the challenge to show that employing the user-cost approach would produce significantly different results (Neumayer, 2000). By contrast, my approach, based as it is on weak sustainability, would deduct from the conventional estimates only the user cost, and would re-estimate GDP itself to purge from it asset sale proceeds as appropriate. Once this has been done, the net product would automatically be adjusted also.

To many environmentalists the user-cost method conjures up mistakenly an unacceptably lower degree of natural resource sustainability. This view has sometimes been exaggerated into the preposterous claim that advocates of the user-cost method actually *urge* the liquidation of natural wealth and investing the proceeds in other forms of capital.[1] It was only too facile for sloppy adversaries of the user-cost method to point out that the two categories of assets, natural and produced, are not good substitutes for each other, let alone being *perfect* substitutes as some authors have even claimed to be implicit in the method. All this will be discussed in detail in the following pages.

Once again it is worth emphasizing that the level of sustainability involved here is the one national income accounting is capable of providing, namely the sustainability of *income* or output, not the sustainability of the *environment*. In any case the national accounts can never be an effective vehicle for environmental protection though if they are properly adjusted they can be a good medium for moving towards that goal. Yet even when properly greened, the *income* sustainability delivered would only be a time-limited sustainability: from one account period to the next. However, if this process were to be replicated year in and year out the sustainability brought about would be stretched over longer periods. The fact remains however that the system of national accounts is an *economic* apparatus, not an environmental one, and covers chiefly only those aspects of natural resources that enter the marketplace.

CATEGORIZING DISSENTERS

It is possible to group misrepresentations of the user-cost method roughly under five headings: (1) the view that the user-cost method is a 'welfare oriented' device; (2) that it is based on 'weak sustainability', whereas strong sustainability would be preferable; (3) the user-cost method seeks to adjust the *net* product and not the *gross* product; (4) the claim that a constant profile of future extraction is implicitly assumed and future prices are projected to remain constant; and (5) that life expectancy of the natural resource being extracted remains constant.

It will be seen in addressing these claims that the periodic (typically annual) accounting process affords the opportunity to revise and update all relevant parameters required to make the calculations. These parameters are (1) the estimated volume of reserves; (2) the volume of extraction during the current period; (3) the life expectancy, which can be obtained by dividing (1) by (2); and the interest rate (or future yield) anticipated from investing the equivalent of the user cost. None of these magnitudes is held constant under my method since they are all perfectly adjustable every account period. Bear in mind also that resolutions on actual extraction, future investments (or just making future price projections) are management matters that normally fall outside the accountant's brief. Any one-year's extraction, whether past, present or future, may indeed range from nothing at all to the entire stock if this were to be liquidated in one go. Usually such decisions are constrained by technical, contractual and other limitations on flexibility. They tend to be guided by knowledge, or merely guessing of rivals' plans and overall business expectations, and cannot in practice follow the optimal profiles favored by the economic theorists who target national accounting reform. The stereotypical model of an entrepreneur with maximum flexibility who seeks to equate marginal costs with marginal revenues and aims to balance short-term benefits against future opportunities lacks practical credibility. Note also that such an entrepreneur is also assumed to be equipped with good or even 'perfect' foresight. While such models of extraction behavior may be valuable heuristically they should not be dragged inappropriately into the often 'messy' process of estimating the national income.

It will be seen that one particular misconception that is repeated ad nauseam in the following sections revolves around the issue of time. I did not use calculus for working out my formula since I was using an accounting approach based on discrete not continuous time. Time for the practical purpose of resource extraction comes in slices, and particularly for accounting purposes, is not at all a continuous stream. It typically occurs in annual segments. And it is in the context of accounting that I assumed the constancy – correctly spotted by critics – of a stream of annual extraction. This constancy I needed only to work out the formula from information that would be available to accountants. And there is a difference between the flexibility of extraction decisions I have just stressed and the formula proposed for estimating the user cost. No inconsistency should be seen in this since the estimation of the user cost is effected afresh every year with the basic parameters in the formula being changeable. These flexible parameters, as by now should be familiar to the reader, are the sale proceeds (R), life expectancy (n), and anticipated future yield (r). I was indeed careful to point the difference between the flexibility of actual extraction and the constancy assumptions within the formula on p. 16 of El Serafy (1989) to forestall possible confusion. Others, notably Hartwick and Hageman (1993) and especially Hartwick (pers. comm.)[2] had found no fault in the assumed formulaic constancy. In fact, Hartwick, whose interest was then focused on optimal (not actual) extraction explored the formula's assumption of constancy, and concluded that:

> The good news is that the El-Serafy's user cost continues to yield the same measure of loss in capital value from extraction as does the economic depreciation concept, $V_{t+1} - V_t$. It is pleasing that the attractive intuition underlying

the El-Serafy measure leads to a concept, which has been traditionally derived from a rather different intuition. There is more than one way to skin a cat, it seems.

This said, it is important to bear in mind continually that my user-cost formula is not meant to sustain natural resources, but only to indicate a sustainable level of income derived from selling the natural assets. Furthermore the method is versatile enough to be applicable to all natural resources whether they are intrinsically depletable or theoretically renewable when the latter are effectively being 'mined'. If extraction persists, the assets being mined will eventually cease to exist, and the sustainability of future income can only be secured with investing the equivalent of the user cost.

To sum up, a constant level of future extraction is not assumed at all, and does not enter the determination of the user cost. No presumption of constancy of either volume or price enters the approach, and constancy was used only to facilitate the derivation of the formula. This may appear as a fine line of distinction, but its *periodic* application, year in, year out, should dispel doubt about the assumed constancy of extraction or the level of future prices. Future prices decidedly play no part in the calculations. Estimating life expectancy by dividing the current year's stock by the volume of extraction does not mean that this life expectancy ('n' in the formula) will remain unchanged. In fact, it is most likely to change. If no extraction occurs in the following year there will be no revenue from the mining activity, no income, and no user cost. On the other hand, if extraction is 100 per cent of the remaining stock the asset will have been liquidated and the user cost will absorb the entirety of the net revenue in the year of liquidation. Future income in the latter case will coincide with the interest (or yield) to be earned from the new investments.[3] Many of these perceived flaws and also a number of scattered misconceptions are taken up for discussion below.

II

DEPRECIATION VERSUS WITHDRAWAL FROM INVENTORIES

Related to the claim that the user-cost method is predicated on the assumption of a constant profile of extraction is the charge that adjusting the accounts for natural resource depletion is akin to the depreciation of fixed assets. I had argued against this faulty interpretation quite early on (see El Serafy, 1989, and specifically El Serafy, 1993). Commercial depletion through extraction should be viewed – along Marshallian lines established a century ago – not as depreciation of fixed assets, but as the drawing down of inventories: as it were 'from nature's store' in Marshall's memorable phrase (El Serafy, 1993).[4] Fixed capital depreciation, practically always, amounts to a small, mainly predictable, fraction of the book value of the asset, whereas using up a depletable resource may vary considerably from year to year following no predictable pattern. For accountants, the distinction between the using-up of inventories and depreciating fixed capital is also of procedural importance. This is because using up inventories shows up in the 'profit and loss' account of a typical enterprise, namely at the initial step of determining *gross* profits or loss. And it is only later, at the stage of reckoning *net* profits or loss that fixed asset depreciation is brought in.[5] At that later stage the presumed depreciation of fixed assets is deducted from the already estimated gross profits (or added to the gross loss) to arrive at the net profits or loss of the enterprise. For national accounting the strong-sustainability stance, which the 1999 *Nature's Numbers* Panel's report (among others) curiously endorsed, led to proposing in effect that the gross output as conventionally reckoned needed little alteration. This contradicts the fact that it inappropriately contains revenues that often exceed income. *Nature's Numbers* (see next section) should indeed be faulted at least for recommending that it is the net output that must bear the brunt of the downward adjustment, besides using the *full* decline in the relevant natural resource stock to effect this adjustment. The adoption of a strong sustainability stance, which appeals to environmentalists often with little understanding of national accounting, would in fact be tantamount to 'over-correction' because it eliminates from the net product all value added specifically pertaining to the natural resource in question. Extraction of course involves the use of other inputs including the services of labor and capital for which wages and interest are paid. But such inputs are usually accounted for without controversy. This flawed approach leaves the *wrong* gross product unadjusted while indicating an equally *wrong* estimate of the net product.[6] It is interesting that the chairman of the *Nature's Numbers* Panel, Professor Nordhaus, in an email to me dated 19 December 2002, thought it was 'going too far' to attach no value added to extraction, obviously failing to realize that the Panel's report actually recommended that 'outlandish' course which I dispute. Am I justified in thinking that membership of a committee does not guarantee that all participants had digested the committee's arguments or appreciated the conclusions put out in their name? The thought occurs to me that lack of progress on green accounting after years of trying might be blamed, at least in part, on mistaken views put forward *inter alia* by such an influential Panel. While the Panel concluded, quite rightly, that greening the accounts should still be pursued, it is clear that pursuit along mistakenly indicated avenues would not be constructive.

III

NATURE'S NUMBERS

I lay special emphasis on *Nature's Numbers* (Nordhaus and Kokkelenberg, 1999) because it is an important report produced under a group studded with well-known analysts, some of whom had produced valuable theoretical work on environmental economics. It also contains much useful historical and analytical information. The familiarity of some members of the Panel with practical estimation methods, however, did not usefully orient in the right direction those academic members who lacked familiarity with accounting methods. This is because the participants with practical experience were obviously not representative of the range of methodological alternatives for greening the accounts. To simplify I would classify this group's membership without exception as 'strong sustainablists' who favored (1) confining the adjustment to the *net* estimates while leaving the gross magnitudes unaltered; and (2) reducing the conventional estimates by the full decline of the resource stocks, thus in effect showing no value added by extraction in the adjusted net accounts. Guardians of national income statistics have been strongly in favor of leaving the gross product practically unchanged, motivated partly by the wish to preserve continuity with historical data, and partly to ward off accusations that the old estimates may in fact have been defective.

Nature's Numbers, it may be recalled, was a project approved by the United States National Research Council and supported *inter alia* by the Bureau of Economic Analysis (BEA) of the US Department of Commerce. As published it had the promising subtitle: *Expanding the National Accounts to Include the Environment*, and when published it carried the editorship of Professor William Nordhaus (the Panel chairman) and Edward Kokkelenberg. To be fair, the Panel was forthright in urging BEA to 'continue to present subsoil mineral accounts in the form of satellite accounts for the near term' until their quality had improved sufficiently for them to be included 'in the core GDP accounts' (p. 102). This praiseworthy recommendation is of great importance, indicating that the satellite accounts should be only a stepping stone towards an eventual full integration of their contents into the core accounts. Whether or not the subsoil accounts will have improved in our lifetime to gain entry into the core accounts is doubtful, and such entry is certainly not aided by the text. Reflecting the expertise of some of its panellists the Report makes many valuable suggestions, but it falls into the trap set by SNA93, which, in essence, treats natural resource concerns as 'non-economic'. Whether temporarily or permanently, relegating environmental considerations to 'satellite accounts' denies them economic significance. It is as if isolating them within a *cordon sanitaire* was needed lest they contaminate the allegedly wholesome economic accounts. And it is as if natural resources should be left out of any production function, to be acknowledged if at all on sufferance as a footnote to economic activity. One may indeed ask: if environmental concerns are not economic, why should they be trespassing at all on the eminently economic grounds of the national accounts?

Significantly, the Nordhaus Panel missed the opportunity to challenge SNA93, which had introduced this questionable dichotomy between what is economic and what is environmental. In fact it managed to confirm it. Why? One may surmise that this was due to the overlapping authorship of both. Once that dichotomy had been established an endless search began to find ways to 'integrate' (or re-integrate) the economic with the environmental. Various attempts were made by the UNSD in cooperation with others to bridge this artificial gap. The natural place for 'integration' was expected in UNSD's series of 'Studies in Method' where concepts would be clarified and procedures laid down for elucidating the role of the satellite accounts and prescribing their contents. But the 1993 guidelines, which had been labeled an 'Interim Version', were found to be too complicated, indecisive and offered little help. The 1993 guidelines were amended seven years later. The new version was again called *Integrated Environmental and Economic Accounting: An Operational Manual* (2000). Later versions have been attempted and efforts are continuing still in various forums, but no definitive edition of the UN manual has emerged. This apparently impossible gap, which had been deliberately created, has proved to be far too wide to be closed.

Note especially that, contrary to economic reality, the *revenues* from commercially extracted natural resources which are market-priced and market-transacted continue to appear in the gross product without any allowance made for their declining stocks. Apparently little thought was given by the arbiters of national accounting methods to those poorer countries that depend considerably on natural resource extraction. Their GDP estimates still continue to confuse revenue with income, and they are made to appear to be growing *pari passu* with extraction when they are merely liquidating their natural wealth. And it is the *gross* product, it should be emphasized, that is the magnitude that is regularly used for macroeconomic analysis, making international comparisons, and for many other economic purposes. It is precisely this magnitude that needs to be adjusted for the deterioration of the resource base.[7]

Nature's Numbers expends much effort on irrelevancies that could have been left out, and fails in the process to deliver a methodical evaluation of BEA's flawed approach. The fact that BEA itself was entrenched in this evaluation raised doubt that an objective assessment of BEA's work on green accounting might not be forthcoming. The emphasis in BEA work is on a periodic valuation of resource stocks, and inferring the flow accounts from these stock values. The text could have been briefer and more to the point had the flow accounts taken the center stage while stocks were left in the background. The intention was indeed salutary to aim for a system of accounts that tightly links flows with stocks, but that could have been achieved by using physical data only. The more useful and less controversial physical information is here obscured by a dubious valuation method taken over from BEA. In order to value stocks, *Nature's Numbers* follows the arbitrary process of predicting imaginary time-bound future extraction, pinning these quantities down with presumptive prices, and then discounting these values at some arbitrary discount rate. To integrate such artificial stock values into the flow accounts does serious damage to the latter which, for macroeconomics purposes, are vastly more important than the stock values, which are hardly ever used by economists. It is as if love of a complicated method trumped common sense and discounted the analytical needs of the macroeconomic users. On the other hand, to its credit, the Report acknowledges the fact that various methods used for stock valuation yield widely different estimates (p. 95). It acknowledged the uncomfortable fact that 'in some cases, the net change in the value of reserves (additions minus depletions) even has a different sign under different valuation techniques'. And yet this valid observation has not deterred the authors from advocating their indefensible approach. It should be stressed here that these were not different techniques, but a single technique that differs only in differing assumptions about future prices and discount rates. This finding alone (i.e. the acknowledged variability of the results obtained) should have alerted the authors of *Nature's Numbers* to the fact that subordinating the flow estimates (including GDP, GNP and their net variants) to a dubious method of stock valuation might not be a wise approach. Had the national income experts on the panel been better versed in economic theory, or had all members perhaps paid more attention to the relevant literature, they might have recalled Alfred Marshall's advice (1920 [1947], p. 80): 'The money income, or inflow, of wealth gives a measure of a nation's prosperity, which, untrustworthy as it is, is yet in some respects better than that afforded by the money value of its stock of wealth.' After all the principal product of the national accounts is national income (or product), not the national wealth.

Despite the high quality of the economic expertise of many members of the Panel little doubt is expressed in this work over integrating such unreliable stock estimates in the flow accounts. To repeat, sight was lost of the fact that stock valuation is unnecessary, and that the valuation of flows is readily provided by the market when the relevant resources come into the orbit of the national accounts. If a value has to be put on the stocks all that is needed is to multiply the physical stock available by any one day's price in the knowledge that the morrow is bound to bring a different price. It should be added that repeated reference in *Nature's Numbers* to Hotelling's model of rising future prices is inappropriate. From the perspective of an individual nation (for which the *national* accounts are obviously being estimated), rising future prices will not be relevant if their natural resource had run out in the interim. Economists may indulge in similar speculative exercises, treating resources in different parts of the world as if they were operated (à la Hotelling) by one owner, but there is no justification for damaging the flow accounts of individual countries by dragging in speculation about rising future values. All told, however, *Nature's Numbers* remains useful in providing a brief history of environmental accounting, with some references to applications that may or may not all be exemplary models to be followed.

It is worth noting that neither the 'user cost' nor 'El Serafy' appears in the index of *Nature's Numbers*, but references to both abound in the text. The 'El Serafy method' appears on p. 222 (Appendix D, Glossary) correctly described, and my formula for estimating the user cost is given on p. 101. On this latter page, it is stated that the 'discussion thus far' aimed to connect the value of depletion with the value of reserves so that natural resource stocks are treated similarly to produced capital, adding as an aside:

> There are yet other approaches that take a 'sustainability' perspective. El Serafy (1989) has devised an alternative approach to adjusting NDP [sic] to account for mineral depletion. As currently measured, NDP is temporarily augmented [sic] during mineral extraction. El Serafy would convert the temporary revenue stream from mineral extraction into the equivalent infinite income stream, likening the latter stream to permanent income from the mineral asset. He thus advocates deducting an amount from the conventionally measured NDP during the extraction period to create an adjusted sustainable NDP.

The inaccuracies in the above quotation are obvious and are examined below, but at least *Nature's Numbers* recognized that 'alternative' ways for greening the accounts existed. In a footnote, it shows my user-cost formula, keeping my own notations before curiously asserting (pp. 101–102):

It may be noted that the production of satellite accounts is intended to address just this type of concern, since those who prefer El Serafy's concept of sustainability to other accounting conventions can make their own adjustments to national output using the information contained in satellite accounts.

It is as if this panel of experts were unsure about their 'concept of sustainability', leaving the matter to researchers' preference. Economists familiar with the user-cost method will spot the inaccuracies made by this 'expert' group that was expected to guide the development of green accounting. Specifically five points should be stressed:

1. Quite correctly there is no mention of *welfare* being the objective of national accounting, and no assertion that my method is welfare-oriented as had previously been asserted by Carson so that *Nature's Numbers* remains focused correctly on the estimation of product or income. This certainly is an improvement on the view previously propagated by the *Survey of Current Business* (1994a, note 4, p. 54) namely that 'El Serafy's approach [is] a welfare-oriented measure';

2. Sustainability cannot be divorced from income estimation; income must be sustainable by definition for it to qualify as income, but as earlier stated it is only a limited sustainability from one account period to the next;

3. *Nature's Numbers* repeatedly misses the point that my adjustment to the accounts needs to be done at the gross- and not the net-product estimation stage, and its repeated references to NDP attributed to my approach are mistaken;

4. Note also the inaccurate statement that my method *converts* revenue into income since the method explicitly identifies income as a component within the revenue – a component that has to be perpetuated to be faithful to the concept of income;

5. The choice of adjustment method should not be left to researchers' preference as proposed in the last passage quoted (pp. 101–102). The Panel should have shown the way to proceed;

6. It is unlikely unless specifically advised that the satellite accounts would include the parameters needed for estimating the user cost such as life expectancy of the resource or the presumed yield on the new investments.

Yet there is even more to say. *Nature's Numbers* shows on p. 140, 'Table 4-4' a 'Summary of forest accounting studies' already made, attributed to Vincent and Hartwick (1997). The table has four columns signifying alternative methods applied, and are labeled successively 'Price', 'El Serafy',

'NPV' and 'Other'. With reference to two studies labeled Malaysia and Malaysia II (the first by Vincent et al. (1993) and the second by Vincent (1997) and Vincent et al. (1997)), the claim is made that Vincent had 'generalized' El Serafy's approach using an 'elasticity of marginal cost' that is less than infinity. The notion that the user-cost method is based on the assumption of perfect substitutability (in other words an infinite elasticity of substitution) between natural resources and human made capital is false as I argue in section X of this chapter, and shall be detailing later. Both authors (Vincent and Hartwick) are formidable analysts, neither of whom is unfamiliar with my work, so that in this instance Vincent's so-called 'generalization' is unexpected. A 'strong sustainability' stance in this case seems to have got the upper hand over Vincent's usually sound judgment. For he must realize that my method is to be applied piecemeal and *ex post*, focusing on the behavior of *individual* resource owners who had already liquidated part of their natural wealth and it is by no means a recipe for future large scale asset liquidation. Accountants, in fact, do not urge any future action, not least the categorical destruction of natural resources, and it would be foolish on my part to advocate the action said to be implicit in my method. Quite early on, Herman Daly, an unquestioned environmentalist, did not see any urging to liquidate natural resources in my approach and generously described my user-cost formula as 'elegant and parsimonious', in the sense that it requires few data for its estimation.[8] Daly was later to propose that instead of investing the user-cost equivalent in just any income-yielding asset, the investment should be made specifically to create a substitute for the very natural resource being depleted. This is a twist that would adjust the method's focus on *ex post* income estimation and orient it towards a normative advocacy for natural resource conservation. In other words it would 'upgrade' my weak sustainability approach to a stronger one – an upgrading that would doubtless garner the approval of many environmentalists. It would, of course, be serendipitous were the new investments capable of generating the indicated non-declining level of income I am seeking. But if the stocks of natural resources are indeed declining, this would be a wise course of action.[9] What is interesting here, however, is that the authors of *Nature's Numbers*, who were considering alternative methods for greening the accounts, had remained silent on this point. They appeared to swallow the accusation that my approach implied a perfect substitutability between natural and produced assets, and further muddying their judgment by leaving the choice of the account-greening method to the preference of the analyst.

All told, consideration of the user-cost method appears in this source almost as an afterthought, being confined to a brief section named

'Alternative Methodologies' (pp. 99–102). Two methods are given serious attention: one is labeled 'net present value' and the other 'current rent method'. The former is based on a prior valuation of stocks using the questionable method described above before deriving the flow accounts from their changes. That such a tortuous exercise is not needed is never contemplated, but creates unnecessary struggles over reconciliation due to new discoveries, and reassessment of reserves in both quantity and value (pp. 90–100). The other method, named the 'current rent method', is split into I and II alternatives which are both 'net present value' (NVP) methods, but are based on the theoretical assumptions of the Hotelling model, taking for granted that growing scarcity would cause the price to rise. Both the NVP method and the Hotelling-based model as applied here are built around estimates of stocks and returns on capital in order to disentangle the resource's contribution to output, which could simply have been derived from estimates of the user cost.

At the risk of repetition it should be stressed that invoking the name of Hotelling in the present context makes little sense and shows an imperfect grasp of the context in which the Hotelling model was elaborated and might be applied. This model, besides being based on ideal conditions of perfect foresight and other simplifying assumptions, refers to a particular setting. The setting is one where extraction reduces the stock and pushes the prices upward in reflection of a higher degree of scarcity. Here, however, we are dealing with a different reality. The focus is on *national* accounting, that is estimating income for one nation at a time. The nation is only a part of the international setting. It possesses a limited quantity of natural endowment, which typically is small relative to the overall global supply. *Ceteris paribus*, as this small national stock diminishes due to extraction, world price cannot be expected to rise à la Hotelling if the aggregate global availability is not diminishing. It is no use to a small country which is running out of its mineral stock, say in five or ten years, to be told that the Hotelling model guarantees elevated prices due to greater scarcity. Global stocks may not be diminishing, or not diminishing significantly, or indeed they could be rising because of new discoveries elsewhere or due to technological advances. The heightened Hotelling scarcity would not therefore happen, and rising prices would not occur. This lack of comprehension of the very context where analytical tools should be used and where they should not be used is astonishing given the composition of the panel and the eminence of some of the pre-publication experts who are said to have vetted the draft.

IV

THE CURIOUS CASE OF THE US BUREAU OF ECONOMIC ANALYSIS

Nature's Numbers was conceived ostensibly to guide BEA in respect of methods covering environmental concerns in the national accounts. But the intimate relations between the Bureau and the *Nature's Numbers* panel precluded a fresh outlook, and in the event reinforced BEA's approaches. Many of the assertions about the user cost in *Nature's Numbers* are lifted almost verbatim from the *Survey of Current Business*. BEA's first contribution to public discussion of the topic appeared in 1994 in two articles in a special issue of the *Survey of Current Business*.[10] A full review of these articles is not attempted here as I focus on what is said about the El Serafy method.

The first article gave a brief history of the green accounting initiative, including collaboration by UNEP and the World Bank in international workshops during the period 1983–86 (see Ahmad et al., 1989), with a reference to the World Commission on Environment and Development's report, *Our Common Future* (1987). The latter had emphasized 'sustainability' as a necessary aspect of development. Realization that the SNA should be amended had set in motion a process in which BEA was closely involved. As stated in Chapter 2 above, an Inter-Secretariat Working Group of five international organizations (Commission of European Communities, International Monetary Fund, Organisation for Economic Co-operation and Development, United Nations and World Bank) was formed to develop a new SNA that would cover the green accounting initiative. Various entities and persons cooperated in that effort before the 1993 SNA was finalized and issued in the name of the five agencies.[11] It was in the pages of SNA 1933 that the satellite accounts for the environment emerged, and BEA wished to explain what these new accounts were, and to disclose its future plans for compiling them for the United States.[12] This BEA article ('Integrated economic and environmental satellite accounts', BEA, 1994b) states on p. 34 that BEA's work on satellite accounts had been given added impetus when in 1993 President Clinton, as part of his 21 April Earth Day address, 'gave high priority to the development of "green GDP measures"' [sic] that 'would incorporate changes in the natural environment into the calculation of national income and wealth'. The following sentence was added: 'At that time, BEA committed to producing initial estimates of natural resource depletion within a year.' But it is the follow-up article, 'Accounting for mineral resources: issues and BEA's initial estimates', pp. 50–72 in the same issue of *Survey of Current Business*, that is more revealing. Ignoring the Presidential direction, to make the adjustment for depletion in the *gross* product, GDP, BEA argued around the target of the re-estimation. On p. 52, note 3, it mentions a 'debate' on whether to view depletion as a reduction in 'the highly visible GDP measure, rather than in the less well known NDP', thus giving the false impression that 'visibility' was a deciding factor for the choice of method. On p. 54, the El Serafy method appears for the first time under 'alternative methods of valuing mineral resources' described as a method that was not used by BEA. A justification for this exclusion is included in note 4 on the same page. This reads:

> Among the methods that have not been used is one suggested by Salah El Serafy. The approach essentially calculates the amount that must be invested in a 'sinking fund' to create an income stream sufficient to replace that produced by the natural resource. The approach although frequently mentioned in the resource accounting literature, is not included largely because it is inconsistent with the concepts embodied in traditional national accounts and the IEEA's. In traditional national accounts, the value of an asset is determined by its market price, or proxy thereof. El Serafy's approach, a welfare-oriented measure [sic], is not intended to estimate the market value of the mineral resource.

Unable to fit my method into the grandiose scheme of integrated stocks and flows covering the period 1947–91, BEA resorted to spurious pretexts for not using the user-cost method. The method was decidedly not aimed at valuing stocks, and anyway it could not possibly lead to any stock valuation, which was at the heart of BEA's scheme to derive the flow accounts from stock changes. The claim that it was welfare-oriented was especially false. Heroically, however, BEA managed to produce 18 pages of tables showing calculated values under five columns: (1) Opening stock, (2) Additions, (3) Depletion, (4) Revaluation adjustment, and finally (5) Closing stock (1 + 2 less 3 + 4) – all this applied to oil, gas, coal and 'all metals'. The labor that must have gone into these calculations was evidently colossal, yet in my view unnecessary and misleading, and could have been more informative and reliable if it had been done with *physical* quantities.

A few years later, the BEA's *Survey of Current Business* of February 2000 contained another article entitled, 'Accounting for subsoil mineral resources' (pp. 1–35) which reproduced parts of *Nature's Numbers* and praised its report as having been produced by:

> A blue-ribbon panel of the National Academy of Sciences' National Research Council [that had] completed a congressional mandated review of the work that the Bureau of Economic Analysis (BEA) had published on integrated economic and environmental accounts. The panel's final report commended BEA for its initial work in producing a set of sound and objective prototype accounts. (p. 1)

This congratulatory pat-on-the-back speaks volumes. Considering *Nature's Numbers* and BEA's articles together it does not take much ingenuity to see that both works came from the same source, and the former's endorsement of BEA's views and BEA's commendation of *Nature's Numbers* carry little scholarly conviction. Digging further back BEA appears to have swallowed whole the Repetto (1989) approach for Indonesia, which I criticized in El Serafy (1993), actually proposing revised estimates for the same Indonesia study. This work appears as a later chapter in this book.

There is yet more to say about BEA's work in this area as a later issue of the *Survey of Current Business* (2000, pp. 26–51). A table on p. 43 shows a 'Summary of forest accounting studies'. This is the same table mentioned in section III above in reference to Vincent and Hartwick in *Nature's Numbers*, but now with an explicit reference to forestry. A considerable number of studies were listed together with their valuation methods. The information given is somewhat hesitant as seven query signs appear in the body of the table, but what is striking is that it mentions Sadoff's work on Thailand (1993, 1995)[13] curiously asserting that Sadoff's valuation was made only with the 'net price' method, the very method BEA favors. Contrary to this assertion Sadoff (1993) had compared the method with the user-cost method and judged the latter superior to its alternative, which I had named the 'depreciation method'. Sadoff concluded in her dissertation, p. 187:

> On a theoretical level, the user cost approach appears the more defensible. The modification of national income accounts following the user cost approach would bring the System more closely in line with the proper economic definitions of production and capital consumption. It would separate the cost of environmental disinvestment from value-added and income. The depreciation methodology would not. Furthermore, in the context of renewable resources, the user cost approach would capture more of the externalities associated with resource exploitation by incorporating the cost of resource restoration, rather than the current market value of the commercial commodities removed.

Whether it was bias or poor scholarship that influenced BEA's preference for what I consider a flawed approach is difficult for me to determine.

V

A DOCTORAL DISSERTATION

John Kellenberg (1996) undertook a comparison of the two methods for greening the accounts: the user-cost method and the 'net price' method in a 1995 doctoral dissertation at Johns Hopkins University. As far as I can make out, he shows no fundamental understanding of the differences between the two approaches, but mechanically compares the adjustment results showing a preference for the net price method. He notes that by using user cost, the disinvestment associated with extracting Ecuadorian oil in the period 1971–90 amounted to $16.7 billion in constant 1987 US dollars or 8.9 per cent of GDP. But using the net price method, the comparable magnitude was $7.8 billion or 4.3 per cent of GDP. He pays little attention to the important feature of the latter method in adding resource discoveries to income. His criticism of the user–cost approach is a repetition of the BEA analysis as covered earlier, even using the same phrases, claiming that the 'User Cost method is discounted by its critics as inconsistent with the concepts embodied in the SNA. In the SNA the value of an asset is determined by its market price, or proxy thereof'. He obviously does not realize that my method avoids putting a value on the asset itself but only on that fraction that is extracted and actually enters the market and valued at market prices. Adding his own criticism he quotes a 1991 joint study by UNDP and the World Bank on Ecuador's public sector to the effect that reserve estimates are of 'dubious quality'. He advances this as an argument against the user-cost method not realizing that the alternative method uses also the same reserve figures. The difference is that the user-cost method focuses on changes occurring in the same reserves and not the absolute stock.

Kellenberg does not appreciate the fact that if a 10 per cent discount rate rather than a 5 per cent rate is used a different user-cost estimate would be indicated. He calls such a difference a 'fluctuation'. While he records the favorable reactions to the user-cost method of 'individuals in the Central Bank in Ecuador, the Ministry of Finance as well as other government ministries' preferring it to its alternative, he remains adamant against their judgment. The contrast between this author's sloppiness and Sadoff's careful work, already mentioned, is quite remarkable.

VI

A CRITIC FROM CHILE

Andrés Goméz-Lobo of the University of Chile decided in 2001 that 'the user cost approach is incorrect and misleading'. This he highlights in the abstract of his disapproving paper. I dwell on this paper because it is a curious combination of mathematical dexterity and economic muddle. It mentions approvingly the 'current value Hamiltonian', which Weitzman

(1976) identified with NNP. Goméz-Lobo's rents are 'optimal' and variously called Hotelling, Hartwick or 'total' rents. He designated my method as having been proposed for a 'small open economy' – a designation that is roughly right, but not quite water-tight (Goméz-Lobo, 2001). His approach is interesting in that he is aware of problems facing a closed economy with significant natural reserves that may be liquidated on a domestically large scale. Clearly, unless investment outlets are sought abroad, the scale of depletion and the profitability of the new investments would be interdependent – an interdependence to which I myself have drawn attention. The economy involved has obviously to be open in order to allow for the investments to be made in foreign economies. Indeed I had once suggested that, in the light of recorded instances of politically motivated financial asset-freezing or outright confiscation by foreign host countries, the safest course for an oil exporter with a balance of payments surplus might be to leave the oil in the ground to appreciate à la Hotelling as the resource scarcity increases. Goméz-Lobo is also cognizant of the fact that while my method is rooted in adjusting the *domestic* product, future earnings accruing abroad to user-cost-financed investments would affect the *national* product – a problem I had not considered because irrelevant, and belongs to future account periods. So he keeps both GDP and GNP in play while failing to realize the temporal incongruity of his period analysis. Consider for instance the following (p. 205):

> In a small open economy, to arrive at a sustainable NNP figure changes in foreign assets must also be accounted for. Once this is done, the main criticism of El Serafy (1989) to the depreciation method – that resource rich countries would not have a consumption advantage over resource poor countries – can be shown to be wrong. In addition, the user cost approach is an ad-hoc method that is not grounded on an optimal resource extraction model. For these reasons it is recommended that only the depreciation method be used in resource accounting methodologies.

Notice that Goméz-Lobo's benchmark for sustainability is NNP not NDP or GDP – with which I have no real quarrel. This is because once GDP has been adjusted downward by the equivalent of the user cost as my method suggests NNP and NDP would adjust by the same amount – other things being equal, of course. The fact that he follows in time the accrual of foreign income is a step I had not taken for I considered it irrelevant for estimating *current* income. Income from investments abroad would only materialize after a lag and would not affect GDP either current or future. Future *national* income will have to wait its turn to be accounted for when the time comes. Mine is admittedly a year-in-year-out approach to which his appellation of ad hoc does not give offense. Needless to say that the income advantage which resource-rich countries do have over the less fortunate nations would be made to vanish with a strong sustainability adjustment that eliminates the resource own value added from the adjusted accounts. But this is by no means a central argument of mine as he seems to assert, and the so-called 'advantage', apart from being observable by the naked eye without any accounting, is maintained through the greened accounts only if the weak sustainability approach of the user cost is adopted. The additional charge that my method 'is not grounded on an optimal resource extraction model' is evidently true. But far from this being a weakness it has been recognized as a distinct merit. For here we are dealing with actual activities not theoretical ones. Income created through resource extraction (which the accountants try to capture in the national accounts) usually follows no theoretical models. The world is much too complex for that. Goméz-Lobo is puzzled why such a 'faulted method' should be considered on par with other alternatives, and fulminates against the alleged gullibility of researchers who have used the user-cost approach for methodological comparisons. His admonition (p. 205) extends to van Tongeren et al. (1993) for the case study of Mexico; Bartelmus et al. (1993) for Papua New Guinea; and Young (1992) for Brazil. Persevering with his period-confusion, Goméz-Lobo writes (p. 209): 'To derive NNP, Hotelling resource rents have to be deducted from GDP, but, in addition, the interest earned on the foreign asset stock has to be deducted.' As mentioned before, that interest will probably belong to another period, and in any case does not affect the domestic product, which is the basic magnitude to be adjusted.

VII

AN AUSTRALIAN PERSPECTIVE

Michael Harris and Ian Fraser of La Trobe University considered the topic in a November 2001 study entitled 'Natural resource accounting in theory and practice: a critical assessment'. In this work the authors take the reader on a wild goose chase where they cover a wide range of issues including definition of income at various hands, the very purpose of natural resource accounting, the optimum models behind the Hamiltonian, with recurrent references to Solow, Hartwick, Weitzman, Mäler and others. No precise crystallization emerges of the position of the authors, who appear to sit on the methodological fence, save when they diffidently offer views uttered by a putative 'devil's advocate' – a phrase they use repeatedly. For adjustment, Harris and Fraser identify two well differentiated methods: (1) the net price method associated as explained above with strong sustainability typified by the pioneering, yet in my view flawed work of Repetto and Associates on Indonesia; and (2) the user-cost method which they name the 'El Serafy method' which is linked to weak sustainability.[14] They describe the former rather grandly as 'derived from a dynamic optimization model where efficient resource pricing (i.e. Hotelling's Rule) is assumed'. Here they cite as a source Repetto (1988). Clearly neither 'efficient resource pricing' nor a future Hotelling vision is relevant to national accounting. Uncritically following Repetto, they consider depletion to be estimated at the stage of reckoning the *net* product and treat it similarly to depreciation of fixed capital, which they present as equal to:

$$NP = (P - MC)Q \qquad (10.1)$$

where NP is the 'net price', $(P - MC)$ price minus marginal cost, and Q is the quantity extracted, adding irrelevantly and obviously wrongly that 'NP equates to the Hotelling rent accruing to the owner of the resource, such that the expected rate of growth of the unit rent would be equal to the discount rate'. Marginal cost as used here, whether or not it covers the mineral itself, is not usually known in practice, a fact that is later acknowledged without lessening the authors' enthusiasm for their unsatisfactory method. Their reference to Hotelling here is pretentious and otiose since the subject is obviously *ex post* accounting. They do not hesitate, however, to cite Young and da Motta (1995) who, however, showed a clear preference for the El Serafy method, stating (that is, Young and da Motta) that 'the erratic results obtained from the net price approach are the consequence of its main conceptual flaw: i.e. both computed output and income depend on variations in reserves' (p. 125) – a judgment that goes to the very heart of the matter. Young and da Motta also perceived correctly (as I had emphasized; El Serafy, 1989) that the 'net price' method where the entirety of the stock decline is removed from income estimation (albeit at the net product stage) may be regarded as a special case of the user-cost method: that is on the assumption that the resource was infinite in size or the interest rate used for the discounting was zero. It is regrettable that the panel that produced *Nature's Numbers* had not apprized itself of the available literature including works of serious scholars such as Young and da Motta who came later, but had researched the topic thoroughly.

Harris and Fraser begrudgingly cite Liu's support of the El Serafy method in two studies (1996, 1998). However, as if unable to make up their minds, Harris and Fraser (2001) move on to discuss the El Serafy method giving the formula for the user-cost correctly using my original notations:

$$R - X = R / (1 + r)^{n+1}$$

Yet they remain unhappy with this method on a number of pretexts. Citing others' misgivings they claim that

> the treatment of rent expectations is unrealistic. Both unit rents and extraction levels are assumed to remain fixed. This implies that UC estimates will be constant whilst prices and extraction costs vary over time. (p. 27)

More tellingly, however, on the same page Harris and Fraser introduce a red herring, which they pick up from another critic and feebly attempt to rebut it in a confused statement:

> the UC method confuses an 'income' measure with a 'product' measure . . . By insisting that 'user cost' does not measure 'capital consumption', and that therefore gross rather than net product should be modified, El Serafy's method violates the production/income accounting identity. A devil's advocate position might be that unmodified GDP should be computed according to the usual accounting restrictions, and GDP as modified by UC calculations should be presented as a more meaningful measure of sustainable income.

But the whole purpose of my method is to show that GDP as conventionally estimated (which treats as income the entire surplus gained from extraction) is wrong and unsustainable, and for the authors to wish to preserve it while incongruously accepting 'GDP as adjusted by UC calculations . . . as a more meaningful measure of sustainable income' does not make sense. There is, of course, no confusion on my part as income and product are one and the same, just as viewed by Keynes, Kuznets, Hicks, Meade and Stone. My argument that the gross product itself should be adjusted downwards by the user cost simply arises from the fact that depletion represents a using-up of stocks unlike fixed capital depreciation, which is relatively limited and follows largely predictable write-off patterns, and thus correctly affects only the net product.

There is also much equivocation in Harris and Fraser's (2001) paper over whether income is a welfare indicator or a 'sustainability device' for estimating the product. True, there is confusion in the literature over this, and hence disagreement over adjustment methods. But the user-cost approach is unambiguous on this score. It is an *ex post* device meant to correct output estimation taken to be synonymous with income with emphasis on the accountant's quest for sustainability, i.e. from one accounting period to the next. Hicks in *Value and Capital* had warned that a precise definition of income in this context is not appropriate: 'a rougher definition is in fact better'.[15] The authors, however, are in one respect right when they state at the very end of their paper that the satellite account system initiated in 1993 under the System of Integrated Environmental and Economic Accounts (SEEA), while it will encourage the collection of data, will not dispel the danger that the data will not be helpful for a clear policy or resource management purpose.

VIII

FROM NORWAY: AAHEIM AND NYBORG

In the *Review of Income and Wealth*, Asbjørn Aaheim and Karine Nyborg (1995) of Norway questioned whether a corrected national income measure would provide useful information for policy makers. From their text it seems that they overlook *economic* policy, limiting their focus to *environmental* policy. In their view a green national product would be difficult to interpret and may even give the impression that stricter environmental policy may not be needed. 'Nor does it indicate', they continue, 'the hypothetical state of the economy after a change in environmental efforts'. Nevertheless, while still believing that environmental and economic policy and analysis are important, they think that the corrected (greened) numbers 'might easily give policy-makers the impression that environmental problems are less *urgent* than they actually are' (p. 70; italics in the original). How this impression could be created is never explained and remains a mystery since that presumption is not argued but is repeatedly asserted: 'When it comes to measuring *observed* environmental changes, this is clearly an accounting task. Valuing such changes *in monetary terms* on a macro level might, however, be more confusing than illuminating' (*loc. cit.*; italics in the original).

Glossing over the fact that the user-cost method was advanced as a first step to be widened in application later when estimation techniques have matured, and crucially that it picks its values from established market transactions and physical changes, the method clearly should escape their strictures. But they get something right where other critics are mistaken, for they realize that the magnitude to be adjusted is the *gross* product not the net product which would not need correction once the user-cost had been deducted from the gross estimates.

Despite their obvious expertise they make fundamental mistakes. Referring to the user cost, their footnote 10, p. 63 reads as follows:

Some of the assumptions actually seem incompatible [sic]. The derivation of the formula relies on constant prices and extraction levels, but at some points he [El Serafy] also seems to assume producer behaviour according to the Hotelling rule. If prices were expected to be constant and the interest rates were positive, the optimal producer behaviour would be to extract all of the resource at once.

To say the least, this statement abounds with confusion. At the risk of repetition it must be clear by now that the derivation of the El Serafy formula does not rely on constant prices. The method is a year-by-year instrument, taking prices from actual transactions during the year of extraction. Further, it does not assume or predict future prices. In fact the method is built on physical quantities throughout, namely the estimated reserve stock and the rate of current extraction. Dividing the stock by annual extraction gives life expectancy in years, a quantity that is to be re-estimated every year. In line with established practice current market prices are brought in for valuing the amount extracted, and the interest rate employed reflects the yield to be expected from investing the equivalent of the user cost. The value of reserve stocks may be estimated (which the user-cost method neither attempts nor recommends) but this should have no bearing on the flows, which are transacted. There is no ambiguity about prices. Accounting is done *ex post* and has nothing to do with future prices or quantities, and since it is done periodically all the quantities involved are subject to change from one period to the next.

The interest rate used for estimating the user cost is certainly changeable. New discoveries or downward reassessment of reserves are taken in the method's stride by changing the reserve to extraction ratio year in, year out, and extraction itself may vary in any one year from 0 to 100 per cent of the remaining stock depending on managerial and other decisions which fall outside the accountant's responsibilities. Hotelling is certainly relevant in that he treated natural resource stocks as assets to be managed rationally – just like any other asset should be managed – whether a financial asset, a piece of real estate or a machine. If the owner predicts rising future prices the resource may be kept unexploited in the current year in expectation of future gain, and if prices are foreseen to fall, then good management would maximize extraction in the current period to take advantage of the current boom. And if interest on investing the user cost is expected to be negative then there is no point in future investment, and in fact the formula itself would indicate a zero level of user cost in that case so that the current year's revenue is all income. Aaheim and Nyborg's (1995) claim that the method suffers from internal incompatibility turns out to be a mirage. Their misunderstanding is palpable. The only constant in the user-cost method is the level of expected future returns assumed within the formula simply to facilitate the calculations. And the last sentence in the quotation above is a total misapprehension: the method does not predict future prices and does not urge managerial behavior whether optimal or otherwise in respect of extraction.

IX

HAMILTON AND RUTA

In a paper entitled, 'Wealth accounting, exhaustible resources and social welfare' Kirk Hamilton and Giovanni Ruta (2009) focus on wealth and welfare. Much of the article is devoted to supporting the notion that 'genuine saving', that is traditional saving adjusted downward by the decline in 'wealth', is the correct indicator of welfare changes.[16] Their approach is a strong sustainability one which has been criticized particularly by Neumayer (2000). Hamilton and Ruta's reference to my work is flattering, going so far as stating that my 1989 paper was 'one of the primary papers in the literature on green national accounting' (p. 54) and further on p. 58 they refer to the 'dominant role of the El Serafy (1989) approach in the resource accounting literature'. However, in parallel with other critics (p. 58) they add that the El Serafy approach requires that both unit total rents (presumably a constituent of price) and the quantity extracted are constant up to the point of extraction. They relax this imaginary constraint in one part of the paper, but restore it in a more detailed section under the heading, 'Practical wealth accounting'. I have already dealt with this constancy issue, which is taken up again in Section XII of this chapter where I discuss weak and strong sustainability. But neither welfare nor wealth had been the purpose targeted in my work. More will be said about this paper later in this chapter.

X

THIRD MEETING OF INTERNATIONAL SOCIETY FOR ECOLOGICAL ECONOMICS

A critique of a sort surfaced at the third meeting of the International Society for Ecological Economics held in Costa Rica in October 1994 (see Vartanián and Peréz, 1994, p. 214). A participant named Timothy Slaper of the American University, Washington DC, described the user-cost method as 'conceptually and empirically inadequate'.[17] The faults he alleged were (1) an imprecise definition of extraction cost; (2) overlooking characteristics of the mineral extraction industries; (3) assuming a fixed stock; and (4) the smallness of the 'fraction of the value added' attributed to extraction. On the positive side, then he expressed the view that 'El Serafy's sinking fund approach may make its greatest contribution in the emphasis it places on policies to invest natural resource rents in substitutes for exhaustible resources'. Clearly these strictures are wrong, immaterial or irrelevant, and the assumption of a fixed stock is based on a misconception. Needless to say the method does not have to define extraction costs whether adequately or not. To be noted also is the mistaken view that the entirety of the surplus realized in extraction is value added which the method specifically aimed at refuting.[18]

XI

A VIEW FROM THE PHILIPPINES

In a paper entitled 'Valuation methods of mineral resources' presented at the self-styled 'London Group' meeting in Johannesburg in 2007, Domingo and Lopez-Dee of the Philippines National Statistical Coordination Board were also critical of the user-cost method on the following grounds. After presenting the algebraic formula for the user cost 'R – X' (where R is revenue and X is income, but changing R for some reason into N), Domingo and Lopez-Dee proceeded incoherently to state that 'several assumptions are needed that are likely to bias the estimates':

> the current level of receipts is held constant during the lifetime of the resource. The rate of extraction is also held constant until the final exhaustion of the resource, thus the life expectancy of the reserve in the present year, n, is not allowed to change over time. It also assumes a constant discount rate. (p. 7)

All their fanciful faults are faulty, as previously argued, simply being based on lack of understanding. Their paper devotes an inordinate amount of space to the valuation of stocks, discussing various approaches including those proposed by the BEA with emphasis on the crucial role of the discount rate. However, the more important point, namely that for estimating the present value of stocks, the future profile of extraction has to be assumed beforehand, and pinned down in time with predicted future prices before doing the discounting, escapes the authors. Needless to say that I consider valuing stocks to be an exercise in futility, and all this projecting and discounting is unnecessary and conjectural, and, of course, bound to be subjective also since the profile of future extraction and the forecast prices will inevitably be arbitrary. As I repeatedly said, if a value must be put on stocks, then these can be multiplied by current market prices to obtain a contingent value that will change when prices change; but see Roscoe (2002), who proposes a speculative yet interesting valuation of potential deposits.

XII

VINCENT AND CASTANEDA

I have not criticized these authors earlier because Vincent has been generally supportive of my approach and has sought to apply it in a number of contexts. In a paper written for the Harvard Institute for International Development in 1997 the authors decided to follow 'the suggestion of El Serafy' (p. 7) in respect of the life expectancy of a depleting resource. This, as the reader must be familiar by now, indicates life expectancy by dividing the stock remaining at the end of each year by extraction in the year that has just ended. They refer to this suggestion as 'workable' but 'crude' as they think it biases Hotelling rent upward presumably because of the use of average rather than marginal cost. Another reason for the upward bias is that the 'quantity extracted should decline over time under an optimal extraction program'. Such a decline, in fact, hardly ever materializes in practice. And they overlook the fact that my approach is not in any way based on an optimal profile of extraction, but on actual extraction, which in all probability does not conform to any theoretical pattern. They are certainly at liberty to compare actual extraction to a theoretically assumed profile, but such a profile has no relevance to the rough and tumble world where extraction is constrained by exigencies of contractual obligations, concessionaires' political uncertainties and many other restrictions. It is actual transactions that make up the national accounts, not any theoretical pattern of activity whether optimal or not.

I have already addressed the claim attributed to Vincent under Section III on *Nature's Numbers* above, namely that since I advocate investing the equivalent of the user cost in other forms of assets, then there must be an underlying assumption that the elasticity of substitution between natural and produced assets is infinite. No such assumption, of course, is involved, but Vincent proceeded nevertheless to 'generalize' the El Serafy approach by reducing this imaginary infinite elasticity to a finite one. Using Hotelling as his standard, Vincent writes:

$$\text{Hotelling rent} = \text{Total rent } T^* (1 + \beta) / 1 + \beta (1 + i) \qquad (10.2)$$

where β is the elasticity of the marginal cost curve, *i* the discount rate, and T the number of years until resource exhaustion.

Again imagining that there is an ascertainable marginal cost curve in resource extraction, and that it has an elasticity that is stable, knowable and could be manipulated to conform to some theoretical value, seems to me a little far-fetched, and flies in the face of reality.

XIII

ANDERS HANSEN

Next to Hartwick's thorough exploration of the user-cost method (see the next chapter) Anders Chr. Hansen of Roskilde University in Denmark scrutinized my user-cost method at length and in great depth (Hansen, 2000). Hartwick's work was available to Hansen, and so evidently was that of Hotelling and Vincent. He shows mathematical dexterity combined with curiosity about alternative computing methods for assessing natural capital consumption. In addition, he pays special attention to discounting, the size of the discount rate, and whether applying logarithmic discounting would make a difference. He pronounced, quite correctly in my view, that the cost functions, which have raised much concern, have little effect on estimating the outcome. He views the so-called 'total rent' approach behind the World Resources Institute (WRI) work on Indonesia (and which is implicitly advocated in Hartwick's rule) as 'unethical' in that it denies any right in the 'rent' to the current generation. This point, of course, I had stressed in El Serafy (1989) without calling it unethical. Despite his evident scholarship, knowledge of sources and mathematical prowess, Hansen, in my view, makes a major error. Unlike Hartwick, who distinguished between the El Serafy 'approach', 'method' and 'formula' (distinctions which I had thought rather overdone at the time, but in retrospect I realize they made much sense), Hansen made no such distinction. Focusing only on the formula, Hansen repeatedly asserted that my approach was based on the double assumption of a constant level of extraction and constant future prices. He missed Hartwick's more careful scrutiny (later also appreciated by Bengt Kriström, 2002), which confirmed that the El Serafy method would give 'accurate' results for the first period:

> If one believes that because of new price information or new discoveries, firms are continually revising their extraction schedules and planning, getting first period depreciation correct may be of the most importance; if EM [El Serafy

method] estimates are found in general to estimate first period depreciation more closely in discrete time, the discrete time version of EM may be preferred. (Hartwick and Hageman, 1993, p. 224)

Three comments may be made here. First, the El Serafy method is not a method to be used by the resource owners for deciding extraction schedules but it is only an accountant's device used for estimating *ex post* income. Since the method is only an accountant's tool, one must not assume that firms necessarily follow that assumed course. Second, the accountant's time is not the continuous time preferred by mathematical economists in pursuit of optimal magnitudes, but discrete time, typically divided in years. Third, each year is a first year for the user-cost method, and if it gives accurate estimates for resource 'depreciation' in the first year it has done its job as intended.

XIV

A VOICE FROM THE PAST: IRVING FISHER

A formidable critic from the past who obviously could not have seen my work on the user cost has a criticism, which should not be concealed. I have maintained that my method is not a normative one that urges the depleting asset owners to save the user-cost equivalent and invest it in new ventures to produce the same level of income. I have maintained that it was a device, devoid of any hint of normative recommendations, and need not be acted upon in respect of actual investment. It was simply a theoretical tool for getting a grasp on the elusive estimation of income. It is amazing that this notable economist, Irving Fisher (1867–1947), seems to have anticipated my 'timidity', and pronounced my approach as 'inadequate' (Fisher, 1906, pp. 111–112): 'To reckon what one *ought* to save in order to maintain capital is not to save it, and a definition of income which depends upon an ideal reckoning instead of a real payment is to that extent inadequate.'

Whether positive or normative, however, the user-cost method indicates that part of receipts that should be put aside and invested. And it points out the magnitude that, if the owner wishes, may be sunk in a 'sinking fund' to yield future income, a procedure which several countries have actually adopted, often without having heard of my formula. All the same, clearly Fisher would be more satisfied if I had pushed my approach more aggressively into a normative direction!

XV

WEAK AND STRONG SUSTAINABILITY: AN ACCOUNTING DISTINCTION

I come back to the differentiation between weak and strong sustainability, which has appeared several times in this chapter. My purpose is to stress the fact that strong sustainability, while desirable in other settings and for other reasons, is incompatible with national accounting (see Chapter 13, where I argue my defense of weak sustainability). In the present chapter these two degrees of sustainability are considered only as adjuncts to national income estimation, and even more narrowly as a sideline to the 'misunderstandings' of the user cost. Economists who advocate reforming the accounts by deducting the user cost from GDP have been described correctly as advocates of weak sustainability. The same appellation is often applied improperly to those analysts who think that 'resource rents' (however accurately or inaccurately defined) should be invested in whole in other forms of capital. Critics have pounced on 'weak sustainability' under the impression that it implies an *injunction* by accountants for natural asset owners to liquidate their natural capital and replace it with human-made capital. In their eagerness to protect the environment critics fail to understand the true function of accountants, which is merely to account. The so-called weak sustainability of which I have been a defender is a concept I urge only for national accounting, and it is well known that accounting in the present context has only an *ex post* descriptive function. It neither commands nor advocates any particular action. In any case, not much of the environment is captured in the national accounts so to believe that reforming national accounting by whatever means would protect or harm natural resources is a belief built on illusion. The 'weak sustainability' to which I subscribe relates only to the resources already captured in the conventional accounts, or are likely in the foreseeable future ever to be brought under the umbrella of the SNA. Relevant to the present discussion is the fairly recent debate that centers on 'wealth'. Increasingly, wealth as a stock is thought to be superior to the flows of income in certain contexts. This is doubtless true when attention is focused on welfare, but wealth estimation and income estimation should be kept separate. Very rarely do accountants face the difficult task of estimating national wealth, but estimating individual and corporate wealth is much easier and done regularly at least for tax assessment purposes. If *changes* in national wealth are sought then the indicator for them would be net investment or the so-called 'genuine saving'. The direction of estimation would run from the flow accounts to the stocks, that is, from income to wealth, and not vice versa.

The criticism I levelled against Hamilton and Ruta in Section IX of the present chapter must be balanced somewhat by a positive note. Their paper usefully separated theoretical speculations about wealth and welfare from the rough estimation practices of the national accountants. In the process they opened up a helpful discussion, which could have been even more helpful, had the concepts they used been more clearly defined. The title of their paper is 'Wealth accounting, exhaustible resources and social welfare' but most of it relates to 'optimal' extraction under ideal conditions, which do not fit well with national accounting. For good reason, welfare looms large throughout their discussion of wealth. For judging welfare, the stock of wealth is obviously a more important quantity that correlates with happiness than a shorter-term income flow, which is liable to fluctuate. But some writers have found it worth their while to prove this self-evident correlation mathematically (see Asheim and Hartwick, 2011). If I understand this paper correctly the authors are saying that weak sustainability, applied through a method such as the user cost, may be appropriate for indicating a sustainable level of *income*, but not a sustained stock of *wealth*, which they would favor. In other words, depletion of natural resources reduces wealth by a larger quantity than a weak sustainability approach would indicate; and it is wealth that denotes welfare not income. I would have no quarrel at all with this position, except that wealth as a stock is almost impossible to estimate even when it is confined to human-made assets. Interpreting what the paper wants to say is, however, made difficult by imprecisely defined concepts, which are highlighted in the abstract. These include 'total resource assets', 'real wealth', 'total wealth' and 'total resource asset value'. While understandably the paper supports 'genuine saving', which people more familiar with national accounting methods have identified as equivalent to 'net investment' (El Serafy, 1992; Dasgupta, 2001), their assertion is not convincing that that quantity is indicative of wealth change without explaining how that quantity could be estimated. Paraphrasing what I think Hamilton and Ruta wish to say: for income, weak sustainability is the more appropriate estimation method, whilst for welfare it is strong sustainability which underlies wealth and welfare change, and would be the more fitting tool.

Another related issue I wish to take up involves 'substitutability'. For there is a false, albeit somewhat popular, claim that the proponents of 'weak sustainability' believe that different categories of capital (e.g. natural and produced assets) are *infinitely* substitutable for each other (cf. Dietz and Neumayer, 2006, p. 117). A starker example of this misapprehension is provided by Peter Victor in his review of the second edition of Neumayer's book, *Weak Versus Strong Sustainability* (2003) where Victor states (2005, p. 127):

Another consideration is the proper measurement of the capital stock. Proponents of WS [weak sustainability] have no problem in principal [sic] using market or shadow prices to aggregate all forms of capital to measure total capital. Since the use of prices for aggregating different components of capital assumes they are substitutable, proponents of SS [strong sustainability] eschew prices for aggregating natural capital . . .

Victor does not seem to realize that the national dividend itself (GDP or GNP) is made up in the language of Pigou (1948) of 'bicycles and beer, bread, meat, and concerts' all grouped together valued at their market prices without any suggestion they can be substitutes for one another (save in the limited sense that they compete for a consumer's income). But more surprising to me is to find Jeffery Vincent interpreting my weak sustainability as implying perfect substitutability between natural and other assets, seeking to reduce El Serafy's alleged infinite elasticity of substitution between natural and produced capital to a finite one as I mentioned in section XII above.

A point that needs emphasis is that my accounting method does not at all attempt to put a value on capital; nor does it rely on either finite or infinite substitutability between natural and produced capital. In any case substitution and substitutability as used by critics have a strange flavor since they lack reversibility. For the critics, substitutability goes only in one direction: from natural resource liquidation to human-made capital formation, and never in the reverse direction. Not much has been heard of calls to demolish roads, buildings or manufacturing equipment and create forests or sources of energy instead. So to invoke an elasticity of substitution in this context seems to me inappropriate. Sanctioning the liquidation of natural resources to finance the formation of other kinds of capital has indeed occurred, and may have even been done collaterally by institutions like the World Bank when financing dams or roads. But this cannot be associated with an accounting procedure such as the user-cost method, which was never meant to assert a normative recommendation to demolish natural assets. To me the very idea is grotesque since most economic activities are built directly or indirectly upon and around natural resources without which economic activity would not be possible. Opposition to the liquidation of natural capital seems to have crept incongruously into the green accounting debate over methods, providing the ostensible defenders of nature with a rickety soap box from which they can harangue their imagined adversaries. To my mind this was yet another artificial barrier erected wittingly or unwittingly to block the path of greening the national accounts properly. To repeat, when it comes to national accounting the so-called 'weak sustainability' is the only level of sustainability that will produce meaningful adjustments to the national accounts.

XVI

A RECAPITULATION

The negative views of the user-cost method enumerated above came from different parts of the world and were as repetitive as they were unjustified. The chapter gave a great deal of space to exposing roughly the same critical views ad nauseam for the unengaged reader. What is remarkable is that editors of journals, the peer reviewers they select, and maybe also economists who supervise doctoral dissertations are so new to the subject that they cannot discharge their responsibilities with the diligence they accord to work in more familiar areas of research. The subject is new, and accounting tends to be a specialized discipline not familiar to economists. It is indeed rare to find national accounting included in the economic curricula offered by institutions of higher education. This chapter purposely dwelt on a large sample of critical views without much reference to the many positive ones that have sustained the user-cost approach and caused it to remain in the relevant literature. But perhaps the most striking finding that came out of the careful juxtaposition of texts is the complicity of the BEA with the panel that produced *Nature's Numbers*. This emerged after piecing together various parts of the passages I cited. It is as if the *Nature's Numbers* panel was carefully selected for the purpose of endorsing the line of thinking that BEA had developed and was reluctant to change. Why should BEA adopt this line? There is a streak in its work, which pays homage to economic theory, sometimes without appreciation of the proper context where theory can be applied. An obvious case in point is the Hotelling model, which is brought in incongruously for the valuation of stocks before proceeding to derive the flow accounts from them. It is well to remember that the flow accounts are far more important than the stocks for macroeconomic analysis. The work of Young and da Motta cited in section VII forthrightly pointed to this conceptual flaw, which underlies BEA estimates, namely deriving the flows from changes in stocks.

The persistent debunking of the user-cost method, and the insistence that it is meant to alter the net not the gross product – an argument that had figured in earlier BEA work and then carried over into the supposedly independent *Nature's Numbers* – may be attributed to eagerness over preserving the historical continuity of the old estimates. Confining changes to the net product, which is not often produced in any case, would mean that the old series of GDP and GNP can be retained. Besides providing continuity, this approach saves the BEA and others from any charge of previous errors of estimation. In fact, preserving the income series continuity seems to be close to the heart of many national account estimators world-wide, whether in Central Banks or Statistical Offices, and is even to be found in professional institutions: national as well as international. To reiterate, this chapter has attempted to refute that:

1. The user cost is based on a constant profile of extraction.
2. It urges liquidation of natural capital and replacing it with other forms of capital.
3. It is a welfare-oriented method.
4. It seeks to adjust only the net product whereas it is the gross product that it targets.
5. It attempts to put a value on stocks, whereas it is based on changes in physical quantities.
6. It aims primarily at building investment funds though that possibility is not excluded.
7. It is in any way connected with welfare.
8. It indicates a slower growth rate for the economy concerned whereas the resulting growth rate may be the same, lower or higher than the one based on the conventional estimates.

This last point is illustrated graphically in Chapter 14.

Having covered a wide range of criticism in this chapter, I turn now to one critic who has made a thorough investigation of my method.

NOTES

1. The World Bank's was certainly one of those voices that argued the case for estimating so-called 'genuine savings' using a strong sustainability method. See World Bank (1997).
2. Letter from John Hartwick to the author dated 19 April 1991.
3. If total asset liquidation takes place at the end of the year the whole of the net revenue will be a user cost, and if the liquidation is at the beginning the user cost would equal (in percentage terms) the net revenue minus the interest earned during the year.
4. This was a contribution to a May 1991 conference in Austria sponsored by the International Association of Research in Income and Wealth (IARIW); the paper had in fact been titled, 'Depletable resources: fixed capital or inventories?' and the meeting was part of the preparations preceding the issuance of the 1993 SNA.
5. The accounting profession had begun before the Industrial Revolution when commerce had dominated economic activity; and the reason why inventory changes should be accounted for at the stage of estimating the gross profits (or loss) may be that buying and selling commodity stocks had been the principal source of commercial income at the time. Stocks had to be replenished continually in order to keep the business concern going, and trading in 'inventories' was therefore viewed by the accountants as the primary activity that generated gross profits or loss. Depreciation of fixed assets (such as the maritime craft that transported traded goods) was viewed as only

incidental to trading, and affected the net profits by deducting an allowance for their depreciation.

6.   Incidentally it is the preferred method advocated by Roefie Hueting, then at Netherlands Statistics, who would keep the traditionally estimated gross magnitudes unchanged while insisting that without adjustment the economy was being steered by 'the wrong compass'. He put his faith in the size of the gap that would emerge between the unadjusted gross product and the [over-]adjusted net product, viewing it as a spur for remedial environmental actions.

7.   It is interesting that in the United States, 'Beginning in 1942 depletion allowances for minerals and timber were deducted from GDP' and that these allowances were eliminated in 1947 due to the absence, it is asserted, of an entry for capital formation. See BEA (2000, p. 51).

8.   See Daly and Cobb (1989, pp. 73–74).

9.   One difficulty, however, is that a natural resource such as oil has multiple uses (fuel, paints, lubricants, textiles, etc.); so what exactly is the new product that should replace it?

10. The first article was entitled 'Integrated economic and environmental satellite accounts' (1994b, pp. 33–49); and the second, 'Accounting for mineral resources: issues and BEA's initial estimates' (1994a, pp. 50–72).

11. The same source (Nordhaus and Kokkelenberg, 1999, pp. 37 and 58), correctly in my experience, states that resort to the satellite accounts was motivated by lack of methodological consensus which prevented a fundamental change in the SNA, and that the United Nations undertook the preparation of a handbook on satellite accounts. Support for the satellite accounts was also urged by the International Association of Research in Income and Wealth which held a special conference in May 1991 (where El Serafy, 1993, was first presented) and further support came from the June 1992 Earth Summit in Rio de Janeiro whose Agenda 21 encouraged the compilation of satellite accounts for the environment. Perhaps more fundamentally, it was the 'guardians' of the old accounts who wished to protect the old series of GDP/GNP estimates against revision by insisting on labeling them 'economic' whilst the 'greened accounts' had to be denied the quality of economic, calling them 'environmental', and therefore could be excluded from the main frame.

12. As mentioned earlier, there was also a political factor in having BEA involved in the new SNA as the international reformers were anxious to build a universal system that would be adopted by the United States and thus would apply to all nations. China and Russia had already signalled their intended adherence to the new system.

13. Sadoff is not referenced in the article at all, so I could not trace the 1995 work that appears next to the 1993 source mentioned in the BEA table, but I can cite her 1993 doctoral dissertation as she had given me a copy.

14. They seem to miss the link of either method to strong and weak sustainability, which is crucial for understanding the difference between the two approaches.

15. Harris and Fraser (2001, p.171). are obviously wrong in describing the so-called 'genuine savings' approach (earlier used by Pearce and Atkinson (1992) and later by Kirk Hamilton and Rota, 2009) as a variant of 'weak sustainability': it is unquestionably oriented towards 'strong sustainability'. See below.

16. Genuine saving is defined as 'net national saving plus education expenditure, minus resource depletion, minus pollution damages' (*op. cit.,* p. 62n).

17. I looked for him at that meeting but he was nowhere to be found.

18. Slaper's name appears in the *Survey of Current Business,* 'Integrated economic and environmental satellite accounts', 1994b, p. 35 under 'Acknowledgements' where he is credited with helping BEA's director (Carol S. Carson) and deputy director (Steven Landefeld) specifically on 'mineral concepts and methods, current rent mineral estimates, and oil and gas replacement cost estimates'. Slaper is also acknowledged on p. *v* of the Nordhaus report (*Nature's Numbers*) as 'explaining the complexities of environmental accounting'.

REFERENCES

Aaheim, Asbjørn and Karine Nyborg (1995), 'On the interpretation and applicability of a "green national product"', *Review of Income and Wealth*, **41** (1), 57–71.

Ahmad, Yusuf J., Salah El Serafy and Ernst Lutz (eds) (1989), *Environmental Accounting for Sustainable Development*, A UNEP–World Bank Symposium. Washington DC: The World Bank.

Asheim, Geir B. and John M. Hartwick (2011), 'Anomalies in green national accounting', *Ecological Economics*, **70**, 2303–2307.

Bartelmus, Peter, Ernst Lutz and Stefan Schweinfest (1993), 'Integrated environmental and economic accounting: a case study for Papua New Guinea', in Ernst Lutz (ed.), *Toward Improved Accounting for the Environment*, An UNSTAT–World Bank Symposium. Washington DC: World Bank, pp. 108–143.

Bureau of Economic Analysis (BEA) (1994a), 'Accounting for mineral resources: issues and BEA initial estimates', *Survey of Current Business*, **74** (4), 50–72.

Bureau of Economic Analysis (BEA) (1994b), 'Integrated economic and environmental satellite accounts', *Survey of Current Business*, **74** (4), 33–49.

Bureau of Economic Analysis (BEA) (2000), 'Accounting for Renewable and Environmental Resources', *Survey of Current Business*, **74** (4), 26–51.

Daly, Herman E. and John Cobb, Jr (1989), *For the Common Good: Redirecting the Economy Toward Community, the Environment, and a Sustainable Future*. Boston, MA: Beacon Press.

Dasgupta, Partha (2001), 'Valuing objects and evaluating policies in imperfect economies', *Economic Journal*, **111** (471), C1–C29.

Dietz, Simon and Eric Neumayer (2006), 'A critical appraisal of genuine savings as an indicator of sustainability', in Philip Lawn (ed.), *Sustainable Development Indicators in Ecological Economics*. Cheltenham, UK and Northampton, MA: Edward Elgar, pp. 117–138.

El Serafy, Salah (1989), 'The proper calculation of income from depletable natural resources', in Yusuf J. Ahmad, Salah El Serafy and Ernst Lutz (eds.), *Environmental Accounting for Sustainable Development*, A UNEP-World Bank Symposium. Washington DC: World Bank, Chapter 3, pp. 10–18.

El Serafy, Salah (1992), 'Sustainability, income measurement and growth', in Robert Goodland, Herman E. Daly and Salah El Serafy (eds.), *Population, Technology and Lifestyle*. Washington DC: Island Press, Chapter 5, pp. 61–79.

El Serafy, Salah (1993), 'Depletable resources: fixed capital or inventories?', in Alfred Franz and Carsten Stahmer (eds.), *Approaches to Environmental Accounting*. Heidelberg, Germany: Physica-Verlag, pp. 245–258.

Fisher, Irving (1906), *The Nature of Capital and Income*. New York and London: Macmillan and Co.

Goméz-Lobo, Andrés (2001), 'Sustainable development and natural resource accounting in a small open economy: a methodological clarification', *Estudios de Economia*, **28** (2), 203–216.

Hamilton, Kirk and Giovanni Rota (2009), 'Wealth accounting, exhaustible resources and social welfare,' *Environment and Resource Economics*, **64**, 53–64.

Harris, Michael and Ian Fraser (2001), 'Natural resource accounting in theory and practice: a critical assessment', available at: http://weber.ucsd.edu/~carsonvs/papers/255.doc.

Hartwick, John (1990), 'Natural resources, national accounting and economic depreciation', *Journal of Public Economics*, **43**, 291–304.

Hartwick, John and Anja Hageman (1993), 'Economic depreciation of mineral stocks and the contribution of El Serafy', in Ernst Lutz (ed.), *Toward Improved Accounting for the Environment*, An UNSTAT–World Bank Symposium. Washington DC: World Bank, chapter 12, pp. 211–235.

Hueting, Roefie (1989), 'Correcting national income for environmental losses: toward a practical solution', in Yusuf J. Ahmad, Salah El Serafy and Ernst Lutz (eds.), *Environmental Accounting for Sustainable Development*, A UNEP-World Bank Symposium. Washington DC: World Bank, pp. 32–39.

Kellenberg, John (1996), 'Accounting for natural resources in Ecuador: contrasting methodologies, conflicting results', Environment Department Paper No. 41, World Bank Environmentally Sustainable Development, The World Bank, Washington DC.

Kriström, Bengt (2001), 'Harold Hotelling (1925) on Depreciation' in Karl-Goran Mäler, Partha Dasgupta and Karl-Gustaf Lofgren, *Economic Theory for the Environment, Essays in Honour of Karl-Goran Maler*, Edward Elgar, Cheltenham, UK and Northampton, MA, USA.

Liu, X. (1996), 'Adjusted coal accounts in China', *Resources Policy*, **22**, 173–181.

Liu, X. (1998), 'Adjusting forest accounts in China', *Ecological Economics*, **27** (3), 283–298.

Neumayer, Eric (2000), 'Resource accounting in measures of unsustainability: challenging the World Bank's conclusions', *Environmental and Resource Economics*, **15**, 257–278.

Neumayer, Eric (2003), *Weak Versus Strong Sustainability*. Cheltenham, UK and Northampton, MA: Edward Elgar.

Nordhaus, William D. and Edward D.C. Kokkelenberg (eds.) (1999), *Nature's Numbers: Expanding the National Economic Accounts to include the Environment*. Washington DC: National Academy Press.

Pearce, David and Giles Atkinson (1992), 'Are national economies sustainable? Measuring sustainable development', Working Paper GEC 92-11, Centre for Social and Economic Research on the Global Environment, University College London and University of East Anglia, Norwich, UK.

Pigou, Arthur Cecil (1948), *Income: An Introduction to Economics*. London: Macmillan and Co., Chapter IV.

Repetto, Robert and Associates (1989), 'Wasting assets: natural resources in the national income accounts', World Resources Institute, Washington DC, June.

Roscoe, William E. (2002), 'Valuation of mineral exploration properties using the cost approach', available at:
http://unstats.un.org/unsd/envaccounting/londongroup/meeting11/LG11_14a.pdf.

Sadoff, Claudia Winkelman (1993), 'Natural resource accounting: a case study of Thailand's forest management', PhD thesis, University of California at Berkeley.

United Nations Statistics Division, Department for Economic and Social Information and Policy Analysis (UNSD) (1993), *Integrated Environmental and Economic Accounting (Interim Version), Studies in Methods*, Handbook of National Accounting, Series F, No. 61. New York: United Nations.

United Nations (2000), *Handbook on National Accounting, Integrated Environmental and Economic Accounting: An Operational Manual. Studies in*

Methods, Handbook of National Accounting, Series F, No. 78. New York: United Nations.

van Tongeren, Jan, Stefan Schweinfest, Ernst Lutz, Maria Gomez Luna and Guillen Martin (1993), 'Integrated environmental and economic accounting: a case study for Mexico', in Ernst Lutz (ed.), *Toward Improved Accounting for the Environment*, An UNSTAT–World Bank Symposium. Washington DC: World Bank, Chapter 6, pp. 85–143.

Vartanián, Daniel and Ana Cecilia Peréz (eds) (1994), 'Down to earth: practical applications of ecological economics', Third Biennial Meeting of The International Society for Ecological Economics, Final Program and Abstracts.

Victor, Peter A. (1991), 'Indicators of sustainable development: some lessons from capital theory', *Ecological Economics*, **4**, 191–213.

Victor, Peter A. (2005), 'Review of Neumayer's weak versus strong sustainability', *Ecological Economics*, **52** (1), 127–128.

Victor, Peter A., Edward Hanna and Atif Kubursi (1994), 'How strong is weak sustainability?', in *Models of Sustainable Development: Exclusive or Complementary Approaches to Sustainability*, Vol. I, International Symposium organized by Université Panthéon-Sorbonne, 16–18 March, Paris, pp. 93–114.

Vincent, Jeffrey and Beatriz Castaneda (1997), 'Economic depreciation of natural resources in Asia and implications for net savings and long-run consumption', Development Discussion Paper No. 614, Harvard Institute for international Development, Cambridge, MA.

Vincent, Jeffrey, R. and John M. Hartwick (1997), 'Accounting for the benefits of forest resources: concepts and experience', Planning and Statistics Branch, Policy and Planning Division, Forestry Department, Food and Agriculture Organisation of the United Nations (FAO), Rome.

Weitzman, Martin L., (1976), 'On the welfare significance of national product in a dynamic economy', Quarterly Journal of Economics, 90, 156–162.

Weitzman, Martin L. (1997), 'On the welfare significance of the national product in a dynamic economy', *Quarterly Journal of Economics*, **90** (1), 156–162.

World Bank (1997), *Expanding the Measure of Wealth: Indicators of Environmentally Sustainable Development*. Washington DC: World Bank.

World Commission on Environment and Development (1987), *Our Common Future* (The Brundtland Report). Oxford: Oxford University Press.

Young, Carlos Eduardo Frickmann (1992), 'Adjustment policies and the environment: a critical review of the literature', Vrije Universitat, Institute for Environment and Development, Amsterdam and London.

Young, Carlos Eduardo Frickmann and R.S. da Motta (1995), 'Measuring sustainable income from mineral extraction in Brazil', *Resources Policy*, **21**, 113–125.

11. Hartwick's contribution

PROLOGUE

The preceding chapter was devoted to misunderstandings of the user-cost method but John Hartwick merits special treatment for three reasons. First, he spent a great deal of time and effort analyzing my method and relating it to his own work, paying special attention to its antecedents; he had dug up my 1981 paper on 'Absorptive capacity, the demand for revenue and the supply of petroleum', which contained my user-cost formula. A second reason for devoting this chapter to him is that he is too important an environmental economist to share my foray against the national accountants and others named in the preceding chapter. Third, many people seem to have read his critique of my method and accepted his interpretations at face value. Some of his interpretations, I believe, distort my approach in important ways. On balance, however, the effect of his comments on my work has been positive for he brought the attention of a large audience to the user-cost method. Initially, his reactions to my ideas were affirmative, but gradually he came to temper his early enthusiasm with reservations.

HARTWICK'S 'CONTRIBUTION'

Hartwick's 'contribution' (1993) actually began in 1991 when the World Bank's Environment Department commissioned him as an outside consultant to 'appraise' the El Serafy approach as expressed principally in 'The proper calculation of income from depletable natural resources' (1989). I had no formal connection with that department at the time, and knew nothing about this assignment. It seems that the Environment Department was seeking to formulate a research program building upon the 1980s' UNEP–World Bank collaboration on green accounting. Hartwick was an excellent choice being a well-known analyst who had thought constructively about the subject and who combined theoretical insight with empirical experience. He also seemed to have a view similar to, but by no means identical with the position I had taken over re-investing the user-cost equivalent in new capital. He had advocated the re-investment of what he called 'resource rent' (my net revenue from extraction) in other assets to sustain the future prosperity of the resource owners after the resource had been exhausted. Yet, whereas Hartwick advocated the reinvestment of the *entire* revenues from exploitation, I had proposed the re-investment only of a part of these revenues. To stress a further distinction, for me his approach was a 'normative' one, expressed in clear policy terms. By contrast, mine was 'positive' in the sense that it implied no policy prescription. It aimed at *describing* in accounting terms what actually has already happened. It is important to keep in mind that neither he nor I urged resource owners to liquidate natural capital although many critics leveled that charge erroneously against both of our approaches. Critics, rather irrelevantly for accounting, would stress that natural resources and produced capital are not substitutes for each other – some even claiming that we hold the view that they were even 'perfect substitutes'. My main quarry all along has been the estimation of income from depletion, and for this purpose I refrained from making any normative policy recommendations – a stance that Irving Fisher, as I mention in the previous chapter, would have condemned as timid. I was simply interested in indicating income out of revenue, performing the role of a positive economic analyst. It should have been obvious that arguing that current income may be more properly estimated by re-investing the user-cost equivalent in alternative income-producing assets was not an injunction for liquidating natural resources. It was a theoretical *ex post* method for estimating past income that must, by definition, be sustainable. Any unsustainable magnitude that passes as income, I am fond of repeating, is simply misnamed.

By contrast Hartwick's approach was explicitly normative (see Hartwick, 1977, in particular). But it was forthright on his part to address an important *policy* issue over which I was reticent. Neither of us, however, had advocated active liquidation of natural resources to be replaced by other forms of capital, but it is important to point out that my approach significantly allowed for some current consumption out of the incoming financial flows, provided consumption remained within the limits of 'true income' as estimated with the user-cost formula. By contrast, Hartwick would disallow any consumption out of current extraction revenues until the new investments had begun to produce income. It was a little unrealistic on his part to expect indigent countries that were beginning to enjoy welcome financial inflows from their depletable natural resources to refrain from allocating any part of their revenues to consumption (and it is this particular stance that motivated Beckerman to call it 'immoral' as I mention elsewhere). Eventually, however, when Hartwick's new investments matured and began to produce income, our projections of future income would converge.

A CHRONOLOGY OF REACTIONS

The sequence of Hartwick's reactions is important. His initial commentary on my approach came out in November 1991 in the form of a World Bank Environment Department Divisional Working Paper No. 27 and was co-authored with Anja Hageman. It carried the title, 'Economic depreciation of mineral stocks and the contribution of El Serafy' – a title that was retained when republished in 1993 in *Toward Improved Accounting for the Environment* (Chapter 12, pp. 211–235). In the process the text had undergone several amendments and added references to some of my other papers.

Hartwick approached my work from a position at variance to my own. First, he rejected my insistence that GDP itself should be adjusted by removing from it the capital elements I identified as a user cost, siding safely with the conventional position of limiting the income adjustment to the *net* product. The fact that the unadjusted GDP, which is much more commonly reckoned, and used extensively in macroeconomic analysis, contains elements of capital that have no business to be there seems to be of little concern for him. Further, he came in his commentary from a position of optimality: optimal extraction and optimal 'depreciation', added to an assumption of smooth total cost functions that enable the estimation of first derivatives indicating magnitudes such as marginal costs. It does not take much ingenuity to realize that such an ideal setting is far removed from the practical conditions prevailing in extractive activities and which the accounts strive to portray. These conditions are often characterized by uncertainty, contractual constraints on flexibility, indivisibility of capital equipment – in addition to many other factors standing in the way of actual optimization. In fact, the accountants who are called upon to estimate income, or profits, from extraction are not usually interested in whether the markets are perfect or not, whether the prices they use for valuation reflect true scarcities or not, and whether the private or public business for which the accounts are being drawn is maximizing its rewards or not. They are called upon only to estimate income *ex post*, which my approach was meant to do. While Hartwick's outlook provides interesting and useful material for the economist, this material is no concern of the national accountant. Thus it should be obvious that to expect idealized behavior to set the standard for judging the validity of accounting estimates – as Hartwick tried to do in his 'Contribution'– is of limited value. Again, this is not to say that Hartwick's approach is devoid of merit, but simply that it is inappropriate for the purpose of the comparisons he made and in no way diminishes my approach. There is obviously no harm in making comparisons between estimation methods provided that one approach is not set up as *the* standard for judging its alternatives.

There is yet another important argument in Hartwick's critique that has unquestionably influenced others. This is his assumption that my method relies on a constant profile of extraction – an issue I dealt with in the previous chapter, but which may merit reiteration here. This assumption allows Hartwick to assert that my method yields 'correct estimates' *only* for the first year of its application. The fact, however, remains that every year, under my approach, *is a first year* since the method is to be applied *de novo* with new parameters every accounting period. If it gives the 'correct' income estimate for the first year, then it has achieved its purpose. This point is not just important for my user-cost formula, but also important against his claim that a constant profile of extraction in practice characterizes my whole approach. Actual extraction is handled by the resource owners, not by their accountants, and every fresh year brings in a different set of parameters, which provides inputs for the income-estimation process. Constancy of future quantities was indeed assumed, but only for devising the simplified formula I proposed, and implied no assumptions regarding prospective actions.

STOCK VALUATION AND IDEAL ASSUMPTIONS

There is yet another difference that separates us. Hartwick derives the flows of income from changes in stock values, a path that many others have also taken, whereas my approach attaches no importance whatever to the value of stocks which I hold firmly in the background. The flows of revenue and income should not be derived from stock values. For estimating income my attention focuses on *physical* quantities that are brought into relevance merely to estimate the resource's 'life expectancy' at current extraction rates. Were the stock infinite there would be no problem for income estimation as there would be no user cost and all revenue would be income – a fact that my formula would indicate. In order to reckon life expectancy the available stock is divided by current year's extraction, and both stocks and extraction in this exercise are gauged in physical terms to show the resource's horizon of sustainability. This is done in the knowledge that life expectancy in the following year is very likely to be different, depending on the remaining stock and the level of extraction in that year as well as any change occurring in the physical stock including new discoveries. Hartwick spends time and space capitalizing projected flows into stocks and unnecessarily addresses problems of stock valuation and changes therein, which simply appear to me as mere conjectures. As part of a changed stock, he has to usher in new discoveries, claiming, rather irrelevantly I believe, that my method implies instantaneous capitalization of such discoveries. Contrary to this assertion, I have absolutely no interest in knowing the *instant* the discoveries are made, and only bring them into view at year-end when income estimation is called for. To say the least, he seems to be splitting hairs over the issue of instantaneity of discovery, which in my view is immaterial and irrelevant for accounting purposes. One might even venture the thought here that Hartwick displays arguments, not for assessing the 'contribution of El Serafy', but to put his own work on show. This is not, however, without value as this display is quite useful on its own. However, to present such arguments in a discussion of how to estimate income in the framework of national accounting is obviously out of place.

As already argued Hartwick's assumption throughout of ideal conditions is very clearly incompatible with the real world of conducting business in extractive activities and provides little accounting guidance for income estimation. The arguments he presents are woven around *optimal* extraction under idealized assumptions of the Hotelling type. But unlike Hartwick, Hotelling was not addressing income estimation, and specifically not national income for *individual* countries. He was considering an extractive industry whose aggregate behavior had clear implications for future scarcity. For the purpose of national accounting, it should be obvious that extraction in any one country – especially a small or medium-size supplier – given the scattered supply among numerous sources can have only a limited impact on overall scarcity and can fail to force international prices to rise. The Hotelling framework, though highly illuminating in its proper setting, is rather irrelevant where the task at hand is how to estimate *ex post* income for individual countries. Hartwick refers repeatedly to variables expected from stylized situations, conceived in optimal setups, and presents these as 'true' and 'correct' quantities to show the faults he perceives in practical accounting. Such assertions on his part should therefore be taken with caution. Hartwick's long Note 17 (*loc. cit.*) is replete with references to 'correct' and 'true' magnitudes against which my estimates are compared and judged by him to be either 'accurate' or 'inaccurate'.

OVERESTIMATING 'DEPRECIATION'?

For Hartwick, the user cost is one and the same as depreciation, which signifies the asset's capital loss due to extraction, and this I can readily accept. However, in his discussion of the WRI study of Indonesia he seems to concur with my argument that WRI 'overcorrected' the adjustment needed for 'greening' the conventional estimates of national income.[1] This is because WRI deducted from the unadjusted GDP the entire drop in stocks whereas I favored deducting only the user cost.[2] But this is not the source of over-correction as he sees it. Instead, Hartwick attributes the over-estimation of the 'resource rent' to its being read from average costs rather than, as it should, 'correctly' from marginal costs – as if these latter could be ascertained in practice, as I have repeatedly disputed. In this he started a long train of followers who have written about the superiority of marginal over average costs for the analysis of 'resource rents'. For accounting purposes, however, average cost does not vary along a cost curve, but is estimated in one step at year-end as a unique number. It is obtained by dividing the product's value by the volume of extraction without any assumption of a continuous cost function from which either average or marginal cost may be derived. Total cost and total output are then usually known at the time when the accounts are being drawn. Whilst I focus on the *adjustment*, Hartwick concentrates on the stock *level* that is being adjusted. In his view if costs along a continuous function are rising as extraction expands, marginal costs will exceed average costs, which is a truism, and 'rents' estimated on the basis of marginal costs will be smaller than the 'profits' or net revenues read on the basis of average costs. Thus he maintains that in this case 'economic depreciation' (or the user cost if we wish) will be overestimated. In other words, this may be construed as saying that my method would underestimate 'true' income – an argument I cannot accept. Note that Hartwick overlooks another practical possibility: that marginal costs (if they were at all identifiable and easily quantifiable in mining activities) may well be *falling*. Why? As output increases unused capital capacity may be taken up, and average (and marginal) costs would be falling progressively as output expands. Initial over-optimism about the richness of an extraction field might have led to overinvestment in facilities that in retrospect do not get fully used so that output expansion would be associated with falling costs. This rather important point is hardly ever considered either by Hartwick or those who have accepted his views, including Vincent.

Hartwick proceeds in the same Note 17:

> The correct way to circumvent this overestimation is to obtain true marginal extraction costs and to calculate correct economic depreciation. In the absence of such true marginal extraction costs one might proceed with average extraction costs, and make some ad hoc adjustment with the qualification that observed profits generally overestimate true mineral stock depreciation. For example one might reduce profits by one-third and then let these reduced profits stand for true economic deprecation.

Where this one-third downward 'correction' comes from is not explained, and to think that that fraction will remain constant at one-third is curious, considering his quest for precision. Along his own lines, when the resource approaches extinction the extraction cost curves would be rising more sharply than before, and the difference between average and marginal costs will widen. This means that the claimed overestimation of 'depreciation' will get progressively larger, and the 33 per cent adjustment offered is thus seen to be not just unfounded but also wrong. In comparison, using my own approach, when the resource is abundant in the early stages of extraction the user cost would tend to be a smaller proportion of revenue – a proportion that grows gradually until extinction when the entire revenue will all be a user cost. A reminder here is that it is market prices that are used in national accounting as a numéraire, approximating average magnitudes to be read by dividing total values by volume without any resort to marginal quantities.

CONTINUOUS TIME

Hartwick is not alone in preferring his analysis in continuous time over discrete time. Many other analysts have resorted also to continuous time, which provides a convenient context for unbroken functions from which to derive such magnitudes as marginal costs. The same device enables Hartwick to incorporate new discoveries *instantaneously* into resource stocks, and to optimize extraction in a way that conforms to the Hotelling model. While all this analysis produces interesting outcomes, it does not belong to the realm of national accounting, which was the focus of my 'contribution'. Hartwick shows admirable patience in comparing results obtained by the user cost method and his 'correct' depreciation, identifying the latter with the decline in 'total Hotelling rent' (THR) between every two successive periods such as V_{t0} and V_{t1}. The comparison is interesting since the disinvestment implied by the user cost could indeed be viewed as 'depreciation' in that way and he has already conceded that my method gave the 'correct results' for the first year. So in his Table 12-5 (p. 224) he compares *income* – the complement of the user cost – with income as estimated according to his preferred method, which means THR minus 'depreciation'. In the same table he expresses all results as 'ratios of true income to receipts' (my X/R). In a sense, he is now playing the game on my home ground, using my own terminology and notations, and in the process confirming that, with the passage of time, as a mine approaches exhaustion, the ratio of income to receipts declines. Having conceded that first year results present no problem (both approaches, his and mine, yielding the same results), Hartwick shows the outcomes at five points of continuous time, at intervals varying from 'year 2.54' to 'year 8.45' with three temporal steps in between. His calculations lead to almost identical ratios of income to receipts under both approaches even when continuous time is used. Thus he concludes that the THR approach and the EM (El Serafy method) yield almost the same estimates of 'depreciation'. All along he reads depreciation from changes in stock values, though some slight differences begin to show when the EM, based as it is on discrete time, is employed.

It is interesting to recall what Hartwick says on the use of discrete time combined with his conclusion that my method renders 'accurate' estimates for the first year 'only' (p. 224 in Lutz, 1993):

> If one believes that because of new price information or new discoveries, firms are continually revising their extraction schedules and planning, getting first period depreciation correct may be of most importance; if EM [El Serafy Method] estimates are found in general to estimate first period depreciation more closely in discrete time, the discrete time version of EM may be preferred.

To recapitulate, continuous time is handy for applying differential calculus and allows for aggregation by integration. A window thus opens for analytical tools to be used. But in order to speak convincingly of marginal costs a smooth, stable and continuous function must exist in the first place tracking the course of costs as the product increases in theoretically infinitesimal amounts. From such functions the first derivative would indicate values at different outputs to be read for example as marginal costs. Marginal costs in mining, however, as repeatedly stated before, make little sense in a field replete with uncertainties, indivisibilities in the form of lumpy equipment, joint products (such as oil mixed with gas) and all kinds of rigidities imposed by contractual obligations, political uncertainties and much else besides. We must not forget also the possibility mentioned earlier, that costs may be falling so the marginal costs would be lower than average costs. Consistent with his stylized approach, Hartwick assumes an 'optimal' extraction profile along Hotelling lines with perfect markets, operators' perfect foresight, and other simplifying assumptions. Such an approach, though highly illuminating to analysis in the abstract is, however, far removed from the practical world of mining, and should be seen as inconsistent with the pragmatic methods of national accounting which are without question 'historical' and descriptive procedures. By contrast, for accounting purposes, the total costs, once ascertained, may simply be divided by output (both quantities should be available to the mine owners and their accountants by the end of the year) to produce *average* costs which several empirical researchers have used fruitfully in their calculations while occasionally (and perhaps a little pretentiously) paying lip service to marginal costs.

A CONSTANT PROFILE OF EXTRACTION?

From the beginning Hartwick was aware that my approach is to be applied afresh ('*de novo*' in his language) each accounting period. The application of the user-cost method afresh every year means that all parameters including the volume of extraction had to be newly ascertained for making the calculations of income and user cost. Yet Hartwick persisted with the assertion that my extraction is assumed to proceed at a constant level year after year until the resource had reached total exhaustion. This assertion of a constant extraction profile has doubtless misled others who have put faith in his interpretation. As the previous chapter shows, so many analysts repeated this alleged constancy of extraction as an implicit weakness in my approach. However, at quite an early stage (in fact in 1991) Hartwick had expressed the opinion that whether extraction was constant or variable the effect on asset 'depreciation' made no difference, or at least no significant difference. Hartwick wrote:[3]

> My present analysis of April 16 [1991] of the El-Serafy user cost generalizes from a constant stream of surpluses $\{R, R,......R\}$ to a variable stream $\{\pi (q(1)), \pi (q(2)),......\pi (q(t)\}$ where q(t) is current extraction from a deposit. The good news is that the El-Serafy user cost continues to yield the same measure of loss in capital value from extraction as does the economic depreciation concept, $V_{t+1} - V_t$. *It is pleasing that the attractive intuition underlying the El-Serafy measure leads to a concept which has been traditionally derived from a rather different intuition. There is more than one way to skin a cat, it seems.* (Emphasis added.)

But this highly supportive judgment appeared nowhere in the final version as published in Lutz (1993).

Another point worth stressing is that all along Hartwick insists on viewing the user cost as 'depreciation' due to extraction, whereas I thought of it as a 'disinvestment' that does not follow the standard patterns used by accountants for the depreciation of different categories assets. Over this point, however, there is no fundamental disparity between our positions, and I can accept that the user cost, properly estimated, could be used as an indicator of 'depreciation'. However, there remains a basic difference between my view and his. I derive this 'depreciation' from physical quantities, pricing them at current market prices in the year of extraction following strict accounting valuation methods. But Hartwick derives 'depreciation' from the fall in *value* of the mining stock concerned between every two periods. It is obvious that his approach does not make accounting sense. A mineral stock may be diminishing in physical terms, which would be a highly significant occurrence that merits accountant recognition, while simultaneously the market price may have risen sufficiently to offset, or even more than offset, the volume fall. And if the price rise more than offsets the volume decline, Hartwick would see a reverse 'depreciation', not a fall. Whether or not he realizes this anomaly, he muddies the waters still further by bringing in 'optimality' of extraction, insisting that '[D]epreciation is the change in value of a mine under optimal use' (p. 224).

IDIOSYNCRASIES?

All things considered, the competence and originality of Hartwick in this field cannot be doubted. That's why a perceptive reviewer of his book *National Accounting and Capital* (2000) took him to task, generously describing what he saw as lapses in Hartwick's book as mere 'idiosyncrasies'. One of these, as just noted, is Hartwick's viewing the flow accounts as changes in the capital stock values – an approach that creates many difficulties for national accounting as discussed in various parts of the present book. In this instance, the reviewer, Michael Harris of La Trobe University (2002), mentions Hartwick's book spotty 'coverage':

> The book has a number of idiosyncrasies. Some of these relate to coverage of material. For example, in the chapter on exhaustible resources, no mention is made of the user-cost approach advocated by El Serafy (1989), an approach that has been widely used in case studies of resource-dependent economies. Hartwick himself, with Anya [sic] Hageman (1993), contributed to this debate, but it goes unmentioned here.[4]

A HARTWICK UPDATE?

Two decades later, Hartwick remains unconvinced by the user-cost approach, and persists in reading natural asset depreciation from the decline in stock values. He continues to view the total decline in stock as 'depreciation', pursuing the green adjustment not in the gross but the net product. In a joint paper with Asheim (Asheim and Hartwick, 2011) the authors discover what they call 'anomalies' in green national accounting: the adjusted *product*, they allege, will differ from the adjusted *income*. Curiously they treat income and product as two separate entities whereas students of national accounting know that they are but two sides of the same coin. Hartwick of all people should know this elementary fact, and it is curious that he associates himself with this argument. Greening the income side using a strong sustainability method and making the adjustment only in net income – an approach Hartwick has for long advocated – negates the contribution that the resource itself makes to net income whilst the product lies uncorrected in positive territory. Instead of finding a solution to their confused position in a user-cost approach that postulates a weak sustainability, they belatedly discover this internal inconsistency in the Hartwick approach. In the greened accounts, the 'correction' for depletion, they now allege, will cause net income from a wasting asset, such as petroleum or fish, appear to be zero while output or product remains a positive number. Clearing up this imagined anomaly they only create another and the paper concludes rather fancifully that only if a social accounting matrix is employed will the anomaly be resolved. Yet even then a new one seems to appear, namely that the estimated investment in reproducible capital will be different on the two sides of income and product (p. 5). They try desperately to solve this new paradox with some unconvincing arguments about investment technology being either stationary or changing, leaving the reader none the wiser. I find Hartwick's association with this paper difficult to understand.

NOTES

1. Strictly speaking national income is the NNP not GDP or GNP.
2. WRI also added new discoveries to the stocks and included them in the adjusted income estimates, thus depriving the adjusted income of economic meaning.
3. In the same letter to the author dated 19 April 1991. In a short note appended to this letter Hartwick explains that his series V at each date represents the maximum present value of the surplus attainable beyond t, the latter being a value associated with an *optimal* extraction profile.
4. Perhaps another 'idiosyncrasy' may be added here which revolves around Hartwick bringing in highly theoretical approaches such as the Hamiltonian into discussions of national income estimation. The Hamiltonian is a dynamic intertemporal model that purports to derive an ideal concept of NNP, which is clearly at variance with the rough approximations of national income estimation. Besides, the Hamiltonian concept in the present context is rooted in the pursuit of 'welfare', perceived as a return on the stock of 'wealth' – a stock that has so far adamantly defied empirical estimation. On a denunciation of the use of the Hamiltonian for national accounting see Usher (1994). But see also Asheim and Weitzman (2001).

REFERENCES

Asheim, Geir and Hartwick, John (2011), 'Anomalies in green national accounting', *Ecological Economics*, **70** (2), 2303–2307.
Asheim, Geir and Weitzman, Martin (2001), 'Does NNP growth indicate welfare improvement?', *Economics Letters*, **73**, 233–239.

El Serafy, Salah (1981), 'Absorptive capacity, the demand for revenue and the supply of petroleum', *Journal of Energy and Development*, 7 (1), 73–88.

El Serafy, Salah (1989), 'The proper calculation of income from depletable natural resources', in Yusuf J. Ahmad, Salah El Serafy and Ernst Lutz (eds.), *Environmental Accounting for Sustainable Development*, A UNEP-World Bank Symposium. Washington DC: World Bank, Chapter 3, pp. 10–18.

Harris, Michael (2002), 'Book review of John. M. Hartwick, *National Accounting and Capital*', in *Australian Journal of Agricultural Economics*, **46** (1), 125–128.

Hartwick, John M. (1977), 'Intergenerational equity and the investing of rents from exhaustible resources', *American Economic Review*, **76** (5), 972–974.

Hartwick, John M. and Hageman, Anja (1991), 'Economic depreciation of mineral stocks and the contribution of El Serafy', Divisional Working Paper No. 1991-27, Policy and Research Division, Environment Department, The World Bank.

Hartwick, John M. and Hageman, Anja (1993), 'Economic depreciation of mineral stocks and the contribution of El Serafy', in Ernst Lutz (ed.), *Toward Improved Accounting for the Environment*, An UNSTAT–World Bank Symposium. Washington DC: World Bank, chapter 12, pp. 211–235.

Hartwick (2000) *National Accounting and Capital.* Cheltenham, UK and Northampton, MA: Edward Elgar.

Lutz, Ernst (ed.) (1993), *Toward Improved Accounting for the Environment*, An UNSTAT–World Bank Symposium. Washington DC: World Bank,

Usher, Dan (1994), 'Income and the Hamiltonian', *Review of Income and Wealth*, 40 (2), 123–141.

PART IV

Methodological tools

12. Depletable resources: fixed capital or inventories?

PROLOGUE

In this chapter I argue the case against treating the declines in natural resource stocks similarly to fixed capital consumption. I advanced a similar argument some 20 years ago in an invited paper I presented at a 1991 conference organized by the International Association of Research in Income and Wealth (IARIW). The original paper (El Serafy, 1993) was later printed in Franz and Stahmer (eds), *Approaches to Environmental Accounting*. The conference at which I first presented this argument was held in Baden, near Vienna, Austria as part of the preparations for SNA93. In some small way my contribution was used for the drafting of that document, and in substance it was used also in the 1993 United Nations Statistics Division's Manual on 'Integrated Environmental and Economic Accounts' (SEEA). The SEEA was intended to guide the implementation of the new SNA, which for the first time, as related earlier, tried to cover environmental issues. When it first came out the manual carried the label 'Interim Version' in expectation that it would be put on a firmer footing later. However, despite a number of attempts since its first appearance, a definitive version has been difficult to produce. This failure, as I have already tried to explain, was inevitable owing to the fact that SNA93 had declared the environment as a non-economic concern. Subsequent versions of the SNA meant for 'reintegration' have not been able to close this breach. In my 1991 address I set out to refute the false analogy between natural resource deterioration and fixed asset depreciation – an analogy that has regrettably dominated the account greening efforts since then.

ACCOUNTING FOR USING-UP INVENTORIES

The extraction of minerals out of the earth's crust, in Alfred Marshall's memorable phrase, is tantamount to taking them out of nature's store. This metaphor, which I have never tired of repeating, at once suggests that extraction comes out of natural 'inventories' and dispels its kinship with capital consumption. I have strongly emphasized the different nature of the two concepts because the capital-consumption match has grave implications for greening the national accounts. The issue here is doubly important because this mistaken view has found popularity among environmental economists and national income accountants leading to what I see as wrong adjustment procedures.

The depreciation of fixed assets is usually made in the accounts at the end of the account period. Typically, this takes the form of an annual exercise that follows bookkeeping norms for depreciating different categories of assets. A building has a longer life than a machine and its periodic depreciation is therefore a smaller portion of its book value than the portion used for depreciating a machine. While this is true as a general rule, it becomes inappropriate if the concern that owns the asset exits the business, or when some unexpected change in technique, for instance, renders a piece of machinery obsolete. In that case total amortization will have to be made. This procedure, however, cannot be applied to commercially exploited natural resources as the diminution of natural assets differs *in kind* from fixed asset depreciation. It does not follow any standard pattern based on an assumed life of the asset, and cannot be anticipated with any accuracy before it actually happens. In fact, at one extreme, it can be nil if the resource is left unexploited. At the other extreme, it can amount to 100 per cent of the stock if the resource is totally liquidated. Wherever actual extraction lies within these two boundaries the user-cost approach will take up the situation and indicate the size of the adjustment needed for greening the resource's contribution in national accounts.

MANY REASONS WHY

There are several reasons why depletion differs basically from fixed asset depreciation. In the first place fixed assets need to be maintained to keep them functioning for the continuation of the economic activity involved. By contrast, a depletable natural resource, if exploited, cannot be preserved in order to serve a similar function. It has to diminish deliberately as it is used, or more correctly 'used up'. While depreciation of fixed assets in bookkeeping aims to keep capital intact, mining a natural resource, whether depletable or renewable, obviously cannot have a comparable purpose. There can be no pretense that a mine needs to be maintained intact for the continuity of operations since the very act of extraction inevitably diminishes the asset. A second difference is that, unlike fixed assets, the natural resource in question does not just perform a supporting role, but lies at the heart of the activity itself. The natural asset occupies the center of the economic activity and is not just a means to enable 'production'. A third reason is that the fixed assets that depreciate are not meant to be sold at all during the life of a going concern, whereas the products of mining are intended for sale. The fixed assets get sold only in exceptional circumstances as when they become obsolete, when the entity is going out of business, or in comparable circumstances which force the termination of the activity. By contrast, commercial extraction of a natural resource is usually a regular and continual activity while the resource lasts, and the product is explicitly marked for sale. A possible fourth reason of some relevance is that natural capital in most cases had existed all along, formed in many cases over decades, centuries or even millennia, and emanates very largely from the 'Bounty of Nature'. By contrast, fixed capital is usually of a more recent formation, and its formation is financed out of savings. Efforts to discover natural capital and develop it, while they certainly do involve costs, sometimes great costs, tend to be modest in relative terms and are not at all on a scale comparable to the costs of financing fixed capital formation. In the case of natural resources, the input of Nature is clearly predominant.

The natural resource 'inventories' I am envisioning here are usually homogeneous, or fairly homogeneous, differing markedly from the diversity usually found in say a manufacturing entity's inventories. But this difference is of no material import for accounting. Inventories held by a manufacturing concern are usually a mélange of raw materials, fuels, final products and goods at various stages of processing, being all held for the purpose of sustaining the activity concerned, and hence assisting in its contribution to the domestic product. And it is not by chance that in standard accounting changes in inventories are incorporated in the estimation of the *gross* profits (or loss), whereas depreciation of fixed assets is only brought in later for the determination of the *net* profits (or loss). For national accounting purposes, therefore, I have been convinced that the adjustment should be made in the gross product itself. And once this has been done, the net product, when reckoned, will be automatically modified with no need for any further adjustment.

AN INTEGRATED SYSTEM OF STOCKS AND FLOWS

A closely related anomaly in national accounting procedures that also needs challenging is the tendency among both analytical economists and national accountants to try to link resource stocks and income flows in a tight embrace that threatens the proper estimation of the flows. I have already addressed this issue in a number of places including Chapter 11 on Hartwick's contribution. The flows, we should bear in mind, are vastly more important for macroeconomic purposes than the stocks – a fact Irving Fisher had told us more than a century ago. In his *Nature of Capital and Income* (1906, p. 324) Fisher had written:

> The Stock of wealth is called capital, and its stream of services is called income. The income is the more important concept of the two, for the capital exists merely for the sake of income, and the ownership of the capital has no other significance than the ownership of possible income from that capital.

Marshall also said the same thing in his *Principles of Economics* (1920 [1947], p. 80).[1]

The misguided approach to which I have taken strong exception begins from the stock end with a value placed on a natural asset, and the flow of product is inferred from the change of this value between the start and end of the accounting period. This method is frequently proposed not just for one natural asset at a time, but for the aggregate of all ecological stocks considered as when a country's national income is estimated. The flaws in such a method are obvious. For one thing, any valuation of the stocks will be contingent on the moment it is made, and most likely would alter the following day. As for a collection of resources in a country situation, a list of these resources will not be complete, and reading national income adjustments from an incomplete list would not be very meaningful. This, of course adds to the controversial quality of the valuation itself.

My reasoning against this kind of integration proceeds at two levels. Concentrating on one particular resource, say petroleum or forestry, and even when confining the argument to a single economy, the initial physical stock will defy precise estimation. Likewise the period-end stock will not be easy to estimate either. What enters the national accounts – what can in fact enter the national accounts – is not the estimated change between these two uncertain quantities, but the flows as they are actually transacted. These flows can of course give some indication, albeit not a precise one, of stock changes if we should wish to pursue these. But the stocks themselves, valued in money, I stress, are neither useful nor needed for national accounting.

The other level at which I wish to take the argument is accounting for a variety of natural assets in a country situation. The country, of course, is the usual unit for which the national accountants attempt to estimate national income. Obviously we cannot make a complete list of all assets. Nor can we make a physical inventory of all such assets – let alone value these stocks meaningfully as already stated. But this comprehensive task fortunately is not needed. All that is needed is to select a few economically important natural resources for the country concerned and see if these can be brought into the orbit of the national accounts. This is exactly the sensible approach taken in the 1989 WRI pioneering study of Indonesia as will be discussed in detail in Chapter 19.[2] The adjustment to the national accounts will evidently be partial – and in fact even with additional adjustments made subsequently and a wider coverage, not all aspects of resource deterioration will be accounted for. However, such an exercise will take us nearer to a realistic appreciation of what is actually occurring in the economy concerned. We should therefore be content if the accounts manage to correct the income estimates to some degree, say for forestry losses, for petroleum extraction, for soil erosion: each resource one at a time, or in the aggregate, anticipating that with the passage of time a broader front will be covered and the adjustment will be expanded. In this I have been mindful once more of Pigou's perception that his quarry, 'human welfare', was too vast a subject to be handled in economics in one stride. So as a first step he selected those aspects of welfare which he judged could be brought into a 'relationship with the measuring rod of money' (Pigou, 1924, pp. 10–11). In time he expected that this vista will expand with the addition of more aspects of welfare. Similarly, for green accounting, I have been in favor of making selective and piecemeal adjustments, gradually expanding them with additions and refinements as our vision of natural resources improves and methods of resource accounting advance.

STOCK REASSESSMENTS

With the realization that stock size cannot easily be ascertained the whole approach of deriving the flows from an uncertain stock is clearly undermined. And since normally the physical stock is of a higher order of magnitude than the withdrawals from the stock, welding the two together can seriously harm the flow estimates. On top of uncertainty about their physical size, valuing the stocks presents a formidable problem. One serious weakness in WRI's study of Indonesia was to bring the changes in stock values directly into the flow accounts, thus preventing the adjusted accounts from making economic sense. It will be seen in Chapter 19 that changes in the estimated stocks of Indonesia's petroleum overwhelm all other adjustments and seriously damage the study's overall conclusions. As I said in El Serafy (1993), *not only* does the adjustment proposed there for petroleum dwarf the adjustments for the other natural resources considered (forestry and Java's soil) but the bulk of the adjustment for petroleum stems largely from reassessments of reserves. With upward re-estimation of reserves vastly exceeding extraction during the relevant accounting periods, the WRI study ends up with the anomalous result that *net* income in some years is greater than *gross* income, and the so-called natural asset depreciation perversely becomes *appreciation.* We have only to reflect upon any usefulness of this revised income estimation, either for indicating a sustainable level of consumption (which should be viewed as the primary purpose of income estimation) or to provide a benchmark for gauging economic performance (in order among other things to guide economic policy) to realize the inadequacy of such an approach.

By following this flawed procedure – which I fear is the one currently adopted by official circles – the so-called 'adjusted' income estimates present an annual stream of undulating flows that bears no relation to economic performance which the accounts had been intended to do. By comparison, the user-cost adjustment method acknowledges stock re-estimation by altering the reserves-to-extraction ratio. This ratio indicates life expectancy, spelling out the resource sustainability, and enables a re-estimation of income that makes economic sense. As I put it in my address to the assembly gathered in Austria by the IARIW in May 1991, WRI managed to show us the path that should not be taken for greening the accounts. But when SNA93 came out the WRI method was in fact endorsed.

STOCK SIZE AND THE USER COST

A critic might justifiably find some contradiction in my position as just stated regarding the indeterminateness of stock size. This is because I do rely on stock size to estimate the user cost. At the risk of repetition the procedure I reject injects stock value changes directly into the income flows so that the adjusted flows become victim to exogenous and fortuitous forces that should play no part in income estimation. By contrast, for reckoning the user cost, while the stock may not be precisely estimated, it enters the calculation obliquely, with much less force, and most importantly in physical not in money terms. Besides, for estimating the user cost only a rough and ready estimate of the stock is needed (El Serafy, 1981).[3] The purpose is to expose the *proportion* of the stock that is being drawn down, and this proportion is only one among other parameters needed for estimating the user cost. In other words, the stock size does not impact the reckoning with the full force that is brought forth by the method I have been criticizing.

A RECAPITULATION

This seems to be as good a place as any to piece together what I have been saying so far. By way of a recapitulation, I would offer the following set of proposals for the treatment of depleting resources in the national accounts.

1. Greening the accounts should not begin from the stock end.
2. Values placed on stocks at both ends of the account period will always be somewhat arbitrary.
3. Fortunately such values are unnecessary for estimating the income flows.
4. If we must have a value for the stock, the physical volume may be multiplied by the price of the day in full knowledge that the morrow's price will likely be different.
5. Even in the context of an individual country a *comprehensive* measurement of environmental change cannot be expected. For account-greening purposes attention should focus on those few weighty resources likely to make a difference to *national* income re-estimation.
6. It is a serious mistake to treat the proceeds from selling natural assets as income and include them in national income. Revenues are not the same as incomes.
7. If the proceeds of natural asset sales are counted in the national product they should be expunged from it and a downward adjustment must be made.
8. The down adjustment should not eliminate the entire revenue, but only the equivalent of the user cost contained therein.
9. The adjustment should be made in the gross product, and no further change will be required in the net product.
10. Any windfalls gained from new discoveries should not be included in the flow accounts; nor should any downward re-estimation of reserves be deducted from them.
11. Withdrawing products out of inventories should *not* be viewed as capital consumption.

NOTES

1. Marshall wrote that 'The money income, or inflow, of wealth gives a measure of a nation's prosperity, which, untrustworthy as it is, is yet in some respects better than that afforded by the money value of its stock of wealth.'

2. Robert Repetto and Associates (1989). See my criticism of this work in World Bank (1993). There I re-worked WRI's adjustments and arrived at very different estimates which are to be found in Chapter 19.
3. There I listed the assumptions on which this formulation was based, including the assumption that exploitation in period n does not yield income until period n + 1. If, however, exploitation and income are simultaneous, falling within the same year, the formula indicating the user cost becomes:

$$1 - \frac{X}{R} = \frac{1}{(1 + r)^n}$$

In practice, however, there is little difference in the calculations between using n or (n + 1) as the power with which to raise the fraction (1 + r). This latter formula had appeared also in El Serafy (1981).

REFERENCES

El Serafy, Salah (1981), 'Absorptive capacity, the demand for revenue and the supply of petroleum', *Journal of Energy and Development*, 7 (1), 73–88.
El Serafy, Salah (1993), 'Depletable resources: fixed capital or inventories?', in Alfred Franz and Carsten Stahmer (eds), *Approaches to Environmental Accounting*. Heidelberg, Germany: Physica-Verlag, pp. 245–258.
Fisher, Irving (1906), *The Nature of Capital and Income*. New York and London: Macmillan and Co.
Marshall, Alfred (1920 [1947]), *Principles of Economics*, 8th edition. London: Macmillan.
Pigou, Arthur C. (1924), The *Economics of Welfare*. London: Macmillan.
Repetto, Robert and Associates (1989), 'Wasting assets: natural resources in the national income accounts', World Resources Institute, Washington DC, June.
United Nations, Integrated Environmental and Economic Accounting (2003), *Handbook on National Accounting, Integrated Environmental and Economic Accounting: An Operational Manual. Studies in Methods*, 'Final draft' circulated for information prior to official printing, to be issued in the series Studies in Methods, Series F, No. 61, Rev.1.
World Bank (1993), 'Country Macroeconomic Work and Natural Resources', Environment Working Paper No. 58, March.

13. Sustainability and substitutability: defending weak sustainability

PROLOGUE

A version of this chapter appeared in *Environmental Values*, 1998, Volume 5, number 1, pp. 75–82. 'Sustainability' has become a desirable objective among ecological economists, and seems also to have found favor with development agencies albeit not always convincingly. It is not surprising therefore that many environmentalists dismiss exclamations of support for sustainability as empty rhetoric. Needless to say different scholars have brought forth different perceptions of sustainability, not all of them reconcilable with each other. Questions are often raised over what exactly to sustain, at what level, for how long and for what purpose. The answers have remained imprecise, variant, and when cogently formulated they have not garnered consensus. For national accounting purposes, and therefore for the benefit of macroeconomics, sustainability relates narrowly to income estimation. But even within this narrow view the question may be asked if sustainability for the poor would mean perpetuation of their poverty? Or should it be taken to mean that they do not become even worse off? And yet, despite all these uncertainties there seems to be agreement that sustainability is probably a 'good thing', obviously superior to its opposite which may be called 'unsustainability'.[1] A related issue is 'substitutability' for in the present context sustainability must also relate to natural resources. These have been subjected to increasing pressure over the past two centuries: what with mounting industrialization and relentless population growth which have been devouring resources as inputs and emitting substantial wastes in the process. These wastes have been going into increasingly clogged-up natural 'sinks' which used to disperse, absorb or assimilate them fairly comfortably before now being overwhelmed by their sheer scale. Signs of ecological stress have been multiplying yet they seem to be unseen by mainstream economists who, besides, rarely question the quality of the national accounts they avidly use. The ability to substitute human-made products for the products of nature would prolong 'sustainability' however defined. That is why discussing sustainability would be incomplete without substitutability being considered also.

TWO CONCEPTS

In the context of national accounting two concepts of sustainability have emerged and the views of them are neither clear nor sharply demarcated. These are strong and weak sustainability. What concerns me here is their applicability to the estimation of national income. National income is of course NNP but here the discussion applies with equal force to gross income. The strong variety is usually favored by environmentalists who regard it as more protective of natural resources. To them, 'strength' indicates superiority over 'weakness' – the latter often seen as a feeble environmental defense stratagem. Strong sustainablists would like to keep the natural assets undiminished, but the less strict among them would favor safeguarding the *services* of these assets if this can be done without keeping the assets themselves undiminished. In this regard sustainability would be achieved by a variety of policy instruments built around persuasion and deterrence. If a fish stock is depleted by exploitation, or a forest reduced by logging, these are to be restored to their original conditions by restocking and replanting.

Weak sustainability does not oppose this approach though it is often disparaged unfairly for advocating that natural resource declines should be tolerated provided other assets are built as a replacement. But support for weak sustainability by its advocates, myself included, is only income-focused, and confined to individual income earners. It would indeed be foolish to 'recommend' natural asset demolition in general as some critics have alleged. The accountant is not a campaigner, but a kind of historian describing past acts and is struggling to estimate income for a period that has already closed. In fact, I have not seen anywhere a recommendation for large-scale demolition of natural assets to be replaced by income generating alternatives as a blueprint for action. The accountant's kind of sustainability is of course different, and it is in no way a weaker or a frailer version of a stronger sustainability. Some thoughtful analysts have sought a compromise. Instead of attempting to sustain income through *any* fresh investments as implied by weak-sustainability accounting, the natural assets should be replaced by 'similar' assets. If trees are cut for timber, then the new investments should aim to create fresh sources of timber. Quite often, however, a natural resource such as petroleum is versatile and has many uses. It is an input for making lubricants, paints, textiles, fuels and other products. Which new asset should be contemplated for replacing it? This argument for specific replacements, though commendable when feasible, is not as firm as it first appears, and it is far removed from the historical nature of accounting. Accounting, in other words, is not 'normative' but 'positive' and descriptive. It should be added here that though *income* sustainability for many poorer countries depends on *environmental* sustainability, the two concepts are fundamentally different when viewed through the lens of national accounting.

In defending 'weak sustainability' I have had in mind all along *income* sustainability not *ecological* sustainability. As I show in Chapter 7 (on income from extraction) strong sustainability is incompatible with national accounting. To remind readers of my argument, the reason is the following. If the portion of the gross product originating in mining, fishing or logging is adjusted downward by the full decline of the stock (an exercise strong sustainablists recommend for re-estimating the net product) the latter would show no value added at all attributable specifically to the natural resource. The user-cost method, with its weak sustainability basis, will always show a positive ingredient of value added. For income accounting purposes, and certainly not for natural resource conservation, the equivalent of the user cost (which is only part of the decline in the stock) should be estimated and 'theoretically' reinvested in any income-producing asset for the specific purpose of estimating current income. Whether or not this theoretical investment is acted upon in practice is altogether a different matter which falls outside accounting. This adjustment method obviously does not aim at, nor indeed is it capable of, sustaining the natural resource stock. However, just reckoning the user cost provides a means for getting a grip on the sustainability of the resource being exploited for it raises the question as to how long will the resource last at the current rate of extraction.

This, in short, is the background to the present chapter, which appeared originally as a paper in *Environmental Values* (1996). It was a reaction to a number of contributions on sustainability published in that journal – contributions I believed were leading nowhere. It is unnecessary to list the specific views to which I took exception, since these will easily be inferred from my argument, which, I must stress once more, was focused on greening the national accounts. So in El Serafy (1996) I wrote the following.

HASTY CRITICS

I thought Herman Daly (1995) and Michael Jacobs (1995) were too hasty to concur with Wilfred Beckerman (1994) that 'weak sustainability' should be dismissed, and especially Daly in offering his congratulations 'for Beckerman's effective demolition of "weak sustainability"'. Now that Beckerman got 'weak sustainability' out of the way, or so he thought, he also proceeded to demolish 'strong sustainability'. Before I attend to 'weak sustainability', which I consider to be an entirely economic concern and eminently worthy of being defended, I wish to commend Beckerman for his helpful distinction between 'complementarity' (as between natural and human-made inputs) pure and simple, and 'gross complementarity'. The latter clearly is the relevant relationship, which underlies the normative concept of 'strong sustainability'. However, though Beckerman is technically correct, he seems to miss the big picture. This is because the debate is not about static substitutability or complementarity at a given level of production or consumption, but about a relationship that seems to describe an observed association between natural inputs and human-made capital along a path defined by an ever-expanding scale of economic activity. It does not in the least matter if the source of the change is endogenous or exogenous. This expansion of production and consumption, which is stressful to the environment, is propelled by a variety of forces. These include mounting population growth and rising material aspirations on the part of most people, particularly in the more numerous poorer nations, as well as by wasteful habits of consumption by the rich the world over. Market signals in many environmental situations are sluggish and unclear, and are often so twisted by political action that the 'endogenous' relationships Beckerman is technically delineating hardly ever have sufficient room to work themselves out, and if they do, can indeed lead the adjustment astray. But exist, they undoubtedly do.

FAULTY MARKET SIGNALS

National accounting apart, I have always thought that 'strong sustainability' is a useful concept when considering economic activity, provided that we temper it with the undeniable possibilities of substitution among inputs, both in the process of production, and also (and this is often forgotten) among the final goods and services that constitute ultimate demand. The scope for substitution, though appreciable in certain areas, may in fact pale in comparison with the rising tide of economic scale that is reinforcing the relationship of Beckerman's 'gross complementarity' and inflicting irreparable harm on the environment. Besides, in order for substitution to work, the market should show more sensitivity than it seems able to do toward the ever-changing patterns of scarcity. And we should also be able to distinguish between price signals that are genuinely produced by the interaction of free and 'socially beneficial' market forces, and those that are the product of monopoly, 'exploitation', political pressure, military intervention, and indeed skewed income distributions. For instance it should be clear to Beckerman that primary commodities tend to be undervalued on the international markets since the market fails to internalize the full ecological costs of their 'production'. Many of the problems of under-development, I fancy, would be alleviated if the poorer countries were to receive adequate compensation for their primary product exports. In this respect Beckerman exhibits a disarmingly simple faith in the ability of the market to indicate 'optimal' prices.

In fact, I view 'weak sustainability' as a first step that must be taken by economists without any normative reference to the environment, and once achieved, perhaps it could lead to the stronger forms of sustainability that the environmentalists cherish. Daly's and Jacobs's strictures against 'weak sustainability' (which incidentally are shared by many others including Victor (2005)[2]) reveal to me not so much a denial on their part of the utility of this concept, but more of an impatience with a weak and diluted objective in the belief, I think, that its pursuit would impede the attainment of their ultimate and stronger goal. Beckerman's reaction to their partial surrender in the face of his initial onslaught should be a lesson to them not to abandon what is in effect their first line of defense!

WEAK SUSTAINABILITY AND SUSTAINABLE DEVELOPMENT

As an economist I have felt much more comfortable to argue for 'weak sustainability' using economic logic and without resort to any value judgment about the environment. But first we should be clear what 'weak sustainability' actually means. Beckerman's definition of 'weak sustainability' is not one that I recognize, although his excuse is that he is following a recent definition proposed by David Pearce. Careful examination, however, shows that Pearce's definition is not that of 'weak sustainability', but of 'sustainable development' – a hybrid concept that, though somewhat related, is quite different. The notion that 'weak sustainability' (as Beckerman asserts) implies that per capita wellbeing does not diminish over time is certainly not what is generally understood by 'weak sustainability'. Assuming that it can be operationally measured, a non-declining per capita level of welfare may well be an excellent benchmark against which *development* should be assessed, but this has little to do with 'weak sustainability'.

It is therefore wrong of Beckerman to say that 'As it soon became obvious that the "strong" concept of sustainable development was morally repugnant, as well as totally impracticable, many environmentalists shifted their ground. A new version of the concept was adopted, known in the literature as "weak sustainability"'.[3]

Daly's and Jacobs's readiness to bury weak sustainability should at least have alerted Beckerman to the possibility that he might in fact be misreading the debate. That is because 'weak sustainability' did not rise from the ashes of 'strong sustainability', but may be said to have preceded it. For 'weak sustainability' has long been recognized as revolving around the correct measurement of income: not income per capita, and certainly not 'development' whether sustainable or otherwise. 'Development' has traditionally been assessed in terms of economic growth, i.e. the rise over time of what passes as the national income and product of a *developing* country. Leaving aside the elementary fact that development is a much wider concept than the mere expansion of economic activity, growth itself will be questionable if income has not been properly estimated. By my drawing attention to the fact that *proper* income measurement is a *sine qua non* for the accurate gauging of economic expansion I, as well as others, have insisted that capital, including natural capital, must be maintained intact.[4] This fundamental requirement which has for centuries been recognized by accountants (namely that capital must be kept intact for the proper estimation of income) and which was later adopted by successive generations of economists, found expression half a century ago in Hicks's (1946) standard definition of income in *Value and Capital*, a definition which is probably acceptable to most economists: in order to ascertain income in the current period, enough from current receipts must be put aside to compensate for capital deterioration so that future income might be sustained. 'Weak sustainability' requires that this rule be obeyed, but also attempts to insert natural capital under the umbrella of the capital that should be kept intact.[5]

CORRECTING THE INCOME MEASUREMENTS

As is well known, accounting for income is fraught with uncertainties. Approximations and short cuts have to be resorted to in order to enable a rough, but eminently useful, picture of income to be drawn. These uncertainties, however, have troubled some economists. But this is not the main point here. The main point is that, in order to satisfy 'weak sustainability', the capital that must be kept intact for sustaining future income is not any specific piece of equipment, or a sub-category of overall capital, but capital in general. This, Hicks (1974) has dubbed 'fundist capital'.[6] If proper measurement of income is to be ensured, capital *in general* must be kept intact. This would mean that the stock of natural capital that contributes to production may be reduced, provided that other forms of capital are increased so that capital in general is kept intact. Two things here should be borne in mind, however. One is that accounting for income is typically carried out once a year so that sustainability of future income implied by keeping capital intact applies to a fairly near horizon, which is defined largely by the life expectancy of existing assets. A corollary of this is that in the process of accounting no view is taken of future technological change, though if and when that change should occur, the necessary adjustment to income (via the adjustment of the capital stock) would be made in the light of the actual change. As stated earlier, while traditionally 'keeping capital intact' has been confined to produced assets, advocates of 'weak sustainability' would extend this concept to cover also natural resources, especially those which are already implicitly incorporated in conventional national income estimates, albeit perversely at a zero value. However, since in the long run, the structure of final demand, as well as production techniques, are liable to change, it is obviously not sufficient to rely on accounting principles to ensure longer term sustainability. In other words, 'weak sustainability' will not satisfy the environmentalists. The other point to remember is that the concern of the national income statistician is primarily focused on income estimation, and only indirectly is this focus shifted to the stock of capital. To the accountant, maintaining capital intact does not spring from any desire to preserve the capital stock as an end in itself, but simply as a stepping stone towards getting a grip on the estimation of income, which must be sustainable if it is to be identified as income at all. Maintaining capital intact, as Beckerman clearly recognizes, is merely a technical artifact. But technical as it may be, however, its lack of observance in practice is rife, especially where natural resources are concerned, and this requires correction. It is 'weak sustainability', I hold, that is the proper instrument for this correction.

For most of the developing countries, the national income accounting methods in use have tended to confuse natural asset liquidation with growth, and the 'development' suggested by a rising national income may not be genuine, in which case it should be characterized as being unsustainable. The growth indicated by those erroneous measurements has often been illusory, since the cardinal rule of keeping capital intact was being ignored. The longer a country avoided incurring the cost of cleaning up its environment, and the faster it cut down its forests, eroded its soil, depleted its aquifers and exhausted its mineral deposits, the faster it appeared to grow as seen through faulty accounting. Economists seldom stop to question the numbers turned out by faulty national accounting methods, and have continued to use such numbers in all kinds of otherwise sophisticated analyses, leading them frequently to misjudge an economy's progress, and to prescribe inappropriate and even harmful economic policies. To economists, 'weak sustainability' in the sense of getting the accounts right, is by no means a redundant luxury.

FROM WEAK TO STRONG SUSTAINABILITY

It was understandable, therefore, that many environmentalists should seize on Hicks's definition of income to point out that measurements of income which ignored environmental deterioration might indeed be faulty and misleading, and to demand that economists be faithful to their own discipline, insisting that capital be kept intact for the purpose of properly estimating 'sustainable income'. I put sustainable income between inverted commas because income, to be income at all, must be sustainable. This totally objective (and 'positive', i.e. value neutral) requirement, that capital, in its 'fundist' sense, be kept intact for the purpose of properly measuring income and its growth, came in time to be called 'weak sustainability'. But this was subsequently 'strengthened' as sustainability got converted to a normative injunction to keep natural capital (a sub-category of Hicks's 'fundist' capital) intact. Thus the focus moved from *income* estimation to preserving the *stock* of natural capital undiminished as an objective not as a means to the estimation of income. If natural capital is a complement to, rather than a substitute for, human-made capital in production, then maintaining production flows requires guarding against running down natural capital and this would favor strong sustainability. But this has nothing to do with income accounting.

Later still, attention to proper national income measurement was extended in another direction to individual extractive projects. Some writers attempted to promote the concept of a 'sustainable project', claiming that part of the project-yield which can be attributed to resource use (such as the user cost) should indeed be re-invested for the purpose of sustaining future income, but it should be reinvested specifically in projects geared to the generation of substitutes to replace the declining natural resource that is being depleted. This move was also in the direction of 'strong sustainability' although it shifted concern from the macro aggregates to individual investment projects. Not only did this extension move the definition of capital away from Hicks's 'fundist' concept towards his 'materialist' capital, but it also introduced (or endorsed) the notion of a 'sustainable project' to which Beckerman seems uncritically to subscribe. To me, projects are good projects if they can produce a surplus – a genuine value-added surplus – over the course of their limited life after which the capital sunk into them, if it had been properly amortized, may be shifted to new projects capable of yielding acceptable future returns for a while, until these too will expire. Beckerman's (1994, p. 193) naïve example of a poor country having to choose between leaving its mineral wealth in the ground and using the proceeds for survival or education is unworthy of serious consideration. For nobody has ever suggested other than making use of such a resource constructively in order to better the life of its owners. The real issue is not whether or not to exploit such an asset, but how much of the proceeds from this finite resource can properly be regarded as genuine income, available for consumption, and how much needs to be reinvested in order to sustain the same level of consumption into the future.[7]

SUBSTITUTABILITY

Some environmentalists claim that natural capital and produced capital are not substitutes but complements – as if these qualities were inherent in the inputs used in production. Can plastic substitute for wood, can synthetic rubber substitute for natural rubber, or can chemical fertilizers substitute for organic farming methods? Such questions are often bandied as if in a vacuum. They can be answered in the affirmative in moderate doses. This happens all the time and is attested to by observation. On a large scale, however, substitutability has its limits, and the world cannot do without natural resources altogether. What is troublesome in the present discussion is that no link is established between the markets for final products and the markets for the inputs used for manufacturing them. Surely if demand declines for a product that is intensive in the use of a natural input the demand for this input will subside. Substitution among goods in final demand works itself back inexorably to the markets of inputs. All the time consumer preferences keep altering, but significantly so do production technologies – the latter both independently and in reaction to changes in relative prices. What I am trying to say is that the qualities of substitutability and complementarity are neither static nor inherent in inputs or outputs. They are flexible and dynamically changing all the time.

CONCLUSION

Defining genuine income is not a marginal issue for economists; and it is the proper measurement of that income that will satisfy the 'weak sustainability' criterion that is the subject of this chapter. This is a technical or value-free requirement that has little to do directly with the environment. 'Weak sustainability' is indispensable for accurately assessing economic performance and estimating income. 'Strong sustainability', by contrast, is a normative concept, and relates to the immensely complex stock of environmental assets and properties. Many of these are not easy (in the famous Pigouvian phrase, 1924, p. 11) 'to bring into a relationship with the measuring rod of money'. Thus for that reason alone they cannot be brought into national accounting. The fact that parts of the environment seem now to lie beyond what economists regard as not their concern does not necessarily mean that such parts do not exist, or that they might not assert themselves as scarce elements in the future. In parallel with Bishop Berkeley's tree, the environment is beheld by society as whole, and it would be imprudent if economists confined their vision to what they mistakenly regard as economic now, and shut their eyes to what is getting progressively economic all the time.[8] For one thing, resources that had once been considered abundant, such for instance as fresh water, have now become so obviously scarce that they present an economic problem. I for one would not dismiss either weak or strong sustainability as cavalierly as Beckerman does.

NOTES

1. I may in fact have picked this line from Eric Neumayer.
2. For instance also by Victor *et al.* (1994).
3. Beckerman (1994, p. 195). See also his 1995 piece in the same journal, 'How would you like your "sustainability", sir, weak or strong' where he tried to ridicule sustainability both strong and weak.
4. See (*inter alia*) El Serafy (1981, 1989).
5. Some environmentalists would even relax this concept arguing that it is not the assets themselves that should be kept intact but only their services. But accountants in their role as guardians of sustainability (from one account period to the next) would rather set aside more rather than less out of current revenue to maintain future income: if in doubt, underestimate income rather than overestimate it to prevent any consumption of capital.
6. Hicks (1974) drew a distinction between 'fundist' and 'materialist' capital in the writings of successive generations of economists. Fundist capital represented a value or a fund covering all forms of capital in the possession of an individual, a corporation or an economy, whereas materialist capital related to specific pieces of machinery, inventories and the like. I made use of this distinction in El Serafy (1991) to argue for the inclusion of natural resources in (fundist) capital, relying also on the argument that the environment may be regarded as a factor of production. The latter notion I borrowed also from Hicks (1983, pp. 121–122) where he wrote:

   > So it is not necessary, in order that a thing should be a factor, that it should have a price. In order that a thing should have a price, it must be appropriable, but it is not necessary for a thing to be appropriable for it to be a factor of production, in the sense that if it were to be removed, production (or output) would be diminished. Or, more usefully, if a part of it were to be removed, production would be diminished. Which comes to the same thing as saying that the factor must have a marginal product.

7. See El Serafy (1989).
8. George Berkeley (1685–1753), Bishop of Cloyne, was an influential philosopher and mathematician of his time. He claimed that the proposition 'to be' is contingent on being 'perceived' by someone: *esse est percipi.* This provoked much merriment in English literature. Critics asked: if a tree had fallen and no one had perceived its fall, would it still exist? Bishop Berkeley's answer was that 'God' had observed its fall.

REFERENCES

Beckerman, Wilfred (1994), '"Sustainable development" is it a useful concept?' *Environmental Values*, **3** (3), 191–209.

Beckerman, Wilfred (1995), 'How would you like your 'sustainability', sir? Weak or strong? A reply to my critics', *Environmental Values*, 4 (2), 169–179.

Daly, Herman (1995), 'On Wilfred Beckerman's critique of sustainable development', *Environmental Values*, **4**, 49–55.

El Serafy, Salah (1981), 'Absorptive capacity, the demand for revenue and the supply of petroleum', *Journal of Energy and Development*, 7 (1), 73–88.

El Serafy, Salah (1989), 'The proper calculation of income from depletable natural resources', in Yusuf J. Ahmad, Salah El Serafy and Ernst Lutz (eds), *Environmental Accounting for Sustainable Development*, A UNEP-World Bank Symposium. Washington DC: World Bank, Chapter 3, pp. 10–18.

El Serafy, Salah (1991), 'The environment as capital', in Robert Costanza (ed.), *Ecological Economics: The Science and Management of Sustainability*. New York: Columbia University Press.

El Serafy, Salah (1996), 'In defence of weak sustainability', *Environmental Values*, 5 (1), 75–82.

Hicks, John R. (1946), *Value and Capital*, 2nd edn. Oxford: Clarendon Press.

Hicks, John R. (1974), 'Capital controversies: ancient and modern', *American Economic Review*, 64 (2), 307–316.

Hicks, John R. (1983), 'Is interest the price of a factor of production?' In *Classics and Moderns, Collected Essays on Economic Theory*, Vol. III. Cambridge, MA: Harvard University Press, Essay 9, pp. 113–128.

Jacobs, Michael (1995), 'Sustainable development, capital substitution and economic humility: a response to Beckerman', *Environmental Values*, **4**, 57–68.

Pigou, A.C. (1924), *The Economics of Welfare*, 2nd edn. London: Macmillan and Co.

Victor, Peter A., Edward Hanna and Atif Kubursi (1994), 'How strong is weak sustainability?' In *Modèles de développement soutenable, Des approches exclusives ou complémentaires de La soutenabilité?* Vol. I. Paris: Université Panthéon-Sorbonne, pp. 93–114.

Victor, Peter A., (2005), 'Review of Eric Neumayer's book *Weak versus Strong Sustainability*, 2nd ed (Edward Elgar Publishing, 2003)', *Ecological Economics*, **52**, 127–128.

14. Growth rate after adjustment

It is often presumed that greening the accounts of an economy will reveal that its growth had been overstated. This short chapter seeks to show that contrary to popular opinion, the rate of growth of an economy consequent upon greening its national accounts need not at all be lower than the growth rate that had been inferred from the unadjusted estimates. The re-estimated growth rate can be higher, lower, or the same as that reckoned before greening. This argument pertains specifically to average annual growth estimated over a period of years as was done under the WRI's study of Indonesia (see Chapter 19 below). This argument, however, does not necessarily apply to any one-year's growth to be derived from two successive national income estimates. If greening the accounts results in downsizing GDP (or as in the WRI study adjusting NDP) for period $t+1$ as compared with period t, then other things being equal, the growth rate will be found clearly to have fallen. This will be true unless national income for period t had itself been reduced – a fact that will obscure the change.

The WRI study of the income accounts of Indonesia that ended with the assertion of a reduced growth rate had left the GDP numbers unchanged while making the adjustments in the NDP and compared average growth in the two series during the period 1971–84. The study concluded that average growth fell from 7.1 per cent a year to an adjusted rate of 4.0 per cent. The focus on the growth rate reflects the familiar obsession with the growth rate as denoting economic success. WRI attention to the growth rate was very much in line with the prevailing economic fashion. Much more important is to watch out for the *level* of national income and its associated magnitudes, such as saving and investment, after the adjustment had been made (see Chapter 18 on the so-called resource curse). In support of my argument I offer the following illustration. It does not matter whether the growth in question is inferred from changes in the gross or net product.

Imagine a country for which conventionally estimated GDP showed an average growth rate of 10 per cent over a period between a base year (year 1 in Figure 14.1) and the end year (year 2). It matters not whether this growth covers a ten-year period or just two, but in order to show the effect

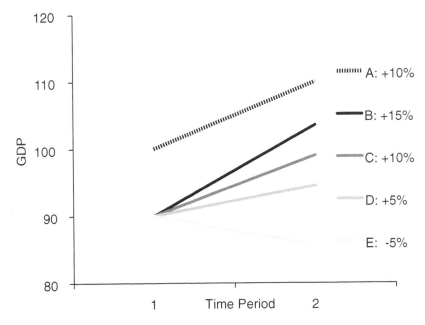

Figure 14.1   Growth after adjustment

diagrammatically with straight lines rather than with concave curves, the shorter the period considered the better. Note also that I am assuming the adjustment to have been made in GDP not NDP – a distinction that is not important for the current purpose.

In Figure 14.1 a line A (A+10%) shows a conventionally estimated GDP growing against time, ascending from 100 to 110 on the vertical axis over the interval between year 1 and year 2. Time is depicted along the horizontal axis. This expresses a conventionally estimated 10 per cent average growth rate.

Now suppose that greening the accounts showed that the level of the re-estimated GDP should be scaled down by 10 percentage points throughout. A line tracing the adjusted GDP, now line C, would be lower than the original line, rising, say from 90 to 100. This line will parallel the original line and will show the same inclination of 10 per cent as before (actually the growth rate will be nearer 11 per cent as the starting base is now 90). The adjustment, though highly significant for the *level* of GDP, is seen in this case not to have affected the growth rate. In other words, greening GDP, while reducing it substantially in absolute terms, has resulted in keeping the conventionally estimated growth rate unchanged.

This particular change, however, is only one of more possibilities. Now imagine another possibility where, owing to rising awareness of resource deterioration, a significant improvement in resource conservation occurred so that the greened GDP is now depicted by line B. Instead of the initial shortfall from the unadjusted GDP of 10 percentage points, the shortfall has by period-end narrowed to 5 percentage points below the unadjusted GDP. In this case the growth is not just the same as in the first case, but has in fact accelerated. If the scale on the vertical line were clearer line B would show that adjusted GDP has now increased from 90 at the outset to 103.5 at period-end, showing a growth of 15 per cent. Far from the greening of GDP reducing the growth rate, it is now seen to be associated with faster growth.

Yet a third possibility is Line D in the graph depicting a growth rate of 5 per cent in the adjusted GDP. In many studies this is generally assumed to occur, signifying a post-adjustment lower growth than had originally been estimated. This is possible, but it is not a general case.

Lastly a more extreme case is the one shown by line E. If post-adjustment GDP growth actually drops this only means that the resource deterioration must have intensified between the base year and the end, by which time the difference between line A and line D is seen to have widened over time so that the adjusted GDP has not only failed to show a slower growth, but actually a drastic decline.

The gist of all this is that the greening process in itself does not invariably show a lower growth than had been previously estimated.

This exposition, it should be emphasized, has been carried out with a focus on the gross product, which I maintain is the variable that should bear the brunt of the adjustment. If this were done, the net product, if estimated, would automatically reflect the adjustment. However, if the preferred medium for the adjustment is the net product the same argument made above applies: greening need not invariably reduce the growth rate of the net product. My preference for adjusting the gross product, as repeated more than once in this book, bears reiteration. As conventionally estimated GDP is inflated by capital elements contained in the proceeds from natural asset sales, and these should have no place in GDP. Besides, NDP and NNP are not always officially estimated in practice, and economic analysis in any case tends to be conducted using the gross estimates. Furthermore, employing a 'strong sustainability' approach for the adjustment as done in the Indonesia study and as favored by many others (including the BEA) deprives the adjusted numbers of *economic* sense. Deducting from the unadjusted product *all* natural asset declines (rather than only the user cost) obliterates from the commercial exploitation of natural assets the entirety of value added specifically attributable to the resource. In my view this faulty procedure exaggerates the downward adjustment of greening the national income and depresses the adjusted net product unduly. It is this flawed result, I maintain, that has doomed more than one official attempt to proceed with national account greening along more appropriate lines.

15. Pricing the invaluable: services of the world's ecosystems

PROLOGUE

As a member of the Editorial Board of *Ecological Economics*, I was invited to comment on an ambitious article published in the journal *Nature* (volume 387, May 15, 1997, pp. 253–260), which put a monetary value on the services of ecosystems, estimating these services at an annual value amounting to nearly twice the conventionally recorded global GNP. The lead author of the article was Robert Costanza.[1] This comment appeared in *Ecological Economics*, 1998, volume 25, number 1, pp. 25–27.

MIXED REACTIONS

It is constructive of *Ecological Economics* to invite comments on this imaginative and stimulating article (*Nature*, 387/15 May 1997), which draws attention to the value of the services provided by ecological systems and natural capital stocks. Such an article should in principle elicit unreserved commendation from ecological economists who are more aware than other specialists of the contribution made by ecology to economic activities and human welfare. Nevertheless, I find my own reactions to the article rather mixed. On one level, I salute this brave attempt at 'pricing the invaluable', but on yet other levels I have some misgivings, which I shall try to summarize below.

The range of valuation offered is considerable (US $38 trillion), amounting roughly to two and a half times the lower estimate, and exceeds significantly the *average* estimate of US $33 trillion. Such a wide range, while perhaps unavoidable considering the current state of knowledge, inevitably detracts from the estimates' worth. We are told that these estimates are 'almost certainly' a minimum. Thus there is the possibility that as these initial estimates are scaled upward, the range might broaden still further. That there is a chance of double counting (in that the ecological services here identified must have been, at least in part, already counted in the global gross product) this, while explicitly admitted by the authors, cannot go away, and should perhaps be quantified at a future date and reconciled with the estimates. The importance of this point derives from the fact that a vivid comparison is made between the estimated value of ecosystem services and the global gross national product (US $18 trillion) – a comparison apparently made to convey the impression that the value of such services is a multiple of the recorded product.

SERVICES AND FUNCTIONS

Table 1 (of the article) appears to make a distinction between ecosystem services and ecosystem functions, listing them under two separate columns. In many cases these are described in identical or near-identical terms. For instance, 'water regulation' is listed as a service, and 'regulation of hydrological flows' as a function; 'soil formation' as a service, and 'soil formation processes' as a function; 'pollination' as a service, and 'movement of floral gametes' as a function, etc. While it is useful to enumerate these services/functions to highlight their contributions, presenting them in two separate columns is not perhaps necessary. On the evidence of the language of Table 1, and in light of the environmental literature, one might venture the guess that the authors' 'service' is really a function, and their function is truly a service or product that is normally produced by the function. Such an interpretation would conform to the standard definition of an environmental function (see especially Hueting, 1980, Chapters 4 and 5). Hueting is nowhere mentioned in the article, nor his terminology followed. He had defined an environmental function as the current and potential use of an essential part of our biophysical surroundings for which a portion of current production, given present technology, has to be sacrificed in order to restore the future availability of the function. At low levels of activity, Hueting argued, while the function is still relatively unimpaired, its supply price is zero. But the supply price rises as the function gets progressively scarce. Under pressure of demand, competition among functions will set in, with the use of one function being at the expense of another or even itself. While still abundant, functions are free goods, falling altogether outside the purview of economics, but with expanding demand they gradually become economic goods, commanding a price that rises as their scarcity increases – a price that should be reckoned as a cost of apparent economic growth.

SUPPLY AND DEMAND

The authors give us their Figure 1, showing supply and demand curves, said to pertain to environmental functions. I find this figure difficult to follow. The empirical derivation of demand at the global level, I submit, is well nigh impossible, and the authors, I believe, drew the demand curve only for illustrative purposes. One is not assured, however, by their reference to contingent valuation, said to be used partly for pricing the functions. Reference to a consumer's surplus (to be read from these macro aggregates) also raises methodological questions and is probably irrelevant in this context. On the supply side, the concept of 'net rent' is equally neither meaningful nor relevant. With no 'producers' it is hard to figure what the authors mean by a producer's surplus even if the supply function is actually as illustrated in Figure 1. Rather than depicting the supply function (in the *Nature* article) by a curve that rises throughout its length, I would expect such a curve to lie initially along the horizontal axis from the origin until the function gets threatened, then to rise gradually with demand until it hits a vertical straight line representing saturation or exhaustion. Afterwards the cost of restoring the function increases *pari passu* with demand pressure. In order properly to illustrate this, Figure 1 in the original article should have shown not one demand curve, but a family of demand curves. As proposed in my Figure 15.1 below, demand shifts upward to the right as the scale of economic activity rises and demand moves from D_1 to D_2 to D_3.

OSCAR WILDE'S CYNIC

The classical economists had battled with the notion that some very useful goods (e.g. water) command prices, or 'values in exchange', lower than those of others (such as diamonds) which apparently are 'less useful' and whose utility, or 'value in use', is perceived as distinctly lower (Daly, 1998). It was not until the last decades of the nineteenth century, however, with the advent of 'marginalism' (involving the application of calculus to economic functions such as costs and utilities) that this apparent 'paradox' was solved.

Total and marginal valuations were distinguished one from the other, and it became obvious that while a commodity may have a high total (use) value for its buyers, its marginal value can be low in reflection of its relative abundance. The marginalist revolution was to lead to the supply–demand apparatus, and neoclassical economists moved from explaining the determination of prices to elaborating how the supply–demand model

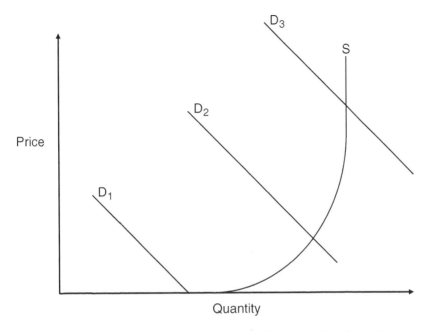

Figure 15.1 The likely shape of a global cost function of ecological services

would function under different market structures: perfect and monopolistic competition; monopoly; duopoly; oligopoly; monopsony; bilateral monopoly; etc. Much less effort began to be expended by economists on the determination of actual prices and the (theoretical) 'theory of value', a basic part of microeconomic teaching, came to dominate price analysis to such an extent that Paul Samuelson, an outstanding leader of the economics profession, once playfully suggested that the economist had become the inverse of Wilde's cynic: he knows the value of everything but the price of nothing! The *Nature* article evidently goes in the opposite direction and thus should commend itself to Samuelson!

FURTHER COMMENTS

Let me in conclusion mention two methodological reservations. Under 'Sources of error', the authors argue that current market prices may be distorted by virtue of the exclusion (inter alia) of 'household labour and the informal economy' from GNP estimates. In this, they give the impression that since these services are not valued in the national accounts, they somehow distort market prices, not realizing that the sheer existence of such activities bears unavoidably on market price determination, whether or not they are counted *ex post* in the national product. The other reservation concerns the authors' suggestion in the section labelled 'Discussion' to inflate conventional GNP by the values they quantify for ecological system services, presumably in order to record their decline when they deteriorate. As the scarcity of these services rises their unit price is also bound to rise, thus offsetting or more than offsetting their volume fall and possibly indicating a value that may be read as indicating an improved situation. Valued in money, the effect on GNP would be obscured or, worse, give spurious confidence in the integrity of the ecological systems. Estimation in physical units may be sufficient to bring their decline to the attention of citizens and politicians, and even economists. It would be useful, nevertheless, to attempt such monetary exercises in analytical studies outside the national accounts orbit, while probing their implications for sustainability and market behavior and valuation. This, of course, is what the authors of the *Nature* article, I believe, set out to do.

The article is clearly thought provoking and should be seen not as an end, but a beginning that would serve as a useful foundation on which to build improved future estimates.

ACKNOWLEDGEMENT

For useful discussions I am grateful to Joseph E. Serafy of the Rosenstiel School of Marine and Atmospheric Science, University of Miami.

NOTE

1. Besides Costanza, the other authors were d'Arge, R.; de Groote, R.; Grasso, M; Hannon, B.; Naeem, S.; Limburg, J.; Paruel, R.V.; O'Neill, R.; Raskin, R.; Sutton, P.; and Van den Belt, M.

REFERENCES

Daly, Herman (1998), 'The Return of Lauderdale's Paradox', *Ecological Economics*, **25** (1), 21–23.
Hueting, Roefie (1980), New *Scarcity and Economic Growth*. Amsterdam: North Holland Publishing Company.

PART V

Policy matters

16. Population and national income

MALTHUS AND THE IRON LAW OF WAGES

What I intend to cover here about population is very limited, and relates only to national income. Population as a source of labor was recognized by the early economists, along with land as being the major creators of wealth. But these wealth creators had claims on the product, and it is labor's claim on the product as consumers that constitutes a potential danger for ecology. Provided that labor's contribution exceeded its claims on consumption the danger remained latent. Situations where excessive labor through diminishing returns has caused labor output to fall short of its consumption is exactly what environmentalists have in modern times been warning against.

Adam Smith gave great importance to this problem and distinguished between a nation's 'gross revenue' and its 'neat revenue', the latter being the portion out of national income available for spending upon subsistence, conveniences and amusements. The difference between the gross and net income of the 'inhabitants of a great country' is equal to what must be deducted as an expense

> of maintaining; first, their fixed; and, secondly, their circulating capital; or what, without encroaching upon their capital, they can place in their stock reserved for immediate consumption, or spend upon their subsistence, convenience, and amusements (Smith, 1776 [1937], Book II, Chapter 2, p. 271).

To Smith, for maintaining society's circulating capital and thus securing the flow of labor services, the subsistence of the workers had to be covered. But it was left to Malthus to link workers' subsistence with the flows of labor services. In his famous *Essay on Population* (which underwent many revisions) Malthus (1826) built up workers' subsistence into a self-balancing mechanism that kept population in check while ensuring that wages remained at a level just sufficient to cover workers' nutrition. If wages rose above subsistence, the population would multiply and depress wages, and if these fell below subsistence, insufficient labor would push up wages. That apparently was an iron law of nature. Malthus, the *laissez-faire* enthusiast, was prepared to endorse the Corn

Laws which restricted the importation of cheap food that might disturb this balancing mechanism, even at the risk of being viewed as a champion of the landowners against the laborers (Pullen, 1987). Numerous factors, however, unsettled this iron law as markets opened up with the 'division of labor' and began to expand with better transport and foreign trade, higher productivity and technological progress – which all led to higher wages. Economic and social developments ushered in by the Industrial Revolution seemed to bury the iron law forever, and apparently Malthus himself realized this (Spengler, 1945).

And yet, a shadow of the Malthusian ghost continued to prevail, or aspects of it continued to prevail, in the less developed world where fertility rates stayed well above mortality rates. In parts of China, India, Africa and elsewhere pressure of population on local resources has periodically threatened workers' subsistence, causing deprivation and famine, and maintaining labor remuneration at levels close to subsistence. Outmigration provided some relief, but this has caused other problems. The pressure of people on the means of subsistence has very much reflected a Malthusian pattern.

THE SEVEN BILLION MARK

In the year 2011 world population passed a landmark when it reached seven billion. Environmentalists had for long warned against the pressure which population growth inflicts on world resources, very much with the Malthusian model in mind. More than four decades ago, when world population was actually still half what it is today, Paul Ehrlich wrote his famous book, *The Population Bomb,* predicting inevitable doom, and his vision was endorsed by the Club of Rome which translated it into futuristic scenarios that spelled alarm, but most people remained unconvinced and apparently unconcerned. The seven billion mark, however, renewed concern over the role of population in activating ecological stress, narrowing the options for economic and social progress. And even if population growth rates have declined in recent decades, and may decline still further, the demographic base is sufficiently large to render absolute additions to total population significant, and much of the increase comes from the poorer parts of the world. Even the sociological changes that had been expected from urbanization, improved female education, greater participation in the labor force and the trend for smaller families seem also to be too slow to make a difference. On the practical level resistance to family planning has been significant among foreign aid recipients, and ominously among the aid donors themselves. On both sides of the divide there is no shortage of pretexts. Where drastic steps had been taken to limit the number of births by force, contrary forces invoking human rights naturally developed, the effects on the gender balance and on the age structure of the population have been disruptive, and the longer term effects have yet to work themselves out in detail.

There are many poorer countries which may be judged to be 'overpopulated' though this latter expression has tended to be disparaged since it denies the possibility of remedial measures that might restore balance between people and productive opportunities. However, there is no scarcity of countries, states within countries, and even regions where the expression 'overpopulation' may not be inappropriate. These exist where the available capital and labor, applied to the limited natural resources in place, fail to provide adequately for feeding, housing, educating and delivering health care services for the inhabitants who are already immersed in poverty but keep multiplying. This situation is of course different in the more industrialized parts of the world depending on official immigration policies, and varies significantly in the developing world from place to place depending on the population density already reached. In the aid-receiving countries where room is available to accommodate a larger population there tends to be more flexibility. In places such as the United States, Canada and Australia where room exists to accommodate larger populations, immigration, when and where permitted, helps to restock the labor force with new bodies, minds and skills – sometimes unfairly taking trained people away from poorer countries that can ill afford to lose them, but seem unable to use them productively. The older countries of Europe represent yet another group where there are signs of aging populations in some, and even declining populations in others. The long-term prospects for some of these countries are opaque with few young workers at the bottom of the population 'pyramid' to provide for the needs of the expanding and often less productive top layers. No doubt importing young workers would be helpful in many ways, and in fact a redistribution of world population among regions and states could provide some alleviation. All such arguments, however, are indeed theoretical, speculative and in many respects 'utopian', given the Nation State system that makes up the world today. But we must not forget that the whole subject of 'national accounting' pertains to this very system of nation states.

Because population issues have deep roots and wide ramifications it is not easy to reduce them to a simple analytical model. They also touch on sensitive matters about which feelings are strong involving religion, psychology, ethnic identity, nationalism and politics, besides, of course, economics. It is probably because of the complexity of the subject that population, which had attracted the attention of major economists in the past, seems now to arouse less interest from the leading economists of today.

POPULATION AND NATIONAL ACCOUNTING

The national accounts do not contain any information about population, though the size of a nation's population and its age and gender structure clearly affect the size of GDP and its subdivisions, both on the side of production and also of expenditure. Though there is little in this book of a demographic import population is of great importance for *interpreting* the national accounts. Without giving thought to population size, the magnitude of a nation's GDP is not in itself meaningful. It defines the scale of an economy and places it in a position to be compared with other economies. It provides a place in a hierarchy of size that helps to correlate it with such things as its contribution to global pollution, ozone layer damage or energy consumption. It also helps in assessing international contributions to development assistance, to financing United Nations activities and in many other ways. But with minimal manipulation, a given GDP can yield much more. And here the population dimension emerges as a most useful vector. In fact GDP estimates begin to make deeper sense when related to population and reduced to a per capita basis. Given the size of GDP a larger population signifies a smaller product per capita than a smaller population does. Below the surface of account estimates, as a population of a country multiplies against its space and natural resource base, and if factor productivity fails to match up to a larger population, output per head will decline, leading to the obvious fact that an increase in aggregate GDP, by itself, signifies little by way of product availability, and even less as an indicator of 'welfare' as commonly understood. GDP is a poor indicator of welfare in any case, though many people expect that much from it. A country spread out geographically has to devote more resources to transport than a closely compacted country and its GDP would be augmented accordingly without necessarily offering greater happiness. Clearly its higher GDP will not mean greater joy. Similarly if its climate is extraordinarily cold so that it has to devote appreciable resources to heating this will inflate its GDP but will not enhance joy; and so forth.

GDP (or GNP) per head of total population is a metric that is often reckoned and widely used for international comparisons. It is taken by many people as indicating a country's level of 'development' or as an index of its inhabitants' 'welfare'. GDP numbers are initially expressed in local currencies and have to be converted to an international standard, such as the US dollar, to enable comparisons. Conversion is most commonly done using official exchange rates, but this practice has been criticized, and many refinements have been introduced to this rough and ready measure, among other methods by using conversion factors based on 'purchasing power parity' and the choice of a varied basket of purchases, which reflect popular local preferences.

In order to obtain a per head estimate, instead of using a country's total population as a denominator for GDP some analysts interested, for instance, in labor productivity have related GDP to the number of people in the work force; or to people actually employed; or to workers in specific occupations. Analysts with different interests have also used other denominators to suit their purpose.

It goes without saying that population is not a homogeneous variable. For economic analysis so much depends on its age structure, gender (at least as gender affects employment and modes of consumption), the distribution of habitation over space and of economic activities between the countryside and the ever expanding urban settlements, and hence the energy intensive transport sector. An economy with large proportions of its population of non-active age, being too young or too old to be productive, has to meet its consumption needs by the efforts of those aged in-between. The pre-work and post-work age cohorts do require housing, schooling, health care and support from the active members of society. Such an economy is obviously at a disadvantage compared with an economy whose population is mostly of active age. Living in the countryside in proximity to primary production activities may have its rewards in terms of personal satisfaction and community interactions, but it may also be associated with reduced availability of many services available to the urban inhabitants. The urbanites may also have their problems of over-crowdedness, lack of extended family relationships, unhealthy air and greater effort, expense and time to reach their workplace through dense traffic. All these factors may seem obvious, but I relate them here to draw attention to the fact that even a simple technique like that of national accounting relates to very complex matters and cannot be reduced to a set of equations or to mechanical regression coefficients. The economic 'universe', unlike that of chemistry or physics, is not uniform, and a reading on the scale of per capita income has not the same quality meaning in different countries. A family's income of $1000 a year is hardly the same for the United States, India and Mali.

REFERENCES

Ehrlich, Paul R. (1968), *The Population Bomb*. San Francisco, CA: Sierra Club, Ballantine Books.

Malthus, Thomas (1826), *An Essay on the Principle of Population*, 6th edn. London: Macmillan.

Pullen, J. M. (1987), 'Malthus, Thomas Robert (1766–1834)'. In *The New Palgrave Dictionary of Economics*, Vol. 3, pp. 280–285.

Smith, Adam (1776 [1937]), *An Inquiry into the Nature and Causes of the Wealth of Nations*, Modern Library Edition. New York: Random House.

Spengler, Joseph J. (1945), 'Malthus's total population theory: a restatement and reappraisal', *Canadian Journal of Economics and Political Science*, **XI**, 234–264. Reprinted in J. J. Spengler and W. R. Allen (eds.) (1960), *Essays in Economic Thought: Aristotle to Marshall*. Chicago, IL: Rand McNally & Company.

17. Green accounting and economic policy

PROLOGUE

The genesis of this chapter was a paper that appeared in 1997 in *Ecological Economics*, **21**, pp. 217–229. Whilst policy matters have been raised in practically all the preceding chapters, here the major policy issues that merit consideration once the national accounts have been greened are grouped together. Drastic excisions have been made in the original paper to avoid more repetition. Some repetition of matters dealt with in earlier chapters remains, but it is the kind of repetition that sheds new light on what has been said before. This is particularly the case with sections II and III on weak and strong sustainability and on the satellite accounts, which are elaborated here to open up the discussion of macroeconomic policy issues.

I INTRODUCTION

GREEN ACCOUNTING METHODS

The course of the green accounting has by no means been easy. Its advocates, as we have seen, have come from different directions pursuing different ends and this has promoted much divergence among greening methods. One result of disagreement on methods has been that macroeconomic monitoring and policy formation continue to be based on the unadjusted numbers, which in some situations are so flawed as to be misleading. Some reformers had come to the greening initiative in pursuit of welfare assessment; others with a desire to protect ecological wealth. My own purpose throughout has been to get a better grasp on the estimation of output in GDP. A divergence of outlook should be stressed once more between rich and poor countries. Greening the accounts will make little difference for the majority of the industrialized economies whose primary product sectors in most cases are modest. By contrast these very sectors loom large in the economies of a large number of developing countries.

Yet the influence of the richer countries on the new SNA has been great. Their experts dominate powerful international bodies that helped to shape SNA93 and they have been in a position to offer bilateral economic aid in support of greening methods they favor. To repeat, the economies that got overlooked in this process are essentially those of the poorer countries where primary production abounds, and where the deterioration of natural resource stocks is ignored in the macroeconomic estimates. Their incomes get exaggerated, their growth record becomes murky, and their balances of payments are often uncertain and fuzzy. Fuzziness in this regard results from including in their current trade balances unrepeatable exports of natural assets (Haberler, 1976).

Though improved measurements of output and expenditure will often serve ecological purposes, they will principally serve economic objectives. Selling natural assets and including the proceeds in the gross domestic product is wrong on both accounting and economic grounds. GDP should be made up of value added, and if it is contaminated through error, or by flawed accounting methods, with elements of a capital nature – elements for instance representing asset sales – these should be expunged from it. In conventional accounting GDP is estimated gross of depreciation of produced fixed assets, just as the 'gross profits' of an enterprise contain asset depreciation until it is removed for the estimation of its net results. Since NDP is not always available, macroeconomic analysis is commonly conducted on the basis of estimates of the gross product: GDP or GNP though these quantities are recognized even by their users as not always sustainable.

There is a fundamental difference in kind between the depreciation of produced assets and the loss of natural resources. This I had elaborated earlier but merits recalling when discussing policy matters. Depreciation of assets – and for green accounting natural resources are part of society's assets – usually amount to a small and predictable fraction of the assets. By contrast, natural asset declines and environmental deterioration have no regular pattern, and vary considerably from one accounting period to the next. Strictly speaking the green accounting I have been espousing all along does not involve value judgment on my part as to the desirability or otherwise of preserving the environment. To me greening the accounts simply invokes economic and accounting principles necessary for correctly estimating the national income. Income, it will be recalled, must be sustainable by definition. To the extent possible, the arguments made here will keep close to national accounting practices, including the traditional focus on transacted activities, the use of accounting methods for the valuation of stocks, and the employment of market prices, however deviant they may be from theoretically optimum prices. For national accounting prices are merely 'weights' used to aggregate heterogeneous economic activities that make up GDP. Thus shadow-pricing, favored by many analysts, including the 'internalization' of environmental externalities, is avoided, and imputations of cost are kept to a minimum. While using shadow-pricing for valuation in place of market-pricing can shed more analytical light on the national accounts, its proper place is in studies outside the formal accounting framework.

EMPIRICAL EXPLORATIONS

It is well known that attempts have been made to 'green' the conventional national accounts for a number of countries in order to capture environmental change or, perhaps more accurately, part of environmental change. Yet not all such adjustments have been made properly, and the revised estimates have seldom been taken seriously to reassess economic progress or influence economic policies for the very countries studied. SNA93 attempted to use some of these as the basis for its modest environmental proposals, but only for 'greening' the accounts, stopping short of proposing policy change. But of course, it was not in the brief of SNA reformers to attend to policy change. So the implications of any adjustments for macroeconomic policies in the countries affected to my knowledge have remained unexplored.

Careful examination of these studies (for Papua New Guinea and Mexico, for instance) shows an exaggerated attention to welfare, which in practice has been distracting to the green accounting initiative. One objective of this chapter is to indicate the kind of economic policies that will have to be re-assessed once the accounts have been properly greened. Before that, however, some important issues need to be disentangled relating to recent efforts to 'integrate the environmental and economic accounts' that had been purposely separated.[1]

It should be stated once more that a comprehensive coverage of environmental deterioration in the national accounts is not possible and should not be expected. Certain aspects of environmental deterioration, such as losses of biodiversity or disintegration of ecological systems, though obviously economically important, will remain difficult to gauge even in physical units, let alone amenable to being valued in money for possible inclusion in the national accounts. Thus even when the accounts are claimed to have been satisfactorily 'greened' we should not expect the greening to be complete or to provide a panacea for environmental ailments. The national accounting system, after all, is an economic apparatus, designed to produce *economic* magnitudes, and even after greening by whatever method, the accounts will continue to have a limited capacity to indicate either the totality of environmental change or to show the way for reform. Physical indicators of environmental deterioration are likely to serve such environmental ends much more effectively than the system of national accounts will ever be able to do. On the other hand, once properly greened, the revised accounts will yield a more truthful level of national income, and describe more accurately the past record of macroeconomic change. But the new estimates will also enable a re-examination of policies, which had been based on the old accounts and may suggest other courses of action for fiscal, monetary, trade and exchange rate management.

ECONOMIC IMPACTS

Environmental deterioration impinges on national economies in multiple ways and to different degrees. Evidently the environment sustains basic life-support systems and provides the overall context within which all human actions take place, whether economic or otherwise. From a narrow economic perspective the environment is the source of raw materials and energy and the ultimate recipient and assimilator of the wastes of production and consumption. When the world population and the scale of economic activity were small relative to nature's abundance it made sense for economists effectively to exclude Nature from their vision, both as 'source' and as 'sink', treating environmental services as free goods. That view is no longer defensible, and in some individual country situations seems obtuse if not actually perverse. Polluted air and contaminated water among many other symptoms of atrophy originate in forces, which inflict harm on society that translates into economic losses. Awareness of this fact, often portrayed plainly by physical indicators, has encouraged the identification of major sources of pollution. And this has led in a number of countries to a successful internalization of the ecological costs of individual activities, and thus to reducing their harm. The drive for pollution-abatement has been strongest and most successful in the more affluent countries – a fact that has led some analysts wrongly to assume that environmental protection, seen as income elastic, will improve as incomes rise, so that pollution will be addressed automatically at least once income per capita has attained a certain threshold. Such optimism – and note that it is not claimed to apply to source resources – which in essence would tolerate passivity in anticipation of the presumed self-adjusting mechanism bringing about the change, had many champions. But this optimism was later to be seen as unwarranted. One influential denunciation of it was led by

Kenneth Arrow.[2] It is however important to remember that for the richer nations environmental concerns tend to be concentrated on pollution. With a few exceptions many of their natural 'source resources' have long been exhausted, and the bulk of their domestic product is now derived from secondary and tertiary activities. Since pollution can be captured in physical indicators and redressed by policing and regulation, green accounting appears to the richer countries as unnecessary or, in any case, of low priority.

Not that pollution is any less important for the poorer countries, especially where large and rising populations are pressing on an already exhausted environment. In the case of many communities in Asia, Africa and Latin America, on top of the damage caused by pollution, the environment *as a source* is also under stress. Agriculture, forestry, fishing, mineral extraction and other primary activities – activities rooted in the natural environment – are usually major sources of employment and well-being. As this environment deteriorates, the very basis of their prosperity, such as it is, gets progressively undermined. The national accounts routinely fail to record natural asset erosion while parading gross revenues as incomes. That economists should pay greater attention in their analyses to the sustainability of natural resources seems to be rather elementary.[3]

II SUSTAINABILITY AND GREEN ACCOUNTING

WEAK AND STRONG SUSTAINABILITY

Attention to 'sustainability' gained much from the Brundtland Report (World Commission on Environment and Development, 1987) and later from the United Nations Conference on the Environment and Development (UNCED, 1992). 'Sustainability' and 'sustainable development' are not easy concepts to pin down without ambiguity, but they seem to have been widely accepted as desirable, even when different meanings are attached to them.[4]

Weak sustainability has certainly been invoked to define a level of sustainability that revolves around the proper measurement of income, which, by definition, has to be sustainable. The main underlying argument is that income, whether gross or net, must be made up of value added, and should not contain the proceeds of asset sales. Thus in order to estimate income from receipts obtained by the sale of natural assets (such as cutting and selling trees in excess of their regeneration, over-fishing, or depleting mineral stocks) capital, including natural capital, must be *kept intact* simply as a device for estimating 'sustainable' income.[5] The accounting principle of keeping capital intact for income estimation in fact predates Adam Smith who certainly recognized it,[6] and has since been endorsed by successive generations of economists. It comes into play for national income measurement through allowance made for capital consumption, which adjusts the gross product into a more sustainable net product. But this fundamental principle tends to be ignored by national accountants when income originates from the sale of natural capital, even when the resource, such as timber or petroleum, is marketable and actually transacted. Receipts derived from such activities are uncritically reckoned as income though in fact they are bound eventually to cease if asset sales continue. Weak sustainability in the sense of ensuring, through proper income estimation, that capital, including natural capital, is maintained intact may therefore be regarded merely as a tool for the estimation of 'sustainable' income. In this sense it can be perceived as devoid of value judgment since it does not prescribe any course of behavior. In other words, weak sustainability is not a normative concept, but positive and analytical, merely required as a facilitating device for the very difficult task of income estimation. It is well to remember that for all accounting, including national accounting, the sustainability thus secured is only a year-by-year sustainability. But extending the process over time, year after year, will lengthen the span of this income sustainability.[7]

Strong sustainability on the other hand aims to maintain the *stock* of natural resources over time, including the capacity of nature to assimilate wastes. It is usually advocated on the argument that natural resources are essential for many purposes including the continuation of economic activities. Natural resources, it is reasoned, provide the ingredients to which value may be added by labor and capital in all kinds of economic activities, and cannot easily be substituted for by produced capital. *Ceteris paribus* if environmental resources diminish economic activity will decline, if not immediately then inevitably later. Thus Herman Daly, an ardent advocate of strong sustainability, has denied 'substitutability', claiming the existence of a complementary relationship between natural resources and produced capital (see, for instance, Daly and Cobb, 1989) and arguing that the latter capital cannot replace the former. This view is opposed by many technology optimists who take a relationship of substitutability for granted. Recognizing the analytical credentials of the user cost, Daly has suggested that weak sustainability could be strengthened by reinvesting the equivalent of the user cost of a depleting natural resource in developing renewable substitutes specifically targeted to replace the natural resource being depleted.

A major misunderstanding over substitutability has certainly emerged in the writings of some of the detractors of the user-cost method, and this I have already covered in Chapter 10. My insisting that capital in general, including natural capital, should be kept intact for income estimation does not mean that all forms of capital are necessarily substitutable for each other. From the perspective of a single productive entity, and specifically for *ex post* accounting, keeping capital intact means that a reduction of one form of capital must compensated for by the formation or acquisition of another form of capital to maintain the stream of income. The purpose here is limited to ensuring that the income *of the entity* concerned may be sustained.

Keeping capital intact for the estimation of income as already said is a rolling process, carried out periodically, typically one year at a time, and because of the near horizon of this process, it is not particularly suitable as a normative long-run instrument for ecological conservation. However, outside the framework of national accounting, 'strong sustainability' comes into its own when a long view is taken, and the perspective is broadened beyond the interests of individual productive units. Indeed the situation would be untenable where every productive unit were to tolerate the decline of its natural capital in the expectation that investing in produced capital would compensate for this decline so that income somehow could be sustained: it obviously could not be maintained in that event. We may therefore conclude that the accounting tool of 'keeping capital intact', necessary as it is for the *ex post* estimation of an income which must be sustained for a single entity from one accounting period to the next, should not be taken as an *ex ante* injunction to liquidate natural capital on the dubious pretext that it can be replaced, without limits, by produced capital (see El Serafy, 1996).

III   THE SATELLITE ACCOUNTING SYSTEM

THE SEEA

The system of integrated economic and environmental accounting, SEEA (1993), recommended by the United Nations Statistics Division as the appropriate venue for greening the national accounts, should be seen as the outcome of a long process of exploration and debate dating back to the mid-1980s. The issue was considered in detail during the workshops organized by UNEP in collaboration with the World Bank, which discussed the feasibility of adjusting the SNA to incorporate environmental change. Some of the ideas generated under that initiative were subsequently applied experimentally to a number of country studies to test the waters, so to speak, for methods to green the accounts. The SNA, which had remained virtually unchanged since 1968, was amended, and this brought in the novel system of the 'satellite accounts for the environment'. As previously stated SNA93 came out in the name of five international agencies whose representatives had collaborated on its revision via an interagency working group.[8] And guidance for the implementation of the environmental proposals was set out in a companion volume, *Handbook of National Accounting*, published, also in 1993, by the United Nations Statistics Division under the title *Integrated Environmental and Economic Accounting*.

Although this handbook was meant to be a practical guide for implementing the proposed 'Integrated System of Economic and Environmental Accounts' its authors were aware that controversy over adjustment methods had not settled. So departing from the role of an 'implementation manual' it had to show details of preparatory work that demonstrated some of the methodological disagreements on how actually to green the accounts. Significantly the 1993 handbook was called '*An Interim Version*'. In that version, adjusting the standard macroeconomic estimates – the very heart of national accounting – was flagged as only one of a number of objectives sought out by the SEEA. But the satellite accounts had been expected to 'integrate' the environment into the national accounts since that integration was denied in the 'mainframe'. In retrospect, however, with no standard format or even clarification of purpose they seem to be depositories of information related somehow to 'points of contact' between the environment and the 'economic system'. With a bias for recoding ecological stocks the tilt towards strong sustainability became obvious. The satellite accounts turned out to be a sop to the environmentalists provided the core accounts remained protected from change.

THE WRONG EMPHASIS ON STOCKS

The over-attention given to stocks in the SEEA seems to accommodate those environmentalists who had wished to use the national accounts to highlight environmental deterioration. Pressure from that source did not target income re-estimation. Under the SEEA the estimation of the stock of natural assets is the initial point from which all environmental accounting must begin. Changes in the stock during the accounting period are taken inappropriately as determining the estimation of the flow accounts (GDP, GNP and their component parts). As it is not possible to compile a comprehensive list of environmental stocks at either end of the accounting period, it should have been obvious to the accounting reformers that this approach cannot be reliable or useful. This is because it tries to infer important flows from changes in an incomplete list of assets of controversial values. Even for produced capital no country, however advanced, has managed to compile such a comprehensive list, which for completeness must include the country's infrastructure.

The inappropriateness of this approach is further enhanced if the stocks are to be valued, as recommended, at current prices that differ between the beginning and end of the accounting period. The standard *accounting* rule – a rule that is overlooked in national accounting – is to value year-end stocks at the same prices of the opening stocks unless the market has declined in the interval in which case the lower prices must be used. This precautionary rule, which is meant to ensure that income is not over-estimated to the detriment of sustainability, has little appeal to economists. Unlike the accountants who, similarly to historians, are retrospective, economists tend to be forward looking, attaching great importance to replacement costs (El Serafy, 1995).[9] When current prices are used for stock valuation and changes in stock values are incorporated in the flow accounts, the integrity of the latter is damaged for *economic* purposes and very little *environmental* wisdom will be gained either. Value changes will obscure the more informative physical changes.[10]

It should be remembered that it is in fact the decline of natural stocks that gets transacted as *a flow*, not the stock itself. And it would be wrong to consider the entire decline in environmental stocks, even valued at the same prices, as a charge against the gross product as it would be equally wrong to incorporate changes due to upward or downward re-assessments of the stock in GDP in the year of the re-assessment.[11] The amount to be charged as capital consumption should be only the imputed cost of environmental resource use, the *user-cost* portion. It would be better still to exclude this capital element from the gross product altogether since it does not represent value added, and no adjustment of the net product would then be necessary. The user-cost approach, it may be repeated, is applicable to both depletable and renewable resources – the latter to the extent they are being 'mined' (i.e. when their exploitation exceeds their natural or human assisted regeneration). Once a user-cost approach is followed, the accounts become sensitive to sustainability through the device of estimating correct, i.e. sustainable, levels of income. This is because the user cost indicates extraction as a ratio of the physical stock being extracted during the year (valued at current market prices) spelling out the resource's life expectancy. The inverse of this proportion, the resource's life expectancy counted in years, is an obvious indicator of the sustainability of current income.[12]

INCOME FROM RESOURCE DEPLETION

How should the depletion of exhaustible resources then be reflected in the national accounts? If we include sale proceeds in the gross product and treat the decline of the stock due to exploitation as depreciation and deduct it for the estimation of the net product, we end up totally wiping out the contribution of this activity from the net product. Besides, the estimated gross product will be kept unaltered, inflated wrongly by the proceeds of asset sales. The proper way to estimate a sustainable income from depletion, as I have been asserting, is by employing the user-cost method, which converts revenue from extraction into a stream of non-declining income. Alternative methods, including the Hotelling–Hartwick approach (Hotelling, 1931; Hartwick, 1977; Hartwick and Hageman, 1993) which seek to estimate 'resource rent' per unit of product as the difference between the market price and the marginal cost of extraction, while theoretically correct and obviously applicable to *optimal* depletion, are not operational for national accounting and are in many respects irrelevant.[13]

TREATING POLLUTION

When a country successfully curtails pollution by regulation and taxation, insisting for instance on removing lead from gasoline, the costs incurred in this process will show up as intermediate inputs to be charged against output. GDP then would be reduced accordingly, and its estimation will come out right without any greening needed. In the more typical case where anti-pollution regulation has not become pervasive, greening the accounts for pollution should best rely on setting standards of acceptable ambience or tolerance of emissions impurity, and calculating the theoretical cost of meeting such standards, to be imputed as a cost of conventional GDP.[14] Such a cost will naturally depend on current technology and may contain elements of subjectivity. Some believe that correcting for pollution will call for only a modest adjustment to conventional GDP estimates, but this generalization will have many exceptions. In comparison, running down natural resources can be on a substantial scale and needs to be carefully assessed and directly expressed in the macroeconomic measurements that make up the family of national accounts. This should not be viewed, as stated earlier, as either environmental or novel, but simply as an overdue correction of the accounts that already contain many natural resource disinvestment elements, albeit often at erroneous, mainly zero, values.

WHAT SHOULD WE BE ACCOUNTING FOR?

It is important to be clear about the purpose for which we seek to green the accounts.[15] If the goal is to describe the state of the environment, emphasis should understandably be placed on assessing environmental *stocks*. But for this purpose the units of account should not be monetary, but physical. Money values fluctuate with the market for individual resources and with the general price level. Little can be gained for environmental conservation from hiding meaningful *volume* changes under the masking veil of money. If a resource gets scarcer thereby pushing up its price, the total value change would not indicate the increased scarcity. But if accounting in physical units, or in indices based on physical units, is best for revealing environmental change, the question may be asked as to why cannot this be done *outside* the national accounting framework? An inevitably partial entering of physical stocks in satellite accounts, deliberately placed away from the 'economic' accounts, does not amount to 'integration', and is in any case of limited utility for income estimation. If environmental deterioration is to be conveyed via the national accounts, whether integrally in the core accounts or peripherally in satellite accounts, the objective should be unambiguously to reach more realistic macroeconomic measurements, with the stocks kept firmly in the background and not as the prime mover of the green accounting process.[16]

IV POLICY IMPLICATIONS OF GREENING THE NATIONAL ACCOUNTS

POLICY MATTERS

If economists accept the measurements of the conventional accounts as valid and set out to analyze the economic problems of a country that is depleting its natural assets on an appreciable scale and counting the sale proceeds of commercially exploited resources as value added, their macroeconomic analysis is likely to be wrong, and the policy cures they prescribe unsuitable or even harmful. When the national output, as expressed in GDP, needs to be adjusted downward because a substantial part of it is not value added, then the economy in fact must be recognized as much poorer than the accounts make it out to be. The degree of output exaggeration may, in some cases, amount to 20 per cent of the conventionally estimated GDP (El Serafy, 1993a), a finding that is corroborated in some sense by estimates of 'genuine savings' made by the World Bank (1995). If in addition unaccounted for pollution is also taken into consideration, this can expose the unadjusted national accounts of many countries to be seriously flawed and misleading. If as economists we are unable to assess the level of economic activity, how can we proceed to reckon the productivity of the various inputs which involve the use of natural assets, whether for projects, sectors, or the aggregate economy? Do conventional estimates of individual or total factor productivity have any value if neither the products (if inflated by assets sales), nor the inputs (where natural resources are treated as costless), fail to be measured properly? What significance can we attach to an incremental capital output ratio (ICOR) that implies that rapid liquidation of natural assets represents high productivity and signifies desirable economic behavior? Would we be able to judge if an economy is genuinely growing? How would we justify building apparently sophisticated macroeconomic models to illuminate the structural workings of an economy when the data fed into the model are flawed? The inadequate estimates of national income may be good enough for short-term demand management, but are highly questionable either for indicating genuine economic progress, or for guiding long-term development.

INTERNATIONAL TRADE AND PRICES

It should be stressed that the unadjusted macroeconomic estimates produced by the conventional national accounts continue to be used for economic analysis and international comparisons. This is because SNA93 has kept the core accounts immune from change, viewing them perversely as 'economic' and in no need of significant change. Participation in world trade, a developmental drive pursued in earnest by the Bretton Woods institutions since the end of World War II, has sought, through conditions attached to the provision of financial assistance, to align domestic prices with international prices. By taking international prices as the norm, the process aims to guide country specialization through free trade to where its 'comparative advantage' lies. But this process, admirable as it is on the theoretical level, will not necessarily lead to the internalization of environmental costs. International prices are seldom Pareto-ideal, and are often also distorted by non-market forces including subsidization of agricultural products by important exporters, and political and military interventions by powerful importers to influence the markets of important products. These actions tend to depress international prices, including the prices of strategic products such as petroleum, and thus distort genuine comparative advantage.

It should be added that the supply reaction of individual developing countries to international prices varies. In some cases the supply curves of primary exports are backward-rising, reflecting negative income effects caused by the poverty of the sellers and lack of substitutes to be offered for export when the price of a natural resource product gets depressed. In this case lower international prices would induce greater rather than smaller volumes of exports – a reaction that with more waves of supply increases leads into a vicious circle of further price declines. The international market for primary products is devoid as a rule of adequate anti-dumping mechanisms similar in effectiveness to those available for internationally traded manufactures and overseen by UNCTAD. Selling natural resources below their full environmental cost by one large source, whether motivated by long-term political or military considerations, or simply by short-term expediency, will, through international competition, cause primary products to continue to be underpriced, and generate a trend for yet lower prices. Awareness of this process is growing among the poorer countries but their ability to restrain it is obviously limited.

ECONOMIC POLICIES AFTER GREENING THE ACCOUNTS

There are at least three important policy issues that would need to be examined once the national accounts have been properly greened. These are first, savings and investment; second, domestic price stability and the exchange rate; and third, the balance of payments on current account. A fourth issue is the fiscal balance which is often inaccurately estimated when natural resource exploitation takes place in the public sector and the receipts from natural resource sales flow directly into the public treasury and are treated as current fiscal revenues. All these issues are obviously inter-connected.

SAVING AND INVESTMENT

It matters a great deal for sustainability whether or not an economy is saving and investing sufficiently for its future. If the downward adjustment of GDP on account of resource depletion and degradation is appreciable, this will directly affect the reckoning of saving and investment. Given consumption, if GDP is significantly reduced in a closed economy, estimates of savings and capital formation must be revised downward as I have shown in Chapter 8 on post-Brundtland adjustments. I had stressed this argument in El Serafy (1981, 1989, 1991). The attention given to 'genuine savings' by the Environment Department of the World Bank in 1995 was certainly welcome though it was obviously imperfect and inadequate for testing 'sustainability'. Saving is only one of several policy issues that have been raised by the national accounting reformers since the mid-1980s, and concern for macroeconomic policy issues should not be confined to a consideration of net savings or net capital formation, but should be extended to the whole family of national accounts. If *produced* capital consumption – perhaps amounting to 10% of GDP which appears as a kind of norm for many countries – is combined with estimated *environmental* depletion and degradation, say of the order of 20 per cent of GDP, then many countries' net saving and capital formation would turn out to be significantly negative – a sure indicator of unsustainability.

PRICE STABILITY AND THE EXCHANGE RATE

When a country is selling its environmental assets and not insulating the sale proceeds from other monetary flows, a phenomenon known as the Dutch disease will take hold, and its domestic terms of trade between non-tradable goods (such as real estate and services) and tradable goods (such as manufactured products) will get distorted to the detriment of traded goods activities. The prices of housing and of many services will appreciate and those of manufactures fall with downward pressures coming also from imports. A process of 'de-development' would set in, shrinking previously productive and labor-employing sectors in the more industrialized economies, and hindering the development of potential secondary activities in pre-industrial countries liquidating their natural assets. To counteract this phenomenon, monetary sterilization (i.e. insulating the foreign exchange export receipts from being mingled with the domestic money supply) becomes necessary. Devaluation is another weapon in the armory to be used against the Dutch disease, often becoming necessary specifically in order to counteract the rising domestic costs of products to be exported from the 'non-booming' sectors of the economy (Corden, 1984).

How do we judge a domestic currency over-valuation? A procedure, quite often used to determine whether or not a country's domestic currency has appreciated vis-à-vis the currencies of its trading partners, frequently fails when applied to natural resource exporting economies. This failure would be due to overlooking the effect on the domestic price level of the availability of cheaper imports paid for by exporting what in effect is natural capital. The application of the procedure begins by selecting a year in the relatively recent past, judged to have been a year when the exchange rate was roughly 'right'. An index of domestic inflation is then calculated to estimate the general domestic price rise from the base year. This domestic index is then compared to a composite index of inflation in the country's main trading partners. So indexes of inflation in individual trading partners are then combined into an overall index using weights reflecting the importance of each partner in trade. Devaluation would be indicated to the degree that domestic inflation, thus estimated, has exceeded foreign inflation. While this method is capable of yielding reasonably satisfactory results in the absence of a Dutch disease and where the national accounts roughly approximate reality, it will not at all be a reliable guide of foreign exchange policy for a resource-depleting economy. If the proceeds from the unsustainable exports of natural assets are employed to finance an import surplus – as they often do – thereby suppressing a domestic inflation that may otherwise have become manifest – then an apparent stability or near-stability of the domestic price level cannot be taken as a genuine barometer of inflation. And devaluation, which had not been suspected as a policy option, could in fact have been indicated. Quite often the domestic currencies of resource-exporting countries become over-valued – a factor that encourages imports and inhibits exports from alternative industries. The effect would be the obstruction of possible industrial diversification away from dependence on the natural resource sectors. When analysing macroeconomic developments economists have rarely given enough thought to this important policy issue.

Before leaving this discussion mention should be made of a scholarly attempt (Sunderlin and Wunder, 2000) to assess the impact of the Dutch disease associated with mineral exploitation on tropical deforestation. Assessing such an impact, however, proved elusive. The authors tested the hypothesis that countries that contained forests while having a high proportion of petroleum and other minerals in their exports experienced low deforestation incidence, and found the evidence wanting for such a hypothesis. Too many factors were judged to be at stake to support this simplified notion.

THE BALANCE OF PAYMENTS ON CURRENT ACCOUNT

Looking at the same phenomenon from a different angle, a free market for foreign exchange may be artificially sustaining an overvalued domestic currency owing to the simple fact that the proceeds of natural capital exports are recorded in the balance of payments on current account, thus hiding a genuine deficit. The market for foreign exchange is often too myopic to distinguish current from capital flows so that the inflow of foreign exchange, irrespective of the account in which it is recorded, will tend to push up the value of the domestic currency in terms of foreign currencies. Analysts should therefore make an effort to discern the nature of these flows in order to get a better grip on appropriate macroeconomic management, and should be on the alert considering devaluation as a policy choice. A cleaned up current account would be an effective tool in this direction.

The question as to whether exports of environmental assets should or should not be recorded in the current account of the balance of payments was raised by no less an authority on international trade than the late Harvard Professor Gottfried Haberler (1976, p. 184, note 12), but his view has since been ignored. If, after adjusting the product accounts, a parallel attempt is made to purge the balance of payments on current account of flows of a capital nature, care should be exercised in this process. This is because conceptually the domestic or national product is made up (or should be made up) only of value added, whereas exports and imports contain within them also non-value added elements used for their production. The 'purging' will not be easy or devoid of controversy: that is why few economists have been prepared to confront it. So it remains a promising field of enquiry that one day should attract (and reward) a risk-taking economist.

It may be added that the process of adjusting the balance of payments flows in the manner just described should focus on exports and not imports. This is because the importing country may be construed as acquiring the imports in question, value added as well as associated non-value-added ingredients, and for this privilege it has to pay for them by exports. In the case of transactions between two industrialized countries, where trade may be construed as being largely made up of value added on both sides, the distinction between value added and other inputs could be ignored for the purpose at hand. Also trade on both sides may be assumed not to be different in composition to make the effort worthwhile. On the other hand, for a developing country where part of exports (and unadjusted GDP) represents a significant amount of user cost of natural resources, this part should be excluded from exports in parallel with its exclusion from GDP. If this is done properly, the current account will look quite different. There will certainly be resistance by conventional economists (and national accountants) to adjusting the balance of payments in the manner just described, but an analytical exercise clarifying the nature of the different strands of balance of payments flows, even if carried out outside the framework of the national accounts, would still be useful for the benefit of economic analysis and for designing macroeconomic policies for natural resource dependent countries.

V OTHER RELATED ISSUES

STRUCTURAL ADJUSTMENT PROGRAMS

Misguided blame has been levelled at policies implemented under stabilization and structural adjustment programs supported, inter alia, by the IMF and the World Bank. The claim is often made that these operations have had harmful effects on the environment. It is undoubtedly true that reducing public expenditure in the name of fiscal balance will trim or abolish public programs friendly to the environment. However, the austerity ushered in by these initiatives is unavoidable if the economy concerned had been living beyond its means, showing deficits both domestic and external, and had in the process accumulated foreign liabilities over and above its ability to service them. Short of the creditors forgiving a significant part of the debt, and most creditors are naturally reluctant to do so, the indebted country must cut its public expenditure as a necessary step towards balancing its accounts. These cuts may fall on the poor, on health programs, on the environment or on other laudable ends, normally worthy of protection. To safeguard these ends against cutting public expenditure would defeat the structural adjustment process itself. But as a way out a set of carefully balanced expenditure cuts may be worked out to safeguard some high priority areas, though environmental concerns, being often of a longer-run nature, may get sacrificed in the short run in favor of more pressing objectives. Sacrificing the environment, at least for a while, is not uncommon since, even without adjustment programs, the poor have often to compromise, running down the sources of their meager livelihood in order to survive: in a kind of a 'Hobson's Choice' imposed on them by the severity of their conditions. That is why poverty mitigation programs if carefully designed will be generally helpful to the environment.

While still on the subject of structural adjustment, it may be suggested that instead of passively examining the deleterious effects of these programs on natural resources it will be more fruitful to try and use this powerful instrument pro-actively to counteract environmentally harmful practices already in place. But these practices have to be identified on the ground through detailed research beforehand. For instance policies leading to the wasteful use of water, the settlement of landless peasants on previously forested public lands, subsidizing cattle raising ventures, and encouraging the exports of underpriced natural resources and their products should be thoroughly scrutinized, their hidden environmental costs estimated and set against the more observable benefits they bring. In Costa Rica, for instance, a minimal level of land tax that had remained unchanged in nominal terms for half a century was judged in a World Bank study to be instrumental in encouraging landowners to expand their holdings, taking land out of the virgin forest through a complex modus operandi of temporarily settling landless peasants in a never-ending mechanism that continually reduces forest cover. While privately profitable, this process is only profitable through tacit and indirect public subsidization at the expense of the national treasury. The land acquired from the forest is converted to arable use for only one or two years after which the soil is eroded. The land then falls in the hands of large-scale ranchers using uneconomic cattle-raising methods. A rational system of taxation instituted under a thoughtful adjustment program would put a stop to this process which appears to be prevalent in Latin American countries with remaining forests and is well known to forestry specialists. I came across this phenomenon first hand when working for the World Bank (El Serafy, 1988).

SHOULD ALL COUNTRIES GREEN THEIR NATIONAL ACCOUNTS?

The question may now be asked as to whether all countries would benefit from greening their national accounts and where the gains would be sufficiently important to warrant the effort. One cannot be categorical a priori, and judgment has to be made on a case-by-case basis to set likely benefits against the net costs of such an exercise. There may be a presumption, however, that countries whose industrial structure is dominated by primary activities, or whose exports are mainly or appreciably made up of primary commodities, would be a priority target for investigation (El Serafy, 1993a, table 2 lists 14 developing countries where three primary commodity exports made up upward of 40 per cent of exports by value around 1990 and this situation is likely to have persisted). But such presumptions will have to be corroborated by detailed expert knowledge at the level of field investigations. The involvement of local economists in such investigations with knowledge of social mores and institutional structures will be necessary. Expatriate economists have to familiarize themselves with local conditions, perhaps apprising themselves of previous environmental studies, the country's 'environmental action plan' if it exists, and any sectoral reports containing relevant information.[17] Above all they should seek the cooperation of local experts including sociologists, ecologists and economists. World Bank economists working on these countries should realize that it makes no sense to produce optimistic extrapolations of exports, say, over a 10-year period, mechanically without carefully examining the resource base from which the extrapolated exports will have to emanate.

THE ROLE OF PHYSICAL INDICATORS

While some industrialized countries have given support to the idea of money-valued 'green accounting', they have tended to view green accounting as an *environmental* instrument – a view that obviously dominated SNA93 and its aftermath. Their major concern on the whole has been focused on issues of pollution. While there have been notable cases where the national accounts were subjected to experimental 'greening' for source-resource changes, I know of no country that has systematically re-examined its economic policies along the policy spectrum outlined above in the light of revised accounts. As I reiterated in various places in this book the process of amending the SNA has been managed by these very countries, and reflects, in my judgment, the biased view that the economic accounts as conventionally compiled have been adequate all along. Any adjustment needed was viewed essentially as a sop to the environmentalists, could be divorced from the central SNA 'constellation', and impounded in peripheral satellites. It is also probably not unfair to add that the national income statisticians, especially those who have been involved in adjusting the SNA, tend to favor leaving the conventional accounts unadjusted to preserve the continuity of historical time series however imperfectly estimated they might have been. Many economists no doubt will resent the kind of criticism made in section IV above, which in effect says that they had in many instances misdiagnosed economic ills, and sometimes prescribed harmful economic medicine based on faulty national accounts. Instead, in my experience when economists are confronted with the inadequacy of the accounts and the kind of criticism I have been making in this chapter they would plead ignorance of national accounting methods, yet keep using the numbers national accountants produce. If they happen to have concerns over the environment they would rather safely refer to physical indicators of environmental deterioration, preferring them to any tampering with the so-called 'economic accounts'.

There is no doubt that physical indicators of environmental change have been instrumental in promoting a cleaner environment in many industrialized countries. They have also directed attention to the scarcity of strategic commodities needed for industrial and defense purposes. See USA President's Material Policy Commission (known as the Paley Report; Paley, 1952). But resort to physical indicators will not be sufficient for addressing the deterioration of natural resources as a source, or reveal implications for economic policies for the less developed countries that depend significantly on natural resources. Physical indicators of deforestation, loss of fish stocks, declining mineral deposits, soil erosion and the like are certainly necessary for drawing attention to environmental decline, and must be available as a basis for any monetary valuation of environmental losses. To repeat: it is not the physical stocks themselves that are needed, but changes in them. Clearly their economic role would be vastly strengthened if monetized, and properly incorporated in an adjusted set of macroeconomic measurements.

VI   A FEW CONCLUDING REMARKS

EMPHASIZING THE ECONOMIC NATURE OF NATIONAL ACCOUNTING

When greening the SNA was being debated, methodological disagreement among reformers largely reflected two divergent views of the sustainability that should be targeted: whether it is income (i.e. weak) or environmental (i.e. strong) sustainability. This divergence of aims remained obscured for a time to surface only when disputes over adjustment *methods* got heated. The disagreements have had many facets and played themselves out at different levels. One of these was whether it is the flows or the stocks that should have primacy as this would affect the reckoning of national income and its components. Adjustments to the flow accounts where made would take their cue from the stock accounts. Under the SEEA, and its parent, the SNA93, the economic and the environmental worlds are set apart. These could only be connected if at all outside the main accounts which must remain immune from change. With powerful backers the unadjusted accounts have continued to be used for economic monitoring, analysis and policy prescription. Considering the lingering lack of methodological consensus about how to green the accounts, confining the greening process to satellite accounts was sensible, but made sense only as a temporary measure until methodological disputes had been settled. This much was confirmed, albeit I sense with little conviction, in *Nature's Numbers* (Nordhaus and Kokkelenberg, 1999), which received detailed scrutiny in Chapter 10 on 'Misunderstandings'.

There is no sight of a consensus promising to appear on the horizon soon, or as I said in Chapter 10 during our lifetime. So what we already have will remain, and active attempts to fill in the satellite accounts will continue. For now debates over adjustment methods seem to have ended prematurely. Some debate has certainly surfaced during the long-drawn and apparently never ending process of finalizing the UN guidelines for the satellite accounts, but this venue is hardly adequate for the purpose.

What is acutely needed is a thorough assessment of the substantial empirical work that has already been done in various countries, much of which has been passing as efforts for greening of the national accounts without being particularly instructive. That methodology is important is obvious: this was clearly demonstrated by the 'greening' experience of the United States. When the BEA of the US Department of Commerce attempted to green the US accounts for the first quarter of 1994, in an attempt to capture the depletion of energy resources it 'over-corrected' the accounts by using a strong sustainability approach – the approach, incidentally that is now favored. On top of an undeviating focus on stocks, it fully integrated upward re-assessments of hydrocarbon reserves into the flow accounts – just as the WRI study of Indonesia (Repetto et al., 1989) had done five years previously – using a method that now dominates the green accounting movement. Since the additions to reserves by new discoveries were modest, the overall result was a diminished net product of that sector. In the light of this negative outcome, the erroneous conclusion was reached that, since depletion (treated wrongly as depreciation) was counterbalanced by new discoveries, the adjustment to the accounts was thought to have been accomplished, and indicated a negligible change from the conventional measurements. But burning fossil fuels also dirtied the atmosphere, which was an added negative. So for political reasons this well-intentioned initiative had to be abandoned. Had it been done properly the outcome would have been different and the initiative might not have been suspended.[18] Later work by the BEA in the same area though apparently extensive has not brought much progress.

Finally, it should be stressed once more that greening the national accounts is more important for economic policy than for environmental policy. Pollution concerns do not need to be addressed through national accounting as they can be indicated directly by physical measurements and addressed, quite adequately, through regulation and inducement. By contrast the natural sources of materials and energy (the so-called 'source resources') are different. Natural resource depletion and degradation unquestionably need the medium of the national accounts, most acutely to distinguish value added from asset liquidation. If this sorting-out were made with the proper methods the resulting macroeconomic quantities would have become more realistic. This will be especially true for those developing countries whose natural resources are rapidly eroding, and the erosion is counted perversely in GDP as value added. Once the accounts have been greened all macroeconomic policies need to be re-examined afresh along the lines elaborated in this chapter.

A PERSONAL POSTSCRIPT

In this book this chapter is perhaps the one most affected by my experience at the World Bank. For many years I labored on country policies and on structural adjustment operations that targeted macroeconomic policy changes. The changes were meant to influence monetary policy, interest rates, the fiscal balance, foreign trade, and *policies* relating to exchange rates.[19] A fine line divided the responsibilities of the Bank and the IMF in this respect and both institutions were naturally anxious to harmonize their interventions. World Bank lending had previously been mostly to finance 'projects' (dams, power stations, roads, agriculture, sanitation, etc.) but moved to supporting macroeconomic changes in 1980. This began with its first SAL to Mexico and was later extended to SECALs (sector adjustment loans) and to IDA credits. The borrowers were usually in financial difficulties, unable to service their foreign debt obligations, and came to the IMF and the World Bank not only to get quick financing, but also to restore their international creditworthiness, which these operations seemed to give them. The policies recommended were later criticized as following a 'one-size-fits-all' pattern, later summed up as the 'Washington Consensus' (meaning a unified policy agenda 'imposed' on the borrowers by the US Treasury, the Bank and the Fund and stemmed from the conservative economic policies of the 'Chicago School'). The common policy recipe advocated for policy reform comprised (1) reducing budget deficits; (2) raising interest rates to become positive in real terms in order to encourage saving; (3) freeing internal and external trade including removing quantitative restrictions on imports; (4) reducing government subsidies; (5) pricing scarce resources such as power and water at levels closer to costs; and (6) improving public management generally. Features of individual adjustment programs naturally differed from country to country depending on the historical context, the severity of the imbalances, the perceived quality of domestic institutions, and the administering procedures and practices in place. From my position on the coterie named 'Economic Advisory Staff' that supervised 'tranche' releases under adjustment operations I could see that policy progress was often insufficient to justify release of funds. But release had to be sanctioned in any case especially as changed circumstances had altered the situation. In some instances the 'conditionality' was met, or went some way towards meeting its objectives, but more often than not it failed. It either failed to be implemented, or simply did not produce the expected outcome. Faults in program design were admitted in retrospect, and difficulties showed up which prevented implementation. But there were also many unforeseen changes in circumstances that frustrated actual policy changes.

One of the most negative outcomes of structural adjustment programs in sub-Saharan Africa was the dismantling traditional food-security types of agriculture and replacing them with commercial crops for export as insisted upon by adjustment operations.

A policy issue that relates to the discussion of this chapter will be taken up in the next. This is the issue of a Resource Curse said to afflict countries allegedly disadvantaged when they discover that Nature had endowed them with commercially exploitable resources.

NOTES

1. The 1993 SNA and its companion volume, *Integrated Environmental and Economic Accounting*, imply that the environment does not raise economic concern. This can clearly be inferred from SNA93, which describes the conventional, unadjusted, measurements of national income as *economic*, a description that denies economic significance to the environmental accounts it prescribed. The subsequent efforts made to 'integrate' the environment back into the national accounts have been an obvious failure, and the so-called economic accounts, however flawed, have continued to be used for the purposes of economic analysis. For the New Proposals see Commission of the European Communities et al. (1993) and United Nations Statistics Division (1993).
2. See, Arrow et al. (1995) for a systematic refutation of this optimistic view. For a conspicuous example of the rosy argument, see World Bank (1992).
3. During my 20-year service at the World Bank, often in close association with International Monetary Fund (IMF) economists, I noticed that the economists of both institutions hardly ever connected the macroeconomic magnitudes they analysed and projected forward (including GDP and especially exports) with the physical base that would produce the macroeconomic numbers. Medium-term macroeconomic projections in particular tended to be mechanical extrapolations of current estimates, and the IMF on the whole appeared uninterested in the long term, which is the proper term for watching out for environmental deterioration.
4. Sustainable development is clearly different from a sustainable natural environment. The former implies a process through time relating to the prosperity of the average individual within a finite natural world, and the natural resource stock *per capita* therefore becomes relevant. Attempts have been made to extend the objective of sustainability to 'human capital' and, less successfully, to a so-called 'social capital', the latter consisting of institutional relationships believed to sustain communities (Serageldin, 1996). For national accounting purposes however the sustainability of environmental capital far outweighs in importance the other forms of so-called capital. What is called 'social capital' is likely to remain hazy and immeasurable. As to 'human capital', this is hardly ever threatened, and it would be wrong to treat expenditure on education and training (though in many respects *economically* justifiable) as *investment* in human capital since not all education leads to higher productivity: many graduates fail to find productive employment commensurate with their training. Besides, improvements in productivity due to education get reflected automatically in the conventional measurements of GDP without further ado. Human capital deterioration on account of infirmity and death do not endanger the intactness of capital since human knowledge and technology enrich the stock of such capital all the time, and are bequeathed without cost to future generations. Admittedly not all produced capital formation can be regarded as productive, but the scale of discrepancy here is different, and sorting out what is productive from what is not goes well beyond national accounting.

5. Income, as already stated, is sustainable by definition. Here the word sustainable is placed within quotes because in a strict sense it is redundant.
6. See Adam Smith (1776 [1937], p. 271).
7. Both Keynes (1936 [1949], especially in reference to *net* income, pp. 56–60) and Hicks (1946) have drawn attention to the difficulties of defining and estimating income. This topic was covered in detail in Chapter 8 on 'Hicks's income and Hicksian income'. Hicks (1946, p. 176) expressed skepticism even about his own definitions of income which revolve around what a person can consume while leaving his capital intact:

    > By considering the approximations to this criterion, we have come to see how very complex it is, how unattractive it looks when subjected to detailed analysis. We may now allow a doubt to escape us whether it does, in the last resort, stand up to analysis at all, whether we have not been chasing a will-o'-wisp.

    Referring to the concepts of 'income', 'saving', 'depreciation' and 'investment', Hicks (1946, p. 171) stressed the fact that '[a]t bottom, they are not logical categories at all; they are rough approximations, used by the business man to steer himself through the bewildering changes of situation which confront him'. In the context of national accounting the user-cost method I proposed for estimating income from the extraction of depletable resources should be seen in the same light as a practical device for estimating income.
8. See Commission of the European Communities et al. (1993). The five agencies are the Commission of the European Communities, the International Monetary Fund, the Organisation for Economic Co-operation and Development, the United Nations and the World Bank.
9. An early proposal that came to my notice recommending the use of current prices for the valuation of stocks for national accounting purposes is to be found in a summary of OECD, Department of Economics and Statistics, Meeting of National Accounts Experts, 29–31 May 1985 entitled 'Treatment of mining activities in the system of national accounts', note by the Secretariat, DES/NI/85.4, distributed 29 April 1985 (*mimeo*). It is interesting that this recommendation that flouts well-established accounting conventions has emerged afresh in the SEEA.
10. This accounting rule for stock valuation derives from standard accounting procedures in respect of individuals and corporations. It applies to entities that hold stocks as 'working capital' usually for facilitating their manufacturing activities. In the present context where environmental stocks cannot usefully be viewed as working capital there is no need at all to put a money value on them. It is only the *changes* in the stocks during the accounting period that need to be valued the flow accounts, and the market does all the valuation needed. Since these changes are directly valued by the market there is no need to derive them from changes in stock values. In fact natural resource stocks (say bauxite or petroleum) may be one or two orders of magnitude larger than annual extraction. By incorporating stock changes in the low accounts there is danger that the more significant transacted extraction will be swamped by irrelevant (and untransacted) changes in the value of a much larger stock and thus undermine the veracity of the flow accounts.
11. Such was the procedure used by WRI for greening the national accounts of Indonesia (Repetto et al., 1989) and this led to unacceptable results. It was also the procedure used for adjusting the US accounts in respect of depletable resources for the first quarter of 1994, an initiative that has subsequently been abandoned, in my view, largely because of adoption of the wrong method. See United States Department of Commerce (1994).
12. See El Serafy (1981, 1989) where the surplus realized in the exploitation of a depletable natural resource, often called rent, is converted under a user cost approach into a sustainable income stream. This process excludes from annual revenues an estimated capital element, the user cost, to be re-invested so that its yield will contribute to the

generation of this income both during extraction and after the resource has been totally exhausted. The so-called El Serafy formula for the estimation of the ratio of true income (X), [and its complement the user cost $(1 - X)$], to net receipts (R), relies on two parameters: (r) a discount rate, and (N) the life expectancy of the resource at the current year's extraction rate. True (i.e. sustainable) income as a ratio of net receipts is given by the expression: $X/R = 1 - 1 /(1 + r)^{n+1}$.

For practical estimation, the discount rate selected r, should be a precautionary real interest rate representing the expected yield from the investment, and should on no account be a wishful-thinking rate of return. It may be varied from time to time in line with market indications. (In one of the exploratory studies organized by the World Bank and the UN Statistical Division for greening the accounts of Papua New Guinea an over-optimistic discount rate of 10 per cent was wrongly employed and this biased the results.) Life expectancy is also variable depending on the resource owner's annual extraction plans, which are usually made in line with market developments and expectations about prices. These plans, depending on technical and contractual feasibility, could range from total liquidation of the natural asset in one year to over a horizon of a hundred years. Some writers have mistakenly interpreted the user-cost approach as relying on the assumption of an invariable rate of extraction until the resource expires. But the only constancy assumed under this approach pertains to the stream of income to be generated from the re-investment of the user cost as derived from a totally flexible annual extraction schedule. Since this is an *ex post* approach, capable of accounting for any entrepreneurial decisions regarding extraction, no optimality of depletion is posited. And if stocks are reassessed upwards or downwards, the reassessment is automatically reflected in the life expectancy of the resource, and incorporated in the estimation of income and the user cost. For details and qualifications of this approach, see El Serafy (1989, 1993b, 1995). Among many applications of the 'El Serafy method' was the 1992 United Kingdom Central Statistical Office's exercise to estimate income from oil and gas exploitation. See Hamilton et al. (1993).

13. Cf. Devarajan and Fisher (1982). The so-called Hartwick Rule (Hartwick, 1977), which incidentally has been endorsed by Solow (1992), recommends that the entire surplus realized from the extraction of a depletable resource be re-invested to generate future income. This, it may be observed in passing, is a normative injunction meant to ensure the sustainability of future income. Such a recommendation, however, would deny any current consumption from the exploitation of a depletable resource until the new investments have begun to yield income. If we allow for a gestation period during which the new investments mature, the Hartwick Rule would eventually converge with the (analytically positive) 'El Serafy rule', which is only an accounting device divorced from any recommendation of desirable behavior. This 'rule' anticipates future income from re-investing the user cost, thus making room, through the estimation of current income, for immediate consumption out of extraction revenues.

14. This proposal was first put forward by Hueting. See, for instance, Jan Tinbergen and Roefie Hueting (1992).

15. At the behest of UNEP an international group of specialists was then at work to produce a simplified green national accounting manual based on the SEEA for use by national statistical offices. An important first task of the manual would be to clarify the objectives for which the national accounts should be greened.

16. Environmental information gathered in satellite accounts can still be useful for the purposes of environmental policy. For instance, data relating to the structure of intra- and inter-industry pollution can, with the help of an input–output framework, direct attention to the sources and impact of pollution, thus enabling the formation of counter-pollution policies.

17. At the same time the World Bank, largely at the behest of the United States Treasury, was urging each of the poor countries eligible for receiving funds on a concessional basis from the International Development Association (IDA, a part of the World Bank Group), to have an 'Environmental Action Plan' each. The Bank often assisted

in drafting those plans and provided loans, called 'credits', at very easy terms to the poorest countries.
18. See United States Department of Commerce (1994).
19. There was at the time a Memorandum of Agreement regarding division of labor over adjustment operations. The IMF would not relinquish its primary responsibility for recommending exchange rate levels, but had no objection to Bank economists discussing foreign exchange policy with the borrowers in general terms.

REFERENCES

Arrow, Kenneth, Bert Bolin, Robert Costanza, Partha Dasgupta, Carl Folke, C. S. Holling, Bengt-Owe Jansson, Simon Levin, Karl-Goran Maler, Charles Perrings and David Pimentel (1995), 'Economic growth, carrying capacity and the environment', *Science*, **268**, 520–521.

Commission of the European Communities (EUROSTAT), International Monetary Fund, Organisation for Economic Co-operation and Development, United Nations; and World Bank (1993), *System of National Accounts 1993*. Brussels, Luxembourg, New York, Paris, Washington, DC: EUROSTAT.

Corden, W. M. (1984), 'Booming sector and Dutch disease economics: survey and consolidation', *Oxford Economic Papers*, **36**, 369–380.

Daly, Herman E. and John B. Cobb Jr. (1989), *For the Common Good*. Boston, MA: Beacon Press.

Devarajan, Shantayan and Anthony C. Fisher (1982), 'Exploration and scarcity', *Journal of Political Economy*, **90** (6), 1279–1290.

El Serafy, Salah (1981), 'Absorptive capacity, the demand for revenue and the supply of petroleum', *Journal of Energy and Development*, 7 (1), 73–88.

El Serafy, Salah (1988), 'Environmental issues and the natural resource base', in Costa Rica: Country Economic Memorandum. World Bank, Report 7481-CR, Washington DC.

El Serafy, Salah (1989), 'The proper calculation of income from depletable natural resources', in Y. J. Ahmad, S. El Serafy and E. Lutz (eds), *Environmental Accounting for Sustainable Development: a UNDP–World Bank Symposium*. Washington DC: The World Bank.

El Serafy, Salah (1991), 'Sustainability, income measurement and growth' in: R. Goodland, H. Daly, S. El Serafy and B. von Droste (eds), *Environmentally Sustainable Economic Development: Building on Brundtland*. Paris: UNESCO.

El Serafy, Salah (1993a), 'Country macroeconomic work and natural resources', Environment Department, The World Bank, Environmental Working Paper number 58, Washington D.C (March).

El Serafy, Salah (1993b), 'Depletable resources: fixed capital or inventories?', in A. Franz and C. Stahmer (eds), *Approaches to Environmental Accounting*. Heidelberg, Germany: International Association of Research in Income and Wealth, Physica Verlag.

El Serafy, Salah (1995), 'Depletion of natural resources', in W. van Dieren (ed.), *Taking Nature into Account: Towards a Sustainable National Income: A Report to the Club of Rome*. New York: Copernicus-Verlag.

El Serafy, Salah (1996), 'In defence of weak sustainability: a response to Beckerman', *Environmental Values*, **5**, 75–81.

El Serafy, Salah (1997), 'Green accounting and economic policy', *Ecological Economics*, **21** (3), 217–229.

Goodland, R., Daly, H. and El Serafy, S. (eds.) (1992), *Population, Technology and Lifestyle, the Transition to Sustainability.*, Washington DC: Island Press.

Haberler, Gottfried (1976), 'Oil, inflation, recession and the International Monetary System', *Journal of Energy and Development*, **1** (2), 177–190.

Hamilton, K., Pearce, D., Atkinson, G., Gomez-Lobo, A. and Young, C. (1993), 'The policy implications of natural resource and environmental accounting', Report to the World Bank. Centre for Social and Economic Research on the Global Environment, Norwich and London.

Hartwick, J. (1977), 'Intergenerational equity and the investing of rents from exhaustible resources', *American Economic Review*, **67** (5), 972–974.

Hartwick, J. and Hageman. A. (1993) 'Economic depreciation of mineral stocks and the contribution of El Serafy' in E. Lutz (ed.), *Toward Improved Accounting for the Environment*. Washington DC: World Bank.

Hicks, J. R. (1946), *Value and Capital*, 2nd edn. Oxford: Clarendon Press.

Hotelling. Harold (1931), 'The economics of exhaustible resources', *Journal of Political Economy*, **39** (2), 137–175.

Keynes, John Maynard (1936 [1949]), *The General Theory of Employment, Interest and Money.* London: MacMillan.

Nordhaus, William D. and Edward D.C. Kokkelenberg (eds) (1999), *Nature's Numbers: Expanding the National Economic Accounts to include the Environment*. Washington DC: National Academy Press.

Paley, William S. (1952), *Materials Policy Commission, Resources for Freedom*. Washington DC: US Government Printing Office.

Repetto, R. et al. (1989), *Wasting Assets: Natural Resources in the National Income Accounts*. Washington DC: World Resources Institute.

Serageldin, I., (1996), 'Sustainability and the wealth of nations', Washington DC: The World Bank, March.

Smith, Adam (1776 [1937]), *An Inquiry into the Nature and Causes of the Wealth of Nations*, Modern Library Edition. New York: Random House.

Solow, R. (1992), 'An almost practical step toward sustainability', Washington DC: Resources for the Future (October).

Sunderlin, William D. and Sven Wunder (2000), 'The influence of mineral exports on the variability of tropical deforestation', *Environmental and Development Economics*, **5**, 309–332.

Tinbergen, Jan and Roefie Hueting (1992), 'GNP and market prices', in R. Goodland, H. Daly and S. El Serafy (eds), *Population, Technology and Lifestyle, the Transition to Sustainability.* Washington DC: Island Press, Chapter 4.

UNCED (1992), United Nations Conference on Environment and Development, Rio de Janeiro, popularly known as 'The Earth Summit.'

United Nations Statistics Division, Department for Economic and Social Information and Policy Analysis, Statistics Division (SEEA) (1993), *Integrated Environmental and Economic Accounting*. (Interim Version). Studies in Method, Handbook of National Accounting, Ser. F, 61, New York: United Nations Statistics Division.

United States Department of Commerce (1994), 'Accounting for natural resources: issues and BEA's initial estimates', Survey of Current Business, Bureau of Economic Analysis, April.

World Bank (1992), *World Development Report: Development and the Environment*. Washington DC: Oxford University Press for the World Bank.

World Bank (1995), 'Monitoring environmental progress: a report on work in progress', Environmentally Sustainable Development Vice-Presidency, Washington DC.

World Commission on Environment and Development (1987), *Our Common Future* (Brundtland Report). Oxford: Oxford University Press.

18. The 'resource curse': institutions and Dutch disease

I

THE RESOURCE CURSE

A fairly extensive literature has grown around a dubious phenomenon called a 'resource curse' – a fable in my view that suggests that countries endowed with commercially exploitable natural resources would be better off without them. Belief in the resource curse and arguments for its existence provide a vivid illustration of an unfortunate blend of faulty national accounting and defective reasoning, leading to an untenable generalization that does not stand up to scrutiny. It is curious, it may be remarked, that the word 'curse' should at all enter the language of economic inquiry in the way it has done, and it is interesting that some of its most serious challengers have come from *outside* economics.[1] In common parlance a curse usually denotes a baffling malevolent occurrence attributable to forces beyond understanding, and has to be driven out, or 'exorcized', by extra-human powers. The recurrent use of the expression in economic discourse gives the impression that neither its origins nor its possible cures are fully understood. Thus there is a presumption that this phenomenon is not amenable to reasoned analysis with the implicit denial that its symptoms can be counteracted with economic policy measures. The result is that several authors, observing the unsatisfactory economic performance of many natural-resource-based countries, seem to abandon economic thinking and attempt to blame what they see as adverse manifestations of extra-economic factors.[2]

The blame tends to focus on *institutional* weaknesses generally, and sometimes on specifically identified types of institutions selected arbitrarily. The selection often omits entities that may be of greater significance such as central banks and ministries of economy responsible for macroeconomic and financial management. There is certainly a germ of truth in the 'institutional argument' as the following discussion will show, but attributing the curse to unsatisfactory institutions rather than to *economic* mismanagement seems to provide a false alibi for the economists. To me, economists who find fault in institutions appear to shed their basic training and reach out for sociological explanations.

ADVERSE MANIFESTATIONS

There are essentially two views of the curse to be found in the literature. A more popular version does not dispute an initial period of prosperity or apparent prosperity to be followed *inevitably* by economic decline. Advocates of this version are too numerous to need identification and include the Norwegian trio Mehlum, Moene and Torvik (2006) whose arguments will be discussed in detail presently. Another more drastic version of the curse regards natural resource endowment as fundamentally inimical to *development*. The latter company includes Sachs and Warner (1995, 1997), as well as many others. These economists view all beneficial impacts of a natural resource bounty as illusory, and believe that the naturally endowed countries would be better off without Nature's gifts. Both groups conflate economic or 'development' success with GDP 'growth' as read from the national accounts, and in both versions of the curse the negative manifestations are emphasized and any positive impacts ignored or suppressed.

There is a familiar pattern to the argument that favors the curse. Its advocates usually begin by establishing its existence to their satisfaction using as evidence the medium of the national accounts. The evidence, such as it is, is a slow or negative economic expansion. Having done that, they seem to think that their case has been confirmed: natural resource exploitation and unsatisfactory economic performance are positively correlated. Should such a correlation amount to a causal relationship? Students of statistical method know very well what the correct answer would be. True, every now and then a curse believer would seek explanations for what the numbers seem superficially to say, but this tends to be done only *after* the existence of the curse had been established. However, such explanations lean heavily towards unsatisfactory institutions, though occasionally the *economic* hypothesis of a 'Dutch disease' is invoked albeit only as an ancillary factor. Methodologically, the reasoning sequence is flawed since the 'evidence' of a phenomenon in this case is launched without theory, and only subsequently is a hypothetical explanation offered.

INFERENCE FROM GDP CHANGES

Believers in the curse fall into the logical trap of induction, which seeks generalizations from limited observations. The induction trap has been recognized for centuries, notably by David Hume (1711–76). But it has also been recognized by innumerable students of scientific method since Hume. Nearer home, Keynes in his *Treatise on Probability* (1921, p. 272) writes that 'Hume's statement of the case against induction has never been improved upon', and in the same breath commends Leibniz for condemning 'generalisations based on mere repetitions of instances'. This is exactly what the believers in the curse seem to have done, piecing together a number of facts and jumping to conclusions without any deductive reasoning.

The defects of induction find ample exposition in the more recent writings of philosophers such as Karl Popper (1961)[3] and Alfred Ayer (1956, 1973).[4] Popper is categorical in his conviction that 'Induction is a myth that has been exploded by Hume' (Popper, 1976, p. 80). Without an explanatory hypothesis mere facts cannot establish evidence. Popper has insisted that scientific inquiry has to begin from the deductive end with an idea formulated as a hypothesis which if married to 'initial conditions' would lead to predictions capable of being tested with experimentation. A. J. Ayer in the same vein asserts that 'For the most part, attempts to solve the problem of induction have taken the form of trying to fit inductive arguments into a deductive mould' (Ayer, 1956, p. 73). Invoking the authority of Hume, he also questions that what we have observed to be conjoined in the past will hold good for the future (Ayer, 1973, p. 139). Some economists will also remember Keynes's strictures against Tinbergen's League of Nations econometric study of the trade cycle, saying that in Tinbergen '[t]here is not the slightest explanation or justification of the underlying logic.'[5] In the same vein Economics Nobel Laureate Koopmans (1947) strongly denounced generalizations from observations judging them to be 'Measuring without Theory'.[6] The curse advocates are evidently reversing the train of reasoning, affirming the primacy of observation over explanation.[7] See also the criticism of reading regression results as evidence in the work of Durlauf (Durlauf and Quah, 1999; Durlauf, 2009).

THE PERILS OF INDUCTION

GDP changes can signify many things and it is rather naïve to read sluggish or negative rates of growth as reflecting solely a resource curse. For one thing, the possibility is overlooked that the GDP estimates at issue may be statistically flawed. In previous chapters the argument has been put forward repeatedly that resource extraction *revenues* are routinely misrepresented as *income* and are offered wrongly as if they were all *value added* and wrongly incorporated in GDP. This point has been a continuous thread in this book and needs no further elaboration. Revenue may indeed be increasing while income, true income, may be falling as argued in Chapter 11. In most cases revenue will exceed income not infrequently by an appreciable margin. On a practical level, if the accounts wrongly proclaim revenue as income, the recipients might be justified in treating their receipts as expendable and proceed to allocate them to consumption. That is in fact what many natural resource owners have done and in the process have contributed to the apparent curse. If they had indulged in wasteful expenditure – a fairly common behavior, which is described in some studies quaintly as 'overconsumption' – they would be behaving within the misleading parameters set for them by the supposedly expert national accountants. On top of the resource owners obviously eroding their natural capital by extraction, there has been the added tendency for them to assume foreign debts in volumes exceeding their capacity to service them. The international lenders may also be deceived by the falsely estimated *income* of these borrowers. Whether the borrowed funds go to finance additional consumption, or are sunk in investment ventures of questionable profitability, the burden of paying interest and repaying principal adds to the borrower country's liabilities. Advocates of the curse are frequently fond of stressing these problems and claim them to be inevitable with it.

Analysts, reading GDP changes as evidence for the curse, ignore the plain fact that there are usually many factors behind the changes appearing in the national accounts. These factors include the whole gamut of fiscal, monetary and foreign exchange policies whether active or passive. Without counteracting policies the economy gets seriously 'distorted' by the inflow of the resource revenues. All economic policies in fact need to be overhauled and adjusted to accommodate the financial inflows and contain their harmful impact. True, necessary economic reform is often paralyzed in practice. More commonly it is deferred in a miasma of deceptive prosperity aided and abetted by false accounting that propagates the illusion of a rising income. Corrective policy steps that could voluntarily be taken with little difficulty in conditions of financial surpluses have later to be forced upon struggling economies when the surpluses have turned into deficits and austerity has become unavoidable.

In sum, curse advocates typically resort to establishing a record of lackluster economic performance first, reading this record crudely from time series of GDP irrespective of whether or not the GDP numbers are reliable. Even if the GDP estimates were accurate in the first place, which for resource dependent economies are often not, there are many possible reasons behind GDP negative changes, including dwindling natural stocks, a deliberate and rational slow-down of resource extraction, and many other possibilities that are rarely if ever considered by the curse-believers. These go on to stress institutional defects without carefully looking first at the validity of the statistical evidence. The fundamental fault in their approach is to try to establish the curse's existence before looking for possible explanations of the evidence they proceed to examine.

II

INSTITUTIONS ARE STILL IMPORTANT

Many of the curse advocates consider nothing else other than alleged institutional inadequacy behind what they read as a record of economic failure. Indeed, it would be foolhardy on my part to deny any role played by institutions, not just in the management or mismanagement of the revenues derived from natural resource extraction, but also in respect of economic and social development generally. Passive inaction or wrong-headed active economic policies are often culpable. And yet I would expect sociologists not economists to stress the role of institutions in this regard. If institutions should be brought into the economic discussion, I would expect them to be relegated to a supplementary role behind the economic argument that should assume pride of place.

Generally speaking economist attention to institutions is well established. One has only to recall the important school of 'institutional economics' that flourished in the United States in the latter half of the nineteenth century and the early years of the twentieth. This school was more or less retracing the footsteps of earlier German and Marxian writers who strove to place economic dealings into a wider framework of societal relationships that needed to be confronted in economic analysis. This wider framework addressed fundamental issues such as the distribution of property, the sociology of powerful groups, the legal system in place, and similar structural factors that ultimately determine the level and composition of production, the makeup of demand for final goods, and ultimately income distribution. According to this line of thinking, if such issues are overlooked while attention is given merely to the outcomes of these powerful forces economists will simply be scratching at the surface. They would be tinkering with superficial details of markets and prices while losing sight of deeper-seated elements. Within the American school of institutional economics, and also without it, the names of Commons, Newcomb, John Dewey, John Maurice Clark down to John Kenneth Galbraith and Kenneth Boulding attest to profound interest by important economists in institutions and their influence on the level and structure of economic activity. Such interest seems to be renewed in the literature on the curse. But interest in institutions may also be spotted farther afield. It can be found at the heart of neo-classical economics. In the theory of value, analysis is made of market forms such as competition and monopoly and shades of market forms that lie in between. It is manifested in the theory of wages when trade unions have to be discussed. Analysis of 'contestable markets'; transaction costs; risk-hedging; forward trading; and many other institutional sinews of economic life become not just relevant but central. Thus while I cannot deny the important role usually played by institutions this chapter nevertheless tries to lay emphasis on the primacy of economic analysis for matters pertaining to the alleged natural resource curse.

ECONOMISTS AS SOCIOLOGISTS

The work of the Norwegian economists Mehlum, Moene and Torvik (2006) is noteworthy in that it typifies the recurrent method based on inference from GDP estimates that may have indicated the wrong growth rates. The authors presented these numbers as evidence, and eschewed economic explanations altogether. They attributed the curse to no other cause save defective institutions, denying any role to economic factors including failure to forge proper economic policies. Possible corrective measures they overlooked would include fiscal, monetary and foreign exchange adjustments that might have suppressed the symptoms and provided more lasting cures. Despite their concentration on growth rates they could not help noticing that not all resource-endowed countries were equally 'cursed'. But they were quick to judge that those countries that exhibited a better growth record must have possessed *better* institutions. 'Countries rich in natural resources constitute both growth losers and growth winners. We claim that the reason for these diverging experiences is differences in the quality of institutions' (*op. cit.* and highlighted in the paper's abstract). The authors, as will be shown below, appear to have based their stance on earlier papers by Sachs and Warner, three of which were cited in their references. In later papers, still pursuing the institutional argument, one or more of the same authors, in collaboration with others, began to pinpoint *political* institutions, subsumed under 'governance', claiming this as the key institutional weakness that allows the rise of rent-seeking groups inimical to progress.

Mehlum et al. may have been thinking that they were introducing a new vocabulary distinguishing between good institutions, which they call 'developers', and bad institutions they name 'grabbers' – a vocabulary that for me echoes an earlier Hicksian distinction between 'stickers' and 'snatchers' in contestable markets.[8] According to these Norwegian analysts, the developers work constructively for the 'public good' so to speak, while the grabbers are predatory rent-seeking sets that seek short term self-enrichment. In an obvious *post hoc, ergo propter hoc* type of argument, the successful countries must have had more of the former groups and the unsuccessful ones more of the latter. To distinguish between these two categories (*loc. cit.*, p. 13) the authors constructed an overall 'institutional quality index' based on the unweighted average of five subsidiary indices: a 'rule of law index', a 'bureaucratic quality index', a 'corruption in government index', a 'risk of expropriation index' and a 'government repudiation index'. Just listing these so-called sub-indexes is sufficient to show how sloppy the components are that make up the supposedly overall institutional quality metric. Using symbolism, as if to cover up a weak approach, the authors designate the overall institutional quality index by the letter λ to which they assign values varying from 0 to 1: 'When $\lambda = 0$, the system is completely grabber friendly such that grabbers extract the entire rent ... A higher λ implies a more producer friendly institutional arrangement. When $\lambda = 1$, there are no gains from specialization in grabbing' (pp. 4–5). This veneer of pseudo-science (which Karl Popper would label 'scientistic' to distinguish it from 'scientific') fails to conceal the fundamental feebleness of their approach. But their dubious path had already been broken for them earlier by others, including Sachs and Warner (1995, 1997, 1999).

An element of my criticism of the kind of approach espoused by Mehlum et al. is that economists are probably not the best sociology analysts, and economists should use their own specialty before turning to other disciplines to sort out and address economic phenomena. Specific charges I also make against Mehlum et al. include (1) the fact that their sub-indices of institutional quality amount to no more than subjective and immeasurable perceptions; and (2) other institutions of decisive importance are left out of their consideration.

Among the institutions left out are the central banks, the ministries of finance, economy and trade, and beyond them universities and research establishments where they exist whose quality would be, not just relevant, but crucial for economic policies. To assess economic policies and to devise cures their role, passive or active, is unjustifiably left out. Such institutions are presumably overlooked because they do not fit into the grabber–developer straightjacket they set up, and perhaps also if brought in may highlight failure of macroeconomic policy which these authors could have been avoiding.

It is interesting that the stress latterly placed on 'governance' echoes what R. C. O. Matthews (1986) had claimed as a major factor determining economic growth rates in general. In his Presidential Address to the Royal Economic Society, Matthews had stressed the role of the State, which he dubbed 'authority'. He enumerated four State components of the institutional argument: 'property rights, conventions, types of contract and authority' (pp. 905 and 910) and these seem to have re-emerged in the literature of the curse.

THE INFLUENCE OF SACHS AND WARNER

Among the proponents of the institutional argument behind the curse the role of Sachs and Warner has been prominent (Sachs and Warner, 1995, 1997, 1999). After initially focusing on GDP growth they adjusted their approach slightly to what they termed 'development', now reading its change not from GDP itself but from GDP per capita. The metric they forge for monitoring 'development' confirms their view that economic prosperity is impeded by resource endowment. But whichever way their 'development' is defined it has to be gauged from GDP growth. And as already stated the conventional GDP estimates for resource-dependent economies tend to be flawed. Furthermore they emphasize the growth rate while failing to observe that resource exploitation elevates the *level* of GDP. How can a higher level of GDP be associated with developmental failure? Whether Nature's gift of resources is a blessing or a curse they have no hesitation in declaring it a curse (Sachs and Warner, 1995, 1997). In a later contribution, however, they seem to entertain some scholarly doubt. The doubt can be gleaned from a paper dealing with Latin America (Sachs and Warner, 1999). Departing from their earlier certainty they begin to show hesitancy over the curse's inevitability (pp. 44ff.). Importantly, however, they continue to be unaware of the weakness I have been stressing in the conventional GDP estimates, which confuse revenue with income. Clearly, the econometric approach they pursue, based as it is on inadequate data, is unconvincing.

For me it is obvious that Mehlum et al. picked up their index of institutional inadequacy from the earlier work of Sachs and Warner. Relying on uncorrected GDP data as a yardstick, Sachs and Warner (1999) conduct several regression exercises testing a rather fanciful array of mostly unquantifiable factors to which they assign arbitrary values, and proceed to combine them into an overall index of institutional inadequacy. The factors they consider are 'a rule of law index', a 'bureaucratic quality index', a 'corruption in government index', 'openness to trade' and 'central government savings'. These are used as sub-indexes that are stitched together into a frail fabric that indicates institutional quality, which guides their analysis of the curse in different country situations. Thus they conclude that the quality of 'institutions' makes a significant difference to whether or not a resource endowment leads to successful development. In that work Sachs and Warner widen their coverage to consider country performance across continents and over long periods, and offer the more balanced judgment that the topic is still worthy of further exploration. While showing new caution they seem determined, however, to prove their unqualified contention that a natural resource endowment is inimical to development.

A NEUMAYER VARIATION ON SACHS AND WARNER

Eric Neumayer who has championed the user-cost method for many years unsurprisingly became a critic of the curse theory. He had successfully used proper GDP data (adjusted for estimated user costs) to challenge the World Bank's claims that many developing countries, which were running down their natural capital, were proceeding on an unsustainable development path (Neumayer, 2000). In its dubious assertions the World Bank was employing a 'strong sustainability' concept that showed no value added in extraction attributable specifically to the resource itself. Neumayer (2004) addressed the resource curse issue scrutinizing the growth record of the countries covered in Sachs and Warner (1997). He followed their approach as closely as possible but now considering the period 1970–98 (instead of 1970–90). Neumayer regressed the average GDP growth rate on the log of the initial GDP per capita, and the Sachs and Warner variable termed 'natural resource intensity' (the share of primary products exports in GDP), while trying faithfully to observe other details of their approach. He called his adjusted GDP 'genuine income'. Not unexpectedly he could 'confirm' the existence of the curse though in a much milder form. Neumayer, just like Sachs and Warner, was focusing on growth rates, paying no attention to the higher *level* of GDP attributable to the resource endowment.

A COMMON MALAISE?

Sachs and Warner (1997, also Sachs and Warner, 1999) have made the pertinent suggestion that easily acquired riches can make societies less entrepreneurial and more prone to rent-seeking. This claim in all likelihood cannot be disputed. The weaknesses they identify, however, are not uncommon to developing countries in general whether or not they are endowed with commercially exploitable natural resources. There are obviously many political factors at play, which certainly make a difference to the development record. Lack of transparency and leaders' proclivity to holding on to power are two characteristics of many developing economies and evidently handicap progress. It is an undeniable fact that in too many instances developing country leaders seem to accord low priority to economic and social development issues, giving more weight to self-enrichment and the interests of supporting political cliques. Moreover, for their own self-preservation they tend to enhance military and police power at the expense of development. Whether these features are political, sociological, institutional or something else, they do affect economic performance and would go some way towards explaining the negation of the benefits natural resources can bring. According a low priority to economic matters in a country's agenda stifles progress and arrests social development including the betterment of its institutions. In this regard the quality of the *institution* of 'national leadership' is certainly of paramount importance – a factor that has certainly to be conceded to the institutional argument though it cuts across the whole range of the development effort and is not confined to resource-based economies. In the light of this reasoning, could the institutional weaknesses behind the resource curse be seen as a manifestation of a partial hypothesis that is only one element in a wider explanatory pattern? Sachs and Warner would likely dismiss this criticism saying that in the instances they consider, their thesis was confirmed. The point remains, however, that for economists, *qua* economists, sociological and political factors should receive from them only secondary attention. They are expected to deploy the tools of their own trade first to analyze the economic symptoms that get wrongly and indiscriminately summed up as a paradox named a curse.

III

CRITICS OF THE CURSE

The record of individual natural resource extracting economies does indeed show a variety of experiences, and this has provided room for different interpretations. In a remarkable paper on the subject Michael Ross (1999) criticizes the paucity of the argument behind the sluggish performance of resource-endowed economies. This political scientist suggests that efforts to explain the curse fall in three categories: (1) booms may cause short-sightedness of policy makers; (2) booms tend to empower interest groups that favor 'growth-impeding' policies; and (3) they weaken state institutions in general. Ross adds two further categories: (4) the inefficiency of state-owned enterprises that control the extractive sector; and (5) inability of the state to enforce property rights. Note that all these factors are indeed institutional in nature. But he goes on further as I have argued above to lay great emphasis on the lack of hypotheses to be tested against the factual record of so-called growth, upbraiding fellow political scientists' efforts that methodologically fall short of the standards of proper analysis. Ross portrays enough economic perception to propose that the same complaint may be levelled equally against those economists who support the resource curse argument.

Another critic of the curse theory, Paul Stevens (2003), a petroleum economist, rejects the term *curse* altogether, suggesting it be replaced by *impact* which varies significantly negatively and positively across countries and across time. He argues that the overall negative record is far from convincing as it reflects sensitivity of the analyst to the period chosen and the fact that some countries managed significantly to avoid the curse altogether. Stevens sensibly recommends a case-by-case approach, not one that indiscriminately lumps all the 'cursed' countries together and over periods of heterogeneous performance. In a subsequent contribution (Stevens, 2005) he considers economic development in the experience of a number of resource endowed countries and finds their experience too complex to yield easy answers though he opts for an institutional explanation behind success or failure. Despite their insight, however, both Ross, the political scientist, and Stevens, the economist, along with many others, seem to fail to appreciate the defective nature of GDP estimates that are taken to support the alleged impacts whether positive or negative. If the professional economists themselves are unaware of the weakness of the GDP numbers the political scientists can perhaps be excused for overlooking this fatal defect in the 'evidence'.

Much more striking in my view is the work of Boyce and Herbert Emery (2005) who astutely argue that the growth rates observed by the curse-advocates may indeed have been sluggish or even negative, but the *level* of income has often been higher (see also Boyce and Herbert Emery, 2011; Busse and Gröning, 2011). They even ventured to dispute the claim by Sachs and Warner that institutions were at all to blame. They followed this up by a more detailed study of states within the United States of America – a study briefly discussed below. For my own part I have always insisted that a resource endowment, far from being a handicap against economic progress, does give a positive advantage to the fortunate country (or region) provided it is sensibly exploited. Impressive as the work of Boyce and Herbert Emery is, however, the authors overlook the weakness of gross domestic product estimates for the entities they consider (see also Cervellati et al., 2008).

In the present context mention should also be made of the work of Jenny Minier (2007) who supports the notion that institutions do indeed matter, especially in respect of 'policy variables', but doubts any direct role for institutions that affects growth. She holds that institutions play a part though a complex one, suggesting the existence of indirect links that work through 'nonlinearities'.

IV

THE DUTCH EXPERIENCE

I turn now to my favorite explanation which derives from the original experience of the Netherlands and which has given rise to the epithet of the 'Dutch disease'. A copious literature exists on the Dutch disease, which believers in the curse, for one reason or another, choose to overlook or underplay. If they bring it into discussion at all it is often at the end of their putative proof of the curse's existence and only in an ancillary capacity. It is debatable if the actual experience of the Netherlands in this respect can be blamed on institutional weaknesses.

The available literature on the Dutch disease describes in clear economic terms the negative impact of 'windfalls' associated with natural resource revenues. The literature does not lack the impact of comparable financial inflows, not arising from a natural endowment, of an 'unrequited' nature. Such inflows may be described as unrequited because they are not paid for directly by current value-added production.[9] These situations have also been discussed with the now 'generic' description of a Dutch disease.

The Dutch disease appellation did not apparently originate in the Netherlands itself. According to Corden (1982) the phrase was coined in Britain around 1975 when it was feared that North Sea petroleum might bring economic troubles similar to those inflicted on the Dutch economy in the 1960s when natural gas and other petroleum deposits were discovered in the North Sea. (See also Wijnbergen, 1984). This attribution makes sense as it is unlikely that the Dutch would coin it in reference to themselves. For the Netherlands, the inflow of petroleum funds encouraged national extravagance, elevating labor remuneration and inflated pension schemes. These funds also helped to initiate and augment varied social programs the financing of which later became an intolerable burden. Among other adverse symptoms deficits began to show in the fiscal and external payments balances. The prosperity that was initially ushered in by the inflow of financial resources had in time seemed to have brought with it unwanted side-effects that tempered the early welcome. What was thought of at the beginning as an unalloyed 'blessing' had in retrospect acquired the features of a 'disease'. One important negative symptom to be elaborated later was the appreciation of the Dutch currency, the guilder, which in turn discouraged exports of a previously thriving manufacturing industry besides encouraging the inflow of imports which displaced previously available domestic products that had supplied jobs to the Dutch workers. This assortment of negative developments reflected itself in unemployed labor, underused capital equipment, and other far-reaching structural distortions of the Dutch economy before the disease was properly diagnosed and counterbalanced by corrective economic policies.[10]

'BOOMING' SECTOR AND MULTILATERAL DEVELOPMENT ORGANIZATIONS

Generally speaking a 'booming' natural resource sector, such as petroleum, offers limited employment opportunities within the domestic economy, crowds out traditional exports and inflicts damage on previously successful activities. These also get handicapped by rising domestic wages, generally high prices of services and the rush to invest savings in real estate. The unfavorable manifestations of the disease tend to follow a familiar pattern and can be explained in economic terms and analyzed with familiar economic tools provided that a Dutch disease has been diagnosed. But this affliction is not always recognized as such, and not early enough to instigate a battery of well-known economic policy remedies.

A complicating factor that tends to impede the rational management of resource proceeds (and is mainly absent in the 'curse' literature) is the volatility of the international prices of natural resource products. From the resource owners' perspective every year seems to bring in a fresh surprise with no clear price trajectory in sight. Whether next year's proceeds will be higher or lower – other things being equal – is in practice often unknown. While it is obvious that many of the petroleum exporters in the past few decades have succumbed to the Dutch disease to an appreciable degree, their economic advisers have not been forthcoming with helpful or timely guidance. In dealing with the oil exporters, even international organizations, including the World Bank and the International Monetary Fund, fell short in their role as economic advisers. They showed far more concern for their major shareholders' interests, essentially the richer OECD members, than the welfare of the petroleum exporters: at the time mostly poorer and less developed countries. These organizations were oblivious to (or preferred to shut their eyes to) the fact that the petroleum exporters were selling their assets to produce *temporary* revenues. The same institutions, to lessen the pressures on the balance of payments of the petroleum importers, sometimes inadvertently encouraged wasteful expenditures by resource-based economies ostensibly to expand their domestic 'absorptive capacity'. I previously argued this in El Serafy (1981). No serious analysis of the development problems of the oil exporters was attempted at the time, and these institutions' overriding interest appeared to be focused on corralling their financial surpluses, especially the OPEC members, for incorporation in their own resources. Unlike the Netherlands, the oil exporters lacked a significant manufacturing sector in place to be damaged, but they had been desirous of establishing one anew, hoping to diversify their economies and create more lasting sources of value added that would generate employment opportunities and enhance their development. For such a promising development strategy they received no constructive advice from the multilateral institutions that would claim responsibility for guiding economic and social development in the developing world. I touched on some of these failures in El Serafy (1979) while serving with the World Bank.

V

THE NIGERIAN EXPERIENCE

Nigeria presents an excellent case for lessons to be derived from the record of a developing country that experienced oil windfalls of considerable proportions relative to its economy. The case also shows an early attempt by analysts to blame institutional weakness for the economic difficulties Nigeria encountered. Generalizing from the Nigerian experience, Sala-i-Martin and Subramanian (2003) asserted the robustness of evidence for (some) natural resources, namely 'oil and minerals in particular', exerting a long-run negative impact on growth. This they claimed does occur through weakened institutions, and not through any Dutch disease. Note the emphasis placed on *growth*, which has typified the economist criterion for judging economic performance for some considerable time. These authors blamed this negative impact on waste and corruption, and advocated policies to distribute the resource gains directly to the public, paradoxically through the very imperfect institutions extant rather than trusting them to the government. This advice would constitute a generally acceptable policy approach, but it is their economic argument that is rather weak. As pointed out before, they assert without qualification the existence of 'robust evidence' for a sluggish growth record simplistically reading growth from inadequate national accounts that confuse asset sale proceeds with value added. Even their arguments regarding the balance of payments and the exchange rate are marred by an obvious flaw. Nigeria's balance of payments is dominated by oil exports that figure as current transactions whereas these contain large elements of natural capital outflow. It is indeed difficult to separate empirically what is current and what is capital in these transactions, but at least some qualification on their methods should have been made which would undermine the robustness they claim for their case. I have in mind here Harvard Professor Gottfried Haberler questioning the appropriateness of showing export proceeds of natural asset sales in the current account of the balance of payments (Haberler, 1976).

THE CASE OF INDONESIA

Indonesia provides yet another clear example (though there are also other countries at different times) of a developing country that has been quite successful in fighting the Dutch disease. See Glassburner (1988) who traces Indonesia's development during the crucial decade that followed the petroleum market upheavals of 1973–74. He describes Indonesia's satisfactory performance as a combination of good fortune and good policies. Indonesia was, of course, the field where the important empirical study of national accounting for 'wasting assets' was pioneered, and this I have criticized and adjusted reaching significantly changed results using a user-cost approach. See Chapter 19 on Indonesia.

POLICY ISSUES AT STAKE

In a situation of a natural resource boom the domestic money supply needs special attention by the policy makers as it will expand with the inflow of foreign exchange, which, if unchecked, gets converted into local currency causing the general price level to rise. Without offsetting policy actions the country in question gradually loses its old trading competitiveness while its industrial structure gets disrupted by new and strong economic currents. Such structural changes might be tolerated if the booming exports were permanent so the country may expect to live contentedly with a changed industrial structure. However, the time inevitably will come when these inflows fade and then entirely cease. One obvious advantage of the user-cost method espoused in this book is that it brings attention immediately to the life span of a natural resource being exploited. It forces the question as to how many years will the resource last at the current rate of exploitation. In the specific case of a developing country that is looking forward to a future of a diversified economy – away from dependence on primary production – the country witnesses its development ambitions frustrated. In practice the incidence of the Dutch ailment would vary from country to country depending on the size of the inflows relative to the domestic economy, and obviously also on the initial industrial structure so that a case by case analysis would be far superior to lumping the varied experiences of natural resource countries together, and hiding their differences under a cloak of an inevitable curse.

Unless the possibility of a Dutch disease is contemplated early on, and handled properly by counter economic policies, the Dutch disease will take hold, and the symptoms of the alleged curse will be inevitable and become difficult to reverse. But once the problem is seen as such, and the disease is recognized early enough, a battery of offsetting economic measures does exist, capable of addressing the affliction's adverse symptoms. These measures will be helpful, if not always totally effective. In the first instance they include avoiding the appreciation of the domestic currency by building up foreign exchange reserves; insulating the domestic money supply from the vagaries of export earnings; and above all being aware of the Dutch disease itself as a source of economic difficulties. With enlightened political vision, and forceful economic leadership, the adverse side effects of a resource boom could be successfully managed, and its disagreeable manifestations suppressed. But above all the phenomenon must be recognized as *economic* in nature, and therefore amenable to treatment by *economic* means, and more fundamentally, that the so-called curse is not a mysterious phenomenon that defies economic treatment.[11]

The appreciation of a domestic currency in reaction to a resource boom has not lacked economic insights. Careful analysis will often reveal some correspondence between 'the real effective exchange rate'[12] and the relative prices of domestic non-traded goods to the prices of traded goods: in other words between the appreciation of the exchange rate and the structural changes that usually force up the domestic prices of non-tradable goods. This deepens understanding of the economic forces at play and helps to calibrate and orient remedial policies. For Indonesia, this dual metric appreciated in a typical Dutch disease fashion quite early on in the life of the boom. To begin with the rupiah appreciated, but economic performance generally improved when that appreciation was curbed. According to Glassburner (1988) several factors worked to the advantage of the economy. Not only was foreign borrowing resisted, but foreign exchange reserves were sensibly built up and partly used to extinguish previously assumed foreign debt.[13] Much of the new windfalls were invested in the rural economy which employed the majority of the population and was also fortunately undergoing a kind of an agricultural revolution based on new rice varieties and an intensive use of fertilizers. Developing agriculture for the benefit of the rural population was pronounced a priority for the economy. An important ingredient of economic policy was also the adoption of a flexible exchange rate policy, in effect resulting in spreading the expenditure of windfalls over time. But there was also a prevailing healthy consciousness that the boom will not last. All these measures and attitudes kept the Dutch disease at bay. Not to be underestimated was the quality of economic leadership and the stability of some key institutions, yet these are rightly not given the pride of place in explaining Indonesia's success story which, in Glassburner's analysis, is principally conducted, as it should, in economic not sociological terms.

VI

RECAPITULATING THE ECONOMIC ARGUMENT

It may not be remiss to try to retrace our steps by highlighting certain aspects of the discussion so far. The fundamental question that has been addressed in this chapter is whether the association between natural resource abundance and unsatisfactory growth is a proven fact. The alleged evidence provided for the existence of a 'resource curse' is simply read from rates of change in GDP, which confuse value added with asset liquidation and thus conceal the fundamental difference between revenue and income. Equally important is that the believers in the curse totally ignore the *level* of GDP, which is usually elevated by access to the resource earnings. Macroeconomic mismanagement at the heart of the alleged curse may indeed be associated with weak, inadequate, predatory and corrupt institutions, but recognition of the adverse symptoms of a resource boom as manifestations of an economic Dutch disease must take analytical precedence over any institutional attribution. Stagnation of economic progress may be due to many factors that should be investigated case by case and not attributed indiscriminately to a common cause. It could indeed reflect a deliberate act on the part of the resource owners to restrain supply as the resource may be approaching extinction. Holding supply back, provided it is technically and contractually possible, could in effect be a rational act of saving, and may also mirror a reasoned decision to wait for a future date when prices become more advantageous. Hotelling (1931) had clearly explained that possibility when considering the time profile of depletion as a problem of asset management. In his vision, if technically possible, extraction would be raised or reduced depending on current prices in comparison with expectations of future prices. Reading all declines in GDP by watching its rate of change as a failure can be gravely misleading. Such declines may well be due to reduced physical extraction, or to a collapse of prices, or to a myriad of other causes.

As argued earlier if the natural resource in question were limitless, the fortunate country that owns it may consider all the sale proceeds of extraction as income. It could then allocate all the extraction revenues to consumption if it so desired. Limitless availability would indicate that the user cost is nil and revenue is all income, but this is a special case that does not represent reality. In practically every other case the resource will have a finite life, and the user cost of extraction will be positive.[14] 'True income' will therefore fall short of revenue, and consumption will have to be contained within this true income, otherwise undue consumption will be taken out of capital. Once the boom has subsided, however, an economy dominated by natural resource extraction may well genuinely regress except to the extent that enough savings – the equivalent of the user cost – had been wisely invested at home or abroad and the returns on the investment could then boost up the depressed income.

The fact remains that many economists to this day are not aware of the unreliability of the economic magnitudes produced by the national accountants, not just on account of ignoring economically relevant ecological changes – but specifically in counting natural capital disinvestment as income. It may be argued in many cases that the GDP numbers in use are sufficiently adequate for economies that do not derive much of their prosperity from primary activities. So with some exceptions the OECD countries seem to be content with their national accounts as they are. However, we should be conscious of the fact that the international arbiters of universal national accounting systems mostly hail from the richer countries, and appear averse to changes in GDP estimation methods. Any adjustments must be made, they hold, not in the core body of the estimates, but in satellite accounts, and confined to the *net* product, leaving the commonly used gross product unaltered. But significantly it is where primary activities abound, and where the natural resource base is significantly decaying, that the conventional national accounts are seriously flawed. They lead to faulty economic analysis that obscures the record of economic change, and misinforms economic policy. And it is the poorer developing countries that are paying the price of this obtuseness.[15]

In my own experience drawing the attention of economists to faulty national accounting has often brought up the response that my interlocutors were 'not expert in national accounting'. The habit of trusting the national accounts had become so ingrained in economist thinking that the macroeconomic numbers of the national accounts have become the window through which economic reality is usually perceived.[16] Thus incorrect interpretations of the course of development have frequently been made, and unreliable GDP numbers have indiscriminately been used as inputs into seemingly sophisticated econometric work out of which false conclusions have not infrequently been drawn. The curse is but one example of this impaired economic vision.

VII

A FINAL PIECE OF PIGOUVIAN WISDOM

To round off the discussion of the role of institutions I end with a word from the founder of Welfare Economics. Pigou (1952) was patiently enumerating the factors behind the size of 'real income'. To Pigou 'real income' was the goods and services that are dressed up with prices and aggregated into the national dividend or national income. Whilst he was aware of the important role of institutions in this regard, he refrained from entering into the institutional 'minefield'. Pigou explained once more that a country's real income derives from its 'productive powers', namely:

- natural resources (such as England's coal);
- material capital (railways, factories, machinery);
- immaterial capital of scientific knowledge;
- the skill, strength and intelligence of its people; and
- 'Government' (law and order; security of contract etc).

This was a list comprehensive enough to need no expansion. The last factor mentioned, 'Government', is obviously 'institutional', and Pigou went on to elaborate the importance of institutions including 'a good system of education' and 'methods by which services are paid for, and ways in which production is organized': namely, he elaborated: private businesses, joint-stock companies, municipal enterprises, nationalized industries (e.g. the Post Office). Though recognizing the important role of 'organization' in determining the size of real income he then poses the question: 'what sort of organization is likely to be most effective' in various industries and various conditions and therefore most helpful in producing a big real income? His response was that it was a very difficult question indeed to ask of an economist and he adamantly refrained from answering it (p. 69). He felt he had already strayed far enough away from the path of economics and was beginning to encroach on other fields of study. He had no wish to go any farther into analysing institutions, adding rather demurely: 'About all that, as Vergil says to Dante in one of the least attractive divisions of hell, 'Do not linger here; look and pass on.'

NOTES

1. See Michael Ross (1999) where this political scientist lists an extensive array of sources throwing doubt on the validity of the curse hypothesis. There is also a very useful survey of the curse literature containing several analytical insights by the petroleum economist Paul Stevens of the University of Dundee (2003).
2. However, there is an interesting view put forward in 2007 by Timothy Besley of the London School of Economics who supports the more recent attention given to institutions by economists. He senses that 'The New Political Economy' where the role of institutions is recognized simply tries to reverse the split between economic analysis and political science – a split that occurred in the late nineteenth century when political economy gave way to economics.
3. I happen to have been a student of Popper at the London School of Economics as I took 'Scientific Method' as part of my BSc Economics degree at London University (1952) and am familiar with many of his works. His 'hypothetico-deductive system' of scientific inquiry is in effect a refutation of the induction argument.
4. Ayer, in *The Problem of Knowledge* (1956) half-heartedly defends those who try to generalize from own experience, but concludes that the defenders of induction simply 'try to fit inductive arguments into a deductive mould' (p. 73).
5. Cited by Robert Skidelsky (1992, p. 618).
6. See also Wisdom (1952) on the defects of inference in natural science. Wisdom also taught scientific method at the London School of Economics at the same time as Popper.
7. There is a slight difference between Popper and Ayer on the methodology of science. Popper stresses that experimentation aims at 'falsification', whereas Ayer seeks 'confirmation' of the tested hypotheses. Popper holds that all scientific 'laws' are mere hypotheses, which with experimentation over time are bound to be falsified or revealed to be special cases of more general hypotheses.
8. Hicks (1954) used comparable terms, but in an entirely different context, distinguishing between 'stickers' and 'snatchers'. He was discussing the behavior of entrants into 'contestable markets' where the stickers had a long term strategy, and the snatchers were after short term gains.
9. The recurrent reference in the literature to natural resource 'extraction' as 'production' is evidently misleading. Nature took geological time to *produce* what we now merely extract. Drawing down reserves involves the selling of assets – a fact that is repeatedly stressed in this book. 'Production', I believe, should be reserved to the creation of value added by the services of land, labor and capital.
10. These negative aspects, it should be noted once again, are not confined to 'windfalls' arising from exploiting ecological resources, but may also accompany similar inflows of 'unrequited' funds including external assistance, foreign financing of large scale infrastructure projects such as dams, and incoming workers' remittances. They are also occasionally associated with commodity booms that develop in faraway locations, travel through international commerce, and affect a country's terms of trade. The intensity of the impact will of course depend on the size of the inflows relative to the receiving economy.
11. There seems to be some correspondence between, on the one hand the real effective exchange rate of an economy experiencing a resource boom, and the prices of traded

goods relative to the prices of non-traded goods and services, on the other. See Gelb, Alan and Associates (1988, especially Chapter 6).

12. This is often estimated by reckoning a weighted average of a country's currency relative to a basket of the currencies of its trading partners, making an allowance for inflation. Obviously this quantity will not remain unchanged.

13. Pertamina, Indonesia's State oil corporation, had assumed excessive short-term foreign debt, and in 1974 actually failed to meet its debt servicing obligations. So the government stepped in and allocated the equivalent of two-fifths of a whole year's oil windfalls to repay Pertamina's debt (Glassburner, 1988, p. 205).

14. Resource stock availability usually refers to quantities that may be economically mined with available technology. Technology of course is not constant but always advances – a fact that would increase availability. In the present context, however, uncertainty about reserve estimates seems to be of secondary importance. Any reasonably approximate number will do.

15. For me, an early experience of such a faulty judgment occurred during my time at the World Bank when in the early 1980s a Regional Chief Economist (as it happened for Latin America and the Caribbean) circulated an internal memorandum claiming that OPEC's restriction of oil supply (which in fact was not true as OPEC's supply had actually increased in 1973–74) did not only harm the oil importers' economies, but also the oil economies as well. He based this judgment simply on reading the slow, or in some cases, negative GDP growth as conventionally estimated. The same impression was shared by many economists within and without the World Bank at the time. In an internal World Bank memorandum I refuted his argument and accused him of being simplistic, unaware of the complexity of the issues involved.

16. One fault of 'American economics' perceived by Hicks on coming to America for the first time in 1946 was that American economists tended to make contact with reality only through econometrics. In the present context we may read 'econometrics' as GDP estimates. See Hicks, 'The making of an Economist' published in *Banca Nazionale del Lavoro Quarterly Review*, September, 1979 and reprinted in his 'Formation of an Economist' in *Classics and Moderns, Collected Essays on Economic Theory*, volume III, Chapter 31, pp. 355–364.

REFERENCES

Ayer, Alfred J. (1956), *The Problem of Knowledge*. Baltimore, MD: Penguin Books.

Ayer, Alfred J. (1973), *The Central Questions of Philosophy*. London: Penguin Books.

Besley, Timothy (2007), 'The new political economy', *Economic Journal*, **117** (524), F570–F587.

Boyce, John R. and J. C. Herbert Emery (2005), 'A Hotelling explanation of "the curse of natural resources"', Discussion Paper 2006-06, Department of Economics, University of Calgary, Canada.

Boyce, John R. and J. C. Herbert Emery (2011), 'Is a negative correlation between resource abundance and growth sufficient evidence that there is a "resource curse"?', *Resource Policy*, **36**, 1–13.

Busse, Matthias and Gröning, Steffen (2011), *Resource Curse Revisited: Governance and Natural Resources*. Hamburg: Hamburg Institute of International Economics.

Cervellati, Matteo, Piergiuseppe Fortunato and Uwe Sunde (2008), 'Hobbes to Rousseau: inequality, institutions and development', *Economic Journal*, **118** (531), 1354–1384.

Corden, W. Max (1982), 'Booming sector and Dutch disease economics: a survey', Working Paper number 079, Working Papers in Economics and Econometrics, Australian National University, Faculty of Economics and Research School of Social Sciences , Canberra, Australia.

Durlauf, Steven N. (2009), 'The rise and fall of cross-country growth regression', in Mauro Boianovsky and Kevin D. Hoover (eds), *Cross-Country Regressions in Growth Economics* (Part 4, Endogenous Growth, The New Growth Economics). *Duke University Ongoing History of Political Economy*, **41**, (Supplement 1), 315–333.

Durlauf, Steven N. and Danny T. Quah (1999), 'The new empirics of economic growth', in John B. Taylor and Michael Woodford (eds), *Handbook of Macroeconomics*, Vol. 1A. New York and Oxford: Elsevier Science, North Holland, Chapter 4, pp. 235–308.

El Serafy, Salah (1979), 'The oil price revolution of 1973–73', *Journal of Energy and Development*, **4** (2), 273–290.

El Serafy, Salah (1981), 'Absorptive capacity, the demand for revenue and the supply of petroleum', *Journal of Energy and Development*, 7 (1), 73–88.

El Serafy, Salah (1993), 'Depletable resources: fixed capital or inventories?', in Alfred Franz and Carsten Stahmer (eds.), *Approaches to Environmental Accounting*. Heidelberg, Germany: Physica-Verlag, pp. 245–258.

Gelb, Alan and Associates (1988), *Oil Windfalls: Blessing or Curse?* Washington DC: Oxford University Press for the World Bank.

Glassburner, Bruce (1988), 'Indonesia: Windfalls in a Poor Rural Economy', in Alan Gelb and Associates (eds), *Oil Windfalls: Blessing or Curse?* Washington DC: Oxford University Press for the World Bank, Chapter 12, pp. 197–226.

Haberler, Gottfried (1976), 'Oil, inflation, recession and the international monetary system', *Journal of Energy and Development*, **1** (2), 177–190.

Hicks, John Richard (1946), Value and Capital, 2nd edn. Oxford: Oxford University Press.

Hicks, John Richard (1954), 'The Process of Imperfect Competition', *Oxford Economic Papers.* Reprinted as 'Stickers and snatchers' in *Classics and Moderns, Collected Essays on Economic Theory*, Vol. III, (1983). Cambridge, MA: Harvard University Press, Chapter 12, pp. 162–178.

Hotelling, Harold (1931), 'The economics of exhaustible resources', *Journal of Political Economy*, 39 (2), 137–175.

Keynes, John Maynard (1921), *Treatise on Probability*. London: Macmillan.

Koopmans, Tjalling C. (1947), 'Measurement without theory', *Review of Economic Statistics*, **29** (3), 161–172.

Matthews, R. C. O. (1986), 'The economics of institutions and the sources of growth', *Economic Journal*, **96** (384), 903–918.

Mehlum, H., K. Moene, and R. Torvik (2006), 'Institutions and the resource curse', *Economic Journal*, **116** (508), 1–21.

Minier, Jenny (2007), 'Institutions and parameter heterogeneity', *Journal of Macroeconomics*, **29** (3), 595–611.

Neumayer, Eric (2000), 'Resource accounting in measures of unsustainability: challenging the World Bank's conclusions', *Environmental and Resource Economics*, **15**, 257–278.

Neumayer, Eric (2004), 'Does the "resource curse" hold for growth in genuine income as well?', *World Development*, **32** (10), 1627–1640.

Pigou, A. C. (1952), 'One Way of Looking at Economics', in *Essays in Economics*, London: Macmillan and Co., Chapter IV, pp. 65–84.

Popper, Karl (1961), *The Poverty of Historicism*, 2nd edn., London: Routledge & Kegan Paul.

Popper, Karl (1974), *An Unending Quest*. Chicago, IL: Open Court.

Ross, Michael S. (1999), 'The political economy of the resource curse', *World Politics*, **51**, January, 297–322.

Sachs, Jeffery D. and Andrew M. Warner (1995), 'Natural resources abundance and economic growth', National Bureau of Economic Research Working Paper Number 5398, Cambridge, Massachusetts.

Sachs, Jeffery D. and Andrew M. Warner (1997), 'Natural resource abundance and economic growth', Center for International Development and Harvard Institute for International Development, Harvard University, Cambridge Massachusetts.

Sachs, Jeffery D. and Andrew M. Warner (1999), 'The big push, natural resource booms and growth', *Journal of Development Economics*, **59**, 43–76.

Sala-i-Martin, Xavier and Arvind Subramanian (2003), 'Addressing the natural resources curse: an illustration from Nigeria', Research Department Working Paper 03/139, International Monetary Fund, Washington DC.

Skidelsky, Robert (1992), *John Maynard Keynes, The Economist as Saviour 1920–1937*. London: Macmillan.

Stevens, Paul (2003), 'Resource impact: curse of blessing? A literature survey', *Journal of Energy Literature*, 9 (1), 3–24.

Stevens, Paul (2005), '"Resource curse" and how to avoid it', *Journal of Energy and Development*, **XXXI** (1), 1–20.

Wijnbergen, Sweder J. van (1984), 'The Dutch disease: a disease after all?', *Economic Journal*, **94** (373), 41–55.

Wisdom, John Oulton (1952), *Foundations of Inference in Natural Science*. London: Methuen & Co. Ltd.

19. Natural resources in World Bank country economic work and Indonesia's experience

PROLOGUE

This chapter reproduces in a shortened form a paper I wrote for the Environment Department at the World Bank and published in March 1993 under the title, 'Country Macroeconomic Work and Natural Resources'.[1] I had just left World Bank service after twenty years of work on macroeconomic matters culminating in a spell at the 'Country Policy Department', followed by membership of a coterie of special advisers then named 'the Economic Advisory Staff' (EAS). This small unit provided direct contact with the highest echelons of Bank management with access to the President's Council. Although this paper originally targeted World Bank economists it was released outside the Bank nine months ahead of SNA93. The earlier draft contained two appendices: one outlining my user-cost method, which is here omitted, and another highlighting relevant World Bank Operational Directives, some of which I had helped to draft and may now be considered out of date. My purpose all along has been to counsel Bank economists dealing with assistance strategies, country economic work and macroeconomic analysis to watch out for significant changes occurring in the physical environment since these directly affect the macroeconomic numbers. This paper attracted much attention within the Bank during its preparatory stages, gaining special praise from the then Director General of the Operations Evaluation Department, Robert Picciotto, who subsequently recruited me to head the World Bank's team which, together with UNEP and UNDP, evaluated the Global Environment Facility, Pilot Phase – publishing its report in 1994. This chapter deals with the actual estimation of green accounting by different methods, and in the process touches on a variety of macroeconomic issues that gain from greening the national accounts. It focuses on the experience of Indonesia's reaction to the petroleum boom and how macroeconomic policy adjustment helped to see the country safely through the petroleum upheavals of the 1970s and 1980s. Its concreteness should provide a welcome contrast with the largely abstract discussions of earlier chapters.

I INTRODUCTION

To some this chapter may appear dated, but it is not for it captures some important historical developments in account greening methods. It is included in this book for at least two reasons. First the period covered (1974–83), though obviously past, is the time span covered by the pioneering national accounting study of Indonesia's wasting assets made by the World Resources Institute (Repetto et al., 1989). I have been critical of that study, and used my user-cost-based approach to alter its conclusions significantly. A second reason for its inclusion is that it carried a strong message to my fellow economists at the World Bank, urging them to pay attention to the physical foundations of the macroeconomic variables they monitor, analyze and project forward in their operations. Unless these foundations are maintained against erosion the macroeconomic numbers in use would not be meaningful. The chapter's concern, it will be noted, is for natural resources *as a source*, and it abstracts from other environmental concerns such as pollution, amenity preservation or habitat protection. Many Bank economists working on concrete projects were clearly aware of the relevance of the physical environment for investments in agriculture, fisheries, animal husbandry, irrigation, drainage, population, health and in other sectors. Besides, at the project level, which had been the mainstay of World Bank operations until 1980, certain progress had been noticeable in ascertaining environmental externalities of these investments and incorporating them in project cost–benefit analysis. Furthermore, attempts have additionally been made in some instances to apply the concept of 'sustainability' to individual projects by tailoring them to the limitations of their physical surroundings and by provision in project design for safeguards that would sustain the project's inputs and outputs. But the one major area of economic work at the Bank, which seems to have been slow in responding to concern over sustainability, is the area of macroeconomic analysis. The various macroeconomic aggregates collected, deployed, analyzed, and projected, and then employed to diagnose country economic weaknesses and prescribe policy cures, have often remained divorced from the economy's physical environment. This may be seriously deteriorating while short-term macroeconomic measurements would indicate spurious progress leading to inappropriate economic policies. Again it would be wrong to presume that all Bank country economists have been oblivious to such pitfalls, but generally speaking a wide gap seems to exist, separating ongoing country macroeconomic work from alarming descriptions of a deteriorating natural resource base as reported by visiting environmental missions.

Better national income and product accounts are obviously needed to reflect significant changes occurring in the natural resource stock as a *sine qua non* for gauging macroeconomic performance properly. This chapter therefore addresses the proper measurement of national income and product at some length before it settles down to discussing some important macroeconomic policy implications of the proposed adjustments. National accounting, it will be seen, is a fertile field where the disciplines of economics, accounting and statistics overlap and interlock, and provide an eminently useful apparatus to gauge the macroeconomic aggregates properly. Understandably the accounts leave out a great deal that happens outside the formal sector, and are sometimes inevitably based on guesses and incomplete knowledge. But for good or ill, the set of GDP and its cohorts has become an established barometer of general economic conditions that provides the basis on which much macroeconomic guidance rests. The attention paid in this chapter to the proper measurement of these variables may seem excessive, but unless we get better readings of these numbers than we seem to be getting at present, economic analysis and policy for many countries will remain seriously defective. An initiative is already underway to adjust the United Nations System of National Accounts (SNA)[2] to cause it to reflect environmental change. Until this process is complete, which will obviously take time, some interim measures – as indicated later – need to be devised and applied without delay in order to improve macroeconomic work at the World Bank.

Slightly digressing I should mention that the writing of this chapter has coincided with the publication of a number of initiatives that probe the negative impact of 'Structural Adjustment' programs on the environment.[3] Such initiatives have sought to cover some of the ground covered here, but they approach the subject from a different angle. In the present study my attention is concentrated on the impact of a deteriorating natural resource base on gauging country macroeconomic performance, and hence on economic policies. By contrast, studies, such as that of WRI of the Philippines (Cruz and Repetto, 1992), had set out to investigate the negative effect of 'structural adjustment' on the environment. They focus on the impact on the environment of reducing public expenditure, changes in taxation, interest rates, tariffs and exchange rates which tend to be common features in adjustment lending operations (*loc. cit.*, p. 1). Both approaches are useful, but the approach adopted here needs to be put forward, not just to correct and improve structural adjustment programs, but more generally and perhaps more basically, in order to improve country macroeconomic analysis and policy recommendations.

II   CHARACTERIZING THE APPROACH

Without ambiguity this work applies the notion of 'sustainable development' (or sustainability for short) to economic work at the Bank at a country level. The sustainability sought here is minimal sustainability consistent with economic orthodoxy. It relies on the twin concepts of capital and income, which are central quantities to economics. In order to reckon income properly (for an individual, a firm or a nation) capital must be kept intact. In other words part of current receipts must be used to repair, restore and maintain capital in order to preserve its ability to create future income before an estimate of current income can be reached. Marketable natural resources are certainly 'capital' which, as this chapter argues, should be brought into the purview of national income reckoning. Like other forms of capital, they should be 'maintained intact' for the purpose of estimating income correctly. This, however, does not mean that natural resources should be left unexploited. Indeed, following the minimal sustainability approach advocated here, they might be rationally 'mined' to extinction, provided that part of the proceeds from their exploitation is invested in alternative capital that would sustain income into the future. It is income, not the environment, which is here being targeted for sustainability.

From the beginning of economic theorizing 'labor' has been considered as the factor of production *par excellence*, particularly in its application to land – another acknowledged original factor of production. Later, the Industrial Revolution came to highlight the role of human-made capital as yet another powerful factor in the productive process. In time the role of entrepreneurship and of technology came to be recognized, and have been occasionally conflated with capital. Land, though treated from the beginning as a factor of production, had a separate and differentiated role. Its returns were only a 'surplus', its role as a factor was merely passive, and its reward, called 'rent', was determined only after all the other factors had claimed their share in the product. Hence the rent of land was not considered a cost, and thus did not contribute to the determination of the produce price. Other than land, the environment received no recognition in economic thought as a factor contributing to production. Unlike the environment as perceived nowadays, however, the distinguishing characteristic of land in classical thought was its presumed indestructibility.[4]

Alfred Marshall, perhaps more than other neoclassical economists, found the demarcation between factors of production rather artificial, inventing the category quasi-rent for the reward of inputs temporarily in short supply. In more recent times work on the origins of growth has indicated the difficulty of attributing progress clearly to any one factor, and it has become convenient to resort to simplified paradigms, captured in models such as the Cobb–Douglas production function, where all non-labor factors, including land, are subsumed under 'capital'. The fact that 'Nature' contributes to the productive process has become abundantly clear with the unprecedented growth of economic activity on our finite planet during the past hundred years or so. Both as a receptor of wastes and as a source of materials and energy the earth is showing signs of stress, some of which appear to be irreversible, or otherwise difficult and very costly to reverse. The previously free services of Nature have come increasingly to be associated with cost, and a rising cost at that. Because much of Nature is not appropriated by individuals, or even nations, environmental stress has for long failed to be counted as a cost of doing business. Sooner or later, however, an environmental price must be paid in order to clean up the high seas, revive polluted rivers and lakes, restore air quality to acceptable standards, repair the ozone layer, and replenish soils, forests, and fisheries so that they can continue to be as productive as before and meet the demands of an increasing population with an eye on raising their living standards. Internalizing the external costs of production so that the full cost of each economic activity can be properly counted has brought environmentalists and economists together. With proper costing, resource allocation will clearly improve, but this is primarily a microeconomic issue which lies a little outside the scope of this chapter.

A main message that should emerge out of this work is that the environment is not a sector, like agriculture or transport, but an envelope that contains all economic activities, and provides the long run context in which economies function and develop. Short-term indicators of economic change abound, and serve useful purposes, but for the purpose of managing development, particularly in so-called developing countries, they are seldom sufficient. For there remains a dimension, which is essentially long-term, which is necessary to keep firmly in mind in order for the analyst to perceive where an economy is heading; and whether the current prosperity if portrayed by short-term economic indicators is sustainable, or else is transitory and will lead inevitably to future economic decline. A long view is obviously indispensable for guiding development strategy for a country seeking to manage its resources rationally.

By stressing the importance of the long term, which is the appropriate time frame for development, the question of sustainability of development assumes prominence. Definitions of sustainability, such as that offered in the Brundtland Report[5] are admirable in their way, but for the purposes of this study the Brundtland definition is complex and overambitious, incorporating too many elements, including income distribution at a point of time as well as over time, and the notion of preserving the natural 'heritage' for future generations.

Such objectives are deliberately left outside this current work in order to focus the coverage on certain basic economic considerations. By contrast with the Brundtland definition, the sustainable development to which this chapter draws attention can be described as a 'weak sustainability', reflecting concerns rooted in economics, and avoiding at this stage issues of ecological conservation and income distribution. Development, it should be stressed, is not a short-term affair, but a long-term process, involving building-up capacities, improving human skills, institutions and infrastructure, while simultaneously attempting to maintain the natural resource base from which many developing nations derive their prosperity. Should the natural resource base of an economy be deteriorating, either deliberately or fortuitously, future consumption is bound to suffer unless a conscious effort is made to offset this deterioration by capital formation in all its varieties, i.e. through investments in machinery and equipment, technological development, institution building, health and education, and of course repairing and restoring the natural resource base itself. Were developing countries as richly endowed with natural resources at present as the United States had been two centuries ago, the scale of the problem for them would be much smaller, and the urgency of the issue much less pressing. In many developing country situations populations have now exploded, concurrently as natural resources supporting these populations have eroded to critical levels, and efforts to build up skills through training and investing in material capital to compensate for the deteriorating environment have been highly inadequate. It is perhaps worth stressing once more that seeking to maintain the natural resource base does not mean that it should be fossilized in its current state – rather that it should be exploited rationally according to sound economic principles, and decidedly not liquidated to finance consumption without due regard to the future.

ALTERNATIVE AVENUES

There seem to be three main thoroughfares available – though these are often crisscrossing – for bringing economic work to bear on environmental concerns. One is a route already started in the World Bank to address the environmental impact of projects, minimize any harm they may produce through better design, and try to internalize environmental costs in project analysis. This can be viewed as a microeconomic approach. Another route, now being explored, is to identify sectoral or economy-wide practices that are harmful to the environment in order to devise offsetting measures and policies, and also encourage practices that are environmentally friendly. This can be a mixture of microeconomic and macroeconomic considerations and may be said also to have been initiated in the Bank. A third approach which dominates this chapter is entirely macroeconomic. This leans heavily in the direction of proper economic accounting, and following this through into the field of economy-wide macroeconomic policy. All three approaches are necessary, and fortunately would tend to be mutually supportive.

But the contention is clearly false that all that is required from economists in this regard is better project analysis that would take into consideration both project externalities and proper valuation of inputs and outputs for the purpose of reflecting their true environmental scarcities and utilities. Better project analysis is certainly essential, but it would not take care of the host of environmental concerns that needs to be addressed on a very wide economic front and cannot be captured in a project-by-project cost–benefit framework. After all, there are many situations where environmental stress has reached acute proportions and where new projects are either not being contemplated at all, or, if being seriously considered, would have little effect on the distressed environment however ideally designed they may be from an environmental point of view.

Another idea worth discrediting is the belief that technological progress is bound to render environmental apprehensions superfluous. This idea can be largely discarded for being as unhelpful in a developing country context as it is unrealistic. Technological progress is bound to continue to be made, both in ridding the earth of harmful emissions associated with production and consumption, and in economizing on the use of, as well as finding substitutes for, materials and energy sources. But technological progress is notoriously slow for the developing countries, being handicapped by many factors including high costs and low incomes (see below). However, if and when technological advances are actually made, they will inevitably reflect themselves in changed practices and productive activities, and will be accounted for in the normal way. Technology, however, is unlikely to be able to repair all environmental damage or to restore species that have become extinct in the process.

The most important message of this chapter is that economic work must try to distinguish between, on the one hand, asset liquidation such as that resulting from overfishing, felling trees without replacing them, and drawing down finite reserves of mineral wealth, and on the other hand true value added created by the services of original factors of production through activities which can be replicated and sustained over time. The argument is worth repeating that although some of the natural resources in question may appear to be getting globally more abundant than formerly believed this provides little comfort to individual countries that are running out of the same resources within their own borders. And it is the *country* that provides the context for Bank operational and economic work, as well as for economic policy prescriptions, so that reference to global abundance in this regard distracts and confuses rather than advances understanding of the economic conditions of many a developing country served by the World Bank.

III   COUNTRY MACROECONOMIC WORK AND THE ENVIRONMENT

The high dependence of many developing countries on natural resource use, including commercial exploitation, raises questions about the adequacy of the current practice of viewing their macroeconomic problems through the short-term prism of fiscal and balance of payments developments, with little emphasis placed on issues of long-term sustainability. This myopic view is compounded by the prevalent lack of discrimination between the genuine creation of value added and the generation of financial receipts through the liquidation of natural assets.[6] Bank economic reports for many natural resource-dependent countries, including Algeria, Tunisia, Egypt, Ecuador, Malawi and Congo during the seventies and eighties may be easily faulted on this score. But it would be unfair to single out these instances since many other country reports suffer from the same limitation. For such countries, the loss of environmental capital, including soil erosion, decline of forest cover, or liquidation of mineral deposits, has been ignored in the economic analysis, and even treated as progress reflected in spurious measurements of economic growth and misleading fiscal and balance of payments surpluses. For such countries the economic measurements of performance and the policy advice based on them have, at times, been dubious at best. Misreading the liquidation of environmental capital as economic progress may in fact have contributed to the obstruction of long-term economic development in some of the countries mentioned, as will be illustrated later. Inevitably the productive base of such economies will give out, and valuable time will have been lost when a more accurate measurement of performance, and hence more appropriate economic policies, could have helped to build up proper economic foundations for future development.

The predicament of such countries is sometimes compounded by the assurance of false prosperity as certified for them by the national income statisticians, and endorsed uncritically by the economists who are only too eager to accept them. This false image gets imparted to prospective creditors who would advance loans over and above the true creditworthiness of the borrowers, thus contributing to later situations of insolvency and loss of national economic policy independence. This has been the story of several petroleum exporting countries that appeared very prosperous during the 1970s, and ended up in the mid-eighties with enormous debts and other economic difficulties, though clearly the oil price collapse that followed did aggravate their problems. Rather than wait until a country's marketable natural resources had become seriously eroded or otherwise the markets for those resources had collapsed and the country was left with an intolerable debt burden, and only then begin to prescribe painful stabilization-cum-structural adjustment policies, economists should have much earlier helped to devise a development-oriented longer-term adjustment strategy. Such a strategy would be based on greater savings, more rational investments, and systematic diversification of economic activities. In conditions of greater abundance, the adjustment would have been less painful and the chances of developmental success brighter. Economic work during the past two decades on some of the countries already mentioned (Congo and Tunisia are conspicuous examples) would clearly demonstrate the importance of this argument. It is however true that during periods of apparent prosperity, built on the liquidation of natural resources, countries normally discount outside economic advice, but Bank economists should nevertheless offer such advice once careful analysis has been made of the deteriorating stock of natural resources.

As will be mentioned later, one of the gravest problems confronting such countries is the 'Dutch disease' which sets in as a result of natural asset liquidation, thereby undermining the tradable goods sectors. A proactive exchange rate policy would be indicated to redress such a distortion as argued in section V below. For developed countries environmental concerns largely relate to problems of pollution, including waste disposal. It may be that pollution receives disproportionate attention for the reason that it is seen as important for the richer countries. Furthermore, pollution makes itself readily observable, whereas the cost of depletion of 'source resources' could remain hidden for a while, to be borne only later. Pollution of course raises formidable issues touching on health and sanitation, recycling, protection of scenic amenities and other related issues. Important among these is how to internalize pollution costs through adequate policies, and properly treating in economic measurements the impact of environmental disasters and the costs incurred for guarding against or mitigating the effects of the harm being inflicted.

Needless to say that pollution problems do confront practically all developing countries also, though in general relatively less severely since pollution tends to be associated with industrialization.[7] For many people, however, the environment seems to raise pollution concerns in the first instance, and sight is frequently lost of the often greater issue for developing countries of natural resource depletion and degradation. Even sector specialists at the World Bank and environmentalists producing 'Environmental Issues Papers' and 'Environmental Action Plans', tend to ignore subsoil deposits in these documents, and fail to highlight their limited life expectancy under current exploitation profiles, either under the impression that such resources are not strictly environmental, or because they appear to them to be so important that they must have already been covered in other country economic work.[8]

NATIONAL INCOME ACCOUNTING

Measurements of income and expenditure for gauging economic performance must be convincing if they are to serve as a useful guide to macroeconomic policy, and they obviously are inadequate especially if significant depletion of marketable natural resources is taking place without being reflected in these measurements. Clearly not all countries need the adjustment of their national income estimates to reflect environmental change. For many industrialized countries the adjustment is needed only for pollution though this problem could be addressed, as frequently it has, outside the framework of national accounting. For some, including the United States, topsoil erosion, depleted aquifers and maybe declining fossil fuel reserves call also for some national income adjustment. But for developing countries the adjustment in many instances has to cover both pollution and natural resource degradation, and its magnitude will therefore normally be larger in relation to their national income. Where countries are dependent to a high degree on activities such as timber extraction, fishing, or drawing out minerals and underground water, and where the stocks of such resources are small relative to extraction rates, the adjustment needed to the accounts will tend to be considerable. There is no *prima facie* standard in such cases as to the degree of overestimation of national income as reckoned conventionally since this depends essentially on the importance of the activity in the economy (roughly indicated by its share in GDP however estimated) and on the number of years the resource will last at current extraction or erosion rates. Generally speaking such countries tend to be poorer than the accounts make them out to be, and their economic growth may be quite different from the conventionally calculated growth. Their true growth could even be negative where positive growth had been indicated by the conventional measurements.

As stated earlier, this chapter will altogether eschew issues of pollution as they affect national income and product estimation, and will attempt to focus on the adjustment needed for the erosion of an economy's capital base through natural resource depletion and degradation.[9] It will explore some of the policy implications of the adjusted accounts, and indicate a number of countries where the adjustments and their policy implications are likely to be significant and therefore worth undertaking. Adjusting the accounts to cover more natural resources, pollution or some aspects of pollution, could later be added when estimates of these have become available. The fact that such adjustments are partial, and will not encompass the totality of environmental change, does not represent a weakness of this approach. This issue is addressed later in the chapter. In fact it can be categorically stated now that it will never be possible to carry out comprehensive adjustments of national income to reflect every aspect of environmental change.

NATURAL RESOURCES AS CAPITAL

Natural resources represent capital that can and should be used to produce goods and services for the benefit of their owners. From an economic viewpoint, it is absurd to claim that all natural resources should be left untouched for use by future generations. If such a preservationist rule were to be applied, the next generation's use would also have to be constrained for the sake of still later generations. Like other forms of capital, however, natural resources need to be *maintained* in order that they can continue to help in the productive process. Toward that end, if such resources are renewable, such as forests or fisheries, annual exploitation should be kept within the natural rate of regeneration of the resource. If it exceeds that natural rate, and the capital stock is therefore diminished, the diminution should be estimated and imputed as disinvestment, and reflected in the measurement of the national product. If exploitation falls below natural regeneration, then the owner would be adding to the final stock through a passive act of investment. Either way, the change in the stock should be assessed. There is a well established precautionary accounting convention not to count any appreciation of stocks in current income, but wait until it is actually realized lest the capital base should get eroded by excessive consumption. On the other hand, declines in the value of stocks must, by accounting convention, be recorded, again on grounds of precaution. The usual way of effecting adjustments to reflect over-exploitation of renewable resources is to treat this as *depreciation*, deducting the depreciation from the gross income or product, in order to arrive at an adjusted level of net income or product. This 'usual' way is taken at its face value in this paper. Strictly speaking the adjustment for over-exploitation should be equal to the 'user cost', which is only a part of the apparent depreciation and applied to the gross product.

Valuation can be a formidable problem in such an exercise, but it is not totally insurmountable. It is more manageable for those natural resources that are marketable, than for pollution, although for the loss of biodiversity the difficulty of valuation cannot be overestimated. Where the market indicates prices for natural resources the economist should, at least initially, base the adjustments on those. But often one has to resort to shortcuts and imputation – such as, for instance, inferring the cost of soil erosion from the decline of crop yields or from the higher cost of increased inputs (such as fertilizers) needed to compensate for the soil erosion. One difficulty, however, is that loss of soil may not reduce crop yields until soil depth has begun to approach 'rock-bottom'. Full and comprehensive adjustment will always remain elusive, and all adjustments will inevitably be partial though useful, and this has to be expected.

Where resources cannot be regenerated and commercial exploitation leads inevitably to a diminished stock, such as in the case of mineral extraction, national account adjustment requires special treatment. Strictly speaking, the income derived from this stock, if it were to be liquidated in one go, is the annuity that can be earned on re-investing the proceeds in income-yielding financial or material assets.[10] However, it may not be possible, or indeed judicious on account of market limitations, to liquidate resources abruptly. It may be more prudent to continue to exploit them gradually over time, unearthing some, and leaving the bulk underground. The owners of the resource if not constrained by contract, will be deciding its annual exploitation rate in the light of their judgment of the resource's current market conditions and likely future prices, and in conjunction with their current financial needs, technical extraction constraints, prevailing yields on alternative investments, etc. The rate of exploitation ultimately decided upon may or may not be judged by the economists to be optimal. But for the purpose of income reckoning this optimality is irrelevant, since the accountant's function is to estimate the owner's income during the year that is already past, whether or not the owner had made ideal decisions and realized gains or suffered losses. I have proposed a method for estimating true income from the gradual exploitation of depletable resources based on the proportion of the known reserves extracted in any one year and the rate of interest at which a certain portion of the receipts, identified as a user cost, must be re-invested in financial or material assets in order to maintain income. 'True income' would be the difference between the net receipts (i.e. net of extraction costs) and the user cost, which represents asset diminution in the course of exploitation.[11]

Since non-renewable (or exhaustible) resources cannot be restored or maintained as renewable resources can, it does not make economic sense to view the decline in their stocks as *depreciation* to be deducted from gross income (or product) in order to arrive at an adjusted level of *net* income.[12] Those who adopted such a faulty approach ended up with wiping out from the net product the entire contribution of the natural resource to income, since that same contribution represents also the magnitude of asset erosion. Instead, as I have suggested, after calculating the proper dimensions of the user cost, this should be excluded altogether from gross income since it represents an inventory drawdown, and no further adjustment of net income would then be required. After some initial skepticism there is now greater appreciation of this method, which has actually been applied in several places.[13] The 'user cost' in any case is the proper magnitude of resource 'depreciation' if the adjustments were to be confined to the calculation of net income.

For the majority of industrialized countries, the adjustment resulting from taking account of natural resource exploitation, whether exhaustible or renewable, along the lines just indicated will not make a sizeable difference to income estimates as conventionally reckoned owing to the limited contribution of domestically extracted natural resources to their economic prosperity. Except for countries such as those exploiting North Sea petroleum deposits, or for regions or states within Canada, the United States or Australia, where natural resources (largely in the form of forests, petroleum and other mineral deposits) currently contribute significantly to economic activity, will the adjustment to the regional or domestic product be appreciable, and therefore worth undertaking. This last statement, however, should not be taken to mean that natural resources are unimportant for the developed countries, since however small the contribution of domestic natural resources to economic activity appears in GDP, the decline of natural resource availability would reduce GDP by a multiple of their presumed contribution. This is because natural resources often provide the base on which value may be added in secondary and tertiary activities.[14] This, however, is quite a different issue.

But for some developing countries the required adjustment to the accounts can be substantial, deriving from a combination of several natural resources, all being simultaneously exploited and eroding at various rates, reinforced by population pressures and the complex impacts of poverty. In an environment characterized by widespread indigence the pursuit of survival can lead to serious liquidation of whatever natural capital there is since, for survival, the future gets discounted by the poor at extremely high rates of time preference. This is not to say that natural capital does not also get destroyed where time preference is relatively low. But it is part of the purpose of this study to indicate a few of those countries where the adjustment needed to the conventionally estimated national product would be appreciable, and to urge country economists in the Bank to be aware of the problem of an eroding resource base and alive to the extent to which natural resources may be deteriorating. The list of countries where the problem is likely to be important can be expected to expand with time as awareness of the problem increases and the necessary work to assess it is done. The adjustment to the accounts could actually be undertaken by the Bank country economists themselves, or with their guidance and cooperation by the national statistical offices of the countries they work on.

It should be stressed once more that we must not expect either comprehensiveness or precision from the proposed process of income adjustment. It is difficult, if not impossible, to ascertain all the stocks of natural resources at a point of time, and in every case to place a monetary value on that stock. Such a value is not actually needed for estimating the user cost. Also, even if the market sets a value on the resource, we may not be able to ascertain the complex gradations of its quality, or fathom the costs of extraction exactly, either in average or marginal terms, or predict their future course with any precision – though we might be fairly certain that future costs will be higher than current ones, which in turn are probably higher still than the costs of earlier periods. Though some of the cost of mineral exploitation may decline over time due to technical progress, the fact remains that early stages of exploitation tend to focus on rich deposits of easy access, and this process will cause later exploitation to be associated with higher extraction costs. Approximation of the relevant magnitudes, however crude, would be an improvement on current practices, and would bring greater accuracy and realism to economic measurements, which are often divorced from what is actually occurring in the physical environment, and would improve the insight of the economic analyst and the relevance of the analysis. In particular country situations the focus should be on effecting the adjustment in respect of those resources that figure prominently in the economy concerned, extending the coverage over time in the direction of comprehensiveness to encompass more and more resources as knowledge of the resource base increases and the methods of estimation improve. Where the market indicates values for such resources, there is really no excuse for the country economist to abstain from undertaking the adjustment, but his or her primary concern should be for the year-to-year change in the stock rather than for the value of this stock at any point in time. To the economist, the flow accounts, the profit and loss accounts, are far more important than the balance sheets.

This last point is important since some analysts, either independently or following OECD (1985) tentative guidelines have focused on the estimation of the opening and closing stocks of proven reserves of exhaustible resources, using market prices current at the time for valuation. And the difference (made up of the diminution due to exploitation and changes due to reserve re-estimation) is carried into the income estimates. Since the resource stocks are normally much larger than annual extraction, re-estimation of their size, as well as incorporation of changes in their value in the flow accounts, can dwarf the adjustment specifically due to extraction, and we may end up therefore with gyrating and economically meaningless adjusted income, and in some cases with estimates of so-called net income higher than those for gross income.[15] My own method brings the reassessment of stocks into the flow accounts through changes in the reserves-to-extraction ratio and consistently indicates a net income level lower than gross income – that is if the user cost method were to be treated as depreciation. Since extraction takes place inevitably out of a finite stock, it is obvious that the 'net' must always be less than the 'gross'.

POLICY IMPLICATIONS

If, as this chapter maintains, economists in some situations are unable to gauge economic performance through accurately estimating national income and its changes over time, how can they tell if an economy is growing, declining or stagnating? How can they indicate a meaningful country level of per capita income for meaningful international comparisons? How can they judge a proper level of money supply, a tolerable level of external debt, or manageable fiscal and balance of payments deficits – all of which need to be related to national income? How can they estimate a balance of payments current account deficit when the *current* account contains unrepeatable exports of environmental *capital*? How can they judge the adequacy of the saving/investment effort? Additionally, the relation of welfare to income raises yet a host of further issues, but, as stated earlier, this chapter will leave welfare considerations aside, focusing only on the proper measurement of output as a national performance indicator.[16]

To sum up, where an economy derives significant parts of its prosperity from natural resource exploitation, and where the resource depletion fails to be reflected properly in the national accounts, including the balance of payments, then (1) income will be overestimated; (2) savings and investment exaggerated; (3) the fiscal deficits (if natural resource exploitation is carried out in the public sector as it often is in developing countries) underestimated; (4) and if natural resources are exported, the current account may in reality be in deficit but papered over by unsustainable exports of assets. Where such phenomena are not recognized, the domestic currency could be seriously overvalued to the detriment of future development. This is because development relies to a large extent on diversifying the economy's productive base and creating employment opportunities outside the primary sector of natural resource extraction. By relying on conventional income measurements such economies may be judged wrongly to be healthy and growing satisfactorily while their natural resources last, but in reality their prosperity will prove to be ephemeral, inevitably giving out when the natural resources being exploited have been depleted or have approached extinction.

A major drawback of faulty economic accounting, as explained above, is its obfuscation at the macroeconomic level of certain symptoms of the Dutch disease phenomenon that sets in as a result of excessive dependence on natural resource exploitation. The inflow of extraordinary financial resources from exports often upsets the domestic economy in harmful ways. Among other things the Dutch disease distorts relative prices in favor of non-tradable goods and services, thus undermining the development of sustainable productive activities that could create employment opportunities and contribute to export promotion and efficient import substitution. With few exceptions, there is still a too limited awareness in the World Bank of the Dutch disease phenomenon among economists working on countries whose prosperity derives from diminishing and degrading natural resources. And little integration has so far occurred in economic reporting or analysis of the detailed environmental work already carried out on such countries – and which indicates some degree or other of resource depletion and degradation. Analytical macroeconomic efforts have tended to give great weight to short term economic aggregates without sufficient attention paid to long-term development. Even when long-term projections of the macroeconomic aggregates are attempted, these often extrapolate from short-term magnitudes and fail to reflect trends in resource depletion and degradation. The policy implications of the Dutch disease phenomenon are further elaborated in Section V below.

STRUCTURAL ADJUSTMENT OPERATIONS AND THE ENVIRONMENT

The Bank has recently tightened the process of assessing its lending operations for their environmental impact, but exempted structural adjustment lending operations (known in the Bank as SALs) from such scrutiny.[17] Some staff concerned with the environment have therefore proposed that structural adjustment operations, including SECALs (a sub-group focused on sectoral policy change) be subjected to the same process of environmental assessment, in order to investigate the environmental impact of such typical loan conditions as the reduction or removal of subsidies on pesticides, fertilizers and petroleum products. Raising the price of gasoline and kerosene, for instance, might encourage the consumption of coal and fuel wood, and could thus worsen emissions and lead to further deforestation. Others have been disturbed by the impact on poverty and nutrition, and hence indirectly on the environment, of the belt-tightening measures associated with stabilization programs which nearly always accompany structural adjustment. But besides such passive scrutiny of SAL impact, which needs nevertheless to be undertaken at least in order to assess any harmful effects these operations may have on the environment, structural adjustment programs could conceivably be used actively and effectively to bring about major changes in policies already in place which are judged to be inimical to the environment, as well as encourage other policies that would be instrumental in protecting the environment.

No matter how desirable such an objective might appear so that SALs could actually play a positive environmental role, it is an objective that cannot at present be realized owing to the lack of sufficient knowledge about the precise linkage between environmental degradation in specific country situations and the policies in place behind such degradation. Special investigations would need to be carried out systematically in the context of country economic and sector work to identify those current practices that enhance environmental deterioration in specific country contexts, and then devise corrective policy actions. This does not deny the possibility that once a certain type of environmental degradation has been traced back to identified factors, the same factors may be at work in different countries, and thus call for identical or similar remedial policy action. A case in point is deforestation, which in various country situations can stem from the same set of factors. These include insecurity of land tenure, subsidization of credit for settlement activities and for cattle ranching, under-taxation of land – besides such policies as export enhancement measures that disregard the under-pricing of exports' content of natural resources.[18]

Thus in order to use structural adjustment operations effectively to change policies that are inimical to the environment, much prior economic work, especially at the sector level, has to be undertaken, specifically to identify the policies that need to be changed, and explore their economic impact before and after they change. Few Environmental Issues Papers or Environmental Action Plans so far produced have succeeded in identifying such policies, which need to be uncovered over time through patient and systematic country economic and sector work. Until this is done, handling environmental issues under adjustment operations will remain *per force* partial, and largely of limited effect.

Just as it may be expected that poverty cannot be eliminated through individual adjustment operations –though of course some poverty alleviation may be feasible through adjustment programs in a partial and limited sense – the same can be said also of seeking to protect and maintain the environment through structural adjustment lending. A great deal of detail has to be unearthed first by country economic and sector work as part of the process of economic reporting, and then thoroughly analyzed for potential policy change. Once the policy changes have been identified, however, structural adjustment operations can be an ideal medium for effecting the desired results. Although structural adjustment programs have sometimes been blamed for damaging the environment, such blame is generally unwarranted. Apart from issues, such as those involving rationalizing and harmonizing alternative fuel prices, or the uncritical encouragement of exports whose natural resource contents are underpriced, the argument seems to be based on the economic hardships apparently imposed by stabilization-cum-structural adjustment programs on an already poverty stricken population, forcing the poor inevitably into environmental disinvestment in an attempt to survive. The same argument is also often used to blame adjustment programs for reducing the living standards of poorer nations when they are called upon to service external debts whose proceeds had not been utilized wisely in the first place to support productive investments. Such arguments wrongly focus on the pain normally associated with the intended cure, without objectively taking into account the origins of the waste, and the inefficiencies and overconsumption which had led to excessive borrowing. The origins of the economic difficulties that emerged, and which the device of structural adjustment is meant to address in an orderly fashion as a temporary and unavoidable measure, should be included in any objective analysis of the harmful impact of structural adjustment operations on the environment. This does not mean, however, that country economists and other specialists should not pay special attention to any harmful effects, which reduced public expenditure or lower private consumption under adjustment programs might inflict on the environment. In this regard, the environment is very similar to vulnerable groups, which should be specifically protected from the impact of adjustment programs through 'safety net' arrangements to enable them to survive the adjustment process.

COUNTRY STRATEGIES

Over the years the Bank has found it productive to expend considerable resources to clarify, rationalize and articulate its country assistance in the form of forward looking Country Strategy Papers. To plan and execute Bank operations in individual countries, Country Departments and Divisions have been set up, with country and other specialists working at various levels on economic and social problems. Within the Bank, the Region, headed by a Vice-President, is required periodically to put forward and justify its lending operations, country economic work, and other activities involving the use of Bank resources in the form of a strategy paper for the approval of Senior Management. Such strategy papers have different guises, some of them being brief and informal, e.g. to signal abrupt changes in country situations, but most of them have a three or four years' perspective, take months to prepare, and get reviewed by various units and at various levels in the Bank before they are adopted. Strategy Papers are often complemented by other efforts, such as Policy Framework Papers, drafted for IDA poorer borrowers by the country concerned in cooperation with the Bank and the IMF. These try to cover development problems and policies in a three-year forward perspective, which gets updated every year.

Generally speaking, it can be asserted that coverage of environmental issues, including natural resources, in strategy papers has until now been pro forma, or otherwise too scanty to be useful, either for illuminating an appropriate strategy for long-term development or for any policy analysis conducive to recommended policy changes. In Policy Framework Papers, although the relevant Operational Directive would state otherwise, environmental considerations tend to be almost non-existent (see Appendix). The reason for this is either that sufficient prior work had not been undertaken to guide movement on policy, or that highly detailed studies of the environment had remained unread by the country economist, or otherwise insufficiently analyzed to be incorporated in economic work.

As argued earlier, the description and analysis of natural resource change should be part and parcel of Country Economic Reports, and seriously and systematically addressed in Country Strategy Papers and

Policy Framework Papers. In particular, environmental change in the form of disasters, loss of forest cover, watershed degradation, soil erosion, mineral deposits depletion and reassessment of subsoil reserves, should be indicated in country economic reports and strategy papers in value terms if possible, but at least in physical terms in the first instance. In fact, because of the volatility and uncertainty of many natural resource prices, the physical measurements would quite often be more informative and dependable than value estimates, since the latter, where they relate to environmental stocks, can obscure what is actually happening to the physical assets. Economic reports should show the rate of exploitation and other declines in relation to the natural stocks available in order to indicate the relative seriousness of the deterioration. Once the extent of environmental deterioration is ascertained, the economists should bring in their expertise in order to assess its economic significance and then adapt their analysis accordingly.

MICRO AND MACRO ISSUES

The attention given in this chapter to the proper measurement of macroeconomic indicators (GDP and NDP levels and their growth, savings, investment, the current account balance, etc.) should not be taken as indicating an absence of need for a parallel movement among sector specialists and country economists aimed at improving the economic analysis of projects to accommodate environmental concerns. Serious attention should be given by them to project externalities, and to the correction for these by setting proper values on them and bringing them into the cost–benefit calculations. Second, many environmental benefits of investments are left out at present because of insufficient knowledge or inadequate efforts to capture them in the analysis. Once these benefits are estimated and internalized in the calculations, many environmental investments would appear more justifiable than before. Third, the process of shadow-pricing inputs and outputs should be extended to environmental goods and services where the market fails to reflect their true scarcities in adequate prices. And lastly, care should be exercised lest border prices of traded commodities, often used as shadow prices in project analysis, should themselves be underpriced and fail to reflect full environmental costs. These are important issues, and country economists, who are often called upon to help with the estimation of shadow prices for project analysis, should be more aware of them than they appear to be.

TECHNOLOGICAL PROGRESS

The belief appears unwarranted that current environmental stress is certain to be alleviated and even eliminated through the accumulation of knowledge and technological progress. Optimists cite the failure to materialize of forecasts of doom, such as those made by Malthus in the nineteenth century, and more recently by the Club of Rome. Optimism seems to be based on the notion that whatever environmental assets get lost, the advent of new technologies, the accumulation of human knowledge, combined with investments in human and physical capital will somehow compensate for them. While nobody can deny that knowledge accumulates and technology will continue to advance and find substitutes for materials that become less abundant (though it is impossible logically to predict technology's future course) the relevance of technological progress to environmental problems in developing countries, to say the least, is unclear. Take, for instance, the problem of population. Many parts of the world are suffering from environmental stress caused by populations that have become too large for their supporting environments. In theory a given space can accommodate much larger populations if these are sufficiently trained and backed by enough capital investments. In theory the application of birth control technology and massive capital injections could break the vicious circle of poverty and dependence from which existing populations are suffering. In practice, however, such solutions remain hopelessly beyond the reach of most impoverished countries. Even the physical problem of stabilizing population size, despite the availability of birth control technology for generations, appears untenable owing to economic, social and political impediments that are not easy to surmount. Technology optimists tend to underestimate the many practical handicaps that lie in the path of applying even already known technologies to actual problems in developing countries, let alone the social and financial impediments against introducing new technologies.

The possibility of advancement through technological progress is doubtless real, judging from past experience. But caution and realism should guard against complacency and single-minded reliance on the notion that technological progress will be a panacea for environmental ills. And it is unrealistic to expect that technological breakthroughs will materialize on time and be applied automatically to remove or alleviate past or future environmental damage. After all, technological progress is discontinuous, cannot be predicted, and will have its costs. And one should not too readily assume that those who will be in most need of technological innovations will be able to afford the cost of acquiring them.

What is the relevance of technological progress to natural resource accounting? We must keep in mind that accounting is an *ex post* function which seeks to describe past behavior of individuals, firms and nations, embodying such a description in a standard format of flow accounts and balance sheets. It has no business predicting the future, although good accounting is indispensable for guiding future decisions. Accounting often has a one-year perspective during which technology can safely be assumed to remain unchanged. When technological progress occurs, the decision-makers may or may not incorporate the new technologies in the activity concerned, thereby improving or worsening their ability to compete and gain profits. This in turn will be reflected in the accounts once the year is over. When a new machine appears on the market, old equipment may have to be amortized prematurely, and the accounts will reflect entre-preneurial decisions in this respect in the accounts. National income is obviously the aggregate of all incomes generated in the various units that make up the economy, and will thus be affected by the behavior of its component units.

One problem that confronts accountants and economists alike is the difficulty of treating capital which, by its very nature, endures beyond a single accounting period. The assumption of unchanged technology during the accounting period, tempered by anticipation of certain obsoles-cence, has been the basis of accounting conventions for capital amortiza-tion, which rely on arbitrary benchmarks regarding the life expectancies of various assets. Such conventions have yielded rough, but perfectly work-able, approximations of asset erosion that are essential for calculating net income. The economist faces similar problems in regard to capital depre-ciation, and hence the estimation of net income. The problem of inflation compounds the difficulty. Just like the index number problem which has not been dealt with satisfactorily in analytical terms, albeit without reduc-ing the usefulness and popularity of index number calculations, rough esti-mates of depreciation, based on the assumption of temporarily unchanged technology, however unsatisfactory, are still worthwhile and are certainly needed for approximating net income.[19]

IV   THE NATURE AND MAGNITUDE OF THE ADJUSTMENT

It is only if the income adjustment is sizeable that such an adjustment will be worth undertaking, and once undertaken, it should be followed through into the policy area. A great deal of the adjustment to national income to reflect environmental change if taken as capital consumption, or depreciation, will only affect the net product or net income, leaving

GDP and GNP unchanged. If the old practice continues, which makes use of conventionally reckoned GDP and GNP as bases for growth measurement and for international comparisons of per capita income levels, the environmental correction will be in many respects futile, since *net* income estimates are not always available. If the gross product remains unadjusted there is a strong case for inviting the attention of economists to focus on NDP and NNP.[20] The habit of using net income rather than gross income for country economic analysis will therefore have to be nurtured among country economists, and indeed all economists.

But the last statement requires qualification. For those countries that derive a significant portion of their prosperity from mineral extraction or from 'mining' their renewable natural resources, depreciation is not the right approach to adjusting income, and reliance on 'net income' as suggested will not be appropriate. The user cost of resource extraction should be excluded altogether from GDP and GNP, and the parallel net variants of national income (NDP and NNP) will, therefore, fall in place needing no correction. However, since a large number of practitioners in this field still prefer to think of such adjustments in terms of *depreciation,* the appropriate magnitude of the relevant depreciation would be the user cost I have earlier indicated.[21] This would be a 'second best' approach which obviously I would not support.

THE ROLE OF THE COUNTRY ECONOMISTS

Economists, including Bank country economists, may not have given enough thought to considerations such as those raised above. Some Bank economists have reacted to informal approaches by taking the position that unless the Bank officially – i.e. through guidelines and directives issued by the offices of the Bank's Chief Economist and the Regional Chief Economists – tells them to do so, they will continue with conventional income measurements and base their analysis on them. Bank economists of course do not themselves carry out national income measurements, and few of them have had the experience of estimating national income on the ground. Some seem to have an exaggerated confidence in the conventional income estimates offered to them by country statistical offices, or feel a justifiable reluctance to venture onto new unfamiliar grounds indicated by the proposed adjustments. When the accounts mix asset sales with value added, as argued repeatedly before, the issue of sustainability, which is a *sine qua non* for proper income estimation, gets lost, and economic reports would sometimes seek a comparability that does not exist between economies as diverse and incongruent as Malaysia and

South Korea, allegedly because of the similarity of their conventionally estimated per capita income levels.

Issues, as important as those emphasized in this chapter, should obviously not be neglected on whatever pretext, even if they appear to raise thorny or controversial problems of measurement. The first step of adjusting the national accounts for marketable resource depletion and other environmental degradation along the road to a better understanding of natural resource-dependent economies has not even been attempted inside or outside the Bank on a significant scale. The work done so far on Indonesia, and also on Papua New Guinea and Mexico with the Bank's collaboration, has revealed many dark areas and has unearthed uncertainties involved in carrying out the adjustment. All this naturally feeds the reluctance of Bank economists to embark on what is viewed as an arduous journey with an uncertain destination. But we should realize also that there are many dark areas and uncertainties in standard national income accounting, where imputation, contingent estimation and short cuts are resorted to on a significant scale and on a regular basis. These, however, seem to be taken rather lightly by economists both inside and outside the Bank.

LIKELY POLICY EFFECTS OF ACCOUNT GREENING

Since the *country* is the focus of the bulk of economic work at the Bank, the country should provide the context in which the adjustments should be made, and in which the policy implications of the adjustments should be pursued. It has been mentioned before that we could not hope for comprehensive adjustments of the national accounts that would capture the totality of environmental degradation, but instead should, along the lines of the WRI study of Indonesia, concentrate on a few resources that are judged to be important for the economy concerned, and be content with partial adjustments in the expectation that as time goes by the extent of the coverage will expand. The main task of effecting the adjustment, and of carrying out the subsequent policy analysis, will have to be part of the country economic work. The country economist should be making use of environmental work already accomplished, and setting in motion a process for collecting and analyzing environmental data so that he or she should have a firm grasp of changes occurring in the environment and the impact of these changes on the economy.

After criticizing World Bank macroeconomic work and sermonizing Bank economists on the need to pay attention to the state of the physical resources which sustain economic activities I turn now to discuss a highly illustrative case, the case of Indonesia, which has been the field of a pioneering and instructive study for green accounting – a study which also brings out some important lessons for macroeconomic policies.

V   WRI AND INDONESIA

EMPLOYING THE USER COST METHOD

At this stage it would be appropriate to ask what kind of magnitudes have been found, or are likely to be found, for greening the national accounts? One of the most important studies in this field is that of Indonesia, made by the World Resources Institute (1989) which calculated a series of adjusted NDP to reflect depletion and degradation of Indonesia's natural resource sectors of petroleum, forestry, and soil (on Java) in the period 1971–1984. Significantly this study gave emphasis to its conclusion that the net adjustment to Indonesia's GDP for environmental 'depreciation' amounted to –9 per cent of GDP per year on average. This, as the study clearly explained, was an unweighted annual average based on calculations shown in Table 1.2, p. 6 of the WRI study over the period covered. The WR1 study concluded that, while the growth rate calculated from the unadjusted GDP series during the same period averaged 7.1% per annum, on the basis of the adjusted NDP it was only 4.0 percent.[22]

I have shown in Chapter 14 (Growth rate after adjustment) that the average growth rate is immaterial in this context. A level of income consistently reduced because of environmental degradation and depletion may have higher, lower, or the same rate of growth as that of the unadjusted GDP. Any one year's growth, not average growth, is more meaningful, and may well tell a different story. More important than the growth rate of the net product is (1) the absolute magnitude of the adjustment itself in any one year, (2) the average of this adjustment magnitude over the period studied, and (3) its *trend* over time.

There is little doubt that the WRI study of Indonesia's national accounts has been valuable. It was an unprecedented attempt to translate theoretical concepts of green accounting into practical measurements, done with boldness and imagination. Moreover, the bases of its calculations are clearly laid out so later researchers could adjust the estimates in light of updated data or by using other methods. The study also hit on the right approach which I have been advocating, namely identifying a few resources that are important for an economy and adjusting the national accounts in respect of these selected resources, at least as a first step, in the knowledge that the sum total of the adjustments, though partial, could be enlarged over time when more resources are covered.

As shown in Table 19.1 below, the WRI annual adjustment of about –9 per cent on average during the period 1971–84 was made up as follows: –2.2 per cent for petroleum, –6 per cent for forestry and –0.9 per cent for soil. Now I try to alter the adjustments with a different approach. Initially I set aside WRI estimates for petroleum which I find flawed[23] – focusing attention on forestry and soil erosion. The adjustment in respect of both factors together adds up to the annual equivalent of about 7 per cent of GDP on average, and this adjustment I shall accept. To this I now add a different adjustment for petroleum depletion applying the user-cost method. Under this approach stock reassessments are not brought directly into the estimation of income as the WRI study did, but indirectly through the reserves-to-extraction ratio.[24] The revised calculations using my familiar formula and a 5 per cent discount rate indicate a GDP adjustment for petroleum of –7.8 per cent on average in the period 1971–84. Combining this with WRI adjustment for forestry and Java soil, the total downward adjustment for all three activities adds up to the equivalent to some 15 per cent of GDP – a very significant change indeed. Table 19.1 shows my amended adjustments to the national accounts of Indonesia built upon the WRI study. The impact of this significant adjustment on the various macroeconomic aggregates is considered in the next section.

As the first column in Table 19.1 shows, the average WRI adjustment was a downward 9.0 per cent of unadjusted GDP to which the petroleum adjustment contributed minus 2.2 per cent (second column). WRI petroleum adjustment was a confused mixture of changes in reserves and a strong sustainability approach that deducted the entire extraction from income and thus in my view was doubly flawed. Note that employing the user-cost approach gives a downward adjustment in every year (column 4), whereas the WRI method yielded positive adjustments in the four years 1971–74. It should be noted too that if the discount factor used for estimating the user cost was 4 per cent instead of 5 per cent the downward adjustment would be sharper. A lower rate is preferable to a higher one to be on the safe side of income sustainability. How greening the accounts may have an impact on macroeconomic policies is investigated in Table 19.2.

Table 19.2 follows up the effect of greening the accounts in the same period on the important economic indicators: investment and the current account of the balance of payments. The results are rather striking. Gross investment which had been reckoned at 24.2 per cent of GDP on average – a respectable enough level – turns out on re-estimation to be only 8.9 per cent of GDP: a drop of 15.3 percentage points. Against this gross figure, capital consumption must be deduced to show net investment. Lacking

Table 19.1   Indonesia: amended WRI adjustments of national accounts as per cent of GDP

Year	1 WRI total adjustment	2 Of which petroleum	3 WRI adjustment excluding petroleum	4 Petroleum user cost	5 Corrected adjustment
1971	+21.7	+28.0	−6.3	−4.5	−10.8
1972	−1.6	+5.6	−7.2	−6.4	−13.6
1973	−4.1	+6.0	−10.2	−9.1	−19.3
1974	−35.7	+44.2	−8.5	−6.4	−14.9
1975	−14.7	−10.3	−4.4	−5.6	−10.0
1976	−8.4	−2.3	−6.1	−9.7	−15.8
1977	−19.3	−13.8	−5.5	−11.3	−16.8
1978	−16.8	−11.7	−5.1	−10.5	−15.6
1979	−21.8	−11.8	−10.0	−9.8	−19.8
1980	−23.8	−14.6	−9.2	−9.3	−18.5
1981	−18.4	−12.9	−5.5	−8.6	−14.1
1982	−14.3	−9.4	−4.9	−6.1	−11.1
1983	−22.3	−14.2	−8.1	−6.0	−14.1
1984	−17.3	−13.1	−4.2	−6.3	−10.5
Average	−9.0	−2.2	−6.8	−7.8	−14.6

Source: Repetto et al. (1989) Table 1.2, p. 6; and own calculations of petroleum user cost based on a 5% discount rate.

an estimate for capital consumption one may surmise that net investment was probably around zero, a level that should be alarming to the policy makers. As to the current account balance, instead of averaging –2.2 per cent of GDP it turns out to be –9.5 per cent – another alarming figure. It is remarkable that neither the WRI study, nor I believe the Indonesian government, followed through with re-examining Indonesia's macroeconomic policies consequent upon greening the accounts. Admittedly they did not have the advantage of the user-cost exercise, but this lack of correspondence between the adjusted accounts and policy is common to all greening accounting work which when venturing into interpreting the results of adjusting the accounts at most single out the often meaningless growth rate. One is tempted to keep asking: What are we greening the accounts for? However, it seems that the unsatisfactory levels of capital formation during the years considered did not detract from Indonesia's overall satisfactory economic record – at least for a while.

Table 19.2   Indonesia: implications of GDP adjustment for investment and the balance of payments

Year	1 Total adjustment (% GDP)	2 Adjustment for oil (% GDP)[a]	3 Gross domestic investment (% GDP)	4 Adjusted gross domestic investment (% GDP)[b]	5 Current account balance (% GDP)[c]	6 Adjusted current account balance (% GDP)[d]
1971	−10.8	−4.3	18.4	7.6	−4.2	−8.5
1972	−13.6	−6.2	21.8	8.2	−3.3	−9.5
1973	−19.3	−9.1	20.8	1.5	−3.1	−12.2
1974	−14.9	−6.4	19.5	4.6	2	−4.4
1975	−10	−5.5	23.7	13.7	−3.5	−9
1976	−15.8	−9.7	24.1	8.3	−2.3	−12
1977	−16.8	−11.2	23.4	6.6	−0.2	−11.4
1978	−15.6	−10.1	23.9	8.3	−2.6	−12.7
1979	−19.8	−8.6	26.6	6.8	1.7	−6.9
1980	−18.5	−7.8	24.3	5.8	3.6	−4.2
1981	−14.1	−7.3	29.6	15.5	−0.9	−8.2
1982	−11	−5.9	27.5	18.5	−5.8	−11.7
1983	−14.2	−5.9	28.7	14.5	−7.5	−13.4
1984	−10.5	−6.1	26.2	5.7	−2.2	−8.3
Average	−14.7	−7.4	24.2	8.9	−2.2	−9.5

Notes:
a.   Oil only; not 'oil and gas'.
b.   First column combined with third column.
c.   Before official transfers.
d.   Adjustment for oil only, by combining the second column with the fifth.

Source: Data on GDP, Domestic Investment, and Current Account Balance are from World Bank, *World Tables 1991*. The Total Adjustment in first column is a combination of WRI adjustment for forestry and soil with author's own estimates of the user-cost of petroleum.

CONCENTRATION OF EXPORTS

Numerous developing countries have a large proportion of their exports concentrated in two or three products. Countries like Uganda, Nigeria, Algeria, Angola, Rwanda, Mauritania, Chad, Malawi, Egypt, Mexico and Panama show a very high degree of such concentration. A study by the World Bank (1992, Appendix E, Table E12) shows no fewer than 54 developing countries where the ratio of exports of three primary commodities to total exports exceeded 40 per cent in 1990. These have their base mostly in natural resources. Depending on the ratio of exports to GDP it is reasonable to expect that diminishing natural supplies will impact adversely on these economies, most of which are already vulnerable in different ways.

ADJUSTING FOR OIL EXTRACTION

Crude oil exporters belong to a group whose exports are highly concentrated and their dependence on this natural resource is often extreme. As a group their national accounts offer a superlatively needed target for adjustment. Their accounts should be overhauled and their economies attract serious macroeconomic analysis to guide their development, and perhaps help to curb the wasteful consumption indulged in by many, which seems to bring amusement but exerts its toll on the world ecology. The magnitude of the adjustment to their income for resource depletion will vary inversely with the life expectancy of the resource. So it will turn out to be minimal for countries with abundant reserves, such as Saudi Arabia. It will also vary inversely with the discount rate used to calculate the user cost – a rate which should also guide extraction policies and the re-investment of the user cost in alternative assets.[25] The effect on the estimation of GDP and its associated magnitudes will vary depending on the share of the oil activity in the national economy.

DRAWBACKS OF TRADE LIBERALIZATION

The place seems convenient here to bring up an issue of great importance for the poorer countries which are pressed to liberalize their external trade policies. International prices of traded goods have been used in project analysis for valuation at the World Bank and elsewhere instead of domestic prices as a standard for valuation. Domestic prices may be adulterated by taxes and subsidies, monopoly elements, the impact of exchange controls, and quantitative impediments to trade. 'Border prices' (i.e. international prices of goods at the national border) have been applied extensively as shadow prices for the economic analysis of projects. It is not necessarily because these prices are judged to be ideal or optimal from the standpoint of economic efficiency, but simply on the grounds that they represent a second-best alternative through which a country can enhance its advantage by trading. This process makes a lot of sense except where these prices fail fully to internalize ecological costs. And the strong drive to reduce trade barriers under structural adjustment programs may in some respects have unwittingly been a vehicle for environmental damage for trade-liberalizing countries.

Artificially depressed prices for natural resources entering international trade can be produced by various factors. These include outside political power pressure on weaker countries to expand supply; contracts with foreign concessionaires conducive to accelerated exploitation without regard to the sustainability of the resource base; and backward rising supply curves. These obtuse supply functions are common for individual commodities exported by developing countries where the low income of the suppliers, combined with a paucity of supply substitutes, distort the normal response of supply to prices. In reaction to lower prices sales are raised rather than curtailed, thus depressing prices still further. Thus if free trade in underpriced natural resources is introduced and left unchecked, it will bring harm to the long term interests of natural resource exporting countries.

Competition between participants in international trade under such conditions could be ruinous to small exporters who, individually, will tend to be incapable of protecting themselves from this so-called free trade. Border prices, therefore, may need to be adjusted by shadow-pricing them *again* in order to take account of natural resource sustainability (i.e. to include in them the cost of maintaining a renewable resource, such as in the case of timber, and the user cost of a depletable resource, such as petroleum). But while this procedure will improve the economic analysis of new projects, it will not bring much benefit to a natural resource-dependent economy that needs to be helped by appropriate macroeconomic policies to protect it from the possibly harmful effects of free trade at less than economic prices. Shadow-pricing apart, it is unlikely, however, that individual countries can put in place the right set of policies that will ensure their protection from such 'freedom' of trade. This would require concerted action by exporters in the same situation, perhaps aided by international development organizations. But until such situations are recognized, free trade in under-priced commodities should not be seen as self-evidently beneficial for primary product exporters. This concern should be considered seriously when policy based programs are designed, containing the now almost standard ingredient of trade liberalization.

VI SOME UNSETTLED QUESTIONS

LACK OF COMPREHENSIVENESS

This issue has been raised before, but seems to need emphasizing. It is clear from the foregoing, as well as from the experience of economists who have given thought to the issues presented in this chapter, that there are a number of unsettled matters that may discourage a serious consideration of the adjustments to conventional national accounting along the lines I am proposing. One of the more important of these is the lack of comprehensiveness of the proposed adjustments. The approach recommended is to focus on those few natural resources that are important in a country context, and attempt a partial adjustment of the economic accounts based on changes in the selected resources. This is commendably the approach adopted by WRI in its study of Indonesia, and later of Costa Rica and the Philippines. This approach, with certain amendments, as suggested above, yields significant adjustments that deserve to be made and can alter the macroeconomic analysis of such countries. In some important cases they may throw doubt on macroeconomic policy recommendations based on the conventional measurements.

Lack of comprehensiveness can conceivably depreciate the value of greening the accounts in the perception of critics. These might pose the following question. Since we are unable to capture all the annual changes in the stock of natural resources in the national accounts, what is the merit, then, of a partial adjustment? Some of those who are averse to proper natural resource accounting within a national income framework would wish to ignore natural resources by analogy with the way conventional national income accounting does not cover changes in the (highly theoretical) capitalized value of the labor force, or variations in the real value of external debt. Changes in 'human capital' derive from changes in population size, gender, age structure, employment, health, education, experience and mortality. Similarly the national stock of external debt may actually decline in real terms if the interest on existing debt is fixed whereas interest rates on new borrowing have risen, and this, some have argued unconvincingly, should be reflected in a higher level of national income.

While these are interesting aspects of changes in economic wellbeing that may one day be incorporated in national accounting, their habitual exclusion from national accounting is not a valid argument for not making income adjustments to reflect natural resource deterioration which is bound to have a negative effect on future income. It has already been mentioned that accounting, being a precautionary device to guard against consuming one's capital, has always avoided counting in income any appreciation of assets until such appreciation has actually been realized, but insists nevertheless on counting *negative* changes even if unrealized. Besides, human capital changes are not easy to express in money terms, and these would tend on the whole to be positive, not negative, and therefore accountants would be justified to exclude them from the accounting framework. As to the impact on real debt of interest rate changes, this first belongs to the realm of welfare not actual performance, and second, whether it is accounted for or not, is bound to affect economic behavior: appreciation of the real value of debt would depress consumption, and its depreciation encourage consumption, and all this will be captured eventually in the accounts in the normal way.

In any case taking declines in marketable natural resources into consideration, however partial the adjustment, will move economic measurements closer to reality, and this must be regarded as an improvement in the accuracy of such measurements.

It may not have been mentioned with sufficient emphasis that standard national accounting is itself never comprehensive, and leaves out by convention certain activities which many agree to or acquiesce in leaving out of economic measurements. Unpaid housework is one example of activities left out. Many subsistence activities, and an unknown (but believed to be growing) quantity of 'underground' or 'informal' transactions, including tax-avoiding and illegal trade, escape enumeration altogether. Such 'leakages' from the measured income stream clearly reduce somewhat the value of the conventional measurements, which focus only on recorded transactions. And yet not many voices have been raised against the continued use of GDP for macroeconomic purposes however incompletely estimated.[26]

DISPUTES OVER METHODOLOGY

Perhaps even more important than the difficulties already cited, the quest for adjusting the national accounts to reflect environmental change, which began hesitantly from seeking to devise an overall physical indicator of ecological change and developed into proposals to revise the UN's SNA, seems to have come up against an impasse. Towards the end of the 1980s, after years of debate and exploration, a certain consensus had finally been reached regarding the SNA that (1) the accounts should be adjusted to incorporate natural capital depletion and degradation; and (2) since some aspects of the new accounting had remained controversial, the adjustment of the SNA would not be made in the 'core' accounts, but only peripherally in so-called 'satellite accounts'.

The machineries for setting up the format of the satellite accounts and for producing guidelines for their realization have been slow and cumbersome, and have involved the participation of many individuals and institutions of diverse outlooks and mandates. The methods used for elaborating the new guidelines have therefore been hesitant and eclectic, and have often suffered from lack of rigor and especially from an unclear economic vision as to the purpose of the exercise. Much attention has been paid to building up an integrated system of balance sheets and flow accounts, while sight has been lost of the relative unimportance of the balance sheet. Besides, balance sheet variations would unsuitably be brought into income estimates to the detriment of the latter. In many cases both the volume and the value attached to environmental assets in a balance sheet would be controversial and certainly partial in addition to being subject to sharp fluctuations from year to year. The integration of such yearly changes into the flow accounts would bring unwarranted elements as well as volatility into income estimation, ultimately producing economically meaningless measurements of income that would obscure true economic performance.

'SATELLITE' ECONOMIC REPORTING?

Until the arguments presented here have been accepted within the Bank and elsewhere, and incorporated in economic and sector work, perhaps a 'fall-back' approach might be suggested. It might be useful as an interim measure, just as it has been decided at this stage to confine environmental adjustments of national income to satellite accounts under the forthcoming SNA, for the country economist initially to confine environmental adjustments of performance measurement to a 'satellite' part of the Economic Report and the strategy documents he or she is preparing. Only a small number of back-of-the-envelope calculations will be needed to gauge the dimensions of natural resource depletion and degradation, and these can be made by the country economist to re-assess income and its growth and explore the implications of these revised estimates for policy prescriptions.

In this task, the economist would be helped greatly if the state of the environment, including natural resources, were given adequate space in Country Economic Reports, and if physical indicators of environmental change were periodically produced. The analysis would certainly benefit if these were used imaginatively in the course of economic reporting, and existing policies affecting natural resources identified. Physical indicators might include, as appropriate, the rate of deforestation, the estimated reserves and life expectancy of mineral deposits, the state of the fish wealth and its change, fresh water quantity and quality, soil, pollution, etc. The implications should then be worked out for saving and investment, the balance of payments, the domestic terms of trade, and then be investigated as proposed above so that more realistic economic policies can emerge.

VII CONCLUDING REMARKS

This chapter has attempted to address the concept of sustainable development from the point of view of improved income measurement that relies unavoidably on the notion of keeping capital intact. It has drawn attention to the poverty of much macroeconomic analysis where the physical base of natural resources is decaying while misleading indicators of growth are recorded. The dichotomy currently existing in Bank work, as well as in the work of others, between the physical environment and measured economic aggregates is false and unhealthy, and the two worlds of economics and ecology should be combined in an attempt to improve the economic analysis and policy proposals especially for natural resource-dependent economies.

In the Bank the problem will not go away simply by improving project analysis to accommodate environmental concerns. Project analysis should improve, but this will not be sufficient to address the macroeconomic issues identified in this chapter, including spurious measurement of country performance; overestimation of the creditworthiness of natural resource-based economies; and ascertaining whether their current account of the balance of payments is in deficit or surplus, and whether the savings/investment effort of such economies is adequate for their sustained development.

Proper national income accounting to reflect natural resource changes is imperative as a first step towards sustainability, and an action program needs also to be devised in order to re-estimate income for a selected group of natural resource-dependent economies with the specific objective of sensitizing country economists to the problem, and to train those who need training in appreciating the implications for economic policy of adjusting incomes and other macro-aggregates to reflect environmental deterioration.

The adjustment to income that needs to be made is likely to be appreciable, and therefore worth undertaking, in the case of a group of developing countries. The calculations advanced here to the effect that income adjustment amounted to nearly 15 per cent of GDP in the case of Indonesia, illustrate that such an exercise will probably yield significant results for many other countries.

If the arguments advanced in this chapter are accepted – and for this, a series of discussions needs to be initiated – these arguments should be incorporated in the relevant operational directives, and a program of application in actual country situations be devised and implemented, and become a major area of environmental concern to be monitored periodically in the process of recording environmental progress within the Bank.

Meanwhile, active preparation should begin without delay of *physical* indicators of environmental deterioration, to complement the numerous short term economic measurements that make up the bulk of the statistical annexes to the various operational directives dealing with country economic reports, policy framework papers, country development strategy papers, structural adjustment loans, and the like. The appendix below briefly surveys some relevant operational directives, drawing attention to the fact that many of them already encourage coverage in Bank reports and analyses of natural resource changes. In some respects certain amendments to the operational directives are proposed in an attempt to address the issues raised in this paper.

ACKNOWLEDGMENTS

The author gratefully acknowledges the comments and suggestions made by two anonymous reviewers as well as by Paul Chabrier, Herman Daly, Sandy Davis, Vinod Dubey, Mohamed El-Ashry, Robert Goodland, Enzo Grilli, Susan Hubert, Maritta Koch-Weser, Desmond McCarthy, Robert Picciotto, Jed Shilling, Andrew Steer, Vito Tanzi, and David Wheeler. None of them, however, should be held responsible for errors of fact or judgment that remain.

NOTES

1. El Serafy, World Bank Environment Department Working Paper No. 58.
2. Culminating in the anticipated SNA93.
3. See for example World Wide Fund for Nature-International (1992) and Cruz and Repetto (1992).
4. It will be recalled that to the classical economists the rent of land derived (in the famous Ricardian phrase) from 'the original and indestructible powers of the soil'.
5. World Commission on Environment and Development (WCED), *Our Common Future*, 1987, Oxford University Press, 1987, popularly known as the Brundtland Report. Several definitions of sustainability are put forward in that report as well as in other works.
6. Commenting on an earlier draft a reviewer suggested that I should distinguish natural 'capital' that is used for production from a broader category of assets which would include also stores of value. This echoed Irving Fisher's distinction between capital proper and the rest of wealth as mentioned in Chapter 4 on 'Income and capital'. Such a conceptual distinction would be difficult to maintain in practice, however. Besides, stores of value (part of which Marshall classified as 'working capital') are usually capable of conversion into productive capital as the need arises. Furthermore Keynes viewed liquid assets, such as bank balances, as serving transactionary, precautionary and speculative purposes concurrently. We also have the added authority of Hicks that the capital (of an economy) is 'its stock of real goods with power of producing further goods *or utilities* in the future.' Hicks suggested that such a definition 'would probably

be acceptable to most economists' (Hicks, 1974, pp. 301–316; emphasis added). It was under the influence of Hicks that I began quite early on to see the environment as akin to a factor of production, specifically capital. In the same work cited above Hicks states: 'In order that a thing should have a price, it must be appropriable, but it is not necessary that a thing should be appropriable for it to be a factor of production.' I therefore continue to use assets and capital interchangeably in this chapter.

7. This is not to minimize the existence of formidable pollution problems in developing countries associated with fuel combustion, urban congestion, untreated domestic, agricultural and industrial wastes, often released in waterways, and vehicular and other harmful emissions in dense urban settlements. Some studies have suggested that the desire and ability to implement counter-pollution policies increase at levels of per capita income above a certain range which, it must be seen, is beyond the reach of a majority of developing countries.

8. Environmental Issues Papers and Environmental Action Plans tended to ignore mineral deposits even when these appeared to be rapidly diminishing and were economically important for the country concerned. Pollution always takes pride of place in these tracts, which normally pay less attention to soil erosion, fresh water availability and deforestation. See for instance the World Bank/European Investment Bank, 'The Environmental Program for the Mediterranean', 1990, which totally ignores the management of petroleum and phosphate deposits despite the dependence of North African countries on these resources.

9. Pollution could of course be viewed as depletion of the environment's capacity to absorb wastes. This line of argument, which was suggested to me by Herman Daly, is interesting and merits investigation.

10. This view, which was from the beginning at the heart of my method to estimate the income content of the receipts obtained from natural capital liquidation, is consistent with the analysis put forward by Robert M. Solow (1974).

11. The method is explained in detail in my 1981 paper 'Absorptive capacity, the demand for revenue and the supply of petroleum,' and Chapter 3, 'The proper calculation of income from depletable natural resources' in *Environmental Accounting for Sustainable Development* (1989), reproduced in this book as Chapter 9. My approach is based on Hicks's definition of income as laid down in his discourse on 'Income' in *Value and Capital* (1946). It also makes use of Harold Hotelling's seminal article (1931). Hicks's approval of my use of his tentative suggestions regarding 'wasting assets' to arrive at 'true' income was expressed in a private communication to me in May 1987.

12. See my 'Depletable resources: fixed capital or inventories?', a paper read to the special meeting of the International Association of Research in Income and Wealth, in Baden, Austria in May 1991 (later published in Franz, Alfred and Carsten Stahmer (eds) 1993, *Approaches to Environmental Accounting*. It should be emphasized that the user-cost approach is also applicable to renewable resources where these are being 'mined', i.e. when extraction exceeds regeneration, thus shortening the life expectancy of the resource. To use the entire decline of the stock during the year as depreciation (in the manner of the WRI study of Indonesia and elsewhere) exaggerates the necessary adjustment to income. The degree of exaggeration will tend to decline, however, as the resource tends to extinction. Where the net off-take is small and the life expectancy of the resource is therefore not much diminished by extraction, the required adjustment can be negligible. However, since the WRI estimation of income from forests is confined to timber production and leaves out the negative effects of deforestation on carbon dioxide absorption, soil stabilization and watershed integrity, some overestimation of the impact of timber extraction on income may in fact bring the estimates closer to reality. I owe this last point to Susan Hubert.

13. See Hartwick and Hageman (1991). See also M. A. Adelman *et al.* (1990), where the authors make use of my user-cost formula. I have given several instances of the application of the 'El Serafy method' in El Serafy (1991).

14. It is very interesting that Gavin Wright (1990) attributes much of America's industrial

success during 1879–1940 to the abundance of natural resources, suggesting that their contribution has been 'underappreciated', adding (p. 665) that 'it is perhaps understandable that Americans have not been inclined to attribute their country's industrial success to what appears to be accidental or fortuitous geographic circumstances'. The record of economic success of many other countries, besides the United States, including Australia, Canada, the USSR and Brazil, appears also to have been boosted by their natural resource endowment and some of them may lately be showing signs of economic deceleration owing to the erosion of this endowment.

15. Such were the estimates proposed for Indonesia by Robert Repetto and Associates (1989). This WRI study produced for two years adjusted net income estimates anomalously higher than the conventionally calculated gross income. See also my 1991 paper.

16. See, however, the qualification made at the end of the first part of Section VI below on 'Unsettled Questions', note 26.

17. Structural adjustment operations were introduced in the Bank in 1980 and were coordinated closely with the IMF. They differed from traditional bank operations that supported concrete project investments in that they sought to induce changes in economic policies thought to be favorable to development. They grew rapidly as they were appreciated by Bank staff and borrowers alike for they disbursed usually large sums in agreed tranches. For the borrowers these disbursements were obviously welcome, and for Bank project staff they lessened the need for monitoring project progress on the ground.

18. See for example my Chapter VI, 'Environmental Issues and the Natural Resource Base,' in *Costa Rica: Country Economic Memorandum*, World Bank, Report No. 7481-CR, dated December 6, 1988. The causes behind the serious deforestation occurring were similar to those found for Brazil in the work of Dennis Mahar (1989) and Hans Binswanger (1987).

19. Many of the issues concerning the definition and measurement of capital and its valuation are considered in Hicks (1974).

20. A parallel movement which departs from convention might also be from the national or domestic product 'valued at market prices' to national and domestic products 'valued at factor costs'. See my Chapter 5, 'Sustainability, Income Measurement and Growth' in *Population. Technology and Lifestyle: The Transition to Sustainability* (1992).

21. See for instance Hartwick and Hageman (1991) who insist on calling their adjustment 'Economic Depreciation of Mineral Stocks' while nevertheless concluding that the El Serafy formula does 'track true economic depreciation (computed by direct methods) quite clearly'. I have insisted that the liquidation of mineral stocks is conceptually *not* depreciation similar to that of fixed capital, but is, instead, tantamount to the using-up of inventories. See my 1991 paper and Chapter 11 (Hartwick) in this book.

22. The end-product of the WRI calculation was the average growth rate of the net product. Clearly, as argued before, the growth rate is much less significant than the average downward adjustment of the *level* of income during the period studied.

23. Every time Indonesia's petroleum reserves were re-estimated in an upward direction, the WRI study would add the whole adjustment, valued in current prices, to net income, thus causing such 'net' income to exceed gross income in an erratic and economically meaningless fashion.

24. It is assumed here that the WRI estimates for resource depletion in respect of forestry products and Java soil are roughly correct. Applying the user-cost approach to this depletion instead would reduce the WRI estimates somewhat, but this will not be pursued in this chapter. Reassessment of petroleum reserves would of course be taken care of under my method through the altered reserves-to-extraction ratio.

25. For an exposition of my method and illustrations of the magnitude involved see El Serafy (1989) reproduced in this book as Chapter 9. As explained there, the adjustment is quite sensitive to the discount rate. The income content of receipts from liquidating an asset that has a life expectancy of ten years is 42 per cent if the discount rate used is 5 per cent and 65 per cent if the discount rate is 10 per cent. I have argued that it is

unlikely that the new investments will offer as much as a 10 per cent annual yield and that 5 per cent seemed more appropriate although the rate could be lowered still to be on the safe side, indicating that saving should be higher and consumption lower. I have also argued that the discount rate to be used in the calculations could be changed periodically to reflect actual market opportunities.

26. Monetary policy analysts in particular do not seem to be too concerned about this issue, justifiably claiming that a partial, but consistent, series of national income measurements can still be valuable for analytical purposes and as a useful guide to monetary policy.

27. The practice had then been established that a summary Bank Country Strategy is included in the President's Report for the first structural adjustment operation in the country concerned every fiscal year; otherwise, if no structural adjustment operation is planned, then this summary would be included during presentation to the Board of the first investment loan in the fiscal year. This practice which applied also to IDA 'credits' extended to the poorer countries was being re-considered to include also IBRD borrowers, but, instead of being so comprehensive, the intention is to present the summary strategy not every year, but following the normal cycle of strategy papers, i.e. every three years or so. IBRD borrowers are the usual borrowers on standard terms for Bank loans. International Development Association (IDA) 'credits' are extended on highly preferential terms.

REFERENCES

Adelman, M.A., Harindar De Silva and Michael F. Koehn (1990), *User Cost in Oil Production*, MIT Center for Energy Policy Research, October.

Binswanger, Hans (1987), 'Fiscal and legal incentives with environmental effects on the Brazilian Amazon', Agriculture and Rural Development Department, World Bank, Washington DC.

Cruz, Wilfredo and Robert Repetto (1992), 'The environmental effects of stabilization and structural adjustment programs: the Philippines case', World Resources Institute, Washington DC, September.

El Serafy, Salah (1981), 'Absorptive capacity, the demand for revenue and the supply of petroleum', *Journal of Energy and Development*, **7** (1), 73–88.

El Serafy, Salah (1988), 'Environmental issues and the natural resource base' in Costa Rica: Country Economic Memorandum, World Bank, Report No. 7481-CR, December 6.

El Serafy, Salah (1989), 'The proper calculation of income from depletable natural resources', in Yusuf J. Ahmad, Salah El Serafy and Ernst Lutz (eds), *Environmental Accounting for Sustainable Development*, A UNEP-World Bank Symposium. Washington DC: World Bank, Chapter 3, pp. 10–18.

El Serafy, Salah (1991), 'Depletable resources: fixed capital or inventories?' Paper read to the special meeting of the International Association of Research in Income and Wealth, Baden, Austria, May 1991 later published in Franz, Alfred and Stahmer, Carsten (eds) (1993), *Approaches to Environmental Accounting.* New York: Physica-Verlag, pp. 245–258.

El Serafy, Salah (1992), 'Sustainability, income measurement and growth', in Robert Goodland, Herman Daly and Salah El Serafy (eds), *Population, Technology and Lifestyle.* Washington DC: Island Press.

Haberler, Gottfried (1976), 'Oil, inflation, recession and the international monetary system', *Journal of Energy and Development*, **1** (2), 177–190.

Hartwick, J. M. and A. P. Hageman (1991), 'Economic depreciation of mineral stocks and the contribution of EI Serafy', World Bank Environment Department, Divisional Working Paper No. 1991-27, November.

Hicks, John Richard (1946), *Value and Capital*, 2nd edn. Oxford: Oxford University Press.

Hicks, John Richard (1974), 'Capital controversies: ancient and modern' *American Economic Review*, **64**, 301–316.

Hotelling, Harold (1931), 'The economics of exhaustible resources', *Journal of Political Economy*, **39** (2), 137–175.

Krueger, Anne O. and Baran Tuncer (1980), 'Estimating Total Factor Productivity Growth in a Developing

Country', World Bank Staff Working Paper No. 422, October.

Mahar, Dennis (1989), *Government Policies and Deforestation in Brazil's Amazon Region*. Washington DC: The World Bank.

OECD, Department of Economics and Statistics (1985), 'Treatment of mining activities in the system of national accounts. Note by the Secretariat: meeting of national accounts experts', Mimeo, May, pp. 29–31.

Reed, David (ed.) (1992), *Structural Adjustment and the Environment*. Boulder, CO: Westview Press.

Repetto, Robert W. Magrath, M. Wells, C. Beer and F. Rossini (1989), *Wasting Assets: Natural Resources in the National Income Accounts*. Washington DC: World Resources Institute.

Solow, Robert M. (1974), 'On the intergenerational allocation of natural resources', *Scandinavian Journal of Economics*, **88** (1), 141–149.

World Bank/European Investment Bank (1990), *The Environmental Program for the Mediterranean*. Washington DC: World Bank/European Investment Bank.

World Bank (1991), *World Tables*. Washington DC: World Bank.

World Bank (1992), *Global Economic Prospects and the Developing Countries*, Washington DC: World Bank.

World Commission on Environment and Development (WCED) (1987), *Our Common Future*. Oxford: Oxford University Press.

World Wide Fund for Nature-International (1992), *Structural Adjustment and The Environment*. Boulder, CO: Westview Press.

Wright, Gavin (1990), 'The origins of American industrial success, 1879–1940', *The American Economic Review*, **80** (4), 651–668.

APPENDIX: OPERATIONAL DIRECTIVES

Much of this Appendix has become obsolete owing to changes in procedures, but at the time of the original draft it was important to include it to pave the way for the internal changes recommended. Its inclusion here gives the historical context of the paper as originally conceived, and imparts a flavor of the World Bank's great concern for improving and standardizing its economic work.

The Role of Operational Directives

Operational Directives provide guidance to Bank staff on how best to organize their various activities and present these in an acceptable and fairly uniform format. The efforts exerted for drafting these directives absorb great resources, and the directives themselves are often written by knowledgeable persons. Besides, they go through many iterations, and benefit from rounds of internal discussions in an attempt to incorporate in them the experience and insights of various Bank units. While it may be true that operational directives could remain unread by many, they nevertheless constitute a stock of reference material to be consulted by new staff, and by all staff when doubt is raised about document contents, formats, methods or procedures. A number of relevant operational directives (ODs) are considered below in order to illustrate their possible role in improving country economic work along the lines suggested in this paper.

Country Economic and Sector Work

Operational Directive 2.00 on 'Country Economic and Sector Work' (CESW), issued in March 1989 rightly stresses that country economic and sector work is 'a key element of the Bank's assistance to its borrowers' and that it should 'provide a thorough understanding of their development problems, of the need for and availability of external financing, and of the analytical framework for evaluating development strategies and donor assistance activities.' This OD further states that an important objective of country economic work is 'to inform the Bank and member countries of the situation, prospects, and creditworthiness of borrowing countries.'

The 'long term quality and sustainability of development' is specifically cited in OD 2.00 (paragraph 2) as depending on factors such as 'the causes, manifestations, and treatment of poverty, the efficacy of economic institutions, and the *environmental effects of alternative policy options*' (emphasis added). The continuity and variability of country economic work and its inter-connections with Bank country assistance strategy is further stressed (paragraph 5) where the OD draws attention to the fact that 'CESW is a systematic, continuous program of investigation and analysis, whose specific objectives are determined within the Bank's country strategy'.

Paragraph 10 of OD 2.00 further states that 'although devoted primarily to macroeconomic policy issues and analysis, the CEM (i.e. the Country Economic Memorandum) also integrates the analyses and policy recommendations flowing from Bank sector work.'

From the foregoing, it can be seen that there is enough material in the OD on country economic reports that can be used imaginatively by a country economist who is aware of the issues discussed in this paper. But the general drift, as well as the structure of the OD, however, shows lack of specific concern for changes in the natural resource base. This omission is highlighted by the coverage specified in the annexes depicting the various variables, parameters, ratios and growth rates that must be worked out in country strategy papers. These clearly ignore physical environment indicators of change, which could conceivably be included in the Country Data Sheet (Annex 1). Once the thrust of this chapter is accepted, a section on 'Macroeconomic Policies and the Environment,' incorporating the arguments presented will need to be added quite early in OD 2.00, preferably under 'Purpose, Scope and Approach'. The addition of a set of physical indicators of environmental change is further considered below.

It would further be useful if every Country Economic Report were to contain a chapter devoted to environmental change, summarizing evidence gathered from environmental reports, Environmental Issues Papers and other relevant documents, and identifying economic policies in place that impinge on the environment.

Country Strategy Papers

Country strategy papers are documents internal to Bank management and not shared with the Board of Executive Directors. These are disclosed outside Bank management only in part as has recently been agreed with the Bank's Executive Board for IDA borrowers.[27] The importance of these documents for marshalling Bank resources in support of its borrowers' development cannot be exaggerated, and much effort and resources are therefore expended in their formulation, again with wide participation from the various units that make up the World Bank. As mentioned earlier, OD 2.00 specifically stresses the importance of country economic and sector work for the formulation of Bank country assistance strategies. Such strategies are expected to pick up the major issues identified in CESW, and mold them into a coherent approach to development in the country concerned, while identifying a role for the Bank in such an approach. Unless the environment is properly covered in CESW, such strategies would be spurious in situations of significant degradation of the resource base.

Operational Directive 2.10 on Country Strategy

Operational Directive 2.10, 'Country Strategy Papers' (CSP), issued in September 1990, is more recent than OD 2.00, and urges staff to focus on key issues of country strategy worthy of senior management's attention. It stresses the need for realism, attention to creditworthiness, and Bank exposure. The revised annexes emphasize country creditworthiness and Bank debt exposure indicators, and contain a new supplementary table on debt 'workouts' for countries with projected servicing arrears, a new table on money and credit with optional projections, and a new optional Private Sector Account. See Operational Directive 2.10: Country Strategy Papers, Manual Transmittal Memorandum, paragraph 2(h). The optional annexes would become mandatory once the training of staff had been completed. The 'Socioeconomic Data Division' (IECSE) of the International Economics Department will ensure that templates for these annexes are available to country economists. Cf. the same Transmittal Memorandum, paragraph 4.

It has been standard practice for CSPs, and their predecessors, the Country Policy Papers, to project the major country economic variables ten years forward in an attempt to capture development trends. In its new version the OD emphasizes the importance of the long view 'for the analysis of external debt issues' (Paragraph 6). But it fails to mention the sustainability of the natural resource base which is essential in its own right for projecting future development, as well as for creditworthiness assessment, and for judging the external debt burden. There is much emphasis in these projections on the usual short-term indicators, albeit extended over the longer term, without specific reference to the state of natural resources. True, population growth is in the background particularly as it affects per capita consumption, but there is no transparency or attempted comprehensiveness regarding natural resource coverage. Nowhere in OD 2.10 is the concept discussed of sustainable development in the context of the natural resource endowment of the country concerned. While 'Natural Resources' are mentioned in Annex A of OD 2.10 as part of the 'Social Indicators of Development', the indicators specified are extremely limited and confined to area, population density, agricultural land and its density, forests and deforestation rates. *Access* to safe water – a legitimate health concern – is curiously included under 'Natural Resources'. Clearly missing in this coverage are subsoil deposits and their life expectancy at current exploration rate, soil erosion, overall water supply, pollution indices, fisheries stock trends, and similar physical indicators of the resource base that supports every economy. As complete a set of environmental indicators as possible should be mandatory in the annexes to strategy papers, and this should be the responsibility of the Environment Department to produce, after preliminary work had been carried out by the Regional Environment Divisions.

Policy Framework Papers

Operational Directive 2.20, 'Policy Framework Papers' (PFP), was reissued in October 1989 in a revised form. Among several changes, this version specifically draws attention to (1) incorporating 'social and environmental, as well as macroeconomic, sectoral, and institutional issues', and (2) 'Setting out priorities for policy action to highlight key policy areas.' PFPs are prepared for all countries eligible for the IMF's Structural Adjustment Facility (SAF) or the Enhanced Structural Adjustment Facility (ESAF). These documents are properly described as 'vehicles' for governments to record agreements with the Bank and the Fund 'on the broad outline of medium-term programs to overcome balance of payments problems and foster growth'. The role of these documents in 'achieving consensus' between the Bank and Fund on appropriate medium-term adjustment programs is highlighted (paragraph 1), but missing is the use of these documents as stepping stones in the drive by the Bank to help realize longer-term development in these countries – a responsibility to which Bank economists, much more so than Fund economists, should be paying special attention.

OD 2.20, however, cannot be faulted for neglecting the longer term perspective of development. Paragraph 3 specifically states: 'Although a PFP focuses on a three-year period, it should indicate in broad terms how the proposed program relates to the country's longer-term development priorities, and what it does to overcome the more fundamental constraints to development'. It goes on to say that 'PFPs should maintain an adequate balance in the coverage of macroeconomic, sectoral, social, environmental, and institutional aspects.'

And yet, owing to the fact that such documents tend to be initiated in the IMF, and are processed swiftly through the Bank's management and the Board in order that specific Fund operations can get approved on time under the SAF or ESAF, Bank staff tend to leave much of the drafting of these documents to the IMF, so that the longer term perspective of development, insisted upon in OD 2.20, tends to get neglected. What is required in this respect is that the country economist should be anticipating the PFP, and preparing in good time a set of issues making up a program that balances short and medium concerns with longer term development considerations including protecting the natural resource base. For this purpose, much preliminary work on the environment needs to be undertaken as part of CESW, and related analytically to the issues of long-term economic and social development.

Adjustment Lending Directives

Two ODs are currently under preparation (8.60 on substance and 9.10 on procedures) intended to guide structural adjustment lending operations. These are not new initiatives, but have antecedents that go back in time to the inception of structural adjustment lending about 1980 and have been periodically updated. Preparation of OD 9.10 is much more advanced than that of OD 8.60, and both drafts are of course still subject to change. As these stand, there is hardly any reference in them to the physical environment within which structural adjustment takes place. Nor do the mandatory annexes that have to be produced for adjustment operations cover the state of the natural resource base even where this is likely to affect future performance. As stated earlier, until country economic and sector work covers this aspect of the economy, properly producing physical indicators of natural resource change, and identifying policies that should be installed or adjusted to maintain the natural resource base, individual structural adjustments operations are unlikely to be an effective vehicle for environmental protection. In other words, it is the quality and coverage of economic work that have first to improve before this can be fed into country strategies and get incorporated in country operations, including those for structural adjustment. Once country economic work has taken care of the issues identified here, the desired changes will fall naturally into place.

Structural adjustment programs have to be placed within a projected medium term macroeconomic framework, and unless future changes in the natural resource base are captured in such a framework, the latter would fail to be very useful.

Standardized Statistical Annexes

During the recent drive to produce a new set of ODs to replace the old collection of Operational Manual Statements on Bank operations, an effort was made to standardize the set of statistical annexes that are

appended to Country Strategy Papers, Structural Adjustment Operations
and similar documents in an attempt to minimize the burden falling on the
country economist who is usually responsible for overseeing the production of such annexes. If it is accepted that a new set of physical indicators
of environmental change should be produced and annexed to economic
documents, including PFPs, this should also be standardized and annexed
without change to the various documents in question.

Environmental Action Plans (EAPs)

The last OD to be considered here is Operational Directive 4.02:
'Environmental Action Plans' which was issued as recently as 21 July
1992. This aims to provide guidance to staff 'for assisting borrowers
in preparing Country Environmental Action plans.' During the IDA-9
Replenishment process it had been agreed that all IDA borrowers should
complete EAPs by the end of IDA9, i.e. by June 1993. Subsequently it was
decided that EAPs would be initiated for IBRD borrowers also. The OD's
Manual Transmittal Memorandum (MTM) adds that if the June 1993
deadline 'proves impossible' the Bank 'must be satisfied that (1) preparation of a suitable country environmental strategy is well advanced, and (2)
preliminary findings from the preparatory work have been incorporated
into the Bank's country assistance strategies' (MTM, paragraph 3).

The incorporation of environmental issues in country assistance strategies is emphasized throughout the OD, together with the understanding
that the EAPs need not be embodied in a specific document. What these
plans should do is 'setting forth a long-term national environmental policy
and investment strategy based on comprehensive environmental analysis'
(OD 4.02 – Annex A, paragraph 1). The OD further stresses that EAPs
should indicate 'priorities and related policy recommendations' in various
areas, including setting 'an information system for monitoring the state of
the environment . . . and . . . the management of natural resources' (ibid.,
paragraph 2). According to OD 4.02, the EAP should recommend an
overall plan for environmental policy and investment strategies affecting
the priority issues defined in the rest of the EAP and the country's overall
development plans (Annex A, p. 4 (h)). Among such priorities, the OD
specifically mentions (emphasis added):

> *Analysis of major development activity and trends in economic growth, resource
> use, and conservation.* This analysis covers major sectors – agriculture, forestry,
> industry, transportation, energy, housing, infrastructure, education, health
> and social services, mining, parks, and tourism – *with special reference to the
> environment in all cases.*

The OD further states that:

> The analysis also identifies specific constraints on future economic growth, including shortages of arable land and water … and … degradation and depletion of coastal zones, forests, soils, energy, and other natural resources … (Annex A, d.)

In sum, this OD is both comprehensive and clearly geared to integrating environmental trends in country strategies. If the EAPs *actually* produced manage to be faithful to the spirit of this OD, all that remains to be done is to ensure that EAPs are produced to the high standards indicated, and to see to it that once done, they are periodically revised and integrated in country economic work along the lines proposed in this paper. It would be interesting to examine some of the EAPs already completed so far to see if any of them can match up to the high standards indicated in OD 4.02. But in order for the provisions of OD 4.02 to affect country strategy as intended, OD 2.10 itself (dealing with Country Strategy Papers) should be amended to incorporate these worthy environmental concerns.

20. Sovereign funds

GENERAL

I do not want to end before I put in a word about what has become known as 'sovereign funds'. Many sovereign funds have been created by or on behalf of economies fortunate enough to have been endowed with marketable natural resources. At least four reasons justify covering this topic here: (1) the funds constitute a policy option for savings during periods of apparent prosperity; (2) they contribute to curbing certain symptoms of the Dutch disease; and (3) critics such as in the United Kingdom, lamenting the projected disappearance of the country's North Sea petroleum resources, have begun to ask: 'Where are our Sovereign Funds?'; and (4) the user-cost method has been described by some commentators as essentially a 'sinking fund' method – a description to which I did not take exception as I stated in Chapter 10 on 'Misunderstandings'.

Fund owners have not always been nations. They have included states within nations, corporations and institutions of many types. In general these funds serve as receptors of financial inflows viewed as temporary. Typically nations hold sovereign funds outside their domestic economies, but entities other than nations have invested within the domestic economy though guardedly placing them in other sectors or activities. For them diversification offered an element of safety about changing markets. When I attempted to refute the existence of a 'resource curse' in Chapter 18, I argued that one way of stifling the curse was to insulate the domestic economy against the financial inflows by keeping them abroad. Otherwise they get mingled with the domestic money supply, distort the domestic economic structure and depress previously productive activities. I have also considered the analytical issue of the possible indeterminacy of the discount rate to be used for estimating the user cost is sizeable portions of the inflows were sunk in a closed domestic economy. Domestic capital formation in this case would depress the rates of returns on the new investments thus causing an interdependent relationship between extraction and investment. Investing abroad is an obvious way out. But the chief factor that speaks to investing these funds abroad is the limited 'absorptive capacity' of many a domestic economy. Time is often needed to break infrastructural bottlenecks, training the labor force and developing communication facilities before domestic investment can begin to show acceptable rates of return. So depositing the revenues abroad for a while would make eminent sense. For many reasons, therefore, the strategy of investing in foreign sovereign funds has a place as a policy choice for natural resource endowed economies. On the other hand for the investors such a strategy is not without risk. Where the funds have been invested, freezing bank accounts and other financial holdings, and even outright expropriation, are not unknown during times of political tensions. And there are also the added hazards associated with also slowing down of economic activity and devaluation of the host country's currency when the value of the funds would decline. The policy balance between keeping the natural resource unexploited on the one hand and extracting it and investing the financial surpluses abroad on the other will always be a vexing entrepreneurial decision.

OPTIONS AVAILABLE

Assuming the decision on extraction has not yet been made a resource dependent society has to confront a number of options:

1. Leave the resource unexploited as an act of saving.
2. Save the entire proceeds from current extraction in the manner Hartwick has suggested, and wait until the investments had matured and then withdraw only the yields they produce as income.
3. Spend some of the revenue and save the rest as indicated by the user-cost method.
4. Consider if the new investments should be made at home or abroad.

Option 1 received much consideration in Hotelling's analysis and depends on future prices among other imponderables, which are not easy to predict and remain difficult to discern empirically in retrospect. Both options 2 and 3 actually specify the portion of revenue that should be set aside: option 2 100 per cent, and option 3 depends on life expectancy and the rate of return expected on the new investments. But many entities that built up sovereign funds have done little computation beforehand and if they had done so they have not spelled it out. And on the whole they appear to have acted intuitively. Many economic decisions, as Keynes said in his *General Theory*, are motivated by 'Animal Spirits', and not based on cold calculation of mathematical probabilities. It should be realized that the revenues do belong to the current owners as much as to their descendants (the 'future generations' frequently mentioned in the literature) so

there should be no assumption of denying benefits to the current generation, which Beckerman characterized as 'immoral'. Without much calculus the Kingdom of Libya enacted the Petroleum Royalties Law of 1958
earmarking 70 per cent of the oil revenues to development. So in effect
the government considered options 3 and 4, decided on the portion to be
saved and allocated this to be invested in domestic development.

CONSUMPTION VERSUS SAVING

Natural resource owners receiving their 'unrequited inflows' will not get
much help from economists on how to apportion their income between
consumption and saving. But there is an earlier stage where natural
resource owners have to sort out income from revenue. Within the income
category what to save and what to consume remains indeterminate. The
user-cost approach indicates a division between income and capital in the
revenue flows without any normative urging, but it does not address the
follow-up question as how to allocate income between consumption and
saving. In the literature on growth, and especially in the context of business cycle analysis, attention has certainly been given by economists to
how to attenuate investment at the various stages of the cycle and how
much investment is needed to secure a given growth rate. More generally the trail leading from capital formation to income growth, and from
growth back to investment, has aroused economist interest for decades
and given rise to a rich literature on the trade cycle, dynamic economics,
the multiplier and accelerator, but these matters need not concern us here.

Development economists – along with much of the profession's teaching – believed that saving as much as possible out of current income and
investing the savings to build up capital was the best way to escape 'under-
development'. But given their low-income levels domestic savings were
meager they had to depend on others' savings – either gifted or borrowed.
This much is evident in the vast literature on development that appeared
in the post World War II era. Capital scarcity figured as the bottleneck
that blocked advancement and it was the one that had to be broken. Some
development economists actually went further to offer blueprints for identifying the types of domestic investment that would best activate growth,
directing attention to backward and forward linkages that would connect
the new capital to the rest of the economy (cf. Hirschman, 1958).[1] As
already mentioned boosting savings for building up capital has generally
been seen as an effective factor that would accelerate growth, and this may
be taken as a general policy view to be applied to all economies. In times of
recession, however, at least since Keynes, 'thrift' has been condemned, and

boosting consumption has been recommended in order to raise 'effective demand'. Policy apart, there is an observed tendency for higher incomes to be associated with a higher propensity save out of income, but in some notable instances this is not always corroborated by the record.

INCOME FROM SOVEREIGN FUNDS

Once the sovereign funds have been built what should the resource owners do with the income produced by them? There is no a priori rule and much depends on the size of the new earnings relative to other regular income. Tempting to the owners is to develop the domestic economy and diversify its structure in the direction of new activities, but local markets may still be too small. Consider the cases of Kuwait, Kiribati or Singapore where the absorption of significant capital amounts in domestic investment is not promising, though enjoying them as consumption is always welcome. The income generated by the Sovereign Funds can also be left to be added to the capital and generate more future income. For many other owners opportunities for investment at home do exist, and many oil rich countries have selected that route. Petrochemical plants have been a priority in many countries including Iran, Iraq, Saudi Arabia and Kuwait. But in many cases even these investments have not been genuinely productive, showing profitability only with preferential input prices and further assistance to exports. In these conditions the economic calculus appears to take a secondary role. The more patient and time-requiring investments that are designed to have backward and forward development impulses in the spirit of Hirschman require favorable conditions. They depend on a national capacity for planning or an institutional setup that would guide such investments. In the prevailing circumstance of the past half century or so planning has been disparaged in favor of market forces, but a free market is not exactly a strategic medium capable of directing such investments. That is why Sovereign Funds came about in the first place.

A PARTIAL LIST OF SOVEREIGN FUNDS

According to the Sovereign Wealth Fund Institute (www.swfinstitute. org/fund-rankings/) the total of deposits accumulated in Sovereign Funds amounted to US $4.772 trillion in December 2011. The largest holders were China, UAE and Norway, see Table 20.1. SWF estimates that 58 per cent was 'oil and gas related'. For many countries, especially the petroleum exporters, it is not easy to convert these numbers to a per capita

*Table 20.1   Estimated sovereign wealth funds in billions, December 2011,
             US$*

China	1,112
United Arab Emirates	782
Norway	560
Saudi Arabia	478
Kuwait	296
Hong Kong	293
Singapore	157
Total seven countries:	3,678

Source: Based on SWF estimates (www.swfinstitute.org/fund-rankings/).

basis to get a sense of average individual ownerships since population data in many cases include migrant foreign workers who do not share in ownership. It may be surmised, however, that the relevant highest per capita holdings belong to Brunei, United Arab Emirates, Kuwait, Saudi Arabia and Qatar – all depletable resource owners. Of special interest are the funds of Kiribati, of bird-droppings fame, and the state of Alaska in the United States. All in all, the Sovereign Funds have a broad range of purposes , including the financing of pensions. Significantly, there is a remarkable degree of concentration among the fund owners, with the seven largest holders making up 77 per cent of the total.

With the great volatility of the financial markets in recent years, it is difficult to set a stable value on these funds but their enormous size may be viewed as a potential danger to financial markets stability. Movements by Fund managers to protect their positions or to seek better opportunities represent imminent dangers.

NOTE

1. To simplify, Hirschman's (1958) imaginative investment strategy relied on the deliberate creation by the government of economic disequilibria that would propel the economy forward through market forces.

REFERENCE

Hirschman, Albert O. (1958), *The Strategy of Economic Development*. Connecticut, NH: Yale University Press.

PART VI

Conclusion

21. An afterword

I

At this stage the reader may expect a distillation of the book's central message or messages. But it is doubtful that a succinct summary is possible or can be sufficiently faithful to the many topics discussed. The coverage of the preceding chapters went far and wide, mixing demolition of what I thought heresies with constructive propositions. But the center of attention has been constant throughout, and all arguments have revolved around a core preoccupation. That is seeking a better estimation of national income, namely a greened national product. My quest for greening the national accounts, it should be obvious by now, has not been motivated by interest in ecological conservation, but to obtain more realistic macroeconomic measurements – which at least to some extent would reflect ecological change.

Although several issues have been broached and many questions raised, they have not all been answered or answered satisfactorily. But just raising them, I believe, has been useful. At a minimum, they identify important issues requiring further investigation, and might inspire exploration and provoke debate. Without false humility I believe that I have supplied some answers to a few vexing questions. Raising questions, even without providing answers, should also keep interest alive in and around this important topic. Concern for environmental matters is still running high, especially where natural resources border on economic activities. And in the background there seems to be a growing awareness that the discipline of economics is capable of infusing analytical insights into this very complex subject.

It goes without saying that the advent of the green accounting initiative has been welcomed by numerous environmentalists, though it has elicited much less enthusiasm from mainstream economists. In stressing the drawbacks of conducting macroeconomic analysis with the unadjusted national accounts I have been aiming also to attract the attention of those economists who entertain no suspicion of the reliability of the macroeconomic magnitudes they use and have shown no curiosity for finding out the connection of these magnitudes with the physical environment that sustains them. If they are built on a decaying physical foundation the economists should at least try to find that out. Enough has been said in the foregoing to show that the inadequacy of the conventional accounts rises *mutatis mutandis* with dependence on primary activities. So for many industrialized economies this inadequacy may understandably not cause concern. I have been very critical of SNA93 and what came in its wake. The new system was meant to be a universal system applying to all countries rich or poor.

It has not been difficult to show that environmental losses double as economic losses; nor has it been hard to press the claim that the national accounting system if properly handled is capable of providing a convenient avenue for merging the economy and the ecology in an economically meaningful embrace. Not only was this embrace sidestepped in SNA93, but the two spheres were artificially detached one from the other on the false claim that the unadjusted accounts are 'economic' and that ecological losses are not economic losses, but *only* 'environmental'. The efforts and time expended since then over re-integrating back the two have been considerable, and the so-called 'integration' has remained stubbornly unachievable.

And yet, in order that this avenue – the national accounts avenue – could lead to more fruitful results fundamental changes will have to be made along the lines that have been explored in the previous chapters. First of all we should be clear why greening the accounts is wanted at all. Its purpose cannot be environmental protection. The ecological field is too vast and too unwieldy to be reduced to a format that the *economic* system of national accounting can usefully cope with. The goal of greening the national accounts as I have doggedly insisted must be seen as economic, not ecological, and should be focused on getting a good grasp on the macroeconomic estimates for serving economic purposes. Viewed in this light, a great deal that has been written about greening the accounts must be seen as unfocused and not very useful. For me it is particularly the neglect of the economic purpose of the national accounts – the missing economic outlook – that in the first place made me appreciate the inadequacy of the conventional accounts and guided my steps toward the user-cost method.

In order to 'reform' the conventional estimates of the national accounts – in order to take in ecological losses – I have for long been championing my favorite greening method. I have favored it over alternative methods showing that it provides a general approach under which other green accounting approaches may be subsumed as special cases. This much I demonstrated quite early on in my 1989 essay on the 'Proper calculation of income', reproduced in Chapter 9. Methods of adjustment apart, it could not have escaped notice that one of my overriding concerns in this book has been the elucidation of relevant concepts – concepts that relate to the fundamental quantities of income and capital. In the unadjusted accounts, as I have shown, confusion of the two still abounds, and survives in SNA93. Thus I have dwelled in detail also on the related concepts of rent and disinvestment; on stocks and flows; on costs, both average and marginal; and on revenue as distinct from income. In all this I have tried to follow conceptual clarification into the area of statistical estimation. To me it is conceptual confusions that have been largely responsible for encouraging endless controversies over adjustment methods, and thus slowed the progress of green accounting. If nothing else this book has accomplished I think clearing up confusion over some fundamental concepts has been one of its major contributions. It remains to be seen, however, if my attempt at conceptual clarification will ease the way to methodological consensus.

II

In the foregoing my arguments have veered between attempted demolition of faulty arguments and construction of preferable replacements. Demolition, I fear, may have been allowed a freer rein, but the ground had to be cleared before any reconstruction could begin. In the process many 'sacred cows' have had to be sacrificed, and several icons smashed in order to clear a way for reform. Some of my arguments have been presented with ferocity that must have antagonized adversaries, and might even prove counterproductive. But I have felt that pulling punches in this arena will not do: better to provoke opposition than risk bored resistance ending with virtual indifference. Thus I strenuously fulminated against the cardinal mistake of including sale proceeds of natural assets in GDP. I vehemently resented conflating revenue with income. I could not abide with the notion that the national product would necessarily indicate happiness. I argued that deriving income estimates from stock changes was inappropriate and often produced wrong results. I presented the notion that greening the accounts will not necessarily lead to slower growth. I exploded the myth of an inevitable curse associated with a natural resource endowment. I showed that a strong sustainability approach – the approach favored by the current greening orthodoxy – will not produce a convincing set of greened accounts. And I have also voiced opposition to the excessive use of mathematics most notably in social accounting.

On the constructive side, I must highlight my championship for green accounting in general, though based on what I view as a more rigorous set

of foundations. In this vein I have been defending 'weak sustainability' –
the only degree of sustainability that will yield acceptable national income
estimation outcomes. I have tried to detail and in the process elucidate
intricacies implicit in the user-cost method in an effort to argue its merits
and shield it against its adversaries. If a better method were identified for
greening the accounts, I would be happy to support it for it is the end
rather than the means that should be targeted.

Additionally I have tried to stress the fact that national accounting is
a *historical* process: it describes the past and plays no part in prescribing
future behavior. To me this issue is important since I have been anxious
to show that accounting is a positive not a normative function, and have
taken this position particularly to fend off absurd claims that the 'weak
sustainability' on which the user-cost method is based on even *urges* the
destruction of natural resources and substituting human-made assets for
them. I have also been eager to draw attention to the fact that substitutability between the two types of assets, the natural and the human-made,
is not an inherent quality in either category, but depends fundamentally
on production processes which are sensitive to prices and respond to
technological changes, and depend ultimately on the composition of final
demand. Thus the reduction of demand for commodities which to be produced require the intensive use of natural resources as inputs will lead to a
reduction in the derived demand for these resources and lighten the stress
on their availability.

As stated in the Preface, the purpose of the book from the start has
been to argue afresh the cause of green accounting towards which I
played an early part. After mulling over its 'progress' so far, I have come
to the conclusion that this initiative is now practically exhausted and,
if seen at all to be active, it is proceeding only along narrow alleys and
generally in the wrong direction. The focus of much of the activity now
being conducted in a number of capitals, mainly in Europe and North
America and perhaps also Australia, seems to seek fodder with which to
fill in the satellite accounts, which were introduced by SNA93. Stuffing
these vessels with ecological information will doubtless be useful one
day, but its limited usefulness is further reduced by failure to establish a
standard format for them. This lack of format blocks the way toward the
much talked-about environmental *integration* into the fold of the national
accounts. The current activity may give the impression that all is well with
account greening, but only if we shut our eyes to the fact that the satellite
accounts have been created to avoid treating ecological losses as economic
losses, and in order to avoid integrating the environment candidly in the
national accounts.

III

There are a few lessons that I wish to emphasize in this concluding chapter as reminders. Of these, I select four, which I now touch upon under four headings: 'Context', 'Welfare', 'Capital Theory' and 'Growth'.

CONTEXT

Context is an important issue and provides one of the clearest lessons to be learnt from the present study. This concerns the need to appreciate the appropriate setting or settings where an economic theory could be applied for empirical measurements. Recent writings on environmental economics, and on green accounting in particular, show confusion in this respect. Examples have been cited *passim* in the preceding chapters, but two may be selected for illustration. First is the notion that growing scarcity would raise the price of a natural product along the lines of the Hotelling model. Quite apart from its simplifying assumptions, Hotelling's scarcity is applicable to actual situations *only* under strict market conditions, and cannot be taken as generally valid to be used in greening the accounts. In a Hotelling setting scarcity obtains only if the world constituted one market, or if the individual supply sources were sufficiently separated to make an isolated island of each. As argued in Chapter 12 *Nature's Numbers* inappropriately invoked Hotelling's theory for greening the national accounts, not realizing that it did not fit well with estimating income for individual countries. A country with a small market share may be running out of its natural resource without this causing a ripple of an effect on international prices. And even if these prices were to rise for some reason the rise would come too late as the country would no longer have a resource left to sell.

A second example of inappropriate application of theory to practice relates to the controversy that has been generated over whether it is marginal or average cost that should be used for greening the accounts in situations where the concept of the margin itself is unrealistic and marginal cost hardly ascertainable. These situations tend to typify natural resource extraction where the inputs and the products are often not single but inseparable multiple items which do not lend themselves easily to be strung along smooth and continuous curves linking costs to output. Blame for this 'incongruity' should probably be shared between the theorists and the pragmatic estimators. The theorists, particularly when their work emphasizes 'National Income', should state unambiguously where and how theory should apply; and the estimators should equip themselves with enough economic understanding to pull the relevant model to employ out of the vast cornucopia of analytical ideas that are available on tap.

WELFARE

I take up *welfare* as a second lesson. It is worth recalling that my aim throughout has been to adjust the measurement of economic output and not the happiness that may be derived from output. The latter purpose though worthy of pursuit must wait until the proper estimation of output has been secured – and so far this has not happened. If we still wish to derive happiness from output the two tasks should be pursued apart. And to be able to do this much more information than is available to the national accountants is required – information regarding population size and income distribution, provided also that we can suppress methodological qualms about inter-personal comparability of satisfactions. True, many people associate national income with happiness and for this we may blame Pigou no less. It was Pigou who had conflated the two, setting up a tradition that has since refused to die down. But surely we have come a long way since Pigou, and the national accountants themselves deny that their estimates signify welfare.

CAPITAL THEORY

A third lesson relates to *capital theory* which has sometimes been paraded to justify deriving flows of income from stocks of natural resources of dubious volumes and conjectured values. This method, which appeals to some formidable environmental economists, has nothing to do with either capital or with theory. It is a crude arithmetical operation that would damage the estimation of the all-important income flows if based on inadequately valued stocks. To me reference to capital theory becomes absurd when current stocks are valued on the basis of projecting their future use year by year and then discounting such an arbitrary stream at some subjective discount rate.

GROWTH

The fourth lesson concerns *growth* but this is important enough to merit elaboration in the following section on its own.

IV

Growth is obviously associated with national income, first in measurement and then in interpretation, and by extension also with greened income adjusted by whichever method. Significantly the pursuit of growth has come to impeach economics and economists in the eyes of its critics especially the environmentalists. For me this issue is particularly important since I have rested my case for greening the national accounts on economic reasoning, employing the tools of neoclassical economics in all my arguments. Taken in a universal sense the economy cannot go on growing indefinitely within the finite biosphere that contains it without inflicting damage – not only ecological damage, but economic damage as well. The growth 'mania' that has pervaded economics for several decades, and still continues in one form or another, has rightly or wrongly attracted opprobrium against all things economic. Leaving aside the current global recession that could in theory be alleviated by growth – and some environmentalists do not even wish to see growth as a cure out of this predicament – most economists have been conflating growth with economic success. In this regard I have raised two questions: (1) can we tell from the national accounts whether an economy is genuinely growing through 'value added', or if it is only expanding at the cost of disinvesting its natural capital? And (2) do the national accounts, even post SNA93, measure growth accurately? Economists who are unable to answer these questions, or even lack curiosity to find out answers cannot be defended. If they plead ignorance of national accounting methods their pleading will not protect them against charges of gullibility – or even worse. The macroeconomic data they regularly use are too important to be accepted by them on trust.

Growth evidently leads to a higher level of GDP, so it is worth asking again if a higher level of GDP is necessarily a Good Thing, even if reckoned properly and reduced to a per capita basis for comparability. Going back to the presumption that a higher level of material consumption, made possible by a larger GDP, will lead 'usually' to a higher level of happiness – a presumption put forward, albeit with some qualification, by Pigou – we should by now entertain some doubts regarding this assertion. Let me recall again a statement I already cited in Chapter 6 made by Sir John Hicks who had devoted a great portion of his economic oeuvre to the analysis of growth:

> Why should we be interested in Economic Growth – in increase in the Social Product, however measured? It is clearly not always 'good' in an ethical sense – not only because greater Production may be accompanied by worse

Distribution, but for many other reasons. A richer society may be a more stupid society, or a more discontented society – one does not have to go far to find examples.

So, after all, even genuine economic growth may not always be desirable. But this issue brings me back unfailingly to Brundtland whose Report had envisaged a great expansion in global economic activity, principally to afford room for the poorer countries to grow out of their underdevelopment. However, there is an obvious absence of a suitable mechanism to actuate any part of this Brundtland agenda – notably for want of any credible instrument to arrest the further enrichment of the more affluent so that the less privileged could have their turn. Generally speaking economists do not seem prepared to pronounce on this issue – perhaps afraid of reinforcing the image of their profession as a 'dismal science'. The politicians do not wish to impair their popularity by advocating consumption restraint. And nobody else wants to appear any less optimistic and dampen the rosy expectations cherished by so many out of economic growth. What is left for environmental economists appears to be sermonizing on the theme of abstinence, and making pious exhortations with the help of an occasional piece of analysis, but at bottom without realistic expectation of effective action. Yet lest the same charge be levelled against the present book it must be said that it was never meant to be an instrument of advocacy – save in the limited sense of backing the green accounting initiative.

V

To reiterate: for this book I have had two major objectives. The first is to breathe new life into the green accounting movement, which seems to me to have become moribund. The second is to indicate the way the green accounting initiative should proceed. Pursuing these objectives I have been quite harsh in my criticism of efforts by many scholars, not only to attract their attention, and the attention of those who have been swayed by their reasoning, but also to induce possible rebuttals of my arguments for the benefit of everyone's enlightenment. Provocatively, I have claimed that the furious activity currently being made to fill in the satellite accounts with information, though not without value, is taking green accounting in the wrong direction and giving the impression of progress, whereas it drives the initiative away from what I think was its intended destination. That original destination, the economic destination, was embedded in the very choice of the SNA, a supremely economic medium, as the appropriate conduit to bring attention to the environment's predicament. I will not shy away from repeating that SNA93 judged the unadjusted estimates of national income and its subdivisions and cohorts to be adequate without much need for adjustment: any adjustment must be confined to ancillary accounts created for environmental purposes. In retrospect, the thought has occurred to me that this may have been a ruse done with a sleight of hand so that the old series of national accounts could be preserved uncorrected. The old system may have been good enough for the richer countries but was obviously inadequate to be preserved as a *universal* system. For the authors of SNA93, preserving the old series would not only serve continuity, but would also be an effective shield against any charge, like the charge I have been making, that the accounts were wrong and economically misleading for many countries. While I rather naïvely thought the satellite accounts were a stepping stone which would serve temporarily until controversies had subsided over rival adjustment methods, they have now developed into what looks like a permanent fixture. And considering the power wielded by the institutions currently involved in bolstering them, this course will not be easy to reverse.

VI

There is enough in the foregoing to indicate the way forward, but there is too much equivocation still about the purpose of green accounting. Foremost is the impression that green accounting is being undertaken only for environmental purposes, and this impression should in my view be eradicated as a matter of priority. To prove what I am saying, consider the version of the guidelines issued by the UNSD – a unit that is in a commanding position for green accounting – a version labeled *Integrated Environment and Economic Accounts, Operational Manual 2000*. Significantly this opined that the case studies of SEEA implementation (i.e. for Papua New Guinea and Mexico) had so far offered few examples of how such accounting 'can improve policy-making'. It is obvious from this statement that UNSD was not considering improving *macroeconomic* 'policy-making', and the policy in mind all along was *environmental* policy. But obviously environmental policy could not be helped, at least directly, by adjusting the macroeconomic estimates. As to *economic* policy the *Manual* curiously added that there were 'perceived negative political and economic consequences of such accounting [which] tend to discourage its implementation' (p. 146). Overlooking for a moment that the two realms of environment and economy should not have been separated in the first place, and therefore would have needed no subsequent integration, the two lame justifications just cited cannot be accepted. It is not environmental policies that should emerge from greening the accounts, but economic policies based on correct monitoring of output and its change. Furthermore, the consequences of greening the accounts need not at all be discouraging. As argued in Chapter 14 ('Growth rate after adjustment') the growth of the downward adjusted GDP could remain the same, increase or decline. I may be mistaken, but I hear echoes here of the reactions leveled at Malthus and Hotelling in their time accusing them of untenable pessimism, and here the very institutions in charge of national accounting seem to be trying to find excuses for not offering useful guidance.

Finally, I must emphasize that the arguments I elaborated in this book should not be taken in any way as revolutionary for they spring from the rich legacy bequeathed to us by earlier economists. I have merely been retracing their steps and interpreting or re-interpreting what we have inherited from the work of Irving Fisher, Alfred Marshall, Arthur Cecil Pigou, Harold Hotelling, John Hicks, Simon Kuznets and Robert Solow. From the work of all of these I must single out the contribution Marshall made presciently to green accounting well before the expression was ever used. In his writings this acknowledged father of neoclassical economics was always sensitive to Nature's contribution to economic activities – a sensitivity that is portrayed throughout his *Principles of Economics*, the last edition of which it will be recalled came out in 1920. I do not have to remind the readers of this book that for natural resource extraction it was Marshall who distinguished rent (income) from royalty (disinvestment) – a distinction that lies at the heart of the user-cost method. A few years ago Perman et al. (1996, p. 370) wrote that:

> Although the user cost approach is to be preferred on theoretical and practical grounds, it is unlikely to dislodge the conventional measures of GDP/GNP at least until there is comprehensive coverage of the depletion of natural resources and agreement on methods of valuation and calculation.

I am hopeful that this book will have cleared some of the fog surrounding the methods of valuation and calculation, and provided a step or a number of steps to revitalize the green accounting initiative.

REFERENCES

Perman, Roger, Yue Ma and James McGilvray (1996), *Natural Resource and Environmental Economics*. London and New York: Longman.

Glossary

Where this Glossary does not involve factual information, it seeks to explain terms as used in this book

Balance sheets   A two-sided snapshot of Assets and Liabilities belonging to a person, business or a nation – the latter frequently cited in the national accounting literature. A one-sided list of assets is sometimes wrongly referred to as a balance sheet.

BEA   Bureau of Economic Analysis of the United States Government Department of Commerce. It is the branch of the United States administration responsible for the national accounts, publishing its estimates in the official publication, '*Survey of Current Business.*'

Bretton Woods institutions The International Monetary Fund and the World Bank (including the latter's affiliates). Keynes once described the IMF as a *bank* that would offer loans to national central banks, and the World Bank as a *fund* for financing reconstruction and development.

Brundtland Report   An influential report, 'Our Common Future', published in 1989 by an international commission created by the United Nations under the chairmanship of Gro Harlem Brundtland, formerly a Prime Minister of Norway. This popularized the phrase 'sustainable development' and called for reconciling current demand for natural resources with future needs, as well as balancing the interests of the poorer nations against those of the affluent countries.

Capital consumption   Used interchangeably with Capital Depreciation or amortization. This covers the periodic downward adjustment of the book value of assets due to wear and tear and obsolescence. Natural resource extraction is qualitatively different from Capital Consumption, being akin to withdrawal from inventories.

Dutch disease   Adverse macroeconomic structural developments which afflict an economy receiving unrequited inflows of foreign funds in the absence of corrective economic policies. This phenomenon is usually, though not always, associated with a natural resource boom leading to excessive consumption and over-valuation of the domestic currency, which encourages imports and shrinks traditional exports. Previously active industries get discouraged and employment falls as the share of untradable activities rises in the economy's structure.

El Serafy 'rule'   This is based on splitting the surplus realized in the extraction of depletable natural resources into two portions: 'true income' and 'user cost' – the latter representing a disinvestment. Unlike Hartwick's rule (see below), the El Serafy approach is not normative, in that it does not urge any particular action, but 'positive': merely proposed to guide income estimation. If taken in a normative sense, however, the identified income portion indicates the maximum that could be allocated to consumption in the current accounting period.

EUROSTAT   A Directorate of the European Commission in Luxembourg that provides statistical information to the European Union and coordinates statistical methods among member states. EUROSTAT was an active participant in the production of SNA93.

G-7   A group formed in 1975 of finance ministers from France, (West) Germany, Italy, Japan, United Kingdom and the United States with the addition of Canada in 1976. The group, assisted by support staff, met intermittently to coordinate economic policies. Later this became G-8 when Russia joined the set. At times larger groups were assembled including G-9, G-20 and G-30.

GDP   Gross Domestic Product. This is the aggregate gross product of a society, usually in a year. It relates geographically to a locality, and provides the first step in estimating the aggregate income of residents before this is adjusted for 'factor payments' across national boundaries to arrive at GNP. When capital consumption is taken out of GDP, the result is NDP (net domestic product).

GNP   Gross National Product. This adjusts GDP for income flows across national or geographical boundaries. Inflows of interest, wage remittances and investment dividends are added, and outflows of interest, wages and dividend payments are deducted. In most cases GDP and GNP do not much differ. When Capital Consumption is taken out of GNP the result is NNP which, strictly speaking, is National Income.

Green accounts These are the traditionally estimated nation accounts, but now adjusted for ecological change.

Hartwick rule A rule advising that no part of the surplus realized in the extraction of depletable resources should be consumed in the current period but invested. Returns on such investment may be considered as income and consumed only in future. This 'rule' denies any rights in the assets to the current owners – a view which Beckerman has described as 'immoral', himself (Beckerman) disallowing any rights to 'future generations' since they do not yet exist.

Hicksian income This is the standard definition of income which has become popular in environmental economics. For reckoning 'Hicksian income', all capital, including natural resources, must be kept intact for the purpose of estimating income. 'Keeping capital intact', though desirable in itself, is only proposed here as an accounting device.

IARIW International Association of Research in Income and Wealth. This was founded in 1947 to promote the study of national accounting. It usually convenes international conferences every other year in different countries and publishes the quarterly, *International Review of Income and Wealth*.

ICOR Incremental Capital Output Ratio. This relates an increment in output to a previous capital increment (or investment) that had 'caused' it. This ratio used to be popular in applied research for estimating the size of investment needed to promote a targeted increase in output.

IDA International Development Association. IDA is an affiliate of the World Bank with no physical presence. It is a 'facility' operated by World Bank staff following Bank procedures. Established in 1960 it offers grants and Credits ('Credits' meaning loans on very soft terms) to the poorest nations with limited access to international capital markets. IDA's funds are replenished every three years through 'subscriptions'. Because of its limited resources an annual exercise identifies eligible recipients and decides their shares, and these will back the investments the Bank decides to make in the country concerned.

IECSE International Economics Socio-Economic data division. A unit of the World Bank currently engaged in improving international income comparisons including using 'purchasing power', rather than official exchange rates, for converting currencies.

IEEA Integrated Environmental and Economic Accounts. SNA93 in effect pronounced that environmental concerns were not economic concerns, after which great efforts have been made to 're-integrate' them via the Satellite Accounts – so far to no avail.

IMF International Monetary Fund, established in 1944 simultaneously with the World Bank, both making up the 'Bretton Woods' institutions.

IS–LM A simplified model devised by Hicks in 1937 giving the gist of Keynes's *General Theory of Employment, Interest and Money*. It connects investment and saving (IS) with liquidity and money (LM) via aggregate demand and the interest rate.

London Group A group of national accountants originating in Statistics Canada that has now assumed the mantle of elaborating the Satellite accounts for the Environment.

Mining Extracting subsoil assets including aquifer waters, metals, petroleum and other minerals usually classified as 'depletable resources'. Renewable resources can also be mined if their restoration is insufficient to offset deterioration. The user-cost method is applicable to mining, whether the resource is depletable or renewable.

NAMEA National Accounts Matrix including Environmental Accounts. This was devised in Statistics Netherlands as an integrated system to indicate interactions between economic activity and the environment (covering both pollution and sources). It is not meant to change estimates of the national income.

Natural resource curse An affliction said to retard economic progress in countries endowed with commercially exploitable natural resources. There is no robust evidence for the curse's existence, and its symptoms are amenable to treatment by economic measures.

Net price method A method for 'greening' the traditionally estimated national accounts by using prices other than market prices for natural products. Advocates of this method deduct from the market price the 'marginal' costs of extraction, including an estimated return on capital. However, failing to obtain marginal costs in practice, average costs have been used instead, and this has attracted the charge that 'resource rents' were being overestimated.

OAPEC Organization of Arab Petroleum Exporting Countries. Established in 1968 OAPEC is based in Kuwait for the purpose of fostering economic cooperation among its members and develop petroleum industries. It publishes *Oil and Arab Co-operation*, a quarterly journal of academic contributions. Its members are Algeria, Bahrain, Egypt, Iraq, Kuwait, Libya, Qatar, Saudi Arabia, Syria, Tunisia and the United Arab Emirates. OAPEC has no authority over petroleum extraction or prices.

OD An operational directive intended for use by World Bank staff in an attempt to guide and standardize policies and operations.

OECD Organisation for Economic Cooperation and Development, based in Paris, France. Established in 1961, its members number 34 rich countries accounting for four-fifths of world GDP. Its proclaimed purpose is to promote democratic and free market policies as a means for improving economic and social wellbeing the world over. OECD staff have made substantial contributions to national accounting methods and estimation.

OPEC Organization of Petroleum Exporting Countries. OPEC, headquartered in Vienna, Austria, was established in 1960 by Iran, Iraq, Kuwait, Saudi Arabia and Venezuela, to be joined later by nine other petroleum exporting countries. Its stated objective is to coordinate extraction policies among member countries and secure better and stable terms for their principal export. OPEC's monopoly power is routinely exaggerated, and when it tried to act as a cartel indicating export quotas it failed to control supply, essentially owing to conflicting interests of its members. In 2011 OPEC accounted for 43 percent of oil extraction and 60 percent of world exports. It issues many publications including an *Annual Statistical Bulletin.*

Resource rent A magnitude that is not always well defined, meant to indicate the financial surplus realized in resource extraction, used analogously with the rent of land as viewed by the classical economists. Unlike classical or 'Ricardian' rent, the gains obtained from extraction are not all income, but partly rent and partly 'royalty'. See THR (Total Hotelling Rent).

Royalty Particularly in the work of Alfred Marshall, Royalty complements Ricardian Rent to make up the net revenue obtained in extraction.

SAL   A SAL is a Structural Adjustment Loan (or Credit if on IDA terms). It is a type of loan offered by the World Bank in conjunction with an IMF operation in support of macroeconomic policy changes. It was introduced in 1980 to assist countries encountering financial difficulties over meeting their external debt servicing obligations, but broadened in purpose gradually later.

Satellite accounts   Subsidiary accounts placed outside the main frame of the national accounts. These were introduced by SNA93 possibly to keep the traditional accounts – described as *economic* – immune or fairly immune from change.

SECAL   Sectoral Adjustment Loan. A policy-based loan which developed as an offshoot of SAL (but sometimes initiated without a SAL) to induce policy changes in a sector, such as agriculture or transport, and not in the economy as a whole.

SEEA   System of Integrated Environmental and Economic Accounts as advocated in SNA93 and expected to be realized through the Satellite Accounts.

SNA   System of National Accounts as distinguished from the national account estimates themselves which are made within it.

SNA93   The System of National Accounts that came out in December 1993, 'prepared under the auspices of the Inter-Secretariat Working Group on National Accounts', and issued in the name of five agencies, namely, (1) Commission of the European Communities – EUROSTAT, (2) International Monetary Fund, (3) Organisation for Economic Cooperation and Development, (4) United Nations, and (5) the World Bank.

Stationary state   In classical thought is the ultimate state an economy can reach given its natural resources and relative position vis-à-vis other countries, and beyond which it could advance no further. Marshall called it 'a famous fiction' and even 'mischievous'. Hicks thought it was worse than a steady state.

Steady state   Hicks thought a steady state was 'a curse', but he envisaged it as describing an economy growing at a constant rate. According to Herman Daly, following a path broken by John Stuart Mill, it means no growth at all. This position was endorsed even by Keynes describing it as an 'ultimate state'. Daly has in mind a state of no growth after all economic problems have been solved, but failing that, no growth in 'throughput'.

Throughput According to Daly throughput is the metabolic flow of resources through the economy beginning with raw material inputs extracted from the ecosystem and ending with waste outputs returned to the ecosystem.

THR Total Hotelling Rent. This is a hybrid expression that mixes Hotelling's scarcity rent (the user cost) with Ricardian rent, and incongruously bestowing the name of Hotelling on the total. Ricardian rent enters the mixture from the fact that mines of different fecundity co-exist – a fact which recalls the differential rents of Ricardo. Extraction typically does not exhaust a mine in any one year so market price will exceed marginal cost by Marshall's royalty (Hotelling's scarcity 'rent').

Time Time in accounting is usually divided in discrete segments such as years or quarters, but to economists, time is a continuous flow through which economic variables change, often in infinitesimal steps. Using geometry and calculus this allows the emergence of such quantities as marginal costs and marginal revenues.

UNCTAD United Nations Conference on Trade and Development. This is a permanent organization headquartered in Geneva, Switzerland, set up by the United Nations General Assembly in 1964 to assist developing countries in matters of development, trade and investment, and in general help them to be integrated in the world economy. Among its achievements has been securing for some of its members trade preferences in a few richer country markets.

UNEP United Nations Environment Programme – a program not an agency – that has played the most sustained role behind green accounting.

User cost A temporal opportunity cost associated with mining or with fixed asset depreciation, perceived to vary with the intensity with which a fixed asset is worked. This is sometimes identified with scarcity rent. Behind the concept of the user cost is the notion that current utilization preempts future availability.

Utility This is the benefit obtained from acquiring or consuming a good or service. In microeconomic analysis it is the force behind demand, just as 'cost' is the force behind supply.

Value added   it is the difference between inputs and outputs which constitutes income, out of which the owners of the factors of production get compensated for their factor services. Value-added contaminated with elements of capital, such as the user cost, does not qualify as income however 'gross' it is described. The capital elements should be removed first before the remainder is considered in gross or net terms.

Washington Consensus   An unflattering description of a consensus among the US Treasury, the IMF and the World Bank. In return for financial assistance, externally indebted countries had to adopt a recipe of free market measures that tended to be similar for all countries.

Wealth   Wealth is a stock and income is a flow. In *The Wealth of Nations*, 'Wealth' was used by Adam Smith as a flow, synonymously with Income. As a stock, wealth is broader than capital, the latter sometimes identified with that part of wealth that is used for production.

Welfare   The pleasure or joy experienced by those who acquire goods and services. Being a state of mind it defies direct estimation. Many people wrongly assume that income estimates denote welfare estimates.

WRI   World Resources Institute in Washington DC under whose auspices the pioneering study for greening the national accounts of Indonesia was conceived.

Index